PERPETUATING POVERTY

PERPETUATING POVERTY

The World Bank, the IMF, and the Developing World

edited by Doug Bandow and Ian Vásquez

CATO INSTITUTE
Washington, D.C.

A slightly different version of chapter 5 of the present work appeared as "A Skeptical Look at Aid to Russia," by Nicholas Eberstadt, in *The National Interest*, no. 29, Fall 1992. Copyright © 1992 by National Affairs, Inc. Reprinted by permission. Chapter 14 of the present work appeared in a slightly different version in *Prosperity versus Planning: How Government Stifles Economic Growth*, by David Osterfeld. Copyright © 1992 by Oxford University Press, Inc. Reprinted by permission.

Library of Congress Cataloging-in-Publication Data

Perpetuating poverty: the World Bank, the IMF, and the developing world /edited by Doug Bandow and Ian Vásquez.
    p.   cm.
Includes bibliographical references and index.
    ISBN 1-882577-06-X (cloth): $25.95.—ISBN 1-882577-07-8 (pbk.): $15.95.
    1. International Monetary Fund. 2. World Bank. 3. Economic assistance. 4. Commercial policy. 5. Developing countries—Economic conditions. 6. International business enterprises. 7. International finance. I. Bandow, Doug. II. Vásquez, Ian.
HG3881.5.I58P48   1993   93-48499
332.1'532—dc20   CIP

Cover Design by Colin Moore.

Printed in the United States of America.

CATO INSTITUTE
1000 Massachusetts Ave., N.W.
Washington, D.C. 20001

In Memoriam

This volume of essays is dedicated to the memory of David Osterfeld, who died on September 26, 1993, in Rensselaer, Indiana, where he was a professor of political science at St. Joseph's College. Osterfeld's tireless efforts to advance free societies earned him the admiration and respect of scholars, students, and others who benefited from his prolific writings and frequent lectures. His efforts to champion the cause of liberty culminated in the publication by Oxford University Press and the Cato Institute in 1992 of *Prosperity versus Planning: How Government Stifles Economic Growth*—an outstanding contribution to development economics that is bound to become a lasting resource. David Osterfeld intellectually enriched many of us during his productive life; it is an honor to include one of his essays in this collection.

Contents

Acknowledgments

This book was made possible by the interest and encouragement of a number of individuals to whom we owe a debt of gratitude. Edward H. Crane, president, and David Boaz, executive vice president, of the Cato Institute recognized the value of this project and enthusiastically supported it every step of the way. We are especially thankful to Ted Galen Carpenter, director of foreign policy studies at the Institute, for reviewing manuscripts and making suggestions that improved the quality of the book. Melanie Tammen also deserves special recognition for organizing Cato's conference on multilateral aid in Washington in May 1991. Many of the chapters in this collection are based on papers presented at that event.

Other individuals to whom we are grateful include Leslie Albin, our copyeditor; Pat Felder and Jeanne Hill, whose word-processing work sped production of the book; and Robert Virasin and Jennifer Amis, who spent many hours checking sources. Finally, of course, we thank the authors of this volume for contributing the intellectual labor that will, we hope, stimulate more debate on this important and timely topic.

D.B. and I.V.

Introduction: The Dismal Legacy and False Promise of Multilateral Aid

Doug Bandow and Ian Vásquez

Multilateral lending institutions—the International Monetary Fund (IMF), World Bank, and regional development banks—have flooded the Third World with hundreds of billions of dollars in aid. Since the early 1950s, the World Bank alone has lent developing countries nearly $300 billion.[1] Those institutions have also played a major role in encouraging Western governments to provide hundreds of billions of dollars more in bilateral assistance to the developing world. Yet after providing advice, loans, and grants to the governments of the world's poorest countries for four decades, the multilaterals can point to few, if any, cases in which their efforts have led to improved living standards and sustained economic prosperity. Instead of growth, the Third World has experienced social disintegration, economic stagnation, debt crises, and, in some regions, declines in agricultural production and incomes.

As their failures have become undeniable, however, international aid agencies have only escalated their lending. In 1992, both the Asian Development Bank (ADB) and the Inter-American Development Bank (IDB) increased lending to record levels, and the World Bank announced the following year that its loan commitments had reached a new high of $23.7 billion.[2] The IMF, after receiving a 50 percent increase in resources from the world's industrialized countries in 1992, played a leading role in shaping and distributing Western aid to Russia.

Moreover, the desire for more multilateral aid has caused the membership in both the World Bank and the IMF to expand. Mongolia,

---

[1] World Bank, *The World Bank Annual Report 1992* (Washington, D.C.: World Bank, 1992), p. 195.

[2] "ADB Lending Tops $5 Billion," *Wall Street Journal*, February 10, 1993, p. A10; Inter-American Development Bank, *Inter-American Development Bank 1992 Annual Report* (Washington, D.C.: Inter-American Development Bank, 1992), p. 11; and George Graham, "World Bank Lending Soars," *Financial Times*, July 14, 1993, p. 3.

1

Croatia, Albania, Namibia, Switzerland, the Marshall Islands, Russia, Latvia, Lithuania, Moldova, Ukraine, and other countries have joined the World Bank group since 1990.[3]

At the same time, the industrialized countries created a new development bank in 1990—the European Bank for Reconstruction and Development (EBRD)—for the sole purpose of lending to the Eastern European states and former republics of the Soviet Union. In the United States, meanwhile, a bill has been introduced in Congress to establish a North American Development Bank for the United States, Canada, and Mexico to complement the North American Free Trade Agreement.[4]

Like many other nations, the United States increasingly relies on the multilaterals as part of its foreign aid program. While U.S. bilateral economic assistance averaged $10 billion per year in the 1980s but dropped to $6.8 billion in 1992, net disbursements of official development assistance by multilateral agencies escalated from $8 billion annually in 1985 to more than $16 billion in 1991.[5]

Several factors have helped cause that trend. First, budget deficits and recession throughout the industrialized world have increased the appeal of "leveraged aid"—donor nations can collectively use their resources more effectively by contributing a relatively small amount to a large multilateral aid pool. At the same time, the collapse of the Soviet Union has eliminated Cold War justifications for many costly bilateral economic assistance programs. Second, the international aid agencies have become born-again advocates of free markets, taking credit for dramatic economic reforms sweeping the globe. Although that liberal revolution has occurred quite independent of the World Bank and the IMF, legislators in industrialized states have bought the new rationale for the multilaterals.

Finally, support for the IMF, World Bank, and regional development banks has grown at least in part because of increased skepticism that the U.S. Agency for International Development (U.S. AID), the principal U.S. bureau that distributes bilateral aid, effectively promotes Third

[3]World Bank, *The World Bank Annual Report 1992*, pp. 15, 21.

[4]Nancy Dunne, "Special Bank May Help NAFTA Win Approval," *Financial Times*, July 16, 1993, p. 4.

[5]Organization for Economic Cooperation and Development, *Geographical Distribution of Financial Flows to Developing Countries 1988/1991* (Paris: OECD, 1993), p. 25.

World development. In 1993, a Clinton administration task force conceded that "despite decades of foreign assistance, most of Africa and parts of Latin America, Asia and the Middle East are economically worse off today than they were 20 years ago."[6] The task force went on to suggest that U.S. AID should, among other measures, establish closer ties with the international lending agencies. Similarly, the *Washington Post*, noting that numerous studies had documented pervasive waste and inefficiency at U.S. AID, recommended that the Clinton administration consider pursuing international development through the World Bank and the other multilaterals "where the record shows American dollars and leadership have been successfully leveraged in behalf of important U.S. interests."[7]

Yet if bilateral aid has proved so disappointing, is there any reason to believe that the world's poor will benefit from strengthened *multilateral* aid initiatives? The answer, provided by 40 years of sad experience, is no.

Has Multilateral Aid Helped the Third World?

For years, the assumption of traditional development economics was that the Third World was poor because it lacked capital. Thus, the suggested solution was to transfer wealth from the developed to the developing world. Since the private sector was believed to be unwilling or unable to bring prosperity to the poorest regions of the globe, governments had to plan and manage their nations' economies. And foreign aid would enable recipients to plan and manage better.

Alas, more than 40 years of international transfers have not benefited the Third World. Latin America's foreign debt stands at an overwhelming $430 billion; per capita incomes in sub-Saharan Africa are lower today than they were in the 1970s; and, according to the United Nations, the 47 poorest countries in the underdeveloped world, many of them heavy aid recipients, have experienced no growth in recent years and are expected to show continuing declines in per capita incomes in 1993.[8]

---

[6]Al Kamen and Thomas W. Lippman, "Task Force Favors Restructuring and Refocusing Troubled AID," *Washington Post*, July 3, 1993, p. A16.

[7]"Is It Time to Phase Out AID?" *Washington Post*, July 13, 1993, p. C6.

[8]United Nations, *The Least Developed Countries: 1992 Report;* cited in Frances Williams, "Poorest LDCs Face Decline, Says Unctad," *Financial Times*, March 10, 1993, p. 6.

Clearly, then, the development economists have been proved wrong: a shortage of capital has not been the problem. Developing countries would not have owed Western governments, multilateral aid agencies, and commercial banks in excess of $1.7 trillion in 1992 had those countries been unable to find sufficient funds.[9] What has obviously been ignored by proponents of foreign assistance is the fact that, as Lord P. T. Bauer observes, "Lack of money is not the *cause* of poverty, it *is* poverty," and that to have money is the *"result* of economic achievement, not its *precondition."*[10]

Not only is foreign aid based on a flawed model of development, but there are other, more practical problems inherent to such transfer programs. One is that most development institutions, including multilateral aid agencies, lend to governments, not people. Thus, the IMF, World Bank, and other development banks have consistently made loans to the very Third World governments that have created the worst impediments to economic growth. As Shyam Kamath explains, foreign aid to India, the recipient of the most international assistance in the post–World War II era, has helped expand the country's bloated bureaucracies, finance centrally planned development, and sustain one of the "world's largest and most inefficient public sectors." As a result, India remains among the poorest nations in the world with increasing numbers of its citizens living in poverty.

India is not alone. Roberto Salinas León explains how the IMF and the World Bank have "played a major role in perpetuating the legacy of statism in Mexico." The World Bank's second largest debtor after India, Mexico relied on World Bank loans to expand its state-owned industries from 300 in 1970 to as many as 1,200 by 1982—when Mexico announced its inability to pay its foreign debt, marking the onset of the world debt crisis. Salinas warns, however, that despite Mexico's recent and impressive free-market reforms, the country continues to rely on World Bank and IDB loans to sustain state monopolies in some of the most important sectors of the economy. Paul Craig Roberts similarly reviews how multilateral aid elsewhere in Latin America encouraged

---

[9]World Bank, *World Debt Tables 1992–93* (Washington, D.C.: World Bank, 1992), vol. 1, p. 3.

[10]Peter T. Bauer, "Creating the Third World: Foreign Aid and Its Offspring," *Journal of Economic Growth*, vol. 2, no. 4 (1987), p. 6.

the growth of the interventionist state, setting the stage for the "lost decade" of the 1980s in which Latin Americans saw their living standards fall.

Unfortunately, the World Bank and the IMF have also been very generous to African states. George B. N. Ayittey describes African dictators who regularly justified the need for more aid on the basis that the funds would be used for "development expenditures." The governments then spent millions on arms and wasted even more on "marble office buildings, show airports, basilicas, and other black elephants."

Since multilateral aid has far more often been squandered than used productively, it has naturally kept recipients on a borrowing treadmill. William McGurn sees this kind of unhealthy dependence in the Philippines. World Bank and IMF subsidies to protectionist governments, writes McGurn, have allowed that country's "nationalists and fat cat businessmen [to] meet on the common ground of keeping out foreign competition." And as the nation has become ever more indebted, its dependence on the multilaterals has also increased.

Few poor borrowers have escaped the debt trap. Doug Bandow documents the addiction of scores of nations to IMF loans. According to Bandow, "Through 1989 six nations . . . had been relying on IMF aid for more than 30 years; 24 countries had been borrowers for between 20 and 29 years. And 47, almost one-third of all the states in the world, had been using IMF credit for between 10 and 19 years."

In short, it appears that multilateral aid, instead of helping developing countries, has actually hindered their economic progress. Throughout the Third World, multilateral agencies have subsidized harmful economic programs, financed the growth of already burdensome public sectors, and increased recipients' foreign debt burdens. Certainly, not all of the aid money has been wasted. Indeed, it is difficult to imagine spending hundreds of billions of dollars and not accomplishing something positive. But the overall record is clear—in the developing world, the IMF, World Bank, and other international financial institutions have done far more harm than good.

Do Multilaterals Believe They Help the Third World?

The development banks naturally argue to the contrary, but it is difficult to monitor their often-secret activities. The World Bank does not make public many of its project evaluations and country reports, while the agreements reached between the IMF and borrower states—known as letters of intent—are all kept confidential. Only when World Bank projects lead to major public protests, massive human rights violations, or widespread environmental damage in Third World countries, or when IMF programs, usually characterized by tax increases and currency devaluations, cause riots in borrowing nations, do the Western media and public see how those lending institutions operate.

Of course, it could be argued that this presents a biased picture of mulilateral aid efforts, ignoring any positive achievements. But it is the multilaterals that have chosen secrecy. Moreover, even official reports—whether leaked to the press or made public deliberately—offer little evidence of the development banks' abilities to finance economic progress. In 1992, for example, the World bank reviewed 1,800 current projects for which it had loaned $140 billion. The bank's internal study, known as the Wapenhans report, judged that 37.5 percent of projects completed in 1991 were "unsatisfactory"—more than double the rate of a decade earlier.[11] And that report was no anomaly. As James Bovard documents, numerous other official evaluations over the years have reached similarly discouraging conclusions about World Bank lending in agriculture, telecommunications, transport, irrigation, credit and finance, and an assortment of other fields. Unfortunately for Third World citizens, when such projects fail, the result is debt, not development.

The ADB and the EBRD have also issued reports admitting to their sorry performances. According to the ADB's 1992 annual report, for example, 60 percent of ADB projects reviewed in that year were deemed failures or only "partly successful."[12] A confidential report by the EBRD meanwhile concluded that the bank has failed to contribute to Eastern Europe's economic transition and that its "impact comes up short as compared to the use of its resources."[13]

To such reports the multinational bureaucracies have responded by laying much of the blame on "external factors" and proposing new

[11]World Bank Portfolio Management Task Force, "Effective Implementation: Key to Development Impact," Washington, D.C., World Bank, 1992, p. ii.

[12]Victor Mallet, "Many ADB Projects 'Failed,' " *Financial Times*, April 20, 1993, p. 6.

[13]Robert Peston, "EBRD Role in Eastern Europe Criticized," *Financial Times*, June 18, 1993, p. 1.

procedures or organizational restructuring.[14] But no improvement of methods can overcome the flawed view of development upon which foreign aid is predicated and the many inherent flaws of assistance programs.

Can Multilateral Aid Help the Third World?

Perhaps for that reason, even many aid officials acknowledge that past aid efforts have fallen short of expectations. They argue that the future will be different, however, since IMF and many World Bank loans are conditioned on borrowers' adopting free-market policy reforms. That theory sounds good in the abstract but has yielded few success stories in practice. After all, the World Bank admits that its officials hate to terminate loans, even after it has become clear that the borrower has not and will not implement substantive policy changes.

Nor, sadly, can multilateral institutions even be expected to provide sound economic advice. For example, in its efforts to induce foreign governments to reduce their budget deficits, the IMF typically encourages Third World states to raise taxes and establish more effective tax collection agencies. Yet how does the IMF expect a poor society to become prosperous if its government seizes even more wealth from its citizens?

Another example is provided by Paulo Rabello de Castro, who accuses the IMF and the World Bank of giving successive Brazilian governments misguided advice that helped to trigger chronic hyperstagflation—a unique mix of hyperinflation and economic stagnation. The IMF, says Rabello de Castro, has repeatedly supported attempts to get the government budget under control by reducing expenditures and raising taxes. Unfortunately, that recipe never worked in Brazil, where the central bank simply financed budget deficits by printing money—an institutional factor consistently ignored by the IMF.

Still, many Third World states are adopting reforms. But countries that have done the most to liberalize their economies—Mexico, Chile, South Korea, and Argentina, for example—have done so in spite of multilateral aid, not because of it. To the extent that developing countries

[14]See Henny Sender, "More for Less," *Far Eastern Economic Review*, May 20, 1993, p. 52; World Bank Portfolio Management Task Force, Insert, p. 2; George Graham, "Action Plan for World Bank," *Financial Times*, July 13, 1993, p. 4; and Robert Peston, "Attali Proposes EBRD Shake-up," *Financial Times*, June 18, 1993, p. 2.

have introduced free-market reforms, they have made such changes out of economic necessity.

By ameliorating the symptoms of economic collapse, multilateral aid is more likely to postpone the adoption of necessary reforms. Governments that receive foreign assistance find it easier to avoid making the politically difficult decisions typically required by economic restructuring. Suspending or reducing aid, on the other hand, is far more effective at inducing governments to implement the liberalization necessary for sustainable growth. For example, Vietnam, which until recently was excluded from receiving World Bank and IMF loans, reacted to the cutoff of massive Soviet aid by implementing economic reforms that led to a "vigorously emerging private sector" and an annual economic growth rate of 3 percent in 1991.[15] New loans from the World Bank and the IMF, however, may delay the reform process. An editorial in the *Far Eastern Economic Review* noted that Vietnam might be better off alone.

> Vietnam has done a remarkable job restoring its economy with its *doi moi*, or renovation policy.... And its isolation from the well-intentioned multilateral lending agencies has been another blessing in disguise. Look at the Philippines, a prime target of these loans, and now saddled with nearly $29 billion in debt and nothing to show for it. Contrast this with the rapid prosperity of say, Hong Kong, left happily unperturbed by the attentions of these lenders. To be sure, the multilaterals mean well and in recent years have urged more open markets.... [But] experience suggests that their usual terms of credit and in-built bias toward a top-down approach to development are no substitute for market discipline.[16]

The same concern is expressed by Nicholas Eberstadt regarding Western assistance for Russia. In his view, conditional loans have even fewer chances of succeeding in Russia than in underdeveloped countries throughout the world where "it is impossible to demonstrate [their] success." Eberstadt concludes that "the economic assistance programs now under consideration in the West may not only prove wasteful, but may even ultimately retard reform worthy of the name."

---

[15]World Bank, *Annual Report 1991* (Washington, D.C.: World Bank, 1991), p. 121, and *Annual Report 1992*, p. 125.

[16]"Think Twice: Hanoi Looks to Aid Agencies," *Far Eastern Economic Review*, Editorial, February 18, 1993, p. 5.

Melanie Tammen presents perhaps the clearest picture of why even "reformed" multilateral aid agencies cannot be expected to promote prosperity in the developing world. The World Bank, after lending to the socialist governments of Poland, Hungary, Romania, and other Eastern European states for years, has now proclaimed its commitment to assisting those same countries in establishing market-oriented economies. Yet by continuing to lend money to government-owned enterprises, such as the major telecommunications industries, the World Bank risks precluding private investment in those areas and helps "finance the Eastern European governments' retention of shares in public-private . . . ventures when they otherwise would be sufficiently financially strapped to make them completely private." Even the EBRD, whose charter requires it to make 60 percent of its loans to the private sector where private-sector finance would not otherwise be available, has done little to contribute to reform. The bank has had trouble identifying good private investment opportunities and has thus made fewer disbursements.

In short, when multilateral aid is destined for government, its effects are likely to be counterproductive. At best, multilateral aid targeted for the private sector is redundant. Thus, multilateral aid cannot be expected to promote development now or in the future, any more than it could have in the past four decades. The fundamental problems, again, are the international financial institutions' misunderstanding of the development process and the inevitable counterproductive effects of assisting governments. Lord Bauer best summed up the contradictions inherent to multilateral and other lending agencies' programs:

> If all conditions for development other than capital are present, capital will soon be generated locally or will be available . . . from abroad. . . . If, however, the conditions for development are not present, then aid . . . will be necessarily unproductive and therefore ineffective. Thus, if the mainsprings of development are present, material progress will occur even without foreign aid. If they are absent, it will not occur even with aid.[17]

The Bureaucratic Incentive

So why, if the evidence against the effectiveness of multilateral aid is so clear, do multilateral lending institutions continue to exist and even

[17]Peter T. Bauer, *Dissent on Development* (Cambridge, Mass.: Harvard University Press, 1972), pp. 97–98.

to expand? Virtually every participant in the process—other than Third World citizens—has an interest in the growth of multilateral aid agencies. Particularly important is the role of the organizations' own bureaucrats.

For instance, Roland Vaubel shows how the IMF's emphasis on increased lending has created the impression that the world urgently needs even more IMF loans. Thus, the IMF has engineered at least eight quota increases and created a number of new lending facilities over the years. Even when the international system of fixed exchange rates ended in the early 1970s—and with it, the IMF's official purpose of maintaining exchange rate stability—IMF lending did not decrease. Rather, it doubled between 1970 and 1975. Since then, the fund has created other new missions for itself.

The World Bank, too, has emphasized the quantity of lending as a measure of its importance and success. James Burnham discusses the bureaucratic forces at the bank and the difficulty faced by even the institution's board in trying to change bank lending practices and overall loan commitments. Burnham explains that "the institutional rewards for consistently asking for fewer financial resources were trivial or negative," even though bank officers were aware that a reduction in loans could actually contribute to economic development.[18]

Unfortunately, that problem is not unique to the IMF and the World Bank. As a top official of the ADB put it: "We have never killed a project. We are a development institution, but we are also a bank. We have got to look for customers."[19] As long as multilateral aid agencies are motivated by such perverse incentives and Western governments buy the contention that those institutions are increasingly needed to promote international development, multilateral lending will continue to increase, despite abundant evidence that it does not work.

Removing the Impediments to Growth

Nations around the world are dismantling their state-owned enterprises, liberalizing their economies, reducing their trade barriers, shrinking their public sectors, and abandoning interventionist policies

[18]The Wapenhans report reached a similar conclusion, blaming portfolio management problems on the "Bank's pervasive preoccupation with new lending." World Bank Portfolio Management Task Force, p. iii.

[19]Sender, p. 52.

that have for so long wrecked their economies. Countries in Eastern Europe, Latin America, East Asia, and even Africa are discovering that prosperity depends little upon the practices of outside countries and almost entirely on policies within their own borders. Chile, Malaysia, Mexico, Singapore, and Taiwan, to name a few, have all demonstrated that a poor nation's economic destiny need not be tied to Western aid.

To the contrary, development can occur without aid, and, indeed, is more likely to result if multilateral aid and the domestic impediments to growth financed by it are eliminated. In fact, the now-rich nations of the West would not have emerged from poverty years ago had they depended on outside help. After spending decades on the wrong (statist) road to development, many Third World countries finally recognize that prosperity depends on the creation of wealth, not its transfer.

Unfortunately, despite dramatic liberalizations in much of the Third World and genuine efforts to achieve economic progress through trade, as opposed to aid, most industrialized countries have been unhelpful, maintaining a patronizing attitude toward underdeveloped nations and hypocritically shutting out their exports. Although Western governments maintain low tariffs on most goods, they impose significant nontariff barriers to trade with underdeveloped countries.[20] The consequences are perverse: James Bovard describes how the United States, while making ever-larger commitments of aid to Eastern Europe and the former Soviet Union (and while stressing the importance of free trade when offering policy advice), has erected a virtual iron curtain against the region's exports, including textiles, steel, and agricultural products. He warns that Washington's trade laws are highly protectionist and risk " 'strangling in the crib' the struggling entrepreneurs of the former Eastern Bloc."

J. Michael Finger also examines the costs of the industrialized world's trade barriers to the Third World. "Developed countries' import restrictions," he writes, "reduce developing countries' national income by about twice as much as developing countries receive in aid." Again, rather than facilitating international development, the

---

[20]Prominent among those barriers are anti-dumping and countervailing duties. The number of such cases filed annually in the United States rose "markedly" from 1980 to 1991. Anne O. Krueger, *Economic Policies at Cross-Purposes: The United States and Developing Countries* (Washington, D.C.: Brookings Institution, 1993), p. 118.

11

governments of rich nations create more impediments to it—and then hand over their own citizens' wealth through foreign aid to help alleviate the resulting poverty.

By opening their borders and allowing private foreign investment, poor countries can nevertheless prosper. David Osterfeld shows how multinational corporations improve the economic conditions of the countries in which they invest. Just as multilateral lending institutions are by their nature ineffective at promoting growth, multinational corporations are effective because they are much more likely to allocate their resources productively. Thus, while multilateral aid agencies concentrate on transferring wealth, multinational corporations actually help spread *prosperity.*

Indeed, the more a country opens its borders and is exposed to outside influences, the more its ordinary people are likely to prosper. Jim Powell documents the seemingly endless examples of nations throughout history attempting to shut themselves off from the world. Such economic nationalism, he writes, has always backfired. "Private, commercial contact with the outside world has proven to be perhaps the most powerful, persistent stimulus for human progress."

Ultimately, Third World nations can emerge from underdevelopment only through their own efforts. They have always had the potential to do so, but inward-looking domestic policies, economic nationalism, and other forms of statism have prevented literally billions of people around the globe from enjoying the prosperity that naturally arises from economic freedom.

The industrialized states can still help. If the West is sincere about aiding the world's poor, then it should open its borders to their goods. Likewise, it should dismantle the multilateral aid agencies that have done so much to perpetuate Third World poverty. With so many developing countries successfully undergoing radical transitions toward free markets and political pluralism, the most important thing the West can do is to get out of the way.

PART I

THE INTERNATIONAL MONETARY FUND

1. The IMF: A Record of Addiction and Failure

Doug Bandow

In the fall of 1989, Michel Camdessus, managing director of the International Monetary Fund (IMF), declared his intention to help the world's poor. How? By doubling his organization's resources. At the annual World Bank–IMF meeting, he argued that hiking the IMF's capital from $120 billion to $240 billion would be "the cheapest way for taxpayers in the richer countries to come to the aid of the poor."[1] If the United States and other member countries were stingy and refused to go along with such an increase, he warned that the IMF would have to borrow money to meet its needs and "that would be a pity."[2] Camdessus need not have worried. The industrialized nations ultimately agreed on a roughly $60-billion jump; after all, for more than four decades they had provided all of the multilateral lending institutions with more money whenever the latter had asked.

But to what effect? Officials at the IMF and other aid agencies constantly proclaim their commitment to international growth and development. Yet the result of the flood of grants and loans is impoverishment, indebtedness, and dependence around the globe. The money of Western taxpayers has gone to fatten the bank accounts of foreign rulers, pacify local interest groups, expand bloated bureaucracies, and underwrite projects whose only purpose is to inflate national egos. Even what were once thought to be the best of loan programs—docks, factories, and roads—are deteriorating and bleeding poor nations dry.

The World Bank, as "America's" institution (by tradition, the United States chooses the bank's president), has always received more press attention in the United States than has the IMF. In contrast, the IMF,

---

[1]Hobart Rowen, "IMF Director Asks Again for Higher Quotas," *Washington Post*, September 28, 1989, p. C11.

[2]Ibid.

whose executive director is picked by the European nations, has eschewed publicity. Although it has the distinction of being perhaps the only international organization that has regularly been the target of riots in foreign capitals, it has kept a low profile in Washington except when asking for money.

In 1982, the IMF wanted a quota increase and had to run a political gauntlet ranging from the free-market Competitive Enterprise Institute to several Naderite groups and the environmental lobby. Only under strong pressure from the supposedly conservative Reagan administration did the House of Representatives narrowly pass the funding measure the following year, after which the IMF quietly faded into the background once more.

In the early 1990s, the IMF has again made news. Although its $120-billion pool of gold and currencies would hardly have seemed inadequate for worthwhile lending to Third World nations, many of which cannot pay back their current loans, Camdessus has lobbied incessantly to increase the fund's activities, especially in Eastern Europe and the former Soviet Union. Indeed, many view the IMF as the leading actor in the ongoing reform struggle in Russia; in 1992, the fund called for $22 billion in assistance for Moscow in the following year alone.

Another reason the IMF wants more money is that it, like the commercial banks, is having trouble collecting on its past loans. By 1993, its arrears totaled about $3.8 billion, almost 10 percent of its outstanding credit of $39.4 billion. Under those circumstances, most people would suggest increased prudence in extending new credit, but an independent international bureaucracy able to lift the wallets of taxpayers around the globe sees the solution quite differently: increase lending. And, naturally, private bankers worried about collecting on their loans, as well as political leaders of the essentially insolvent borrowers, share this view. Thus, it came as no surprise that the fund wanted to double its resources and that the Bush administration agreed to a 50 percent jump, permitting the IMF to lend about $12 billion annually throughout the early 1990s.

The Changing Functions of the IMF

The IMF was created as part of the Bretton Woods system at the close of World War II to help nations suffering balance-of-payments difficulties. When Richard Nixon closed what was left of the gold window in 1971, ending the international system of fixed exchange rates, the original function of the IMF disappeared, but that had no impact on the organization's lending. Indeed, the fund soon ended up providing more credit than ever before—new loans increased nearly sixfold from 1973 to 1974. During that period, observes an official history of the fund, H. Johannes Witteveen, the IMF's managing director, "took several innovative steps to increase the fund's lending activity and capacity."[3] Total outstanding credit went from about $1.3 billion in 1973 to $45 billion in 1985 (it has since declined to $39.4 billion). That caused one observer to ask, "Is this an example of Parkinson's Law? Is IMF lending growing although the need for it has diminished?"[4]

What does the IMF do with its money? In contrast to the World Bank, the fund does not back individual projects, such as a power plant or a redevelopment program. Instead, the IMF makes loans to governments, theoretically to assist them in promoting overall economic development. The fund imposes a variety of policy conditions on borrowers that are supposed to improve their economic performance and ensure repayment of the loans.

Once the World Bank began its massive expansion of lending during the 1970s, the IMF's only plausible justification for existing was that it was the sole international institution concerned with borrowers' overall economic policies. By the mid-1980s, however, the bank was providing billions annually in so-called structural adjustment loans, which looked suspiciously like fund programs. Observed World Bank vice president Ernest Stern, "The difference [between the two forms of credit] lies primarily in the orientation of each institution's staff and the experience and expertise it is capable of mustering."[5] In short, not only does the bank lend more than the IMF every year, but it uses much of its resources for the same purposes, which means the fund has lost its last conceivable raison d'être.

---

[3]Margaret Garritsen de Vries, *The IMF in a Changing World 1945–85* (Washington, D.C.: IMF, 1986), p. 118.

[4]Roland Vaubel, "The Moral Hazard of IMF Lending," in *International Lending and the IMF: A Conference in Memory of Wilson E. Schmidt,* Allan Meltzer, ed. (Washington, D.C.: Heritage Foundation, 1983), p. 66.

[5]Ernest Stern, "World Bank Financing of Structural Adjustment," in *IMF Conditionality,* John Williamson, ed. (Washington, D.C.: Institute for International Economics, 1983), p. 102.

A Look at the IMF's Record

Unfortunately, the World Bank has achieved little with annual lending in excess of $20 billion.[6] And the IMF has had no more success in promoting real market-oriented policy reform than has the bank. Instead, all the IMF has done is create yet another ongoing subsidy for corrupt rulers of statist regimes, irrespective of the destructiveness of their policies.

The best test of the effectiveness of the IMF is whether any troubled developing country has ever "graduated" because of the IMF loan program. Alas, success stories are few. South Korea has collected IMF loans, but it began using fund credit only in 1974, after that nation's economic miracle was under way. New Zealand and Great Britain have both borrowed on occasion, but they industrialized long before there was an IMF.

Even friends of the IMF and the other multilateral lending organizations have found few successful cases to praise. Richard Feinberg and Catherine Gwin, for instance, concluded in 1989 that "the record of IMF-assisted adjustment efforts in sub-Saharan Africa is discouraging. Many IMF-assisted programs, adopted in response to steep economic decline, have broken down."[7] Economist Jeffrey Sachs contended that most agreements "are now honored in the breach."[8] Sidney Dell of the United Nations wrote that "the frequency of breakdowns indicates in itself that there is something wrong with the system of pinpoint targetry."[9] Raymond Mikesell of the University of Oregon reported that "most oil-importing [less developed countries] are not pursuing policies associated with successful adjustment and growth" despite the IMF's efforts.[10] Several other commentators have found what Sachs describes as "mediocre compliance at best."[11]

[6]See, for example, Doug Bandow, "What's Still Wrong with the World Bank," *Orbis*, Winter 1989, pp. 73–89.

[7]Richard Feinberg and Catherine Gwin, "Reforming the Fund," in *The International Monetary Fund in a Multipolar World: Pulling Together* (Washington, D.C.: Overseas Development Council, 1989), p. 9.

[8]Jeffrey Sachs, "Strengthening IMF Programs in Highly Indebted Countries," in ibid., p. 102.

[9]Sidney Dell, "Stabilization: The Political Economy of Overkill," in *IMF Conditionality*, p. 42.

[10]Raymond Mikesell, "Appraising IMF Conditionality: Too Loose, Too Tight, or Just Right?" in ibid., pp. 57–58.

[11]Sachs, p. 107.

Indeed, a major review of a score of detailed studies of IMF programs yielded little cause for cheer. The best economist Mohsin Khan could say in an article printed in an IMF journal was, "First, there is frequently an improvement in the balance of payments and the current account, although a number of studies show no effects of programs. Second, inflation is generally not affected by programs. Finally, the effects on the growth rate are uncertain, with the studies showing an improvement or no change being balanced by those indicating a deterioration in the first year of a program."[12] Even the IMF has admitted to a declining rate of compliance in recent years.[13] (However, the fund has studiously ignored the paucity of studies demonstrating its effectiveness, declaring that "the general conclusion of studies of the effects of fund-supported programs is that they have had a positive effect.")[14]

Not surprisingly, then, the IMF has been subsidizing the world's economic basket cases for years, without apparent effect. Through 1989 six nations, Chile, Egypt, India, Sudan, Turkey, and Yugoslavia, had been relying on IMF aid for more than 30 years; 24 countries had been borrowers for between 20 and 29 years. And 47, almost one-third of all the states in the world, had been using IMF credit for between 10 and 19 years. (See appendices A and B.) Since 1947, Egypt has never left the IMF dole. Yugoslavia took its first loan in 1949 and was a borrower in all but 3 of the succeeding 41 years. India was another of the IMF's first customers and, aside from short intervals, has been on IMF programs for four decades.

Bangladesh, Barbados, Gambia, Guinea-Bissau, Pakistan, Uganda, Zaire, and Zambia all started borrowing in the early 1970s and have yet to stop two decades later. IMF loans to Argentina, Bolivia, Brazil, Costa Rica, Dominican Republic, Haiti, Peru, and Uruguay have helped turn those nations into permanent debtors without doing anything to solve their economic ills. Particularly striking is the fact that of the 83 developing states that have been using IMF funds for at least 60 percent of the years since they started borrowing, more than half, 43 nations, have relied on the IMF *every* year. While the fund has

---

[12]Mohsin Khan, "The Macroeconomic Effects of Fund-Supported Adjustment Programs," International Monetary Fund Staff Papers, June 1990, p. 210.

[13]Sachs, p. 107.

[14]International Monetary Fund, *Ten Common Misconceptions about the IMF* (Washington, D.C.: IMF, 1989), p. 10.

not necessarily caused nations to become permanently dependent on foreign funds, its efforts have not appeared to help any nation achieve independence through self-sustaining growth.

There are several problems with IMF lending, though the organization makes it hard to judge its activities. Sachs, for instance, has complained about IMF secrecy that "makes it extremely difficult for outside observers to prepare a serious quantitative appraisal of IMF policies."[15] The details of IMF standby agreements are not reported, and the organization refuses to release audits of its loans. Ultimately, however, the best test of the IMF's achievements is whether borrowers seem to be making progress as a result of the fund's activities. Alas, the fund appears to flunk that test, for several reasons.

Inappropriate Conditions

The IMF has often focused on narrow accounting data, causing its advice to have perverse consequences. As a condition for a loan the IMF will, for instance, demand that a nation reduce its current account deficit—so the borrower restricts imports. Insistence that a country cut its budget deficit may cause the government to raise taxes, slowing growth. In fact, the IMF has explicitly lobbied for higher levies, pushing Argentina's Menem administration to increase the value-added tax, for instance, and advocating that Mauritius adopt "a series of new taxes."[16] Even where the budget deficit does not actually grow as the economy shrinks, the fund has succeeded in reducing the budget deficit only by reinforcing the very borrower policies, such as high taxes, that block growth.

There are obviously some cases in which the IMF does push for sensible reform.[17] However, the "toughness" of the fund's conditionality has varied over time. Economist John Williamson reported that analysis showed "enormous variation between one program and

---

[15]Sachs, p. 102.

[16]Alan Reynolds, "Taxes and Growth in the LDCs," Paper presented to Conference on Global Disequilibrium, May 17–19, 1989, p. 3.

[17]It is hard to judge the ratio of good to bad conditions. Economist Alan Reynolds is a severe critic of the fund. See, for example, "The IMF's Destructive Recipe of Devaluation and Austerity," Hudson Institute, May 1992. Arnold Harberger of the University of Chicago is much milder, saying that "the IMF, while on the whole tending to give good advice, sometimes makes mistakes," "Panel Discussion," in *IMF Conditionality*, p. 579. Even if the agency's errors are few, however, its conditions are neither well enough enforced or sufficiently comprehensive to achieve significant results, as is argued later.

another."[18] Among the factors causing the fund to vary its conditions was, admitted Williamson, pressure "to lend money in order to justify having it."[19]

Moreover, even setting some useful conditions may have little impact if other policies still cause serious distortions in the borrowing country. Observed Raymond Mikesell, who in 1983 estimated that more than half of the less developed countries were following self-destructive interventionist economic policies, "The continued existence of these conditions [such as price controls] in a substantial proportion of the [less developed countries] suggests that not enough attention is being given to policy reform in the negotiation and implementation of the IMF conditionality programs."[20]

Lack of Enforcement

Moreover, the IMF, like the World Bank, does not do enough to enforce its conditions. If a country violates its agreement with the IMF, the organization may simply grant a waiver, modifying the offending conditions. Or the fund may suspend the loan, only to later negotiate a new agreement. Money will start to flow again, the borrower will violate the new conditions, the IMF will hold up payments, the loan will be renegotiated, and the process will begin anew. How else can one explain 17 different arrangements with Peru between 1971 and 1977, 8 separate standby programs for Brazil between 1965 and 1972, decades' worth of credit for Zaire, and so on? In fact, the largest Third World borrowers between 1947 and 1987 were India, Brazil, Argentina, Mexico, and Yugoslavia, all of which maintained state-managed economies throughout the period despite the fund's loan conditions.[21]

The IMF seems to measure success by making loans. The assumption is that financial input into poor countries automatically translates into growth output; thus, to not extend credit is to fail. Members of the Bush administration obviously had a similar view; Treasury Secretary Nicholas Brady, for instance, proposed a new World Bank fund

---

[18]John Williamson, *The Lending Policies of the International Monetary Fund* (Washington, D.C.: Institute for International Economics, 1982), p. 48.

[19]Ibid., p. 50.

[20]Mikesell, p. 58.

[21]David Driscoll, *What Is the International Monetary Fund?* (Washington, D.C.: IMF, 1989), p. 15.

supported by the IMF.[22] President Clinton, a fervent backer of increased aid for Moscow, appears to share the same credit-equals-growth assumption. Yet shoveling more money into essentially insolvent states that have squandered billions in prior loans makes no sense. IMF conditionality would likely be more effective if the fund's refusal to make new loans were based on factors other than a country's inability or unwillingness to repay past IMF loans.

Statist Subsidies

As noted earlier, however sensible the IMF's conditions, they mean little when a nation's overall policy climate is badly askew.[23] In general, the fund asks countries to take too few of the steps necessary to promote growth; nevertheless, the left still regularly attacks the fund for allegedly advocating capitalism. But Williamson has defended the IMF against the criticism that it is too market oriented.

> It has also been charged that the fund is biased against socialism. That the fund welcomes those governments that are willing to work with market forces cannot be doubted. At the same time, the fund clearly does not have an evangelical zeal for spreading "the magic of the market" parallel to that of, say, the Reagan administration. Its attitude, it would claim, is nonideological: it seeks to promote economic rationality, and it just happens that under a wide range of circumstances the readiest means to that end involves harnessing, instead of fighting, market forces.
>
> What is surely true is that the fund does not refuse to provide financial assistance to members with left-wing governments. On the contrary, [in late 1989] some 16.5 percent of IMF credit was directed to the six communist member countries (China, Kampuchea, Laos, Romania, Vietnam, and Yugoslavia . . .) and Michael Manley's Jamaica was at one stage the heaviest *per capita* borrower from the fund. . . . Moreover, the fund continued to give the Allende government [of Chile] the

---

[22]Karen Riley, "IMF, World Bank Suffer from Insufficient Funds," *Washington Times,* April 30, 1991, p. C1.

[23]For a summary of the sort of policy changes that are necessary in developing countries, see Alvin Rabushka, "From Austerity to Growth: A New Role for the IMF," in *The Political Morality of the International Monetary Fund,* Robert Myers, ed. (New York: Carnegie Council on Ethics and International Affairs, 1987), pp. 143–47. In fact, the IMF is not ignorant of the importance of such market-oriented policies. See, for example, Bahram Nowzad, "Promoting Development: The IMF's Contribution," Washington, D.C., IMF, n.d.

benefit of the doubt in drawing from the compensatory financing facility.[24]

The IMF similarly disclaims a bias against collectivist systems: "The fund has had programs in all types of economies and has worked with their authorities, identifying the best way to achieve external balance or exercising its function of surveillance over the payments and exchange system. . . . In many instances, fund-supported programs have accommodated such nonmarket devices as production controls, administered prices, and subsidies."[25] Yet how is a country with such policies going to achieve self-sustaining economic growth? It is hard to take seriously an organization's claim to be "pro-development" when it regularly pours large sums of money into the worst economic systems on earth. One friend of the fund has argued "that to the extent that programs succeed in their objective of establishing macroeconomic stability in the economy, they can be expected to have a positive impact on growth in the longer run."[26] But how often has the IMF been able to transform *dirigiste* policies that are bad in almost every way?

In an assessment of lending to communist states, for example, Valerie Assetto wrote that "Romania's economic reforms were superficial and actually worked to increase the power of the state. The ensuing economic crisis quickly eclipsed the 'reform' movement, and it quietly expired. Fund and [World] Bank support of the Romanian development effort continued throughout this period."[27] Similarly, she found that the "Yugoslav authorities actually retreated slightly from the market orientation of the 1960s" despite generous assistance in following years.[28] As late as 1990 Camdessus lauded the fact that the IMF remained engaged in Yugoslavia, supporting "a comprehensive and bold program to stop inflation in its tracks and to reform the economy over the medium term."[29] Yet economists Jeffrey Sachs and

[24]John Williamson, "The Lending Policies of the International Monetary Fund," in *IMF Conditionality*, p. 653.

[25]*Ten Common Misconceptions about the IMF*, p. 8.

[26]Khan, p. 219.

[27]Valerie Assetto, *The Soviet Bloc in the IMF and the IBRD* (Boulder, Colo.: Westview, 1988), p. 149.

[28]Ibid., p. 132.

[29]Michel Camdessus, *The IMF and the World Economy in the 1990s* (Washington, D.C.: IMF, 1990), p. 19.

David Lipton blamed the fund's conditions—particularly its commitment to continued devaluations—for helping to "cause Yugoslavia to drift from high inflation into hyperinflation."[30]

At times it would appear that the more perverse the policies, the more generous the IMF. The problem is not just the former Soviet bloc, but the many Third World regimes that followed statist economic policies for decades. For instance, India collected more money than any other developing state from the IMF, which acted more as a lender of first rather than last resort, during its first 40 years. Yet while India was borrowing prodigiously from the IMF (and other multilateral institutions), it was pursuing a Soviet-style industrialization program. Catherine Gwin of the Carnegie Endowment for International Peace observed the country's economic orientation:

> India's economy is continental in scope; highly industrialized and extremely poor; centrally planned—some would say overly planned; administratively encumbered and rampant with corruption; caste-bound and socialist-inspired; determinedly self-reliant; and, though guided by principles of social democracy, protective of the interests of politically powerful, propertied groups.[31]

India has also devoted a large portion of its budget, well supplemented by foreign aid, to its military. In the fall of 1981, for instance, India was simultaneously negotiating with France for a $2-billion Mirage jet deal and with the IMF for a $3.6-billion loan.[32]

In the 1970s, the Mexican government was destroying its economy even as it was a regular IMF customer. When Mexico's threatened default on its vast international obligations essentially set off the debt crisis in 1982, the IMF came to the rescue, a role extolled by the fund.[33] Yet the loans did little to improve Mexico's economic performance; that nation did not begin making major market-oriented reforms until the

---

[30]Jeffrey Sachs and David Lipton, "How Yugoslavia Can Save Itself," *Washington Post*, December 31, 1989, p. C5.

[31]Catherine Gwin, "Financing India's Structural Adjustment: The Role of the Fund," in *IMF Conditionality*, p. 513. As for the stultifying effect of India's economic controls, see her discussion on p. 515.

[32]See Doug Bandow, "Aid Money That Just Buys Guns," *Wall Street Journal*, June 14, 1988, p. 34.

[33]De Vries, pp. 186–87.

end of the decade after squandering billions more of foreign money on counterproductive state-led development schemes.

The IMF has some 32 programs operating in Africa, yet nowhere have national economic policies been worse or past lending more misguided. In 1974, for instance, the IMF negotiated a loan to Tanzania, which agreed to adopt a package "of compromises that might be called socialist realism," in the words of one observer.[34] But the government, which had ruined the economy through such policies as forced agricultural collectivization (the *ujaama* program), refused to cut spending, and the IMF terminated the program, having done no more than subsidize the leading example of "African socialism." In 1983, Reginald Herbold Green, of the Institute of Development Studies, concluded that "IMF *influence* on Tanzanian action has, to date, been fairly modest. Direct impact since 1976 has, arguably, been negative. Indirect effects are hard to assess."[35]

Kenya, which borrowed roughly $130 million in 1988 and owed more than $380 million total at the end of 1989 was then building a 60-story, $200-million office building—complete with a larger-than-life statue of President Daniel arap Moi—in Nairobi. Earlier lending programs to Kenya also proved disappointing.[36] In his analysis of IMF lending to these two African states, Stanley Please of the World Bank was particularly critical of Tanzania's failure to review programs that were not working. In his view, Kenya suffered from some of the same difficulties and, he concluded, "the problem of the inadequate use of pricing and the overextension of the public sector" was "a pervasive one in Africa."[37]

Only after its Marxist revolution did Ethiopia begin borrowing from the IMF, yet it was the government's collectivization of agriculture that dramatically worsened the famine during the mid-1980s. The loans to Ethiopia exhibited another damning aspect of IMF lending. The fund underwrites any government, however venal and brutal. Naturally,

[34]William Cline, "Economic Stabilization in Developing Countries: Theory and Stylized Facts," in *IMF Conditionality*, p. 204.

[35]Reginald Herbold Green, "Political-Economic Adjustment and IMF Conditionality: Tanzania, 1974–81," in *IMF Conditionality*, p. 373.

[36]See, for example, Tony Killick, "Kenya, the IMF, and the Unsuccessful Quest for Stabilization," in *IMF Conditionality*, pp. 400–405.

[37]Stanley Please, "Comments," in *IMF Conditionality*, p. 418.

the loans are not earmarked for repression. But the IMF extends credit directly to governments and money is fungible. Whether Ethiopia took its IMF cash and directly bought bombs for use against Eritrean rebels or shifted its accounts around in Addis Ababa first made no real difference: in either case, the fund (as well as other lenders, such as the World Bank) was an accomplice to murder. Another good IMF customer was Nicolae Ceausescu's Romania, which, in contrast to so many other poor nations, regularly paid its debts. China owed the fund $600 million as of the end of 1989; in January 1990, just a few months after the blood had dried in Beijing's Tianamen Square, the IMF held a seminar on monetary policy in the city. Other clients include or have included Burma, Pinochet's Chile, Laos, Nicaragua under Somoza and the Sandinistas, Syria, Vietnam, Zaire, and so on—the IMF has rarely met a dictatorship that it didn't like.

Reduced Political Pressure

There is an even more insidious problem with IMF lending. Countries such as Bangladesh, China, Mexico, Tanzania, and Vietnam have all moved unsteadily towards more market-oriented policies because they have felt the consequences of disastrous economic failure. For years they operated money-losing enterprises and bloated public bureaucracies and manipulated credit, money, prices, and trade for the benefit of well-connected elites. But the day of reckoning finally came.

Naturally, the IMF claims credit for today's reforms. Camdessus explained that his organization currently has a record number of arrangements with African countries. "Discussions are at an advanced stage with several others. Do you think that this number would be so high if it were not recognized by these countries that the way we offer is really the most promising? Do you really think that countries such as Algeria, Tanzania, and Nigeria would be engaged in programs with the fund if they did not have strong evidence that this approach works?"[38] But once governments have decided that they have to either adopt reforms or perish, it is no surprise when they are willing to accept the IMF's money, even with conditions. The real question, which Camdessus ignored, is, Has the IMF advanced or retarded the reform process in borrowing states?

[38]Camdessus, p. 5.

26

While good advice may help persuade governments to change policy, the IMF has eschewed pushing for tax rate cuts, for instance. In nine instances "where the ignition of economic growth followed cuts in marginal tax rates," including in Bolivia, Chile, Colombia, and Mauritius, wrote former World Bank analyst Melanie Tammen, the fund was unhelpful. "None of these nine were 'benefiting' from IMF loans and advice when they undertook the decisive reforms."[39]

In any case, the IMF's financial assistance is unlikely to be enough to persuade governments without the will to reform to do so. For instance, John Williamson believed that in only three of nine post-1975 loan programs "can the fund program plausibly be given credit for securing a measure of adjustment."[40] India made some tentative steps toward market reform during the 1980s, but later regressed. Catherine Gwin accurately predicted in 1983 that "there is some reason to doubt that the government will actually carry through on the politically difficult decisions that adjustment requires. Politicians, bureaucrats, and entrepreneurs do well under the present licensing system."[41] More recently, India has adopted serious economic reforms, but its new course had nothing to do with IMF lending.

Jamaica is an example of "a country which allowed conditions to deteriorate dramatically before a last-ditch recourse to the fund" in 1977.[42] Even then, however, the prospect of IMF assistance was not enough to ensure compliance; wrote analyst Jennifer Sharpley, a "lack of consensus about Jamaica's economic strategy and wavering political commitment to stabilization were to persist throughout 1977–80."[43]

Loans can, in fact, undermine the will to reform by reducing the pain caused by politically popular but economically harmful policies. Indeed, argues Roland Vaubel, "the prospect of cheap IMF lending is likely to generate a moral hazard by reducing the incentive to stay

---

[39]Melanie Tammen, "How the IMF Plays the Bailout Game," *Washington Times*, December 15, 1989, p. F1.

[40]Williamson, "The Lending Policies of the International Monetary Fund," p. 650.

[41]Gwin, p. 516.

[42] Jennifer Sharpley, "Economic Management and IMF Conditionality in Jamaica," in *IMF Conditionality*, p. 240.

[43]Ibid., p. 239.

solvent. It would pay a potential borrower to pass the international means test."[44]

Is Russia Different?

The IMF risks creating just such disincentives to reform as it and other organizations and governments step up lending to Russia. True, international aid bureaucrats proclaim that they have learned from the past failures of foreign assistance. They insist that they are now committed to market reforms and will be tough taskmasters, ensuring compliance with loan conditions. For instance, the Russian reform program, exulted Michel Camdessus when he announced approval of a $1.5-billion loan to Russia in July 1993, "represents a milestone in their efforts to move the economy to a sustainable noninflationary growth path."[45] (Alas, barely two months later the IMF had to suspend its loan program because of noncompliance with fund conditions.)

Even when the money flows again, as it undoubtedly will, it is not likely to markedly advance the cause of reform. Russia has abandoned totalitarianism despite, not because of, Western lending, which was, after all, quite generous to Brezhnev's Soviet Union. Indeed, Boris Yeltsin, well-nigh idolized in Western capitals, moved from party boss to democratic reformer only because of the economic failure of communism. And it is only Russia's desperate straits that continue to force him and his aides to advance reforms in the face of serious resistance. Thus, alleviating some of the worst symptoms of Russia's 70-year bout with the collectivist illness through large-scale aid transfers could paradoxically slow the move towards freer markets. In particular, pouring funds into the Russian government—the recipient of almost all foreign assistance—is likely to strengthen the position of the still-powerful economic bureaucrats, who would prefer to subsidize than privatize money-losing state enterprises, and nationalist politicians, who want to return to authoritarianism rather than move toward freedom.

Western aid programs may hinder economic change in another way. Reformers, like their counterpart apparatchiks, already face manifold temptations involving the prospect of great wealth; the liberal-minded mayor of Moscow, Gavriil Popov, for instance, resigned under an

---

[44]Vaubel, pp. 68–69.

[45]"IMF Board Approves Russian Loan," *IMF Survey*, July 12, 1993, p. 209.

ethical cloud for questionable financial dealings. Thus, aid programs, so often looted by leaders of *dirigiste* regimes, may also ensnare believers in freer markets. Warned Karen LaFollette of the Institute for Political Economy, "In Russia the danger is that reformers could be distracted by the opportunities for graft presented by large-scale financial transfers, and then there would be no one to undertake the transition."[46] Spreading corruption would also discredit the case for reform in the minds of moderate politicians and average citizens.

In any case, Western aid seems only marginally relevant to the unfolding drama in Russia. With great difficulty, the Yeltsin administration has made significant economic strides—*before* receiving substantial Western aid. In fact, the IMF's Camdessus admitted as much when he announced the following in July 1993.

> The Russian authorities have not come to the fund with empty hands. The very high rates of inflation in the last several months have been reduced, and thus the very real danger of hyperinflation seems so far to have been averted. They are resisting with determination various pending populist initiatives. They have implemented various concrete measures to reduce subsidies to importers, the coal sector, and grain producers. They have tightened monetary policy and increased interest rates. The program for the rest of 1993 aims at achieving substantial progress toward financial stabilization.[47]

Consider the important step, lauded by Camdessus, of reducing the inflation rate. That required, not a special Western assistance program, but domestic restraint in the printing of rubles. Moscow took this and all of the other steps cited by Camdessus *without* IMF lending and conditionality. Moreover, the Yeltsin government seemed committed to maintaining a reform course—after all, what other choice did it realistically have, given Russia's precarious economic situation?—irrespective of the amount of aid received from abroad.

At the same time, the Russian Congress of People's Deputies, later forcibly disbanded, voted to resist the Yeltsin program, particularly industrial privatization, *even after* the IMF loan announcement. Nor did those legislators yield when Moscow cashed the IMF's check. Indeed, nationalists criticized Yeltsin in the past for begging for aid; sizable

---

[46]Karen LaFollette, "Soft Assistance for Hard Russian Reform," Cato Institute Foreign Policy Briefing no. 25, June 3, 1993, p. 2.

[47]"IMF Board Approves Russian Loan," pp. 209, 213.

new Western credits may ultimately increase opposition to reform. Imagine the reaction if the IMF or other international organizations had arrived in Washington in October 1992, promising low-interest loans if the American people reelected George Bush. Thus, even if foreign financial support helps bolster the Yeltsin government in the short term, it may both sap its will to adopt tough, new reforms and simultaneously prove to be a rallying point for his opponents.

Perverse Global Impact

The IMF's potentially perverse impact is heightened because of its perceived role as a global leader. The problem is twofold. In general, the commercial banks have not placed any serious conditions on their loans, relying instead on the multilateral lending institutions, particularly the fund. Wrote banker Irving Friedman, "The IMF is, at times, the most visible outside influence with standards deemed acceptable to lending banks."[48] Moreover, the private banks have viewed IMF lending as a form of implicit financial guarantee. Alvin Rabushka of the Hoover Institution argued that perceived guarantees encourage private banks to make bad loans.

> The fund's own resources are insufficient to finance inflationary and other irresponsible economic policies adopted by developing countries, but are large enough to induce private banks to provide huge loans to the governments of developing countries by seeming to remove the risk of default. Many private bank loans have not been for particular projects or enterprises that might earn sufficient profits to repay interest and principal, but simply general loans to governments. The IMF promised implicitly that if debtor countries could not raise the hard currencies to pay back or service loans, the fund would step in with needed funds. On this implicit guarantee, banks have lent hundreds of billions of dollars to developing

---

[48]Irving Friedman, "Private Bank Conditionality: Comparison with the IMF and the World Bank," in *IMF Conditionality*, p. 119. Perhaps the best case that the IMF can make is that in some cases—Turkey, for instance—the IMF provided an official imprimatur for a far-reaching reform program that convinced commercial banks to provide additional credit, helping the government to proceed with its policies. See, for example, Osman Okyar, "Turkey and the IMF: A Review of Relations, 1978–82," in *IMF Conditionality*, p. 556. The truth of this contention is not self-evident: the IMF has been lending Turkey money for 38 years, apparently irrespective of Ankara's specific economic policies. Moreover, the fund seems to have far more often persuaded banks to lend to countries that are now effectively insolvent.

countries, little of which found its way into productive, private-sector enterprises.[49]

For years, foreign money has helped cover financial losses and sustain economies throughout the Third World, pushing off the borrowers' days of reckoning. More loans and aid today, by reducing the pain of continuing bad policies, will only further retard the adjustment process. Economic reform is, of course, often painful, but it is also unavoidable. More IMF lending is only likely to prolong the agony.

The IMF is not the sole offender. The World Bank, which relies heavily on project loans, has regularly provided billions of dollars to countries while simultaneously denouncing the borrowers' domestic economic policies. Moreover, for years the commercial banks, acting on the assumption that sovereign nations could not go bankrupt, were even worse. Observed Mikesell, "In many cases large-scale external borrowing from the private international financial markets has enabled countries to postpone resolution of their payments imbalances for a number of years, and the country approaches the IMF only after it is faced with default."[50]

This is not to ignore the seriousness of the international debt crisis—Third World states owing roughly $1.7 trillion to Western governments, multilateral institutions, and commercial banks. The problem, however, obviously is not inadequate lending. Rather, many, if not most, of the earlier loans have been wasted. Once borrowers have adopted the sort of reforms that will allow capital to be used productively in their nations, foreign credit and investment will flow in naturally. Until then, additional money will be wasted.

In the meantime, U.S. officials should give up trying to fashion a global solution to the debt crisis. Countries and banks should be left to negotiate together; selective write-downs, extensions, and debt-equity swaps should be adapted to the countries involved. Moreover, the Clinton administration and Congress should reject any further funding increases for the IMF, World Bank, or other international financial institutions.

Michel Camdessus insists that expanding his organization's budget is the most effective way for the rich in the West to help the world's

[49]Rabushka, pp. 151–52.
[50]Mikesell, p. 50.

poor. But the poor rarely attend the lavish receptions that mark the annual World Bank–IMF meetings. Indeed, it is the one time of the year when Washington finds itself short of limousines and the driveways of luxury hotels are almost continuously gridlocked as finance ministers and private bankers crisscross the city.

What the world's poor really need are governments that no longer strangle and loot their economies. But as long as the IMF helps fund regimes that are responsible for impoverishing their people, it will remain a large part of the problem.

Appendix A: Use of IMF Credit by Eligible Countries, 1947–89

Country	First Year Used	Number of Years Used	Percentage of Years Used[a]
Africa			
Algeria	1989	1	100
Benin	1989	1	100
Burundi	1968	16	73
Cameroon	1974	11	69
Central African Republic	1974	16	100
Chad	1970	20	100
Congo	1977	8	62
Equatorial Guinea	1980	10	100
Ethiopia	1949	12	29
Gabon	1978	10	83
Gambia	1977	13	100
Ghana	1962	25	89
Guinea	1969	20	95
Guinea-Bissau	1979	11	100
Ivory Coast	1974	13	81
Kenya	1963	25	93
Lesotho	1988	2	100
Liberia	1963	20	74
Madagascar	1974	16	100
Malawi	1975	15	100
Mali	1964	26	100

[a]Based on number of years country was eligible for IMF credit.

Country	First Year Used	Number of Years Used	Percentage of Years Used[a]
Mauritania	1976	14	100
Mauritius	1969	14	67
Morocco	1968	17	77
Mozambique	1987	3	100
Niger	1983	7	100
Rwanda	1966	5	100
Sao Tomé and Principe	1989	1	100
Senegal	1975	15	100
Sierra Leone	1967	19	83
Somalia	1964	14	54
South Africa	1976	9	82
Sudan	1958	30	94
Swaziland	1983	5	100
Tanzania	1974	16	100
Togo	1964	20	77
Tunisia	1964	15	58
Uganda	1971	19	100
Zaire	1972	18	100
Zambia	1971	19	100
Zimbabwe	1981	9	100
Asia			
Afghanistan	1964	13	100
Bangladesh	1972	18	100
China	1981	3	50
Fiji	1977	11	85
India	1949	34	83
Indonesia	1956	24	71
Kampuchea	1972	18	100
Laos	1975	12	80
Malaysia	1976	6	60
Myanmar	1967	21	100
Nepal	1976	14	100
Pakistan	1965	25	100
Papua New Guinea	1976	10	100
Philippines	1955	29	83
South Korea	1974	14	100

Country	First Year Used	Number of Years Used	Percentage of Years Used[a]
Solomon Islands	1981	9	100
Sri Lanka	1962	28	100
Thailand	1976	14	100
Vietnam	1977	13	100
Western Samoa	1975	15	100
Europe			
Cyprus	1974	11	100
Hungary	1982	8	100
Romania	1973	16	100
Turkey	1953	34	92
Yugoslavia	1949	38	93
Middle East			
Egypt	1957	33	100
Iran	1955	6	86
Iraq	1967	1	100
Israel	1957	13	50
Jordan	1971	8	42
Syria	1960	26	87
Yemen Arab Republic	1983	4	100
Yemen People's Democratic Republic	1974	13	100
Western Hemisphere			
Argentina	1957	23	70
Barbados	1977	13	100
Belize	1983	7	100
Bolivia	1959	25	81
Brazil	1951	23	59
Chile	1957	33	100
Colombia	1954	16	89
Costa Rica	1961	23	79
Dominica	1979	11	100
Dominican Republic	1960	26	87
Ecuador	1957	19	58
El Salvador	1956	22	69
Grenada	1975	13	93

Country	First Year Used	Number of Years Used	Percentage of Years Used[a]
Guatemala	1962	14	50
Guyana	1971	17	89
Haiti	1958	29	91
Honduras	1957	23	70
Jamaica	1973	17	100
Mexico	1976	12	86
Nicaragua	1957	24	86
Panama	1968	18	82
Paraguay	1956	5	100
Peru	1958	21	66
St. Lucia	1980	5	100
St. Vincent	1981	4	100
Trinidad and Tobago	1988	2	100
Uruguay	1962	23	82
Venezuela	1989	1	100

Appendix B: Use of IMF Credit, 1949–89

30 Years or More (6)

Chile, Egypt, India, Sudan, Turkey, Yugoslavia

20 to 29 Years (24)

Argentina, Bolivia, Brazil, Chad, Costa Rica, Dominican Republic, El Salvador, Ghana, Guinea, Haiti, Honduras, Indonesia, Kenya, Liberia, Mali, Myanmar, Nicaragua, Pakistan, Peru, Philippines, Sri Lanka, Syria, Togo, Uruguay

10 to 19 Years (47)

Afghanistan, Bangladesh, Barbados, Burundi, Cameroon, Central African Republic, Colombia, Cyprus, Dominica, Ecuador, Equatorial Guinea, Ethiopia, Fiji, Gabon, Gambia, Grenada, Guatemala, Guinea-Bissau, Guyana, Israel, Ivory Coast, Jamaica, Kampuchea, Laos, Madagascar, Malawi, Mauritania, Mauritius, Mexico, Morocco, Nepal, Panama, Papua New Guinea, Romania, Senegal, Sierra Leone, Somalia, South Korea, Tanzania, Thailand, Tunisia,

Uganda, Vietnam, Western Samoa, Yemen (People's Democratic Republic), Zaire, Zambia

100 Percent of Years since First Use (43)[51]

Afghanistan, Bangladesh, Barbados, Belize, Central African Republic, Chad, Chile, Cyprus, Dominica, Egypt, Equatorial Guinea, Gambia, Guinea-Bissau, Hungary, Jamaica, Kampuchea, Madagascar, Malawi, Mali, Mauritania, Myanmar, Nepal, Niger, Pakistan, Papua New Guinea, Paraguay, Romania, Rwanda, St. Lucia, Senegal, Solomon Islands, South Korea, Sri Lanka, Swaziland, Tanzania, Thailand, Uganda, Vietnam, Western Samoa, Yemen (People's Democratic Republic), Zaire, Zambia, Zimbabwe

80 Percent to 99 Percent (26)

Bolivia, Colombia, Dominican Republic, Fiji, Gabon, Ghana, Grenada, Guinea, Guyana, Haiti, India, Iran, Ivory Coast, Kenya, Laos, Mexico, Nicaragua, Panama, Philippines, Sierra Leone, South Africa, Sudan, Syria, Turkey, Uruguay, Yugoslavia

60 Percent to 79 Percent (14)

Argentina, Burundi, Cameroon, Congo, Costa Rica, El Salvador, Honduras, Indonesia, Liberia, Malaysia, Mauritius, Morocco, Peru, Togo

[51]Based on at least five years of borrowing. Several countries, such as Algeria and Benin, began using fund credit only in the late 1980s.

2. The Political Economy of the IMF: A Public Choice Analysis

Roland Vaubel

The International Monetary Fund (IMF) has long been criticized by free-market economists. Gottfried Haberler commented in 1974 on the irony of the IMF's continued growth and expansion after the collapse of the Bretton Woods system (i.e., the system of fixed exchange rates), pointing out that "international institutions may change their names or lose their function, but they never die."[1] Milton Friedman advocated its dissolution: "I strongly oppose any increase of the IMF's quota and prefer to move in the opposite direction to see how we can dismantle the IMF and get rid of it."[2]

Beyond the simple conclusion that the IMF's function was no longer needed after the collapse of fixed exchange rates is Jurg Niehans's argument in 1985 that the IMF actually causes harm: "The fact that IMF lending, despite the collapse of the Bretton Woods System, still is largely conditional on a balance-of-payments crisis creates an incentive for a country to let itself slip into such a crisis whenever IMF lending is desired." Karl Brunner and Allan Meltzer pointed out in 1988 that the IMF's economic forecasts have been less accurate than comparable forecasts by governmental and especially private institutions in the member countries.[3]

Why has such criticism by economists borne no fruit? What can explain the IMF's practices and perennial quota increases, indeed, its continuing existence? The IMF's lending practices and economic policy

The author would like to thank Joe Cobb, John M. Ohlin fellow in economics at the Heritage Foundation, for his assistance in editing an earlier draft of this chapter.

[1]Gottfried Haberler, *Economic Growth and Stability* (Los Angeles: Nash, 1974), p. 156.

[2]*Journal of Commerce*, October 13, 1983.

[3]Karl Brunner and Allan H. Meltzer, "Money and the Economy: Issues in Monetary Analysis," *The Raffaele Mattioli Lectures* (Cambridge, England: Cambridge University Press), Table 4.5.

conditions are of particular interest for a case study from a public choice perspective—that is, from the perspective that bureaucrats behave in their self-interest according to the incentives or disincentives they face.

Why Did the IMF Expand after the Collapse of Bretton Woods?

When the Bretton Woods fixed exchange rate system collapsed in 1973, many economists expected the IMF to stop granting loans and perhaps to disband entirely. However, its real credit volume doubled between 1970 and 1975. IMF officials used the 1973 oil price hike to give the fund a new function: financing the resulting current-account deficits. In that way, the justification for IMF credits shifted from monetary adjustment to optimal real adjustment. In practice, the IMF helped to temporarily compensate for economic disturbances and postpone necessary adjustments. Then, as discussed later, the international debt crisis of the 1980s became a second golden opportunity for the IMF to surge in size and importance.

It is not enough to observe that IMF officials had a vested interest in the survival of their institution. Why did the member governments that are net lenders, under whose critical supervision IMF officials operate, approve the IMF's new role and not instruct borrowers to turn to the capital market? Were member states simply ignorant of the facts? Were they unaware that IMF credits are not a suitable form of development aid? Or did all member governments have an interest in being able to postpone real economic adjustment with the help of the IMF when their popularity was low and elections were near?

Why Are Foreign Exchange Interventions Subsidized?

Under a system of fixed exchange rates, the IMF's balance-of-payments credits were used to keep exchange rate fluctuations vis-à-vis the dollar (then the pivot currency) within the agreed-upon bounds through interventions in the foreign exchange market. Some have justified the extension of low-interest loans under those conditions by arguing that every central bank that keeps its currency's exchange rate stable vis-à-vis another currency improves the other currencies' quality and thus generates positive externalities or benefits that spill over to other economies. There would be something to that line of reasoning if a system of fixed but adjustable parities was desirable at all. In such a case, however, the IMF should subsidize not only foreign exchange interventions but all forms of monetary adjustment that promote exchange rate stability. That would include the exchange-rate-oriented growth of the domestic component of the monetary base.

It is important to note that foreign exchange interventions give a government some leeway for domestic demand management in spite of exchange rate fixity. (Lord Keynes must have been aware of this when he negotiated the Bretton Woods agreement.) Even if the central bank of the pivot currency country gears its monetary policy or its domestic credit expansion toward maintaining domestic price stability or gold convertibility, the governments of the other countries can use foreign exchange interventions to affect their domestic business cycles in spite of exchange rate fixity. Ruling politicians try to influence the domestic business cycle in their favor by generating a boom before elections and reversing course afterwards.

IMF lending can facilitate a business cycle expansion, and IMF conditionality may promote a subsequent contraction. The money supply increase that is compatible with a given fixed exchange rate is larger, the larger the central bank's sales of foreign exchange. How much difference they make depends on whether they are "sterilized" by the foreign central bank. An unsterilized intervention that increases the foreign money supply gives more leeway than a sterilized one, which merely augments the supply of bonds denominated in the foreign currency. But even a sterilized intervention still makes a difference as long as bonds in different currencies are imperfect substitutes in a portfolio of risky assets. In that way, the IMF tended to contribute to political business cycles before 1971.

Even with today's flexible exchange rates, eligibility for IMF credits continues to depend on the state of the balance of payments. Article V, section 3.b.ii, of the IMF's Articles of Agreement states the following:

> A member shall be entitled to purchase the currencies of other members from the Fund ... subject to the condition [that] it has a need to make the purchase because of its balance of payments or its reserve position or development of its reserves.

That condition is regarded as fulfilled if, for example, the country's gross hard currency reserves have declined. But a drop in foreign exchange reserves can be deliberately induced—in the case of fixed exchange rates, by increasing the domestic component of the monetary base, and in the case of adjustable parities, by revaluing the domestic currency. Neither choice of economic policy indicates an emergency situation.

In fact, there is considerable evidence that IMF borrowers are largely responsible for their own balance-of-payments problems. Sebastian Edwards's study of 23 developing countries under fixed exchange rates in 1965–72 confirms that excess supply of money tended "to result in international reserves dropping below desired levels."[4] An unpublished IMF study conducted in 1981 even concluded that, in 1964–73, overexpansionary demand policies were the principal cause of balance-of-payments problems in borrowing countries, while exogenous factors were least important.[5] A study by Thomas Reichmann shows that overexpansionary demand policies were the major factors in 15 of 21 developing countries that had standby arrangements with the IMF during 1973–75.[6]

An analysis by Mohsin Khan and Malcolm Knight concluded that over the whole period of 1973–80, the budget deficit (relative to gross domestic product) was the second most important factor, after their terms of trade, in explaining developing countries' current account balances.[7] An internal IMF working paper by Donal Donovan demonstrated that overexpansionary monetary and fiscal policies also contributed to a country's debt-servicing problems. In the five years before the debt crisis of the 1980s, the rescheduling countries shared the following characteristics:

- considerably higher rates of net credit expansion to government (13.4 percent annually) than the nonrescheduling countries (5.9 percent annually);
- considerably higher rates of M2 monetary expansion (31.9 percent annually) than the nonrescheduling countries (22.8 percent annually); and

[4]Sebastian Edwards, "The Role of International Reserves and Foreign Debt in the External Adjustment Process," in *Adjustment, Conditionality, and International Finance*, Joaquin Muns, ed. (Washington, D.C.: IMF, 1984).

[5]Tony Killick, "IMF Stabilisation Programmes," in *The Quest for Economic Stabilisation: The IMF and the Third World*, T. Killick, ed. (Aldershot, England: Gower, 1984), p. 188.

[6]Thomas M. Reichmann, "The Fund's Conditional Assistance and Problems of Adjustment, 1973–75," *Finance & Development*, vol. 15, no. 4 (December 1978), pp. 38–41.

[7]Mohsin S. Khan and Malcolm D. Knight, "Determinants of Current Account Balances of Non-Oil Developing Countries in the 1970s," IMF Staff Papers no. 30, December 1983, pp. 819–42.

- not surprisingly, considerably higher consumer price inflation (23.8 percent annually) than the nonrescheduling countries (14.3 percent annually).[8]

If it is true that the IMF wants to maximize its lending and supervision, it cannot be interested in legal restrictions on eligibility that might effectively bar potential borrowers. The criterion of balance-of-payments need is not an effective barrier. The IMF admits that "the requirement of need is in the nature of a portmanteau concept. It is a term of art rather than of law.... Reliance on judgmental factors is unavoidable."[9] The governments of the typical borrower countries obviously share an interest in lending conditions that are as easy as possible to meet. But that arrangement is also advantageous for the influential creditor countries, since it permits them to use IMF lending in pursuit of their own foreign policy objectives, as the United States did in 1982 when the debt crisis caused the Reagan administration to reverse its opposition to an IMF quota increase.

Why Should the IMF Lend at Subsidized Interest Rates?

Member governments can borrow from the IMF at favorable interest rates instead of resorting to the international capital market. According to its Articles of Agreement (V.8.d and XX.2), the fund has to charge uniform interest rates to all borrowers, effectively paying the largest subsidies to the least creditworthy. The IMF also tends to give the greatest benefits to long-term debtors, because, contrary to the Articles of Agreement (V.8.b), the rates are normally independent of loan duration. The uniformity of interest charges not only aggravates the moral hazard problem, it also results in adverse selection of borrowers, a "lemon" problem.

Under the Bretton Woods system, the aim of maintaining stable exchange rates was used to justify cheap IMF credits. Many IMF

---

[8]Donal J. Donovan, "The Sources of Current External Debt Servicing Difficulties: Some Empirical Evidence" (DM/84/15), (Washington, D.C.: IMF, 1984); the study is not for public use and could not be obtained from the author. For a short and incomplete summary see Donovan, "Nature and Origins of Debt Servicing Difficulties—Some Empirical Evidence," *Finance & Development*, vol. 21, no. 4 (1984), pp. 22–25.

[9]Anand G. Chandavarkar, "The International Monetary Fund: Its Financial Organization and Activities," IMF Pamphlet Series, 1984, p. 33.

borrowers, however, especially during the Bretton Woods era, were perfectly capable of acquiring foreign exchange via the market.

If, on the other hand, a member government is not creditworthy, the question becomes why it should be granted loans at all. There are two possible answers: to overcome imperfections of the capital market or to provide development aid. With imperfect information, the capital market would function imperfectly as well. However, if the IMF really has better information than potential private lenders about the true creditworthiness of its member governments, it could try to improve the market's information rather than to extend credit itself. Surely the fund has an obligation to make such information public for the protection of other lenders. Alternatively, subsidized IMF lending is a poor form of development aid since the IMF's criterion for extending credit—i.e., balance-of-payments difficulties—is not a suitable indicator of need.

Moreover, the interest rate subsidy creates an incentive to delay adjustment once a credit has been obtained—article V, section 7.b of the Articles of Agreement specifies that each member is normally expected to repay its credits (even before maturity) "as its balance-of-payments and reserve position improves." That runs directly counter to the objective laid down in article I.vi that the fund should "shorten the duration . . . of disequilibrium in the international balances of payments of members."

The interest rate subsidy might be regarded as an insurance benefit against economic instability, but "premiums" do not differ according to risk. From 1960 to 1982, for example, 42 member countries accounted for 78 percent of all standby and extended credits from the IMF.[10] That is not an outcome to be expected if members had been hit by random accidents. In fact, cross-section regressions by Lawrence Officer and Peter Cornelius showed that between 1974 and 1980, the flow of IMF credits to member governments tended to be significantly correlated with the outstanding stock of previous IMF credits.[11]

[10]Roland Vaubel, "The Moral Hazard of IMF Lending," in *International Lending and the IMF*, Allan H. Meltzer, ed. (Washington D.C.: Heritage Foundation, 1983), pp. 65–79; and in *The World Economy*, vol. 6, no. 3 (September 1983), pp. 291–303.

[11]Lawrence H. Officer, "The Differential Use of the IMF Resources by Industrial, Other Developed, and Less Developed Countries: A Historical Approach," *Journal of Developing Areas*, 1982, Table 4; and Peter Cornelius, *Das Prinzip der Konditionalitat bei Krediten des Internationalen Wahrungsfonds* (Munich: VVF, 1988), pp. 197–204.

Richard Goode presented a list of 24 countries that have obtained fund credits for more than 10 *consecutive years*.[12] The maximum is 27 years (Chile and Egypt). He also reported that, in 1974–84, drawings from non-oil-producing countries accounted for 85 percent of fund credit.

In short, the IMF is a continuous provider of aid, in the form of subsidized insurance, to a limited group of member governments. That raises four questions:

- Why do donor governments grant this form of aid?
- Why do they give the largest subsidies to the most negligent members?
- Why is the insurance offered to governments rather than to individuals?
- Why is the subsidy confined to insurance with an international public monopoly, the IMF?

The government treasury origins of the IMF are indicative. As John Makin has noted, the IMF serves the interests of the treasuries of its member governments by flexibly accommodating their borrowing and debt-servicing "needs" at minimum cost.[13] By charging low and uniform interest rates, the IMF protects its members against market judgments and helps insure them against the electoral damage that a visibly poor credit standing might otherwise cause. The policy conditions imposed by the IMF may also be unpopular, but political leaders have occasionally made them scapegoats for unpopular economic reforms. The IMF at least provides politicians with a choice between high-risk premiums (lack of creditworthiness) in the private capital market and the IMF's policy conditions.

The IMF's professional staff also has a vested interest in subsidized, uniform interest rates. Low rates increase the demand for IMF credits. Uniform rates help avoid conflict with potential borrowers. For similar reasons, national social insurance systems and public insurance schemes for export credits and foreign investment do not usually charge premiums according to risk. Moreover, paying larger subsidies to the least creditworthy allows the fund, like national social insurance

---

[12]Richard Goode, *Economic Assistance to the Developing Countries through the IMF* (Washington, D.C.: Brookings Institution, 1985), Table 2.

[13]John H. Makin, *The Global Debt Crisis: America's Growing Involvement* (New York: Basic Books, 1984), p. 183. The treasury origins of the IMF distinguish it from the Bank of International Settlements, which is a central bankers' club.

schemes, to justify its activities on humanitarian grounds. As is well known from social insurance economics, however, the poor are often not the worst risks. The debt crisis of the 1980s is a case in point: the governments of the richer developing countries, such as Mexico, proved to be the least creditworthy.

Can the IMF's Role in the International Debt Crisis Be Explained?

When the international debt crisis broke out in 1982, the IMF again seized a completely new role, changing the justification for its lending activity.

First, it was said that the IMF had to help guarantee the stability of the international banking system. But the only institutions that were in danger—if any—were a few major American banks. If there had been a liquidity crisis, as was then maintained, it should have been up to the U.S. central bank (i.e., the Federal Reserve Board) to grant those banks discount window loans at penalty interest rates. Granting subsidized IMF credits to borrower governments was not an efficient way of saving the endangered banks, since IMF credits benefited not only those banks but also all other creditors of the debtor countries, including the vast majority that were not in danger.

Second, it was argued, the IMF was in a better position than the creditor banks to identify and promote necessary policy reforms in debtor countries. However, that argument does not justify granting subsidized credits; it can only justify the fund's negotiating and approving adjustment programs.

Third, the IMF was supposed to coordinate the policies of the creditor banks and prevent free riding. But, again, it did not have to make loans itself for that purpose.

It seems that there must have been other reasons for the IMF's playing its new role in the debt crisis. Clearly, fund officials were interested in increasing loan volume. The years since 1977 had been difficult: credit had declined by 36 percent until 1980, and the second oil price shock did not lead to the creation of a new oil-lending facility because the first oil facility was thought to have delayed the adjustment process for too long. At the same time, the new Reagan administration was calling for a more restrictive IMF policy. Much like the first oil price shock in 1973, the international debt crisis in 1982 provided the IMF officials with an opportunity to secure the survival and growth of their organization. The debt crisis was well suited to that purpose, since it generated particular problems for the U.S. government—the fund's chief critic at the time.

To the U.S. Treasury, the IMF became a "convenient conduit for U.S. influence," as Assistant Treasury Secretary Marc Leland put it, because the fund's credits especially benefited U.S. banks and several Latin American governments of particular interest to Washington policymakers.[14] The burden of financing, on the other hand, was more widely dispersed and thus barely noticed by politicians and voters in the other industrialized countries. Also, the IMF's interest subsidies do not show up as expenditures in national budgets but instead as diminished central bank profits.

Within the U.S. government, the driving force for increasing the IMF's lending ability was Treasury Secretary Donald Regan, a former investment banker, assisted by Under Secretary Beryl Sprinkel, likewise a former banker, and the chairman of the Federal Reserve Board, which would have faced some difficult decisions without the IMF's intervention. In congressional hearings and elsewhere, American banks, too, pushed hard for increased IMF quotas.[15] That was to be expected, since the endangered loans were concentrated among a few leading banks, which could easily organize themselves and wield the biggest gun. The banks would benefit from IMF action in three ways:

1. Subsidized IMF lending would improve the prospect for current and future debt service to the banks and thereby increase the market value of their loans.
2. IMF conditionality might improve the creditworthiness of the debtors.
3. The IMF would provide free information, negotiation, and enforcement services to the banks.[16]

The tasks national governments delegate to international organizations are often unpleasant activities ("dirty work") that the national

---

[14]Quoted in Benjamin J. Cohen, *In Whose Interest? International Banking and American Foreign Policy* (New Haven, London: Yale University Press, 1986), p. 231.

[15]David F. Lomax, *The Developing Country Debt Crisis* (Houndsmills: St. Martin's Press, 1986), p. 237.

[16]Paul de Grauwe and Michele Fratianni, "The Political Economy of International Lending," *Cato Journal*, vol. 4, no. 1 (Spring–Summer 1984), p. 168.

politicians consider necessary to gain or maintain the support of some interest groups, but for which they do not want to take direct responsibility:

> International organization raises information costs more for the general public which has to pay than for the well-organized pressure groups which benefit. If some countries receive more than they pay, international organization may also serve to disperse the costs of such programmes more widely than would be possible on a national basis.[17]

A nice example is the European agricultural policy, but the same point seems to apply to the IMF's role in the debt crisis. The IMF has served as a smoke screen for subsidies to major U.S. banks. By hiding those transfers, it has increased the opportunities for lobbying and "rent-seeking." More generally, the debt crisis confirms the rule that pressure groups are the natural allies of international organizations (and government bureaucracies in general) because they lobby for transfers and regulations and thereby increase the demand for the institutions' output.

How Has the IMF Turned the Debt Crisis into Opportunity?

Since the outbreak of the debt crisis, the IMF has established several new credit facilities. Two of them, the Structural Adjustment Facility (SAF), established in March 1986, and the Enhanced Structural Adjustment Facility (ESAF), established in August 1988, are confined to low-income developing countries. The latter has effectively tripled the amount of concessional IMF resources that can be made available subject to policy conditions.[18] Both facilities focus especially on the sub-Saharan African countries "whose difficulties in repaying the Fund . . . appeared to threaten the system."[19] The British chancellor of

[17]Roland Vaubel, "A Public Choice Approach to International Organization," *Public Choice*, vol. 51, no. 1 (1986), p. 48.

[18]International Monetary Fund, *IMF Annual Report* (Washington, D.C.: IMF, 1988), p. 47.

[19]Miles Kahler, "Organization and Cooperation: International Institutions and Policy Coordination," Paper presented at the Conference on Blending Economic and Political Analysis of International Financial Relations, Claremont Colleges and University of Southern California, May 1988, p. 270.

the exchequer frankly recommended "backdated drawing on the Enhanced Structural Adjustment Facility to help clear arrears."[20]

Yet, the fund, unlike most private banks, remains politically dependent on the very governments to whom it lends.[21] Thus the fund's lending role impairs its credit assessment role.[22] At the end of the financial year 1988–89, 11 member countries were in arrears by six months or more. Their overdue obligations amounted to SDR 2.8 billion (Special Drawing Rights) or 11.0 percent of outstanding IMF credit (compared with 4.1 percent of arrearages for the World Bank). One year later, the IMF's overdue loans had increased to SDR 3.3 billion. According to David Finch, "An examination of the arrears shows that, in some cases, at least, loans have been given in amounts that went well beyond any normal calculation of risk."[23]

Until the end of the financial year 1988–89, the number of loans outstanding under the SAF and the ESAF rose to 30 while the number of the traditional Standby and Extended Arrangements was halved from 31 (at the end of 1986) to 16. The terms of the former are much more liberal: SAF credits are granted for 10 years at a 0.5 percent interest rate and failure to implement the three-year adjustment programs does not affect the disbursement or duration of the loan. IMF credits under Standby or Extended Arrangements, by contrast, are

---

[20]*IMF Survey*, October 17, 1988, p. 323.

[21]Jeffrey D. Sachs, *Conditionality, Debt Relief and the Developing Country Debt Crisis*, National Bureau of Economic Research Working Paper no. 2644, 1988, p. 20.

[22]Fred L. Smith, Jr., "The Politics of IMF Lending," *Cato Journal*, vol. 4, no. 1 (Spring–Summer 1984), p. 220.

[23]David C. Finch, *The IMF: The Record and the Prospect, Essays in International Finance* (Princeton, N.J.: Princeton University Press, 1989), p. 19. That is also the view of other authors: "The typical case in recent years is that the Fund and the country would sign a program based on full debt servicing, even though both parties fully expect that the agreement will break down in due course." Sachs, p. 16; and "In many cases, by approving standby programs whose targets everyone knows will not be met, the IMF is participating in a big charade; it is implicitly saying that, according to the Articles of Agreement, the resources have been provided on a temporary basis, and there is a high probability that the country will attain balance of payments viability in the near future. For many countries this is not the case, and everybody knows it." Sebastian Edwards, *The International Monetary Fund and Developing Countries: A Critical Evaluation*, Carnegie-Rochester Conference Series on Public Policy, Karl Brunner and Alan H. Meltzer, eds., vol. 31 (Amsterdam: North-Holland, 1989), p. 35.

more short-term (one to three years), more expensive, subject to phasing, and can be canceled if the borrower does not honor its commitments.

Thus the SAF and ESAF induced the eligible least developed countries to shift their demand from Standby and Extended credits and helped the fund to increase lending: it could grant more credits to the least developed countries, which had not been very successful in implementing policy conditions, and free resources for other potential borrowers. While the total amount of SAF and ESAF credits approved continued to increase in 1989 and 1990, there was a marked shift from SAF Arrangements to the much more concessionary ESAF Arrangements. In all those respects, the increase of IMF lending is associated with, and indeed driven by, a weakening of conditionality and an increase in interest rate subsidization.

The problem of growing arrears also led to the introduction of the Rights Accumulation Program (RAP) in 1990. Under that scheme, member governments with overdue obligations to the fund can acquire borrowing rights up to the equivalent of outstanding arrears at the beginning of the (three-year) RAP if they adhere to an adjustment program monitored by the fund and remain current on repayments to the fund and the World Bank. Upon the successful completion of a RAP, prior clearance of the member's arrears to the IMF, and fund approval of a successor arrangement, the member may take its accumulated borrowing rights as the first disbursement under the new financial package.

Thus, if the member government clears its arrears—possibly with the help of a lender to whom it pledges its accumulated drawing rights—it receives its money back from the fund and is no longer ineligible for future IMF credits. In short, the fund transforms the arrears of cooperative members into additional loans. In 1990, the fund also began to lend to member governments overdue on commercial loans; under the Brady plan, rescheduling with the banks is no longer a prerequisite for additional IMF loans.

Finally, in August 1988 eligibility was extended under the Compensatory Financing Facility, which is now called the Compensatory and Contingency Financing Facility. As a result of that change, the IMF may also lend to debtor governments to compensate the effects of deviations from projected interest rates, and it enjoys more power because contingency financing is now subject to policy conditions.

Is There Evidence of "Hurry-Up Lending" at the IMF?

Eight general quota increases, new credit facilities, the introduction of Special Drawing Rights, and fund borrowing have hiked IMF credit lines far faster than the growth of world trade or current account balances. How has the IMF generated member government support for these increases?

If the IMF staff is interested in more resources, it is likely to demonstrate its urgent "need" of them by increasing the utilization of its lending capacity more rapidly when the next regular quota review approaches. According to article III.2.a, the IMF quotas have to be reviewed every five years at the latest.

Table 2.1 shows the dates on which the IMF board of governors concluded its regular quota reviews up to 1983. An earlier assessment in 1950 did not lead to a quota increase. The table shows that, in the third year after the termination of the last general quota review by the board of governors, the use of IMF credit relative to quotas rose on average by 26 percent. In the following year, the last before the conclusion of the review, the increase averaged 52 percent. By contrast, in the first and second year after the review, credit use decreased by 9 and 15 percent. That suggests the IMF staff tends to engage in "hurry-up lending" for political purposes.

I have also tested the hypothesis that the fluctuations in the growth of IMF capacity utilization could be due to fluctuations in the growth of demand for IMF credit. (I have assumed that the demand for the IMF loans depends on the gold and foreign exchange reserves— excluding IMF credits—or the real current-account deficits of those member countries whose reserves are below the international average relative to their imports.) Since the first quinquennial quota increase was approved in 1965, the analysis has been conducted for the period 1964–65 to 1982–83. The statistical tests are consistent with the hypothesis of hurry-up lending. It turns out that the variables that capture the demand for IMF credits do not have a significant effect on the IMF's use of its lending potential, but the increase of the IMF's capacity utilization is significantly larger in the fourth year after the last regular quota review.

The years 1986–88 provided an interesting exception to the IMF's pattern of behavior—which may explain why there was no quota increase in 1988 as implied by the normal five-year pattern. But when,

Table 2.1
HURRY-UP LENDING BY THE IMF

Date of Resolution on Quota Review by Board of Governors	Percent and Index	Used Fund Credit/Quota at the End of				
		t	t+1	t+2	t+3	t+4
Jan. 1956[a] (2nd quinquennial review)	Percent	.05	.11	.12	–[c]	–[c]
	Index[b]	9	45	100	–[c]	–[c]
1960[a] (3rd quinquennial review)	Percent	.03	.10	.07	.07	.09
	Index	43	143	100	100	129
Mar. 1965 (4th quinquennial review)	Percent	.25	.15	.12	.17	.19
	Index	208	125	100	142	158
Feb. 1970 (5th general review)	Percent	.11	.05	.04	.04	.13
	Index	275	125	100	100	325
Mar. 1975 (6th general review)	Percent	.26	.43	.45	–[c]	–[c]
	Index	58	96	100	–[c]	–[c]
Dec. 1978 (7th general review)	Percent	.26	.20	.14	.22	.32
	Index	186	143	100	157	229
Mar. 1983 (8th general review)	Percent	.33	.39	.28	.37	.32
	Index	118	139	100	132	114
	Index average	128	117	100	126	191
	Change in index average		−9%	−15%	+26%	+52%

SOURCES: IMF International Financial Statistics; Chandavarkar, p. 13.

[a]Board of executive directors concludes quinquennial review without proposal to increase general quotas.

[b]t + 2 = 100.

[c]Antedated quota review (resolutions in 1959 and 1978).

in financial year 1989–90, the IMF more than doubled its new credit commitments, it soon secured another quota increase of about 50 percent, this time on the grounds that it had to cover the payments needs of Eastern Europe.

Why Discretionary Ex Post Conditionality?

The IMF's economic adjustment programs may be theoretically justified in that they generate new knowledge (an international public good), reduce the moral hazard among borrowers, and can be more easily imposed by the IMF than by private lenders. Whether or not those reasons are sufficient, the manner in which the IMF designs and implements its adjustment programs raises a number of questions.

The fund imposes its conditions after the member country has gotten into trouble. The requirements are supposed to prevent borrowers from hanging on to their subsidized IMF credits longer than necessary. But the fund could more effectively accomplish its goals if the conditions addressed the causes of the crisis. Nations that have negligently, or even deliberately, created a difficult situation should be barred from receiving IMF credits at all. Ex ante conditions could, for example, include a requirement that domestic credit expansion may not exceed the growth of production potential, that the budget deficit may not exceed a certain percentage of the gross national product, that the rules of the General Agreement on Tariffs and Trade must be strictly observed, and that there may be neither controls on capital movements nor expropriation of investors.

Of course, such "ex ante conditionality" would greatly limit the number of member countries entitled to borrow from the IMF. It would reduce the power of fund officials. Such reform, moreover, would be in the interests of neither borrower governments inclined towards negligence nor lender governments that like to use the IMF to promote foreign policy goals or satisfy domestic interest groups.

Even in the case of purely "ex post conditionality," moral hazard could be reduced if the IMF would at least issue—and apply—strict rules for its conditions. The governments of typical debtor countries would then have no hope of getting away with weak conditions thanks to good relations with IMF officials or special negotiating skills. At present, however, the IMF practices ad hoc conditionality, or a case-by-case approach. Fund officials oppose strict rules about the application of IMF conditions because they limit the fund's discretionary power. Influential lenders and borrowers feel the same way.

Why Is the IMF's Conditionality Not More Transparent?

If the IMF adjustment programs are justified on the grounds that they constitute "new knowledge" and thus an international public good, their terms should be made known. Publication might also increase the probability of the fund and its borrowers adhering to their programs, which seem to be less and less effective.

Why are agreements not published? Secrecy helps a borrower government that does not intend to meet the stipulated conditions save face. If a borrower intends to fulfill the conditions, secrecy enables it to make the IMF a scapegoat for additional reform measures the IMF did not demand. IMF officials avoid unwanted public supervision and a serious assessment as to the effectiveness of IMF programs. Broken conditions suggest that the fund is ineffectual. If, on the other hand, the fund's conditions are minimal and therefore easy to fulfill, it would become evident that the IMF has little impact on borrowers' policies.

Monitoring by the IMF, the banks, and the general public would also be easier and more effective if policy conditions were simple and few. But the fund seems to prefer a multitude of policy conditions. Moreover, policy targets, to be effective, must relate to easily controllable variables—either policy instruments or close intermediate economic targets. Otherwise, it is not clear whether a violation is due to policy failures or unforeseeable disturbances. Without controllability, there can be no responsibility. Targets for relatively uncontrollable variables are not only likely to be missed, as IMF experience shows, they are also unlikely to exert much influence on the conduct of economic policy.

The fund's policy targets, however, tend to include remote, endogenous variables, such as the current account balance, that depend heavily on any number of uncontrollable factors. A public choice perspective suggests that the IMF staff prefers those sorts of requirements because they reduce potential outside control and criticism of the fund's effectiveness. Further, a multiplicity of conditions, without weights attached to them, makes it difficult to evaluate the efficiency of any program, raises the cost of monitoring for external observers, and permits the fund to attribute the low degree of successful program implementation to target conflicts.

The fund's desire to protect itself against outside monitoring may also explain why it prefers highly variable ad hoc conditions to simple rules. Once more, the customary borrowers and the most influential lenders share the IMF staff's interest. The choice of remote endogenous target variables can serve a similar purpose. Missing a target can almost always be attributed to unforeseeable disturbances. In that way, the debtor governments can conceal their noncompliance, and the IMF staff can conceal the ineffectiveness of its conditions.

Why Are Conditions Procyclical?

Several authors have noted that IMF conditionality varies procyclically: it is stricter when the world is in a recession than when there is a boom.[24] The period from 1979 to 1982 is a particularly good example. There is also econometric evidence that tightening of conditionality reduces the volume of IMF credits.[25] One need not be a Keynesian to criticize the procyclical effect of such variations in conditionality. Why does the IMF reinforce the cycle?

Fund officials have a vested interest in lending extensively and imposing strict economic policy conditions because both constitute an exercise of power and a source of prestige. At a time of worldwide recession, when the demand for IMF credits increases, fund officials can maximize their authority by tightening lending conditions, but not more than is compatible with some increase in credit volume. In boom times, on the other hand, the decline in demand for credits leads to eased conditions—as exemplified by the SAF and the ESAF.

Varying conditionality thus becomes a substitute for altering interest rates, since the rates the IMF can charge are fixed in advance. If that explanation is correct, it follows that Richard Cooper's 1983 proposal for countercyclical use of IMF conditionality is not feasible because it runs counter to the bureaucratic interest of the IMF staff.

Why Has the IMF Staff Grown?

Since 1960, the fund's personnel have increased at an average annual rate of 5.1 percent. In contrast, the staff growth rate at the Bank for

---

[24]John Williamson, "The Lending Policies of the International Monetary Fund," in *IMF Conditionality*, John Williamson, ed. (Washington, D.C.: Institute for International Economics, 1983), pp. 605–6; Richard N. Cooper, "Panel Discussion," in *IMF Conditionality*, pp. 569–77; and Cornelius.

[25]Cornelius, pp. 197–207.

International Settlements and at the Organization for Economic Cooperation and Development has been 2.1 percent. Is the IMF a textbook case of Parkinson's Law, or can its personnel growth be explained by a rising balance-of-payments need?

If the balance-of-payments need is again measured by the real decline of gold and foreign exchange reserves or by the real current account deficits of those member countries whose reserves are below average relative to their imports, those factors have no significant effect on the size of the IMF staff. Nor does staff size react significantly to changes in the IMF's relative salaries—compared, for example, with salaries at the U.S. Federal Reserve Board, which is also located in Washington, D.C. In 1986, the last year for which all relevant data have been published, IMF salaries were on average 64 percent higher than those at the Federal Reserve Board. (This comparison does not take account of possible differences in quality or the 7 percent deduction for the IMF pension fund; it also does not reflect the fact that, for non-American employees, IMF salaries are free of income tax.)

There is, however, a significant positive effect on staff growth due to IMF quota increases and a significant negative effect of the combined quota share of the 10 leading member nations on the size of the IMF staff. Since the voting weight of these countries has declined along with their quota shares, the latter finding is in line with Mancur Olson's hypothesis that the incentive to supervise and control a bureaucracy diminishes when the number of members increases and leading members derive a declining share of any benefits of such control.

Conclusion

This analysis has been confined to IMF lending and conditionality. Fund surveillance and coordination also deserve scrutiny but too little is known about them, which may indicate that they are ineffective. Analysis of IMF forecasts revealed an optimistic bias with respect to output growth and, for the industrial countries, also with respect to inflation, which serves the interest of the incumbent member governments.[26] Similarly, Edwards noted that the fund's projections of the

[26]Peter Kenen and Stephen B. Schwartz, *An Assessment of Macroeconomic Forecasts in the International Monetary Fund's World Economic Outlook,* Working Paper in International Economics no. G-86-04 (Princeton, N.J.: Princeton University, December 1986); and Michael J. Artis, "How Accurate Is the World Economic Outlook?" Staff Studies for the World Economic Outlook, IMF, July 1988, p. 39.

main debt-related indicators have been far too optimistic, which was in the IMF staff's interest.[27] For these and other reasons, Michele Fratianni and John Pattison have suggested that international organizations such as the IMF should not publish forecasts or policy commentaries.[28]

The fund's other practices, such as inviting the ministers of finance to give well-publicized public speeches at the annual meeting, also serve to please the fund's principals and to ensure its survival. Invitations to academic economists to spend a research leave at the IMF increase the fund's prestige and reduce the likelihood of scholarly criticism. The periodic country visits, reports and recommendations, and other activities not provided for in the Articles of Agreement evidence the fund's drive for expansion and influence.

All this is not to deny that many dedicated civil servants work at the IMF. But they are exposed to a perverse bureaucratic incentive, as can be predicted by a public choice analysis. While there is little else on which four IMF economists from five countries can agree, expanding their institution is where their interests meet.

[27]Edwards, "The International Monetary Fund and Developing Countries," p. 33.

[28]Michele Fratianni and John Pattison, "International Institutions and the Market for Information," in *The Political Economy of International Organizations: A Public-Choice Approach*, Roland Vaubel and Thomas D. Willett, eds. (Boulder, Colo.: Westview Press, 1991), p. 29.

PART II

THE WORLD BANK

3. The World Bank and the Impoverishment of Nations

James Bovard

The World Bank is helping Third World governments cripple their economies, maul their environments, and oppress their people. Although the bank was started with the highest ideals almost 50 years ago, the bank now consistently does more harm than good for the world's poor.

The World Bank's raison d'être in the early years was to encourage development. From the bank's creation in 1946 until the late 1960s, it was a conservative institution that primarily funded infrastructure and other basic investments in less developed countries. Then, in 1968, Robert McNamara became bank president and dedicated himself to continually raising loan levels. By 1981, when McNamara resigned, lending had increased more than 13-fold, from $883 million to $12 billion. Loan levels have continued soaring: now the bank exists largely to maximize the transfer of resources to Third World governments. According to the bank's own auditors, bank projects have suffered from "unseemly pressure" to lend more money.[1]

Unfortunately, in that way, the bank has greatly promoted the nationalization of Third World economies and increased political and bureaucratic control over the lives of the poorest of the poor. True, bank officials are now leading a rhetorical crusade in favor of the private sector. But every time the bank loudly praises the marketplace it silently damns its own record. The bank, more than any other international institution, is responsible for the Third World's rush to socialism and economic collapse. While the bank has been very effective at expanding government control of Third World economies, it has unfortunately been extremely ineffective at encouraging private-sector-oriented reform.

[1]World Bank, "Twelfth Annual Review of Project Performance Results," 1987, p. 48.

The only thing the bank has left is the moral nobility of its original purpose—to spur development in the poor nations of the world. But the bank provides far more help to Third World politicians and bureaucrats than to Third World citizens. And, most of all, the bank continues helping itself as it doles out ever-larger amounts of money.

The World Bank's Disrespect for Human Rights

Perhaps most striking is that, irrespective of the bank's impact on economic development, it has a long and dismal record of underwriting human rights atrocities. Despite the bank's persistent self-righteousness, it often shows little or no concern for the welfare of poor citizens. As the bank began dramatically boosting lending in the late 1960s and early 1970s, its standards for lending consequently nosedived. One of McNamara's favorite foreign leaders appeared to be Julius Nyerere, ruler of Tanzania, which received more bank aid per capita than any other country. That unconditional support for Nyerere's dictatorship is a major cause of the Tanzanian people's current misery.

In the early 1970s, with bank aid and advice, Nyerere implemented his *ujaama*, or villagization program. Nyerere sent the Tanzanian army to drive the peasants off their land, burn down their huts, load them onto trucks, and take them where the government thought they should live—where they were ordered to build themselves new homes "in neat rows staked out for them by government officials."[2] Nyerere wanted to curb the people's individualistic and capitalistic tendencies and make them easier to control.[3] He even outlawed people sleeping in their own gardens at night—which meant monkeys were free to help themselves to the crops. In many cases, the new government villages were far away from the farmers' lands, so the farmers simply quit tilling the land. Food production has fallen and hunger has proliferated in recent years.

Similarly, the bank helped finance brutal policies of the government of Vietnam in the late 1970s that contributed to tens of thousands of boat people dying in the South China Sea. After North Vietnam invaded and conquered South Vietnam, there was widespread dissent in the south against the new government's forced collectivization

[2]*Washington Post*, May 1, 1976, p. B8.

[3]See John P. Powelson and Richard Stock, *The Peasant Betrayed* (Boston: Oelgeschlager, Gunn, and Hain, 1986), pp. 49–66.

policy. In August 1978, the bank loaned $60 million to the government of Vietnam—even after widely circulated reports in the West of massive concentration camps and brutal repression. The bank announced the loan would finance "an irrigation project that will boost rice production." But, a confidential bank report admitted, "The main effort to deal with the employment problem [in the south] consists of the creation of New Economic Zones—agricultural settlements that are intended to resettle 4 or 5 million people by the end of 1980."[4] The report conceded that the project was risky because of the possibility of rebellion among farmers. Farmers who resisted the government's "reorganization" were sent out in leaky boats and thousands drowned in the South China Sea. Yet, despite the undeniable atrocities that were occurring, the bank planned on giving five more loans to Vietnam until the U.S. Congress vociferously objected.[5]

The bank has loaned the government of Indonesia more than $600 million to remove—sometimes forcibly—several million people from the densely populated island of Java and resettle them on comparatively barren islands in Indonesia. Despite widespread reports of violence, the bank continues lauding the project as "the largest voluntary migration" in recent history. The Indonesian government is simultaneously resettling Javanese on the island of East Timor—which the army seized in 1975. The army's subsequent butcheries and forced starvation policies killed between 100,000 to 200,000 of the island's inhabitants who numbered fewer than 700,000.[6]

Transmigration is a good example of the bank's hypocrisy. Official bank policy states that it will assist projects "within areas used or occupied by tribal people only if it is satisfied that best efforts have been made to obtain the voluntary, full and conscionable agreement of the tribal people." But official Indonesian law states that tribal people's right to their lands and autonomy "may not be allowed to stand in the way of the establishment of transmigration settlements."[7] The govern-

---

[4]Quoted in Shirley Scheibla, "Asian Sinking Fund; The World Bank Is Helping to Finance Vietnam," *Barron's*, September 3, 1979, p. 7.

[5]Ibid.

[6]Arnold S. Kohen, "Massacre on Prime Time: Making an Issue of East Timor," *Nation*, February 10, 1992, p. 162; and James Bovard, "Behind the Words at the World Bank," *Wall Street Journal*, September 30, 1985.

[7]Jack Anderson, "World Bank and Indonesian Colonization," *Washington Post*, June 24, 1986, p. E9.

ment has even locked up people who have abandoned their new homes and returned to Java to "prevent them spreading negative reports and reduce the enthusiasm of others to transmigrate," according to an Indonesian newspaper.[8] The Indonesian minister of transmigration proclaimed on March 20, 1985, that "by way of transmigration, we will try to realize what has been pledged, to integrate all the ethnic groups into one nation—the Indonesia nation. . . . The different ethnic groups will in the long run disappear because of integration and there will be one kind of man."[9] As one Australian critic noted, transmigration is largely "the Javanese version of Nazi Germany's *Lebensraum*."[10]

The World Bank provided massive assistance to the Ethiopian Marxist regime of Mengistu Haile-Mariam. In the midst of the 1984–85 famine, when starvation reportedly threatened 7 million Ethiopians, the government launched a massive "resettlement" program to forcibly move hundreds of thousands of people in the north of the country to the south. According to Doctors Without Borders, a French medical assistance group, the resettlement program may have killed more people than the famine itself.[11] *The Economist* cited Ethiopia in 1986 for the worst human rights record in the world.[12]

Yet, the bank kept open its money spigots for the oppressive regime. Bank commitments to Ethiopia in 1985 equaled roughly 16 percent of the government's budget.[13] A $39-million handout in 1987 went for "Ministry of Agriculture institutional development," among other things,[14] even though the Agriculture Ministry was heavily involved in the brutal villagization program.

According to the U.S. Congressional Research Service, "Any loan from the World Bank provides some measure of support for the

[8]Ibid.

[9]Ibid.

[10]Kenneth Davidson, "Pathetic Attitude to Indonesia," *Melbourne Age*, June 1, 1986.

[11]Blaine Harden, "Ethiopia Bars Relief Team," *Washington Post*, December 3, 1985.

[12]Cited in Martin Sieff, "Toting Up the Human Rights Score," *Insight*, July 28, 1986, p. 30.

[13]Congressional Research Service, "World Bank Activities in Ethiopia," May 12, 1987, p. 7.

[14]World Bank, "770,000 Ethiopian Farm Families to Benefit from Livestock Project," IDA News Release no. 87/61, March 5, 1987.

borrower country's economy."[15] Even when World Bank funds do not directly support oppression, by supplying large amounts of capital they free up other scarce government resources that can be used for that purpose. The World Bank financed the Ethiopian government while the government was herding people into concentration camps and collective farms that doomed Ethiopia's prospects for feeding itself and avoiding recurrent famines.

Throughout India, South America, and elsewhere, the bank is creating thousands of "development refugees," as Environmental Defense Fund attorney Bruce Rich calls them. In India, at a bank-financed project at Singrauli, "200,000 to 300,000 of the rural poor have been subject to forced relocation twice, three times, in some cases four or five times in 25 years, each time with little or no compensation. Their livelihood was the land, which has now been totally destroyed and resembles scenes out of the lower circles of Dante's Inferno," Rich testified to the House Committee on Banking, Finance and Urban Affairs.[16] The same violations of the rights of citizens forcibly resettled have often occurred in Brazil, another recipient of much World Bank aid.

The bank does not have anything against human rights—many bank employees and officials are outstanding individuals with high moral codes. But the bank is driven to meet its lending goals. And if that means bankrolling oppression, so be it. Forty-seven years ago at Nuremberg, the excuse was, "I was only following orders." Now, at the World Bank, it is, "I was only meeting my lending quota."

Consistent Incompetence

If one looks only at bank press releases, one might think that the bank has at least done a wonderful job at promoting economic development. But a closer examination of bank documents shows that the institution itself is aware of its pervasive failures in many areas.

The 1987 annual review of project performance results, published by the Operations Evaluation Department, noted the following:

---

[15]Congressional Research Service, p. 12.

[16]Testimony of Bruce Rich, House Subcommmmittee on International Development Institutions and Finance: Hearing on Environmental Performance of the Multilateral Development Banks, April 8, 1987.

- Seventy-five percent of World Bank African agricultural projects were failures.[17]
- Despite endless pleading by the bank, many Latin American and African governments still refuse to make available sufficient money to maintain bank-financed roads and infrastructure. As the report asked, "Does the ready availability of [external] funds to rebuild ill-maintained roads in any way sway the decision on maintenance funding?"[18]
- The majority of small enterprise borrowers from bank-financed development finance companies are in arrears on their debt repayments.[19]
- Bank projects to encourage increased credit activity in Third World countries are routinely sabotaged by government regulations that hold interest rates below inflation rates, thereby destroying any possibility of a self-propelled credit market.[20]

The World Bank in recent years has formally encouraged its borrowers to provide more support for and tolerance of the private sector. But the bank's actions speak more loudly than its words. The bank has consistently financed and approved the massive expansion of government power throughout the Third World. Bank aid has gone almost entirely to governments, or has been channeled through governments, thereby increasing political control over the private sector. And despite the bank's new, more market-oriented rhetoric, the vast majority of bank aid continues to pour into government coffers, increasing the dominance of politicians and bureaucrats over their economies.

The World Bank probably made its biggest impression in Africa. Between 1973 and 1980, the bank plowed $2.4 billion into agriculture.[21] For almost 15 years, the bank has concentrated on boosting food production; in the late 1970s and early 1980s, 92 percent of bank projects were for this purpose.[22] Yet per capita food production has fallen almost 20 percent since 1960.

[17]World Bank, "Twelfth Annual Review of Project Performance Results," p. 28.

[18]Ibid., p. 84.

[19]Ibid., p. 68.

[20]Ibid., p. 71.

[21]World Bank, *Accelerated Development in Sub-Saharan Africa* (Washington, D.C.: World Bank, 1981), p. 47.

[22]World Bank, "Tenth Annual Review of Project Performance Results," 1985, p. viii.

A 1981 bank analysis of Africa concluded that "much of the investment in agriculture, especially the domestic component, has gone into state farms, big irrigation schemes and similar capital-intensive activities. These have turned out to be largely a waste of money: their impact on output has been negligible in most cases."[23] Moreover, bank aid was crucial in creating and perpetuating African government agricultural boards. A bank report noted, "In Tanzania, the grower . . . is always voiceless and marginal in the system, and everybody's costs are considered except the farmer's." The bank went on to concede that before the Sierra Leone Rice Board lost its exclusive right to import rice, "half of its imports were being allocated to influential politicians to distribute at their discretion." An official of the West African Rice Development Association observed, "There are deliberate efforts by management to reduce purchases so as to reduce costs of subsidies." The report added, "Marketing margins of public marketing institutions are usually very high compared to [those] of private traders because of high overhead costs, large permanent staff, expensive head office facilities, poor management."[24] In sum, World Bank aid has helped deliver African farmers into state serfdom.

The bank's subsidies to governments to run agricultural projects often produce little food. One West African project to promote coffee and cocoa production failed partly because of "soil unsuitability."[25] That is, the bank encouraged farmers to grow crops that were unsuited for their soil. With friends like the World Bank, African farmers don't need enemies.

The bank also played a major role in nationalizing the development process throughout the Third World. For instance, development finance companies (DFCs) have largely taken the place of commercial banks in many countries.[26] As the bank noted, "A number of DFCs owe their existence to an initial World Bank commitment and continue to exist largely as favored channels for bank financing." After the bank began lending to DFCs in 1968, "several companies that had originally been largely private [in India, Pakistan, Singapore, Sri Lanka, and

---

[23]Malcolm Gladwell, "Harnessing World Bank to the West," *Insight*, February 9, 1987.

[24]Keith Marsden and Therese Belot, "Private Enterprise in Africa," World Bank Discussion Paper no. 17, 1987, pp. 4–5.

[25]World Bank, "Tenth Annual Review of Project Performance Results," p. 19.

[26]David I. Gordon, "Development Finance Companies, State and Privately Owned," World Bank Staff Working Paper no. 578, 1983.

Nigeria] came effectively under state control. Today the great majority of DFCs in the developing world . . . are state owned." The bank study concluded that private DFCs were more efficient, had higher profits, and had "been more active in the development of capital market institutions and instruments."[27]

Poor investments financed by the World Bank not only waste money in themselves but also help drag down the entire economy. A confidential 1986 bank study quoted a Kenyan government report, which stated that "troubled investments have required an inordinate amount of the time of government administrators, managers and policymakers, hence diverting their attention from the more basic development needs of the nation."[28] The bank went on to note that "Kenya is another country suffering from having accepted many offers of foreign assistance not well suited to its needs. The recurrent costs of efficiently maintaining and operating projects constructed with donor assistance are beyond the budget capacity of central and local governments."[29]

Unfortunately, more recent World Bank reports continue to paint a dismal picture of the bank's impact on the world's neediest citizens. A 1993 World Bank Operations Evaluation Department report observed, "In general, the performance of public enterprises—whether in mining, steel, DFCs, telecommunications, or transport—was disappointing. This suggests that the bank, when supporting such enterprises, should insist on proper and accountable management working to commercial objectives, free of government interference."[30] Perhaps next year's evaluation report will suggest that bank agricultural projects should be based on the presumption that cows can jump over the moon. By law the bank lends solely to governments. How, then, can the bank suggest that its loans be targeted for projects that are "free of government interference"? The evaluation report's blunt statement is basically a confession of the bankruptcy of the bank's strategy of promoting development. For over a decade, bank reports have been urging that bank projects and Third World governments "get the

[27]Ibid., p. 38.

[28]World Bank, "Structural Adjustment Lending: A First Review of Experience," 1986, p. 18.

[29]Ibid., p. 50.

[30]World Bank Operations Evaluation Department, *Evaluation Results for 1991* (Washington, D.C.: World Bank, 1993), p. xviii.

incentives right" for development. But as long as the World Bank is willing to pour new money into many of the same incompetent, interventionist Third World governments, what incentives do the governments themselves have to cease mangling their own economies? The World Bank gives foreign governments the financial means to increase their control of their economies at the same time that it lectures them on the need to reduce their control.

Similarly, in its analysis of World Bank–supported development finance companies, the 1993 evaluation report noted that "two were regional institutions, two were quasi-public entities, and the rest were state institutions."[31] The DFCs continue to have a poor record. The report noted that one "common problem was government interference in decisionmaking."[32] But to complain of government interference in the decisionmaking of a government-owned institution is pointless. If the World Bank does not want to see political control of Third World industries, it should cease giving so much money to Third World politicians.

A 1990 World Bank evaluation report concluded that less than one-third of the World Bank–financed projects in Africa were likely to be sustainable (i.e., able to maintain an adequate level of net benefits after the investment phase is completed).[33] In other words, for the majority of World Bank projects in Africa, once the bank stops pouring in the money, the project ceases to be of benefit to the country. Unfortunately, a failed project is not simply another bank-financed boondoggle, but represents a potential drain on the nation—and another disappointment to the struggling poor of the Third World.

While irrigation projects continue to be a favorite bank activity, little mention is made of the poor performance of many of the projects. The Operations Evaluation Department surveyed bank-financed irrigation projects and found that the cost recovery of the system's investments from the system's users "had not been satisfactory because of poor government commitment, unreliability in the supply of irrigation water, which had made users reluctant to pay irrigation fees, and the

[31]Ibid., p. 27.

[32]Ibid.

[33]World Bank Operations Evaluation Department, *Evaluation Results for 1988: Issues in World Bank Lending over Two Decades* (Washington, D.C.: World Bank, 1990), p. 7.

often heavy burden of direct and indirect taxes already imposed by governments on the farming sector."[34]

Since the early 1980s, the World Bank has poured billions of dollars into the reform of state-owned companies and enterprises. However, as a 1992 World Bank evaluation report points out, "Public enterprise reforms . . . were often limited to improving the firms' financial positions vis-à-vis the central government budget rather than introducing more fundamental changes to improve efficiency. . . . For the most part, the financial requirements of public enterprises were not reduced as a consequence, but were merely shifted from the budget to the [often-government-dominated] banking system."[35]

Other Highlights from Recent Bank Lending

The bank's obsession with maximizing its lending causes the bank to shower funds on relatively wealthy nations that have easy access to the world credit markets without bank assistance. Chile, for example, received four subsidized loans in 1992: $95 million for a program of technology transfer and provision of credit for farm investments; $71 million for investments in port facilities; $170 million to improve "the efficiency, quality, and equity of primary education"; and $17.2 million for the development of key government institutions responsible for economic management.[36] The last loan is especially ludicrous, because Chile has succeeded economically by reducing state control of the economy.

The bank is also continuing to provide subsidized credit to South Korea. In 1992, South Korea received $100 million to finance the infrastructure for a liquefied natural gas project and $40 million to build sewage treatment plants in Pusan and Taejon. South Korea also received $30 million to upgrade the training received in some of its high schools. Ironically, most international educational tests reveal that South Korean students already score far above U.S. students in mathematical and other skills.

[34]Ibid., p. 43.

[35]World Bank Operations Evaluation Department, *Evaluation Results for 1990* (Washington, D.C.: World Bank, 1992), p. 60.

[36]World Bank, *World Bank Annual Report 1992* (Washington, D.C.: World Bank, 1992), pp. 165–73.

The World Bank characterizes a 1992, $25.8-million handout (a 30- to 40-year loan with zero interest) to the Central African Republic as a means of upping food production: "The government's new agricultural strategy, which relies on producer groups as channels for the delivery of input and services to farmers, will be assisted through a project that aims at the institutional strengthening of the Ministry of Rural Development, the National Agricultural Research Service, and the National Agricultural Development Agency."[37] But the World Bank has long financed the Central African Republic's agricultural ministry—and that ministry has long borne heavy responsibility for the people's hunger.

The World Bank gave the Sudan $16 million to finance "policies directed at mitigating the recurrence of food insecurity." The bank's annual report—which lists the loans and their intended uses—neglected to mention that the Sudanese government itself is intentionally starving much of that nation's population. The country now has roughly 3 million refugees, according to the United Nations' estimate, and, as Freedom House noted, "many were threatened with starvation as [a recent government military offensive] cut the overland supply routes from Kenya and Uganda that relief groups use to supply the south."[38] The Sudanese government also drove 750,000 refugees out of the capital city of Khartoum and into squalid camps in the desert. "One U.S. official referred to the deportations as a virtual 'death sentence.'"[39]

The bank is now providing ample financial aid to the Islamic Republic of Iran, considered by many to be the world's leading financier and promoter of terrorism. In 1992, the bank provided $77 million for a stormwater collection system for Tehran and $57 million for a flood control system elsewhere in the country.[40] In March 1993, the bank added a $165-million loan to allow Iran to upgrade its electrical power system.[41] However laudable those goals, the fact is that aid is fungible: the more of Iran's infrastructure needs are financed by the bank, the more easily the Iranian government can finance truck bombs around the globe.

[37]Ibid., p. 172.

[38]Freedom House, *Freedom in the World: The Annual Survey of Political Rights and Civil Liberties, 1992–1993* (New York: Freedom House, 1993), p. 466.

[39]Ibid.

[40]World Bank, *World Bank Annual Report 1992*, p. 173.

[41]Douglas Jehl, "U.S. Seeks Ways to Isolate Iran," *New York Times*, May 27, 1993.

The bank gave a $180-million handout to the government of Mozambique to subsidize the country's economic and social-rehabilitation program. (The nation's economy has been destroyed by the government's commitment to Marxism, which the bank also financed.) Mozambique also received $35 million "to implement long-term farm-gate and factory-gate pricing mechanisms for cotton."[42] If the government actually intends to pay Mozambique farmers a fair price for their cotton, however, it is difficult to understand why bank aid is needed. Moreover, it is important to note that the Mozambique government continues to have an extremely poor human rights record. Freedom House, in its 1993 *Annual Survey of Political Rights and Civil Liberties*, noted, "Members of militia units, soldiers, and military counterintelligence agents continue to violate basic human rights; there are persistent reports of torture, rape, summary execution, and other abuses of those taken into custody."[43]

In April 1993, the bank announced that it was considering a $250-million loan to finance large-scale economic restructuring in Romania.[44] The bank in 1992 gave a $100-million loan to the Romanian government for "private-sector development in agricultural areas" to be "supported through a project that will finance credit to private businesses to improve input supply and food-processing, marketing, and distribution services."[45] Ironically, in the 1970s and early 1980s the bank funded a herd of industrial white elephants and provided more than $600 million for the government's perverse economic programs. While the government was wrecking its own agricultural sector and building scores of uncompetitive factories, the bank continued to give Romania its seal of approval. And now the bank is underwriting Romania's attempt to rebuild its agricultural sector.

The bank has had a devastating effect on Third World agriculture and bears some responsibility for the starvation plaguing many nations. A 1990 World Bank report on the impact of the bank's agricultural lending concluded the following:

---

[42]World Bank, *World Bank Annual Report 1992*, p. 160.

[43]Freedom House, p. 375.

[44]Roxana Dascalu, "Romania Seeks World Bank Loan to Heal Financial Ills," *Reuter Asia-Pacific Business Report*, April 13, 1993.

[45]World Bank, *World Bank Annual Report 1992*, p. 161.

> From the perspective of the late 1980s, the dominant role of
> parastatals as the beneficiaries of marketing components in
> World Bank projects is striking.... Parastatal projects were
> easy to design and appraise. Parastatals often had a legal
> monopoly of trade, so that assistance was clearly being pro-
> vided to the only organization available—and one that was
> approved and supported by the government.[46]

Bank projects scorned the need to permit or assist the development
of private markets for farm goods. The evaluation report noted that the
World Bank's agricultural projects lacked "any measures for providing
a framework within which markets could operate more efficiently—
commercial legal code, regulation or inspection—and any attempts at
privatizing. While attention was given to the supply of inputs and the
collection of products, the availability of incentive [consumer] goods
seems to have been ignored."[47] Even worse, "Some World Bank
projects have created processing and marketing monopolies for export
products, so small holders have been compelled to use them. Examples
include cotton, tobacco, meat, tea, coffee, coca, oil palm, and rubber."
The evaluation report noted that, although many World Bank studies
were done on agricultural pricing and marketing issues, "there is
virtually no evidence that any study was subsequently acted on."[48]
Despite the failure to achieve policy reform, the World Bank keeps the
money rolling.

Conclusion

Has the World Bank helped the Third World? Some countries have
benefited—but most of the long-term aid recipients have only ended
up with heavy debt loads, swollen public sectors, and overvalued
exchange rates. Instead of spurring reform, most "aid" has simply
allowed governments to perpetuate their mistakes. In the words of one
International Monetary Fund official who assessed the effect of foreign
aid on Zambia, "It is fair to say that what we have done is to allow
Zambia to maintain a standard of living for its civil servants [whose

[46]World Bank Operations Evaluation Study, *Agricultural Marketing: The World Bank's Experience, 1974–85* (Washington, D.C.: World Bank, 1990), p. 2.

[47]Ibid., p. 4.

[48]Ibid., p. 3.

payroll amounts to 20 percent of the country's gross domestic product] which is totally out of synch with the rest of the economy."[49]

After scores of structural and sector adjustment loans, and after thousands of "reform covenants" in bank project loans, most less developed countries still have policies that are inimical to economic growth. If the bank has not straightened out Third World economic policies after disbursing nearly $300 billion in loans and handouts, what chance is there that increased bank lending will correct the problems in the future?

Moreover, the bank has had a net destabilizing influence on the international financial system by encouraging a huge expansion of doubtful loans, even when its research departments should have spotted warning signs, and dogmatically viewing all transfers of resources as inherently beneficial. But the ultimate question is, are more bad loans good for the world economy?

Bank loans always either go directly to the recipient government or must be guaranteed by the government. Thus, World Bank aid inevitably increases the politicization of Third World economies—even while bank economists lecture on the need for politicians to stop throttling the marketplace. The costs of politicizing aid are far greater than the cost of interest payments on private credit.

The bank claims that it needs to provide more aid to Third World economies to help them grow. But the bank itself is based on an outdated and always invalid theory of development economics—that all that Third World economies need to grow are handouts of capital and modern technology. Since it has become obvious to all that domestic economic policies are more important for growth than international welfare, the World Bank no longer has a meaningful rationale for existing.

Indeed, in a 1993 report the bank itself admitted that private foreign investment was sharply increasing in the Third World. But, stated the bank, many foreign governments have reputations that are too shady to win investors' confidence: "The risks of doing business are much increased in countries where the rules of the game are unclear or where the state does not ensure that private contracts are enforced and where the judiciary system does not function well. . . . Inadequate administration of justice, deficient property rights, frequent political interfer-

---

[49]Blaine Harden, "Zambia, Trapped in Poverty's Vise," *Washington Post*, September 26, 1985, p. A1.

ence in private business, corruption and excessive red tape are among the most serious obstacles to private investment."[50] Yet if foreign governments seem so untrustworthy that investors hesitate risking their capital in those countries, why are the same governments trustworthy enough to use handouts from the World Bank productively? No amount of bank lending can buy a government a reputation for honesty and trustworthiness—and without such a reputation, the country's hope for long-term development will remain dim.

Still, the case is often made that lending to less developed countries should be increased because capital can be better used in the Third World. That may sound good in theory but is not convincing to anybody who has visited, say, Zaire. As Harvard economist Nicholas Eberstadt observed, "The rights to private property, personal liberty, due process and even to life itself are routinely ignored or violated by the overwhelming majority of sub-Saharan states."[51] Such governments are neither trustworthy nor creditworthy.

Even so, Third World economic development would be aided more by foreign investment, based as it is on economic considerations. Yet as World Bank aid has increased, recipient countries have felt more able to create barriers against foreign investment.

The only thing that the bank can do that private lenders and investors cannot or will not do is provide money on easy terms to uncreditworthy borrowers. But every bank handout increases the government's ability to act irresponsibly and sabotage its own economy—and reduces its need to rely on private credit markets that impose fiscal discipline on borrowers.

A few years ago, the bank was considering setting up a commercial affiliate that would borrow and loan to less developed countries at a profit. This is a good idea—for the entire bank. If the bank never received another dollar from the United States or other government treasuries, it could still lend more than $13 billion a year because of its huge reserves and repayment of previous loans. If the bank were

[50]Quoted in Stanley Meisler, "Private Money Pours into Third World Business," *Los Angeles Times*, March 2, 1993, p. H1.

[51]Nicholas Eberstadt, "Helping Hand Won't Solve Africa's Problems," *Wall Street Journal*, April 30, 1986, p. 32.

required to support itself by selling bonds based on its own creditworthiness, it would have to focus less on loan levels and more on sound economic decisionmaking.

Today, the bank has an incentive to back unproductive projects and incorrigible kleptocracies. Yet empowering corrupt and inept politicians to rule over their people does not promote real development. Indeed, giving countries money that is badly used is worse than not giving them money.

For that reason, the less money the bank has, the more likely its net effect on development will be positive. As long as the bank suffers from a "have money, must lend" syndrome, it will continue pouring billions into floundering socialist regimes, inefficient government corporations, and odious forced migration schemes. A poorer bank would be a wiser bank—and a better friend of the Third World.

4. Understanding the World Bank: A Dispassionate Analysis

James B. Burnham

What is a reasonable set of expectations regarding the activities and performance of the World Bank? Since dispassionate analysis along these lines of inquiry is rare, this chapter seeks to add to an infrequent literature.[1] I will use some of the insights provided by students of political economy and draw on three years of personal experience in working with the World Bank as the U.S. executive director.

It should not be surprising that a governmental agency with assets of well over $100 billion, a yearly lending program in excess of $20 billion (including World Bank–administered International Development Association, or IDA, credits), and an administrative budget of more than $1 billion should attract a good number of critics and supporters. The fact that it attracts more controversy than, say, the $110-billion Federal National Mortgage Association, a rather free-wheeling U.S. government–sponsored housing finance enterprise, I would attribute more to the international dimension of the bank and its wide range of lending activities than to any inherent differences in the behavior of governmental organizations.

However, one unusual dimension of the World Bank is the extent to which knowledgeable, articulate critics are to be found—and even, to an extent, encouraged—within the bank itself. It is the only organization, large or small, public or private, with which I am familiar that has institutionalized a process with a fair degree of independence for asking "How well did we do?" long after each project is considered completed. While some of the output of this process is of questionable value, and a certain talent is required for reading between the lines, a surprising amount of it is straightforward and candid in describing and analyzing why bank projects fail.

---

[1]An exception is Bruno S. Frey, *International Political Economics* (New York: Basil Blackwell, 1984), chapter 8, which tests several hypotheses about World Bank behavior and finds evidence in favor of a "politico-economic" model.

Of course, the work of the Operations Evaluation Department is not normally available outside the World Bank, and that is a matter of some concern to a wide spectrum of outsiders. But any elementary model of bureaucratic behavior (or professional experience) would predict accurately how the institution would respond if forced to publish routinely what had previously been restricted and relatively candid internal documents.

The World Bank as a Government Bureau

One of the more frustrating dimensions of bank controversies is the tendency for most discussion to focus on the intellectual rationale behind its lending programs. The assumed working model of the World Bank is of an institution managed by a set of perfectly responsive agents in the employ of a homogeneous group of shareholders, all of whom are interested exclusively in the economic growth of developing countries. Anyone who starts with this model of the bank is doomed to frustration.

The starting point for any serious discussion of the World Bank should be an acknowledgment that it is a government bureau, although of a very special kind.[2] To paraphrase economist William Niskanen, it specializes in providing services that some people prefer to be supplied in larger amounts than would be supplied at market prices.

What are the actual interests of the resource-providing governments? It is instructive to recall the specific objectives of the original founders of the bank. The physical destruction caused by World War II, the disarray of world capital markets, and the memory of the post–World War I reparations difficulties were three primary considerations in establishing the bank. Season such concerns with a strong, if erroneous, belief in the inherent capacity of government-sponsored institutions to improve on normal market solutions, and you have the political basis for the World Bank.

What has replaced this original set of rather pragmatic sponsor objectives? At one level, the World Bank is seen as playing a useful role in assembling and administering multilateral aid consortia, research

[2]Although the model must be substantially modified to be applied to the World Bank, the approach developed here is influenced by William N. Niskanen, *Bureaucracy and Representative Government* (New York: Aldine-Atherton, 1971).

projects, and similar activities benefiting developing countries. Moreover, many government sponsors (including, to some extent, those in the U.S. executive branch and Congress) believe that if the bank assists economic growth in developing countries, those countries will be more politically stable, democratic, and friendlier to donor states than they otherwise would be. No matter that this belief remains unproven despite many attempts to do so, it is a powerful belief with measurable consequences.

The major resource providers—particularly those elements within governments responsible for foreign relations—also see the bank, and the other multilateral development institutions, as valuable instruments for rewarding friendly or useful governments or for disciplining politically wayward countries. The promise of additional finance, or the threat of less assistance, is treated as another useful lever for achieving broader diplomatic objectives. Economic performance, recent or prospective, can become a secondary consideration.

On a more operational level, with varying degrees of intensity, governments seek to promote their nationals in both staff positions and as recipients of bank-awarded contracts. Thus, the essential nature of the World Bank, and its cousin institutions, such as the Asian Development Bank and the recently organized European Bank for Reconstruction and Development, in almost all of its manifestations, is political. It cannot be otherwise, given those organizations' constitutions and modes of operation.

The World Bank is an unusual government bureau, however, in that it has multiple governmental sponsors, although power is heavily weighted towards those governments that provide resources to the bank. The existence of multiple resource-providing sponsors gives bank management significantly greater freedom to maneuver than would be the case with a single sponsor.

That latitude has increased in recent years as the relative weight of the largest single shareholder, the United States, has declined from 37 percent in 1947 to under 20 percent today. Although the United States retains its potential veto over any amendment to the bank's charter and the (unstated) right to appoint the bank's president, the dilution of its original power means that the organization is not as responsive to U.S. desires as it was in its early years.

Of equal importance in terms of sponsor control is the globalization of world capital markets over the past 15 years, which has permitted the bank to borrow in a wide variety of currencies other than the U.S. dollar. Because the bank is required to obtain the permission of each country's authorities for its frequent borrowings, denial of permission has traditionally been a useful and discreet technique for major sponsor control. But the ability of the bank to now borrow in sizable amounts in a variety of major currencies, as well as its acquisition of a large liquidity reserve (amounting to $17 billion in 1990, or about 47 percent of its prospective net cash requirements three years forward), has also served to reduce U.S. (and other sponsor) leverage.

In common with other successful government bureaus, the bank cultivates the constituents of resource-providing governments. It conducts an active external publications program, maintains a staff of specialists in media and government relations, and hosts frequent conferences and informal gatherings for legislators and other influential citizens in key contributor countries.

Of equal importance, the World Bank is fully conscious of the potential political leverage on resource-providing governments that bank-funded contractors, consultants, and nongovernmental organizations can exert.[3] With the emergence of a substantial number of World Bank bondholders throughout the world, another influential constituency has been established. Finally, while relatively few in number, the role of the permanent ministerial and legislative staffs in resource-providing governments with a vested interest in the bank and similar institutions should not be underestimated.

What precisely does the World Bank attempt to do? According to the bank, its objective is "to help raise living standards in developing countries by channeling financial resources from developed countries to the developing world."[4] Thus, there is a formal congruence between the bank's stated objective ("to help raise living standards in developing countries") and a key assumption in the resource-providing governments' support of the bank (lending leads to economic growth, which in turn means political stability and democratic governments).

---

[3]The Bretton Woods Committee, an organization of U.S. supporters of the World Bank (and the International Monetary Fund), makes frequent use of bank-supplied data on awards to U.S. contractors as an argument in favor of World Bank appropriations by Congress.

[4]World Bank, *Annual Report 1989* (Washington, D.C.: World Bank, 1989), p. 3.

Of course, there are ample grounds for serious error in the bank's chosen strategy of "channeling financial resources," particularly since the bank, by its charter, is required to lend only to governments or with a government guarantee. It may be that more and better bank advice and technical assistance on how to attract private investment, rather than bank loans, would be the most productive way in which to increase the overall flow of funds.[5] In fact, overstimulation of external finance might discourage saving and productive investment in developing countries.

However, since measurement of the desired output of the World Bank (its contribution to economic growth in the developing countries) is impractical, the bank officially grades itself primarily on the amount of financial resources that it shifts to the developing world. This means, then, that "bigger is better" by definition. The first table in the World Bank's annual report, before any text, always starts by listing volume data, such as the value of new commitments to lend, net disbursements to countries, and number of borrowers.

The emphasis on lending is further evidenced by the bank's expression of concern when borrowers with good access to the private capital markets, such as South Korea or Thailand, choose to forgo bank credit. Moreover, for a number of years, management actively discouraged borrowers from prepaying loans when attractive alternatives were available to them. When the policy was finally relaxed in 1989, prepayments soared to $2.7 billion. In Niskanen's terminology, the measure of activity (lending) has become the measure of output (economic growth).

The Bureau at Work

My experience as World Bank U.S. executive director between 1982 and 1985 amply supports this model of the bank. The first incident was the debate over the bank as "lender of last resort." For many years, particularly during Robert McNamara's presidency, the bank gave wide credence to the notion that it acted as a "lender of last resort" to developing countries.

[5]Putting a priority on this operational mode at the expense of direct lending would be fully consistent with the original charter of the World Bank. See article I(ii).

Such a notion flows easily from the bank's articles of agreement. The first article makes it clear that the bank's purpose is to "supplement private investment."[6] The third article states that for the bank to make a loan, it must determine that "in the prevailing market conditions the borrower would be unable otherwise to obtain the loan under conditions which in the opinion of the bank are reasonable for the borrower."[7]

When I became executive director in 1982, I was interested in the volume of lending to countries such as South Korea and to projects that yielded high financial rates of return, such as gas field development programs. Since the World Bank was frequently stressing the limited amount of "official finance" available for the developing countries, it occurred to me that if we started to screen out loans intended for countries or projects that could secure financing in private markets, more might be available for genuine "lender of last resort" situations.[8]

I pursued this issue rather aggressively and found that I had overturned a hornets' nest. Calling for a fundamental policy review based on clauses in the articles of agreement is taken seriously by many of the World Bank's staff. And that particular review was obviously questioning the rationale for a measurable portion of the bank's lending program—and the consequent justification for its next capital increase. Based on the staff work in response to my request and the resulting debate at the board level, I realized no one had taken this article seriously for many years because if they had, the World Bank would have been a very different institution.

I also realized that to have any chance of succeeding in the debate, I would have to call upon the direct intervention of the U.S. secretary of the treasury, who, in turn, at a minimum would have to devote considerable time to cajoling other important finance ministers. So formal discussion of the overall policy issue was put to sleep in a "seminar" of the directors. But not before the World Bank staff

---

[6] Article I(ii).

[7] Article III, section 4(ii).

[8] It seems likely that World Bank lending to middle-income developing countries during the 1960s and early 1970s was an important factor in the failure of a private international bond market for such countries to reemerge. If such a bond market had reemerged, the less developed country debt problem would have been closer to a repeat of the 1930s (with individual investors directly bearing the losses) rather than a massive, government-supported commercial bank rescheduling effort.

produced a marvelous document of high bureaucratese that, in effect, stated that since the bank was interested in "policy change, institution building and technology transfer" it could ignore the terms and conditions of alternative private-sector finance whenever it wished.

Did I accomplish anything? Yes, two, even if fairly minor, things. The first was purely cosmetic. I do not think the bank has described itself as a lender of last resort since 1983. Second, I educated myself about how enormous the job would be to curb the bank's institutional appetite for more capital.

Having mounted a frontal attack on a central issue and been largely repulsed, my alternate, George Hoguet, and I redoubled our efforts on the weakest flank of the lending program—the oil, gas, and coal projects. Such projects had been encouraged by many sponsor governments, especially the Carter administration, in the late 1970s. Some of them made sense in my opinion.

For example, loans to some countries for such activities as establishing a legal framework, inventorying known data on hydrocarbon possibilities, and financing elementary mapping in preparation for negotiations with large international oil companies seemed reasonable. To work well, the market needs informed sellers as well as buyers. From the bank's institutional point of view, however, such loans were not terribly important, because they were so small.

In contrast, most hydrocarbon projects involved bigger loans but were eminently unsuitable for World Bank financing. The largest loans were for putting known reserves into production. Although such projects required very substantial finance, the returns were normally extremely high: reserves were well established and the geological and developmental risks were small. Private-sector oil companies, including some in the developing countries themselves, were therefore more than willing to undertake the projects with their own funds if the investment regime was appropriate. Why not concentrate on the petroleum and foreign investment laws and tax codes, rather than lend billions for projects that could be financed elsewhere, we asked.

The second set of projects was at the other end of the spectrum. These were high-risk seismic and exploratory drilling programs with very uncertain payoffs. Why, we asked, is the World Bank encouraging developing countries, such as Morocco or the Philippines, to borrow for a 30-year period to finance the type of activity that should be handled with 100 percent equity capital? What if little or nothing comes from those programs, as is most likely, and the countries are on the hook for 30 years paying off the loan?

At first, those questions raised eyebrows mainly among a number of borrowing-country executive directors, whose governments were taking out the loans. The British were mildly helpful and the French figuratively sighed. Bank staff suggested another seminar and trotted out the "country considerations" argument again: "One has to look at individual projects in the context of the overall country lending program; repayment terms for an individual project are not germane."

On that particular issue, I felt we had a strong case on which the World Bank could give ground without calling into question the entire rationale for its existence. Thus, I engaged U.S. treasury secretary Donald Regan in the struggle, and he was most supportive. Did our efforts result in any policy changes? The strongest and most honest statement I can make is, "I think so." A number of projects apparently were removed from the "pipeline" on the basis of our criteria and the volume of this category of lending fell from $840 million annually in the 1980–84 period to an average of $580 million in the subsequent five years. No doubt weaker energy prices also played a role in this trend, but if we accelerated a change in lending policy by 18 months, I think it was a productive fight.

Last is the issue of funding. Although the World Bank does not have to return to its sponsoring governments annually for an appropriation of funds, if it consistently lends more than internal reflows and profits, it must eventually turn to its shareholders and their legislatures for additional capital. This "return to the well" is ensured by the Bretton Woods founders' prohibition, through the bank's articles of agreement, of any leveraging.

Perhaps because bondholders are more concerned about such matters than governmental shareholders, that particular constraint has received substantially more attention from the bank than those bearing on "lender of last resort." The Treasurer's Department is, after all, one of the largest nonsovereign sellers of bonds in the world. A conservative technical interpretation of the "leveraging" article was an important and successful objective of mine during the negotiations for a selective capital increase in 1983.

A central objective during my tenure as U.S. executive director was to require bank management to make a coherent argument, in the context of assisting economic growth in developing countries, as to why it needed another capital increase. Was it not possible to do more with existing resources, such as selling off loans to well-rated, "graduated" borrowers already on the books? What was the rationale for suddenly increasing a loan in preparation from $50 million to $90 million? What would it mean for capital requirements to give genuine content to the phrase "lender of last resort"?

Despite the occasional success on several of these aspects of the capital issue, it became clear that the bank as an institution could not focus on increasing the effectiveness of its lending if the prospect of a capital increase was in the offing. Just as its client borrowers saw little reason to undertake genuine reform if the bank was likely to continue lending regardless, so the bank saw little reason to alter its priorities if a capital increase was always waiting in the wings.

While individual bank officers were quite cognizant of how the bank could contribute to economic development in many countries by granting fewer loans and insisting on better economic policies, the institutional rewards for consistently asking for fewer financial resources were trivial or negative. And as for cutting off lending entirely on economic grounds, that was normally out of the question, because the "need to maintain contact and credibility with those who support sound policies is vital, even if no one of significance in their governments is currently listening to them."[9]

The bottom line, of course, was that the World Bank never did make a coherent case for a general capital increase while I was in office. In consequence, however, it did not receive U.S. government support for an increase during that period.

Two Proposals for Reform

One proposal for reforming the World Bank and channeling its energies toward more effective promotion of economic development is to rule out any capital increase for a minimum of 10 years. Such a constraint would turn bank managers' minds and energies toward using existing resources in more productive ways and lead to alterna-

---

[9]The World Bank does, however, delay individual loans or a country lending program if major policy issues are not resolved to the bank's satisfaction (and key sponsor governments are indifferent or support the bank's position). However, the broad institutional incentive to make loans over time subsumes individual situations.

tive methods of measuring the effectiveness of the bank. There is no question in my mind that such a situation would lead to a considerably greater "bang for the buck" in terms of the bank's contribution to economic growth.

The great difficulty with such a proposal is the proliferation of multilateral lending institutions, of which the European Bank for Reconstruction and Development is the latest example. If the World Bank were the only game in town, the proposal might prove effective. As it is, I suspect the political process in the United States and elsewhere would simply reallocate taxpayer-backed support to other multilateral lenders. Only an agreed-upon cap for all the institutions could prevent the problem.

A more radical, but in some respects more politically practical, proposal would be to merge the World Bank with the International Monetary Fund (IMF). Such a proposal can be justified on efficiency grounds, because both institutions have largely identical missions today with considerable overlap in staff activities and duplicate demands on borrowing countries.

As a bank executive director, I spent considerable time on issues involving World Bank–IMF coordination and grew to appreciate the extent to which the missions and operations of the two institutions had converged over the years. Since then, I have carefully reviewed many of the technical issues and likely arguments against such a proposal and have grown more convinced of its essential soundness. A merged institution, with a tight cap on its combined resources, would probably evolve into a more constructive force for economic growth in the developing countries than the two separate institutions as currently operated. And it would clearly be in a class by itself when measured against other multilateral financial institutions.

Conclusion

Effective performance by any public agency depends largely upon the incentives and constraints that the agency's sponsors impose on it. These incentives and constraints, in turn, reflect an uneven mixture of political, financial, and intellectual considerations on the part of the agency's sponsors. If there are a number of significant sponsors with varying interests, effective performance becomes increasingly difficult to measure or even define, and the staff's own agenda becomes increasingly predominant within the constraints imposed by the sponsors.

The World Bank appears to have evolved into an institution with a performance criterion (lending money to governments) increasingly at variance with its basic formal objective (helping to raise living standards in the developing countries). However, to date, the bank's sponsors appear to believe that the political benefits that accrue from being able to influence the allocation and timing of lending operations outweigh sufficiently any dissatisfaction with the bank's performance in raising developing country living standards or promoting private investment (as called for by the bank's articles of agreement). At the same time, the World Bank staff has independently established a broad set of constituencies to help influence key sponsors to support the staff's own agenda.

None of this behavior should be considered unusual or particularly shocking. But major reforms will be required to focus bank energies and resources on significantly more effective policies that encourage economic growth in the developing countries. No matter how energetic or talented a new World Bank president may be, the institution's behavior probably cannot be altered meaningfully without fundamental changes in the bank's underlying incentive structure. A coordinated capital freeze or a merger with the IMF are two examples of the type of changes that are necessary to make the bank behave differently.

Thus, the answer to the question that initiated this essay, What is a reasonable set of expectations regarding the World Bank?, is simply, given current shareholder makeup and readiness to supply capital, "about what we are getting." Only if one of those two factors is changed are we likely to get a World Bank that more effectively discharges its role to assist economic growth in the developing countries.

PART III

CASES

5. Western Aid and Russian Transition

Nicholas Eberstadt

If Western leaders press forward with their present plans, the principal focus for international development assistance in the 1990s promises to be the former Soviet Union. Indeed, the scale of aid now being contemplated could easily make the Commonwealth of Independent States (CIS) the largest single recipient of development assistance transfers. At the Munich economic summit in July 1992, the leaders of the seven major industrial democracies ratified a $24-billion aid program—a one-year package for Russia alone. "Never before," noted analysts at Germany's Deutsche Bank, "has a comparable amount been made available to one single country."[1] Yet less than one year later, in an emergency meeting, the so-called G-7 governments offered an even larger one-year aid program to Russia; at the April 1993 session in Tokyo, the ratified total exceeded $28 billion.

These initiatives, moreover, are meant to be only a beginning. The managing director of the International Monetary Fund (IMF), for example, stated in 1992 that the 15 countries of the former Soviet Union will require an average of at least $25 billion a year in economic aid for at least the next four years—and by implication, very possibly longer. Such a sum would substantially exceed the present volume of aid for all of sub-Saharan Africa or for all of low-income Asia. In fact, a program of that size would absorb nearly half of all Western official development assistance (ODA) disbursements at current levels of giving.

Whether such an ambitious international aid program can actually be arranged and implemented remains to be seen. (Only about half of the 1992 aid package for Russia was actually disbursed.) But the ultimate magnitude of the West's pending bequest is by no means the only question that arises in reviewing the many plans and packages for CIS aid now under discussion. One major question can be posed

---

[1]Hans W. Mueller and Andreas Gummich, "A Fund to Stabilize the Ruble," *Deutsche Bank Focus: Eastern Europe*, no. 46, May 26, 1992, p. 1.

bluntly: Apart from the immediate symbolism of the gesture, just what is Western "development assistance" to the former Soviet Union supposed to accomplish, and exactly how is it expected to achieve these results?

Obvious as the question may appear, it is not easily answered, for that particular aspect of the various aid initiatives in question seems to have received remarkably little consideration from prospective donor governments. The oversight in itself is revealing. And unfortunately, it is consistent with a pattern that is all too familiar.

To a disturbing degree, Western bilateral and multilateral aid agencies treat objectives and strategy as peripheral to the real business at hand. Throughout the so-called donor community there is a pervasive tendency to equate performance with "moving money": to judge aid not by the effectiveness with which it is spent, but simply by the *fact* that it is spent. Needless to say, that does not augur well for the impact of development assistance on recipient economies.

Examined in its particulars, the actual record of bilateral and multilateral development assistance should not inspire confidence among potential new beneficiary populations. In recent decades the international aid community has subsidized wasteful or even positively destructive economic policies in many countries; it has underwritten a transition to self-sustaining economic growth in very few. By comparison with assisting most developing economies, moreover, the task of restoring economic health to the CIS looks truly imposing. Why the donor community should be expected to succeed in this challenge when it has conspicuously failed in many easier tests is far from obvious.

The Record of Development Assistance

Any realistic assessment of the likely impact of economic aid on the former Soviet Union must take a measure of the performance of Western bilateral and multilateral aid in the developing regions over the past few decades. Though the self-evident diversity of the Third World and the limited reliability and availability of data for these countries must temper any generalization about overall performance, several distinct tendencies nevertheless stand out.

First, the donor community has succeeded in transferring vast amounts of potentially productive capital to the various governments of Africa, Latin America, and low-income Asia. According to estimates by the Organization for Economic Cooperation and Development (OECD), net disbursements of official development assistance, at 1989 prices and exchange rates, totaled nearly $600 billion for the period 1980–90 alone.[2] (If one needs a concrete image to put that figure in perspective, think of two-thirds of the entire U.S. farm system.)[3]

Second, the economies of ODA-receiving countries are today characterized by severe structural distortions—distortions that have become steadily more pronounced over the past generation. To be sure, the developing regions as a whole witnessed considerable improvements in both per capita output and life expectancy during the past quarter century. Yet paradoxically, despite this progress, many Third World economies seem ever less capable of maintaining self-sustained economic growth. Investment without growth and industrialization without prosperity are today widespread phenomena among aid-receiving countries. According to the World Bank, for example, Jamaica's investment ratio over the past generation was much higher than the average for OECD countries—yet per capita growth in Jamaica over the 1965–90 period was negative. By the same token, despite its manifest poverty, Peru's industry reportedly accounts for a greater share of its national output than does Sweden's, and sub-Saharan Africa now appears to be more "industrialized" by this measure than Denmark.[4] During the era of massive aid flows, many Third World economies have evolved in directions that neither generate high rates of return on their scarce capital nor satisfy the demands and needs of their consumers.

Finally, the performance of development assistance programs over the past generation may be judged by the very nature of the continuing resource transfers to Third World countries. According to the OECD, despite four decades of economic assistance premised on helping countries help themselves, concessional ODA still accounts for over half the net flow of funds from the West to the developing regions. Moreover, the share of direct private investment within this overall

[2]Derived from Organization for Economic Cooperation and Development, *Finance and External Debt in Developing Countries 1990 Survey* (Paris: OECD, 1992).

[3]Derived from U.S. Bureau of the Census, *Statistical Abstract of the United States 1992* (Washington, D.C.: Government Printing Office, 1992), p. 648.

[4]Comparisons taken from the Statistical Appendix of World Bank, *World Development Report 1992* (New York: Oxford University Press, 1992), Tables 1, 3, and 9.

flow actually declined between the mid-1960s and the late 1980s.[5] If many recipient states seem incapable of attracting, or unwilling to attract, voluntary private investment from abroad, they seem correspondingly reluctant to embrace financial self-reliance. The roster of governments accepting American development assistance, for example, is virtually the same today as 20 years ago. According to one report by the U.S. Agency for International Development, "Only a handful of countries that started receiving U.S. assistance in the 1950s and 1960s has ever graduated from dependent status."[6] What is true of the U.S. program also obtains for other bilateral and multilateral efforts.

The unavoidable fact about development assistance—indeed, its defining characteristic—is that it is a bequest transmitted not to a population at large but to a presiding government. Some governments choose to use aid funds in economically productive ways; others do not. More than a few Third World states have used their aid funds to finance wasteful policies or even obviously injurious ones. The donor community, for its part, has continued to finance otherwise unsustainable policies and practices by numerous beneficiary governments.

The economies of today's long-term ODA recipients are typically distinguished by a variety of features: external debt obligations they cannot or will not repay, chronic budget deficits and price inflation, nonconvertible currencies and restrictive trade regimes, abnormally swollen investment and industrial sectors, far-reaching economic planning apparatuses, and pervasive state ownership of capital assets. These same features are characteristic of the economies of CIS countries. The variants in the former Soviet Union, of course, are generally more extreme than those found in most developing countries. That being the case, one may well wonder if aid policies have financed milder versions of the CIS members' current afflictions among so many current long-term aid recipients, why should these transfers be expected to restore the CIS republics to economic health?

---

[5]Comparisons derived from Organization for Economic Cooperation and Development, *Geographical Distributions of Financial Flows to Developing Countries, 1987–1990* (Paris: OECD, 1992), and from the predecessor volumes in this series.

[6]U.S. Agency for International Development, *Development in the National Interest: U.S. Economic Assistance into the 21st Century* (Washington, D.C.: U.S. AID, 1989), p. 112.

Is Aid Stabilizing?

To the extent that the Western economic aid packages now being fashioned for the former Soviet Union have been publicly explained, they are apparently meant to underwrite two major efforts: stabilization and policy reform. Let us examine these in turn.

Russia and the other former Soviet republics are today wandering in a no-man's-land between Leninist central planning and the market order. As a system, those current arrangements are inherently unstable; it is far from obvious why one should wish to stabilize them. In its IMF and World Bank usage, however, stabilization has a more limited focus: it refers to the objective of restoring balance or reducing volatility in specific macroeconomic indicators, such as aggregate output, price levels, and external accounts. Traditionally, the IMF has underwritten stabilization programs that move recipients toward economic health through austerity measures (such as budget cuts, elimination of subsidies, and currency devaluation). Traditional stabilization policies, unfortunately, are fundamentally miscast for economies like those of the CIS. The reason is simple: economic activity in these countries is dominated by state-owned enterprises that do not behave like firms in a competitive market setting. In these postcommunist societies, the macro response to stabilization policies will be different from those evinced in a market-oriented society precisely because their macro environments are so very different.

Poland already offers an example of what can be expected from stabilization without privatization in a postcommunist economy. Three-and-a-half years ago, the Polish government embarked upon a bold program of "shock therapy." Prices were decontrolled, the budget was very nearly balanced, and a trade surplus was achieved. Despite strenuous stabilization efforts, however, the Polish economy has not yet been stabilized. By the IMF's reckoning, inflation in Poland throughout 1992 was consistently running at over 40 percent a year—a much more rapid pace than in such traditionally inflation-prone countries as Mexico or Venezuela. Though technically convertible (for transactions within Poland), the zloty has weakened almost continuously against all the major currencies, and a balance-of-trade deficit has emerged. Official data on Poland's domestic economy remain problematic for a variety of reasons, but they indicate that industrial production may have fallen by two-fifths between early 1989 and late 1992.[7]

Why has this shock therapy ushered in such disappointing results in Poland? In the main, it is because the country's vast and predominant network of state-owned enterprises was neither constrained nor motivated by the rules of the market. Accountable essentially only to themselves, the enterprises could grant themselves credit as they saw fit, thus thwarting the government's monetary policies. Similarly, they could refuse to pay their bills with impunity, thereby adding to the budgetary burden. Producing for themselves rather than their customers, they proved to be largely indifferent to the incentives and signals evoked by price decontrol. And by continuing to suck capital into money-losing activities, they effectively strangled much of the supply response that would have been expected from Poland's competitive private sector.

Prospects for stabilization are hardly more auspicious for the CIS states than they were for Poland. To the contrary: the economic situation in the former Soviet Union is, if anything, even more thoroughly distorted. Unlike Poland, the CIS states own the farms as well as the factories. And an arrangement linking (at this writing) 14 separate central banks and 14 separate budgets to a single currency creates a situation in which the temptations of "beggar thy neighbor" policies may prove overwhelming. Even the comparatively modest objective of moving the ruble to the status of technical convertibility within Russia may prove elusive in the absence of far-reaching privatization and genuine economic reform.

To be sure, under current conditions Western stabilization aid (or other sorts of balance-of-payments support) could have an immediate impact on the economies of Russia and the other CIS states. It could pay for imports from abroad. It could subsidize local consumption. It might even provide the illusion of price stability and ruble convertibility until the stabilization funds or balance-of-payments supports run out. But until there is domestic and international confidence in the

---

[7]International Monetary Fund, *International Financial Statistics*, vol. 46, no. 4 (April 1993), pp. 57, 432–33.

governments—and the economic arrangements—*behind the ruble*, neither convertibility nor stabilization can be feasible propositions. Without the sorts of measures that would lend credibility to Russia's money and her economy, stabilization aid, no matter how generously it is provided, can only postpone the ultimate hour of reckoning.

The Myth of Policy Reform

The other concrete suggestions for economic aid to Russia concern subventions for policy reform. It is argued that by offering the CIS governments assistance as they privatize state assets, eliminate expensive subsidies, and veer toward more liberal economic arrangements, Western governments can help speed the transition to a market economy and reduce the attendant social pains.

In the abstract, one may wonder why it should be necessary to reward governments for desisting from demonstrably unwise economic practices or for embracing policies that stand to improve the well-being of their citizens. Such philosophical issues notwithstanding, it is far from obvious that policy reform aid for the former Soviet Union is capable of achieving its desired results.

Unlike dams, irrigation networks, or even family-planning programs, policy reform aid is not associated with a tangible product. When such aid is extended in the form of subsidized loans—as is the common practice at the World Bank and some other institutions—these loans are contracted without identifiable collateral. In return for immediate infusions of cash into their treasuries, recipient governments simply promise to amend their current practices.

Since policy reform aid is by design untied to any specific project, it is virtually impossible to evaluate. Indeed, judged by its own terms of reference, it is impossible to demonstrate failure for any policy reform loan or grant. After all, if conditions improve after a government accepts policy reform aid, lenders can take credit for the changes; if conditions deteriorate, lenders can argue that things would have been still worse but for their intervention. (That fact may not have escaped prospective recipients and may help explain why that particular type of aid is in such demand today.) But if a policy reform loan cannot be shown to fail, it is correspondingly impossible to demonstrate that it has succeeded.[8]

Yet there is one indirect indicator of the efficacy of policy reforms by governments that have accepted money for this undertaking. That is the price of their debt on the secondary market—i.e., the amount that private purchasers are willing to pay for a given dollar of outstanding commercial debt obligations contracted by a sovereign government. The price of a government's debt on this secondary market speaks to the credibility of its policies in the eyes of those who are not directly involved in accepting or dispensing policy reform aid.[9]

Almost all of the governments whose bonds are traded in this secondary debt market have been recipients of structural adjustment loans or other types of policy reform aid at some point during the past decade. Despite these agreements and infusions, the overall price of secondary sovereign debt dropped drastically during the 1980s. By 1989, the unweighted average for these issues was down to barely a third of their nominal face value. (Prices have improved a bit over the past three years; some portion of this improvement, however, may be due to the stimulating effects of lower international interest rates on *all* bond markets, including this one.)

Despite the generally poor performance of sovereign debt in the secondary market, certain issues have witnessed a vigorous recovery in recent years. The secondary price for Mexico's debt, for example, has risen steadily since early 1989, after having fallen for years. The date of the turnaround is significant: it coincided with the assumption of power by a new president. Under the previous president, Mexico had attempted to muddle through its economic crisis with a series of pseudoreforms. Confidence in Mexico's debt issues grew only as the international business community gradually concluded that his successor was both intent on, and capable of, leading his country to economic health.

Is Boris Yeltsin willing and able to do for Russia what Carlos Salinas de Gortari has been doing for Mexico? The question is central to the

---

[8]For a more detailed discussion of structural adjustment lending, see Nicholas Eberstadt, *Foreign Aid and American Purpose* (Washington, D.C.: American Enterprise Institute, 1989), chapter 4.

[9]For an informative discussion of these issues, see Mark R. Stone, "Are Sovereign Debt Secondary Market Returns Sensitive to Macro-Economic Fundamentals? Evidence from the Contemporary and Inter-War Markets," *Journal of International Money and Finance*, vol. 10 supplement (1991).

efficacy of the policy reform aid pending for the CIS republics. What is equally apparent, unfortunately, is that the former Soviet Union suffers by comparison with contemporary Mexico in a number of significant respects.

For one thing, the road to economic health is vastly longer for Russia and the other CIS states than it was for Mexico in 1989. The CIS economies are far more distorted, and they lack the civil-legal infrastructure that Mexico could take for granted. For another, it is not yet clear that Russia's leadership is ready to confront the enormity of the effort that will be required to establish a competitive market economy. And although there have been some changes for the good, there is no shortage of reason for concern.

To date, Russia's "privatization" program has been almost entirely talk; there has been almost no action. (The most recent stab at privatization, a complex and timid "voucherization" scheme, seems at this writing to be going nowhere.) Despite its huge burden on society, the military industry maintains an unjustifiably high level of activity, the civilian government's determination to decommission or convert it notwithstanding. A host of restrictions continues to discourage international trade. High taxes and a hostile regulatory atmosphere discourage foreign entrepreneurs from risking investment in the Russian market. Enormous subsidies are still being granted to money-losing state-owned enterprises.

Nor do the forensics of the reform process inspire confidence that the Russian regime is ready to take the steps necessary to make its economy viable. In spring 1992, when it finally seemed clear that the West would soon be granting the CIS members a major aid package, the Yeltsin government did not redouble its efforts at transformation. Quite the contrary, it restricted the portfolio of the adviser then perhaps most closely associated with radical reform, Yegor Gaidar; it backtracked on price decontrols; and it granted further subsidies to money-losing state ventures.

After spring 1992, moreover, Yeltsin's own control over government policy seemed to have weakened (results of the April 1993 referendum notwithstanding), at least until his showdown with parliament. Although the Russian Federation's initial tempo of reform was hardly breakneck, it has subsequently decelerated since the announcement of major Western aid.

Ultimately, this reversal may prove to be akin to Lenin's *peredyshka*: a tactical retreat for "breathing space" while the government gathers strength to push forward. So we may certainly hope. Yet however events may unfold, such temporizing only underscores a simple but basic fact about aid for policy reform: depending on the disposition of the government in question, such funds may be used either for financing the reform process or for postponing it.

An End to All Aid?

The preceding review should not be taken to suggest that *all* forms of state aid to Russia and the other CIS republics would be wasteful or unwise. Humanitarian aid—temporary relief during famines or after natural disasters—has an impressive record of saving endangered lives. If a catastrophe were to strike within the CIS, Western aid could certainly help to contain its human toll and suffering.

Political aid or security assistance could also serve useful purposes. At the moment, for example, the United States is providing a program of limited aid to help dismantle outmoded Soviet nuclear warheads. And at the July 1992 economic summit in Munich, the G-7 leaders agreed to assist (both technically and financially) in the cleanup of nuclear and toxic chemical sites in the former Soviet Union.

Further aid and cooperation of that general nature are easy to imagine. Japan, for example, might wish to offer an aid package to the Russian government in explicit exchange for the return of the Northern Territories that Moscow has forcibly occupied since 1945 or for a peace treaty to end the formal state of war that still exists between Japan and Russia. South Korea might premise future grants or loans to the CIS republics upon a full disclosure of past cooperation in, and current knowledge about, Pyongyang's nuclear program. Western states might also consider extending aid to the CIS states in return for the removal of atomic, biological, and chemical weapons from their territories.

But humanitarian aid and security assistance, we must remember, are motivated by very different considerations—and evaluated by very different criteria—from development assistance. Humanitarian aid reflects the Western view that life is precious and is to be protected. Political and security aid, for their part, are meant to further the international policy, and enhance the safety, of the states and citizens dispensing it. Neither form of aid needs to be justified by its prospective impact on the economic health of or the pace of material advance in the recipient state.

Unlike humanitarian aid and security assistance, development assistance *must* be justified on economic grounds. Until Russia's business climate is favorable, rates of return cannot be high on physical or human capital—or for that matter, on official development assistance offered by well-meaning foreign friends. Barring changes in legal and commercial arrangements that only the Russians—and other CIS peoples—can make, the economic assistance programs now under consideration in the West may not only prove to be wasteful, but they may ultimately retard reform worthy of the name.

6. Fostering Aid Addiction in Eastern Europe

Melanie S. Tammen

In 1990, the Bush administration and other Western governments opened a gushing pipeline of subsidized, government-to-government loans to the new democracies in Eastern Europe. In 1991–93, the International Monetary Fund (IMF) extended more than $3 billion to the region. The World Bank—undaunted by a woeful lack of development success stories among its borrowers in Latin America, Africa, and Asia—projected a lending program of $8 billion to $9 billion in Eastern Europe over the 1991–93 period. The United States also joined other nations in founding yet another multilateral development bank in 1990—the $12-billion European Bank for Reconstruction and Development (EBRD).

The strong support from the Bush administration and much of Congress for such a large-scale subsidized loan program for Eastern European governments stems from official Washington's captivation with the leveraged aid feature of multilateral institutions. Every year, with a relatively modest (by U.S. federal budget standards) annual payment of $70 million to the World Bank, Washington facilitates $15 billion in new World Bank loan approvals—thus seeming to leverage U.S. taxpayers' "investment" 200 times. Reagan and Bush administration officials persistently promoted that leveraging aspect of the multilateral lending agencies on Capitol Hill. Since 1989, as a result of the tempting notion that such aid produces more bang for the buck, congressional and other proponents of a Marshall Plan–like program for Eastern Europe, noting the tight federal budget, have looked to those institutions to deliver massive levels of aid.

Advocates of government-to-government loan programs for the Eastern European nations should take a long, hard look at the past record of such aid efforts. From the post–World War II efforts to the ostensibly new and improved World Bank of recent years, the record has been one of far more harm than good. The United States and other

101

Western nations should not sidetrack Eastern Europe's opportunities for a true free market through support for such rearguard socialist planning efforts.

Persistant Myths of the Marshall Plan

In a 1990 *Washington Post* article, Senator Bill Bradley (D-N.J.) applauded the "genius of the Marshall Plan" and called on Congress to "set aside an amount of up to one percent of the defense budget as a catalyst for East European reconstruction."[1] Similarly, financial management guru Henry Kaufman proposed a Marshall Plan whereby the major industrial countries provide "grants, aid and soft loans [because] meeting Eastern Europe's financing needs is a political priority and not a matter that can be left to a standard market determination of risk and reward."[2] In 1993, then, the United Nations Economic Commission for Europe called on the G-7 Western industrialized nations to commit to a long-term aid program for Russia on the scale of the Marshall Plan.[3]

Yet, contrary to conventional wisdom, the 1948–52 Marshall Plan, a $1.7-billion program of grants and loans to European nations to buy U.S. products, was not the linchpin for West European postwar recovery. In fact, as research by George Mason University economist Tyler Cowen has revealed, the administration of the aid program influenced many European nations to increase economic planning and controls.[4]

For example, for every Marshall Plan dollar that the United States gave a European government, that government had to set aside an equivalent amount of domestic currency to be used for public works or other state projects. As a result, every U.S. dollar sent to a foreign government caused that government to take another from its own

---

[1]Bill Bradley, "We Can't Afford Not to Help East Europe," *Washington Post*, March 28, 1990, p. A23.

[2]Henry Kaufman, "Where's the Cash for Eastern Europe?" *Washington Post*, July 7, 1990, p. A19.

[3]Frances Williams, "Moscow Needs Own Marshall Plan," *Financial Times*, April 14, 1993, p. 8.

[4]Tyler Cowen, "The Marshall Plan: Myths and Realities," in *U.S. Aid to the Developing World: A Free Market Agenda*, Doug Bandow, ed. (Washington, D.C.: Heritage Foundation, 1985), pp. 61–74. This section relies heavily on Cowen.

private sector.[5] That procedure closely parallels a fundamental feature of the multilateral development banks. Each World Bank dollar borrowed for a state investment project must be matched by the recipient government with, on average, two dollars of local currency.

More directly to the point, Cowen examined the recovery records of Marshall Plan recipients and found that those receiving relatively large amounts of aid per capita, such as Greece and Austria, did not recover economically until U.S. assistance was winding down. Germany, France, and Italy, on the other hand, began their recovery *before* receiving Marshall Plan funds. As for Belgium, it embarked on a radical monetary reform program in October 1944, only one month after liberation. Belgium's economic stabilization and recovery were well under way by 1946, fully two years before the arrival of U.S. aid. Great Britain, conversely, received more Marshall Plan aid than any other nation but had the lowest postwar growth rate of any European country. The critical problem facing Europe was not the "dollar shortage," Cowen concluded, but simply bad economic policy.

In Germany, suffering in the initial years after the war resulted primarily from the Allied Control Commission's continuation of the Nazi system of economic controls. The West German economy hobbled along until mid-1948 when the Allies instituted currency reform, quickly followed by Ludwig Erhard's secret weekend abolition of most Allied economic controls. These key reforms predated the arrival of Marshall Plan funds. In fact, Allied occupation costs and reparations absorbed two to three times the Bonn government's Marshall Plan receipts.[6] U.S. policies thus *caused*, rather than alleviated, German resource problems.

In Greece, American advisers exercised considerable control and pushed for tighter price and exchange controls instead of a move to freer markets. As more U.S. aid was funneled through the government, graft and corruption increased. Greece began to recover only in 1953—the year that U.S. aid was cut to $25 million. This was also the first postwar year that the Greek government balanced its budget. In

---

[5]Ibid., p. 67.

[6]Ibid., p. 64. American aid never exceeded 5 percent of West German gross national product (GNP), while Allied occupation costs and reparations absorbed from 11 to 15 percent of West German GNP. The net economic transfers out of West Germany even exceeded that because throughout the mid-1950s Bonn repaid half of its Marshall Plan aid.

addition, Marshall Plan–financed exports of U.S. tobacco to Europe seriously damaged the Greek tobacco industry. Before the war, tobacco accounted for 50 percent of all Greek export earnings. The first year of the Marshall Plan funded the export of 40,000 tons of American tobacco to Europe. Greek tobacco exports fell from 17,300 tons in 1947 to 2,500 tons in 1948 and never recovered.[7]

Austria, perhaps the most economically devastated by the war, received $280 million in the first year of the Marshall Plan, the largest sum per capita in Europe. Yet the Austrian economy failed to recover, not only because the Nazi system of economic controls remained basically intact, but because of flawed monetary and fiscal policies and U.S. discouragement of trade with Eastern Europe.[8] From 1951 to 1953, then, Marshall Plan aid to Austria was cut drastically, from $127.6 million to $38.5 million. At the same time, the government changed monetary and fiscal policies, and the economy started to improve. Even Marshall Plan supporter Franz Nemschak admitted, "The radical cuts in foreign aid in the last year of the Marshall Plan and the stabilization tendencies in the world economy forced Austria to make a basic change in economic policy."[9]

Bogus Studies on Eastern Europe Discredit World Bank

Relations between the World Bank and Eastern Europe go back to 1945, when Yugoslavia and Czechoslovakia became members at the bank's founding. (Czechoslovakia, which withdrew from the World Bank in December 1954, rejoined the IMF and World Bank in 1990.) Poland joined the bank in 1946, withdrew in 1954, and rejoined in 1986. Romania joined the bank in 1972. Hungary joined in 1982. Bulgaria joined the IMF and World Bank in 1990.

Perhaps what most spectacularly disqualifies the World Bank as the indispensable facilitator of market-oriented economic reform in Eastern Europe is its rubber-stamp analyses of the region's self-destructive economic policies over the years. In an interview with *Forbes* magazine, Sir Alan Walters, former top economic adviser to British prime

[7]Ibid., p. 68.

[8]K. W. Rothschild, *The Austrian Economy Since 1945* (London: Royal Institute for International Affairs, 1950), pp. 14, 58, 71; as cited in Cowen, p. 69.

[9]Franz Nemschak, *Ten Years of Austrian Economic Development 1945–55* (Vienna: Association of Austrian Industrialists, 1955), p. 28; as cited in Cowen, p. 70.

minister Margaret Thatcher, quotes from a 1979 World Bank country study entitled, *Romania—The Industrialization of an Agrarian Economy under Socialist Planning:*

> Between 1950 and 1975 the economy grew rapidly within the framework of comprehensive economic planning made possible by the state's control of the major productive resources and its monopoly over foreign trade.... According to official statistics, Social Product and National Income grew at 9.8 percent per annum for 25 years.... Picture for 1981–90: The prospects indicate a constant growth in the standard of living.... National income should grow at 8 percent to 8.9 percent per annum.[10]

Such analysis was not worth the paper it was printed on. As Walters told *Forbes*, "In 1975 Romania's per capita income was $800 or $700. If they grew at 10 percent per annum for the previous 25 years, then in 1950 they must have all been dead from starvation!"[11]

The World Bank also produced a country study on Yugoslavia in 1979. It offers this bit of good news:

> Since 1950 Yugoslavia has continually extended and refined workers' self-management as the institutional framework for decision-making on all social and economic matters. The country has had a predilection for innovation and testing novel organizations and systemic relations. Its innovativeness has been characterized by a blend of pragmatism and flexibility and by an irreverence for institutions and policies that fail to meet expectations.[12]

In 1985, the World Bank asked Hungarian economist Janos Kornai to review papers prepared at the bank on socialist economies. His report firmly criticized World Bank economists for their adherence to "the wishful theory of prices." As Kornai explained, when an excessive demand for a good is perceived, the conclusion of the bank's economists is to increase the price. For example, when an excessive demand

---

[10]"Poland, Another Argentina," *Forbes*, February 5, 1990, p. 48.

[11]Ibid.

[12]Martin Schrenk, Cyrus Ardalan, and Nawal A. El Tatawy, *Yugoslavia—Self-Management and the Challenges of Development: Report of a Mission Sent to Yugoslavia by the World Bank* (Washington, D.C.: World Bank and Johns Hopkins University Press, 1979), p. 4.

for investment resources is recognized, the conclusion is to increase the real rate of interest. Kornai pointed out the problems with that methodology:

> This is wishful thinking—"get the price right"—perhaps that can be adequate advice in a system where profit incentives and markets dominate the coordination of economic activities [but not in] a highly centralized bureaucratic-hierarchical command economy. . . . Similar wishful thinking is behind the suggestion to make investment decision-making less "politicized" and more efficiency oriented. This is not a change which can be achieved by preaching the reasonableness of such a shift.[13]

Given the World Bank's record of propping up socialism in Eastern Europe—its past lending program there as well as its analytical apologia for state intervention—there is little reason to be optimistic about either the World Bank's accelerated lending in the region or the EBRD's lending there. The EBRD, too, deals primarily with governments, lending them the wherewithal to pursue a variety of undertakings in the public sector.

The EBRD: Assisting the Ailing State

On April 14, 1991, the EBRD formally opened its doors in London. It was initially capitalized at $12 billion. The European Community's 12 member states and its institutions among them hold a 51 percent share, the United States holds a 10 percent share, Japan (like the four largest EC members) holds an 8.5 percent share, and the nations that emerged from the disintegrated Soviet Union together account for a 6 percent share.

During early 1990 negotiations over creation of the EBRD, Senator Robert Kasten (R-Wis.) questioned why the world needed yet another development bank, why U.S. taxpayers should contribute to a bank from which the Soviet Union could borrow, and how European officials, many of whom still believed socialism could be reformed, could be expected to aggressively promote free-market principles at the bank.[14] In response to such criticism, Treasury Department officials

---

[13]Janos Kornai, "Comments on Papers Prepared in the World Bank about Socialist Countries," World Bank, Country Policy Department, Discussion Paper no. 1985–10, March 1985, pp. 12, 22.

[14]See *Congressional Record*, March 22, 1990, pp. S 3089–90.

portrayed the EBRD as a new and improved development bank. For example, Treasury under secretary David Mulford told a Senate Foreign Relations subcommittee in March 1990:

> We pressed for and achieved agreement that most of the EBRD's lending should support the transition to a market-oriented economy and in particular the private sector. By charter 60 percent of the EBRD's aggregate annual lending by country over the first five years must be to the private sector or state-owned enterprises that are shifting to private ownership and control.[15]

Mulford's final reference would appear to suggest that the EBRD will play a large role in the badly needed privatization of state enterprise in Eastern Europe. But, in fact, there is no precedent of a multilateral development bank's making significant levels of its assistance contingent upon the privatization of developing countries' bloated and loss-making state enterprises. The World Bank's dominant emphasis, vis-à-vis state enterprise, has been rehabilitation—not privatization. Among World Bank loans focusing on state enterprise, outright privatization has been promoted in a small number of cases; privatization has been achieved in yet fewer cases.

One World Bank review of 10 years of policy-based lending listed 39 loans tagged to reform of state-owned enterprises. In only three cases was divestiture an explicit bank condition.[16] The vast majority of conditions attached to those loans involved what the World Bank terms "institutional reforms," such as

- "prepare strategy plans,"
- "create intervention fund,"
- "coordination of SOE [state-owned enterprise] investment plans,"
- "increase prices,"
- "organization to increase productivity,"
- "realign salaries,"
- "new tariff [price] structure,"
- "restructure goals,"
- "revise parastatal labor laws,"
- "improve control of SOEs,"

---

[15]Statement by Honorable David C. Mulford, Under Secretary of the Treasury for International Affairs, before the Senate Foreign Relations Committee, Subcommittee on International Economic Policy, Trade, Oceans, and the Environment, March 22, 1990, p. 4.

[16]World Bank, Country Economics Department, *Adjustment Lending: An Evaluation of Ten Years of Experience* (Washington, D.C.: World Bank, 1988), pp. 42–43.

- "establish new State Enterprise Commission,"
- "develop skills mobilization scheme,"
- "improve management and delegation of authority,"
- "implementation of appropriate public sector wage policy," and
- "introduce modern management techniques."[17]

In recent years, such World Bank state enterprise loans have been used to pay off the arrears of state marketing boards in the Ivory Coast and to cover the "development expenditures" of Senegal's state agriculture boards. In Mexico, a $400-million loan to the money-losing state steel sector in 1988 supported, not the privatization of that loss-making state industry, but its purchase of new capital machinery. Also in 1988, Mexico's state fertilizer monopoly received a $265-million World Bank loan—not for privatization, but to bail it out.

In short, despite all the market-oriented rhetoric, the World Bank continues to tinker with socialism and central planning. If not for the World Bank gravy train of stopgap loans for ailing state firms, many could not continue to drag down their economies; they simply would no longer exist.

Early Record Suggests EBRD's Irrelevance

From the EBRD's opening in April 1991 to the end of 1992, the bank approved equity and loan projects with an EBRD contribution totaling $2.17 billion. Of that, it actually had disbursed only $151 million by the end of 1992.[18] Compared with the $7 billion in equity investment that the Czech Republic, Hungary, and Poland received from multinational companies and private investors from 1990 to 1992, the EBRD's disbursement level makes it appear irrelevant to the region's development.[19]

In addition, the EBRD's $151-million disbursement level is barely half what it has spent on administrative overhead and outfitting its London offices—$302 million—since its founding. That amount includes $192 million for operating costs (April 1991 to year-end 1992)

---

[17]Mary Shirley, *The Reform of State-Owned Enterprises: Lessons from World Bank Lending* (Washington, D.C.: World Bank, Country Economics Department, 1989), pp. 52–57.

[18]Robert Peston, "EBRD Spends More on Itself Than It Hands Out in Loans," *Financial Times*, April 13, 1993, p. 1.

[19]Robert Peston, "President Rejects Criticism over Slow Pace in Committing Funds," *Financial Times*, April 13, 1993, p. 6.

and $110 million to outfit the two office buildings the bank has occupied since it opened its doors. (It spent $27 million of United Kingdom government funds outfitting its first headquarters, which it occupied for only 20 months; in early 1993, it was expending another $83 million to outfit its new headquarters.)[20]

The money the bank has spent on itself has payed for lavish expenditures.[21] For example, the travertine marble in the lobby of the new headquarters was replaced with specially imported slabs of more expensive Carrara marble at a cost of $1.1 million. The point of the exercise, the bank's budget director Pierre Pissaloux told the *Financial Times*, was that the marble represented what the EBRD was trying to do for Eastern Europe—"Changing them from something rough into something polished."[22] That is, marble slabs are set in a sequence ranging from rough rock to polished marble. "We knew we didn't like it [the travertine marble]. It didn't give us the right feeling," the budget director added.

Other questionable expenditures included $900,000 in 1992 for hiring private planes for EBRD president Jaques Attali and $78,000 for a 1992 staff Christmas party at London's swank Grosvenor House Hotel—or $120 for each of the 650 employees and consultants in attendance.[23]

To be fair, it can be expected that the costs of running the bank in relation to its provision of finance would be high initially. Further, all expenses noted above were approved by the EBRD's board of directors, who are government officials representing the 53 countries that are the bank's shareholders.[24] Still, such oppulent expeditures appear starkly out of place in a taxpayer-financed organization trying to prove its relevance to the development needs of a region where people are facing great personal hardship.

[20]Robert Peston, "The Bank That Likes to Say Yes to Itself," *Financial Times*, April 13, 1993, p. 6.

[21]The new headquarters contains nine dining rooms, including the main staff dining room called the "Mozart," which is specially fitted with sycamore-lined walls and linen-covered chairs. Artwork costing $375,000, which the EBRD purchased, is scattered throughout the building. Robert Peston, "Reconstructing and Developing a New Working Environment," *Financial Times*, April 13, 1993, p. 6.

[22]Peston, "The Bank That Likes to Say Yes to Itself," p. 6.

[23]Jimmy Burns, "No Place for a Party Pooper," *Financial Times*, April 13, 1993, p. 6.

[24]Peston, "The Bank That Likes to Say Yes to Itself."

As for the EBRD's startlingly slow disbursement record, this is largely due to its charter's requirement that at least 60 percent of its investments be to the private sector on commercial terms, at market interest rates, and made only if private-sector finance cannot do the job alone. One EBRD loan, for example, did not appear to meet the rule in practice—a loan of 61.4 million European Currency Units (about $48 million) to General Motors' Hungarian car and engine plant. General Motors admitted that it could have arranged a loan elsewhere.[25]

A 1992 *Financial Times* editorial noted:

> So far there have been few suitable projects on a large enough scale to interest the EBRD, which meet these criteria. Those that have arisen have been snapped up by private investors. The EBRD, where it has been invoked, has tended to be a minority partner with large Western multinationals, which is not quite what Mr. Attali had in mind.
>
> It is not that private sector investment opportunities do not exist given the relatively high levels of education and low real wages in these countries. But they tend to be small-scale, grass roots projects which private banks find too risky. The EBRD was always going to be too remote to fill that gap.[26]

A confidential report commissioned by EBRD president Attali, and leaked to the press in June 1993, seemed to confirm those observations. According to the report, "The bank's impact comes up short as compared to the use of its resources," and has not made a "coherent . . . contribution to the [Eastern European] economic transition process."[27]

In short, the EBRD's charter—together with the abundance of private finance available in Eastern Europe for viable, large-scale projects—has the bank between a rock and a hard place in terms of proving its relevance. "The bank has more money than it has projects," EBRD president Attali admitted at the time of the EBRD's first annual meeting in April 1992.[28] Thus it is little surprise that Attali proposed, at the April 1992 meetings, to relax the bank's stringent commercial

[25]Nicholas Denton, "East Europeans Attack EBRD for Failing to Meet Their Needs," *Financial Times*, April 15, 1992, p. 14.

[26]"No Soft Option for the EBRD," editorial, *Financial Times*, April 15, 1992, p. 16.

[27]Quoted in Robert Peston, "EBRD Role in Eastern Europe Criticized," *Financial Times*, June 18, 1993, p. 1.

[28]Nicholas Denton, "U.S. Set to Block EBRD Expansion in East Europe," *Financial Times*, April 13, 1992, p. 2.

criteria and set up a facility for "soft loans" similar to the World Bank's International Development Association loans (which are lent at a zero interest rate and 35- or 40-year maturities, effectively making them outright grants). Attali proposed that the EBRD be allowed to make such loans directly to Eastern European governments, thus circumventing the current rule that 60 percent of the EBRD's investments should be to competitive private-sector projects.

Despite support from several Western European governments, the Bush administration strongly opposed the proposal and it appears to have died at the April 1992 meetings.

No Successful Development Bank Model for Lending to the Private Sector

As noted above, the EBRD's charter earmarks a large share of lending to ostensibly support Eastern Europe's nascent private sector. But what models exist for the channeling of multilateral development bank funds to private-sector borrowers? The principal World Bank vehicle for some 30 years has been directed credit via development finance institutions. DFIs are various types of financial intermediaries, most often state-run development banks, which receive large (e.g., $200 million to $400 million) World Bank loans to relend to small- and medium-scale borrowers, primarily in the private sector. Most World Bank–supported DFIs are run by government bureaucrats who allocate the credit by picking "winners"—or, in reality, picking anyone.

The World Bank began lending to DFIs in the 1950s with the stated aim of supporting the development of individual financial institutions. In the 1970s, the goal of DFI lending shifted to the promotion of growth in priority sectors. Since the mid-1970s, the World Bank has lent some $30 billion to DFIs throughout the developing world.

During the mid-1980s, World Bank reviews first began recognizing the sorry record of the bank's DFI lending. One 1985 report noted that, among a sample of DFIs, at the end of 1983 almost half had more than 25 percent of their loans in arrears and almost one-fourth had more than 50 percent. The report offered plenty by way of explanation.

> The DFIs were, in the 1970s, increasingly viewed as tools of development policy, channeling resources to publicly promoted or owned enterprises and to priority sectors which commercial lenders were unwilling to finance. The managements of DFIs that were heavily dependent on government

resources and operated in highly regulated financial markets were unable to make lending decisions based on independent assessments of business risks and profits. In addition, the intermediaries' spreads often did not reflect the true costs and risks involved in long-term lending to higher risk projects.[29]

The 1985 report noted that, of the 153 DFIs financed by the World Bank since the 1950s, 132 remained active borrowers. Many DFIs had received four or five World Bank loans. Yet, the report admitted that "few DFIs have become financially viable, autonomous institutions capable of mobilizing resources from commercial markets at home and abroad." The reasons for this sorry record are scattered throughout the study:

- "Much of the subsidized credit went to wealthy individuals."[30]
- "In many cases, neither creditor nor debtor had sufficient incentive to follow sound business practices."[31]
- "Recipients were induced to use overly capital-intensive production methods."[32]
- "Many governments used credits from DFIs for low interest rate lending to public and quasi-public institutions."[33]
- "On loans made at the behest of government, financial discipline was often poor, and for political reasons the DFIs were not able to foreclose on delinquent loans."[34]
- "Rather than remove real sector distortions, [World Bank–financed DFIs'] financial subsidies were often used in an attempt to offset them."[35]

Second World Bank Self-Indictment in 1989

Despite this embarrassing record assembled at the World Bank in 1985, the bank continued to extend about $2 billion in new loans to DFIs annually. So it was little surprise that in 1989, the World Bank's

[29]World Bank, Industry Department, "Financial Intermediation Policy Paper," July 8, 1985, p. ii.
[30]Ibid., p. iv.
[31]Ibid., p. 12.
[32]Ibid., p. iv.
[33]Ibid., p. 12.
[34]Ibid.
[35]Ibid., p. 8.

annual *World Development Report* rendered another damning verdict on the bank's experience with DFIs. According to the 1989 report, among a sample of 18 DFIs worldwide, on average nearly 50 percent of their loans were in arrears. The report further noted that the poor performance of "industrial DFIs" (development banks that lend to manufacturing enterprises) had caused them "to rely on government and foreign donors for funding."[36] Echoing much of the earlier review, the 1989 report described how World Bank support for DFIs had actually retarded the development of efficient capital markets in the borrower countries.

> It is clear [directed credit programs] have damaged financial systems. . . . Acquiring subsidized credit could sometimes add more to profits than producing goods. . . . The ability to borrow at cheap rates encouraged less productive investment. Those who borrowed for projects with low financial returns could not repay their loans. In other cases, borrowers willingly defaulted because they believed creditors would not take court action against those considered to be in priority sectors.
>
> . . . Moreover, by encouraging firms to borrow from banks, directed credit programs have impeded the development of capital markets. . . . Equity finance is a more appropriate way to finance risky ventures than bank loans. If governments establish the conditions necessary for equity finance, intervention will not be necessary.[37]

Still undaunted, the World Bank continued to use the DFI lending model and in 1990 made it the largest component of its lending program to Poland's new government. Two World Bank loans, for $245 million and $100 million, were to finance subloans to export-oriented industrial projects and agricultural processing industries, respectively. The borrower-intermediary was the National Bank of Poland (NBP), Poland's central bank and monopoly credit provider. To be sure, the development of a commercial banking system is an avowed priority of the postcommunist government. But World Bank loans funneled through Poland's central bank will only facilitate a continued role for the NBP as principal credit allocator within the economy.

---

[36]World Bank, *World Development Report 1989: Financial Systems and Development* (Washington, D.C.: World Bank, 1989).

[37]Ibid., pp. 58–60.

The replication in Eastern Europe of the World Bank's destructive record with funding financial intermediaries has already begun. Part of that $345 million to Poland funded the creation of a new development bank, which the Polish government directed to manage a public sale of shares of several state firms. In 1991, when there was nearly no interest in the shares of two particular firms—no doubt because the public perceived them as worthless—the development bank bought the shares instead. In short, DFI took valuable investment capital made available by Western taxpayers and jettisoned it into a black hole.

Directed Credit Was World Bank Modus Operandi

In Eastern Europe, Yugoslavia was unquestionably the World Bank's favorite son, allowed to borrow more than $5 billion as of 1991. In the 1980s, Yugoslavia borrowed an average of $280 million annually. World Bank loans financed state projects for roads, electric power, railways, agriculture, petroleum development, and other areas. Since the late 1970s, a substantial part of the World Bank's program had been loans to Yugoslavia's state-run banks. Since 1981, the World Bank funneled about $700 million in loans through seven of the Yugoslavian government's nine regional banking groups, in full knowledge that the banks' lending rates were highly negative in real terms (minus 10 to minus 20 percent) throughout the 1980s. A 1989 internal World Bank review of Yugoslavia's financial sector calculated these banks' net worth by adjusting their 1987 financial statements to account for deferred foreign exchange losses and an estimated 50 percent collectibility ratio on problem loans. The result: the banks were all insolvent, with red ink varying between $300 million and $1.2 billion.[38]

Under Yugoslavia's system of "worker self-management" introduced in the 1950s, enterprises operated with a strong built-in incentive to maximize workers' income share while limiting saving for reinvestment in the enterprise or in other companies. As part of the ownership system, moreover, enterprises established and managed banks. The basic objective of those banks had always been to provide

[38]World Bank, Country Operations Department IV, EMENA Region (classified document), "Yugoslavia Financial Sector Restructuring: Policies and Priorities," November 30, 1989, vol. 2, annexes, pp. 46–108 ("1987 Financial Results of the Nine Commercial Bank Groups").

credit to their founder enterprises at the lowest possible cost with little regard for the profitability of banking operations.[39]

While Yugoslavia's banks loaned funds at highly negative real rates of interest for decades, the credit subsidies simultaneously effected a fiscal and monetary expansion. When state banks increase their lending to distressed enterprises on demand, lend at subsidized rates, or relieve the foreign exchange losses that the borrower enterprises incurred on earlier overseas borrowing—all of which Yugoslavia's state banks did regularly—the effect is the same as printing more currency. That explains how Yugoslavia was able to run a modest federal budget surplus in the 1980s yet experience 2,765 percent inflation in 1989.

The expansionary sequence begins with the fact that enterprises are bound to be badly run because of a lack of private property or, as *The Economist* observed, "capital has no representative in the system." Enterprise losses are shifted to the banking system when banks are required to grant soft credit on demand. Eventually, the losses move again to the central bank, where they are financed by the printing of money.[40] That process also characterized the Polish and Hungarian economies.

World Bank officials knew full well Yugoslavia's rigged contraption of a banking system into which they poured hundreds of billions of dollars annually for decades. In 1983, Yugoslavia was the beneficiary of one of the World Bank's much-touted structural adjustment loans. The loan, $275 million to "improve the efficiency of investment selection and resource allocation in the economy," was disbursed to Yugoslavia's Udruzena Beogradska Banka (UBB), a large state bank. The loan certainly did not improve the UBB's own resource allocation—by the World Bank's estimation, this bank was $1.2 billion in the red in 1987.[41]

Among the major policy recommendations of the World Bank's November 1989 review of Yugoslavia's financial sector: "recapitalization [bailout] of the banking system."[42] Five months later, the World Bank began transferring resources to this end. On April 16, 1990, the

[39]Organization for Economic Cooperation and Development, *Yugoslavia: OECD Economic Surveys* (Paris: OECD, 1990), p. 36.

[40]"Survey: Perestroika," *The Economist*, April 28, 1990, p. 16.

[41]World Bank, Country Operations Department IV, vol. 2, p. 94.

[42]Ibid., vol. 1, *Main Report*, pp. 60–61.

bank approved a second structural adjustment loan for Yugoslavia—$400 million to "make public enterprises more financially viable, strengthen the country's financial sector, and streamline the process for identifying and selecting [state] investment projects."[43] In other words, the World Bank continued to bankroll Yugoslavia's socialist experiment until shortly before the country disintegrated into secessionist republics and civil war.

Hungary, since joining the World Bank in 1983, has borrowed about $300 million annually. As with Yugoslavia, much of that finance has been for directed credit, particularly for export-oriented industrial projects. The World Bank channeled its funds through Hungary's central bank. Today, the situation with Hungary's (and Poland's) state-run banking system closely parallels the situation in the former Yugoslavia. Those countries' "commercial" banks—in fact, only extensions of their central banks—loaned funds at negative real rates of interest to inefficient enterprises year after year to keep them from defaulting on previous loans. World Bank estimates in 1991 put central bank losses in Yugoslavia, Hungary, and Poland at 30 percent of their gross domestic products.

As with Poland, the World Bank's current lending program to Hungary continues to rely heavily on credit infusions through the central bank to other state banks. One 1990 loan, for $100 million, was to be reloaned by Hungarian state banks to agricultural enterprises, including state farms and cooperatives.[44] As part of another directed credit loan ($140 million) from the World Bank, Hungary's Ministry of Industry and Trade announced a list of 16 companies that were finalists for subloans of up to $10 million each. According to a publication of the *American Banker*, the list included several prominent firms that are competitive in world markets, including the Raba Hungarian Railway Carriage and Machine Factory, which it described as "the biggest axle-maker in East Europe and highly competitive in Western markets."[45]

[43]World Bank News Release no. 90-71, April 16, 1990.

[44]*Socialist Economies in Transition*, newsletter of the World Bank (CESCE Division), July–August 1990, p. 12.

[45]"Hungarian Firms to Get Aid," *The World Bank Watch* (an *American Banker* weekly publication), March 25, 1991, p. 6.

The largest portion of private international capital flowing to Eastern Europe has been going to Hungary—$1.4 billion in 1992 alone. (The Czech and Slovak republics attracted $1.2 billion that year, and Poland just $210 million.)[46] In fact, various American press reports over the last year have suggested that considerable private capital remains bottled up in several private investment funds in Hungary awaiting attractive investment opportunities. The Hungarian firms noted above should be able to tap that pool of capital. The $140-million World Bank loan only continues the bank's distortion of private capital market development through provision of cheap loans when equity investment may be more appropriate.

World Bank Infrastructure Lending Defies Global Trend

As cash-strapped governments and angry, ill-served taxpayers are warming to privatization across the globe, a lot of "strategic" enterprises and sectors (sacred cows) once reserved for state ownership are going private. This trend is particularly evident with publicly owned infrastructure—multilateral development banks' defining area of activity for decades. A Reason Foundation survey noted that

> around the globe, governments have begun a major shift of the responsibility for financing, building, operating, and, in many cases, owning major capital-intensive infrastructure projects. . . . The 1990s may well go down in history as the decade of privatized infrastructure.[47]

Indeed, from 1990 through 1991, 12 nations undertook sales (or partial sale) of their state telephone companies—Argentina, Australia, Canada, Gibraltar, Guyana, Israel, Jamaica, Malaysia, Mexico, New Zealand, Thailand, and Venezuela.[48] As for the nations of Eastern Europe, interest in global expansion by the cash-rich U.S. regional Bell telephone companies and several European companies means that they need only undertake the necessary reforms to capture that source of private investment. The *Financial Times* of London reported in 1990 that, as a result of liberalization in the region, "West Germany's

[46]International Finance Corporation, as reported in Tim Carrington, "What to Do with State-Run Dinosaurs," *Wall Street Journal*, April 12, 1993, p. A7.

[47]P. Fixler, Jr., R. Poole, Jr., L. Scarlett, and W. Eggers, *Privatization 1990: Fourth Annual Report on Privatization* (Los Angeles: Reason Foundation, 1990), p. 19.

[48]Reason Foundation, *Privatization 1992: Sixth Annual Report on Privatization* (Los Angeles: Reason Foundation, 1991), p. 44.

Siemens, France's Alcatel, Sweden's Ericsson, AT&T of the U.S. and Canada's Northern Telecom are actively negotiating joint ventures with local telephone companies across Eastern Europe."[49]

That reality renders totally unjustifiable the $1 billion the World Bank slated for lending to state telecommunications enterprises in Eastern Europe over the 1991–94 period. That $1 billion includes loans totaling $300 million for Hungary, $120 million for Poland, and $200 million for Czechoslovakia.

What has been U.S. policy in the face of the World Bank's being so laggard in adjusting to the global trend toward privatized telecommunications? Instead of pointing out that governments everywhere are getting out of the telecommunications business, in 1991 the U.S. Treasury Department's top official at the World Bank, E. Patrick Coady, organized a seminar to help dozens of U.S. firms get the upper hand in bidding on the forthcoming procurement contracts. Coady, according to an *American Banker* newsletter, was "working hard with the Department of Commerce to increase the volume of business U.S. firms do at the World Bank."[50]

Not only did all the major U.S. firms (AT&T, GTE, MCI, and the Bell affiliates) attend the 1991 seminar, but so did their competitors, including Alcatel, Ericsson, Siemens, and Northern Telecom.[51] Notice the overlap with the list of firms prospecting in Eastern Europe identified above. In short, the World Bank is spending Western taxpayers' money to modernize and expand telecommunications networks in Eastern Europe when the world's major private companies are eager to seek equity stakes and carry out the investments themselves. The World Bank telecommunications loans' primary result will be to finance the Eastern European governments' retension of shares in public-private telecomunications ventures when they otherwise would be sufficiently financially strapped to make them completely private.

In addition to privatizing telecommunications, governments across the globe are also selling (or allowing private-sector new capacity creation of) airports, bridges, highways, tunnels, ports, rail-

---

[49]Reason Foundation, *Privatization 1991: Fifth Annual Report on Privatization* (Los Angeles: Reason Foundation, 1991), p. 36.

[50]"$1 Billion in Telecom Loans May Go to East Europe," *World Bank Watch,* March 11, 1991, p. 1.

[51]Ibid.

roads, water systems, oil companies, and more. In 1992, Malaysia, Singapore, Argentina, and Venezuela were moving ahead with plans to privatize their postal services; and Argentina, Malaysia, and Thailand had either embarked on railway privatizations or had new, privately financed railway systems under way. Also in 1992, the privatization of ports was completely under way in Argentina, Mexico, Panama, Venezuela, Brazil, Malaysia, and Singapore; and private tollways were initiated in Mexico, Colombia, Venezuela, Argentina, Malaysia, Hong Kong, China, Hungary, Poland, and Czechoslovakia. In the energy sector, Argentina has sold the electricity corporation in Buenos Aires, the state gas distribution company, and the state oil company.[52]

Particularly given that dynamic trend toward private infrastructure throughout the so-called developing nations, there is no compelling justification for the following loans approved by the World Bank in recent years:

- $250 million to "develop and rehabilitate" Poland's gas fields and advise on "gas pricing" policies (loan approved in 1990),
- $90 million to "help fix roads and bridges" in Hungary and to "replace outdated maintenance equipment" (loan approved in 1992),
- $246 million to "support operation of cleaner and more efficient power plants" in the Czech and Slovak republics (loan approved in 1992).[53]

The Leveraged Harm of "Leveraged Aid"

In congressional testimony soon after the Bush administration pledged its support for the proposed new European bank, Treasury under secretary David Mulford explained, "The [EBRD] was also viewed as a vehicle which could, through its borrowing in capital markets, leverage contributed funds into larger loanable resources."[54]

[52]Reason Foundation, *Privatization 1993: Seventh Annual Report on Privatization* (Los Angeles: Reason Foundation, 1993), p. 39.

[53]*Socialist Economies in Transition*, newsletter published by the World Bank (CECSE Division), 1990; "Power Plant Upgrading in Czechoslovakia," *Transition*, newsletter published by the World Bank (Socialist Economies Reform Unit), May 1992, p. 12; and "Road Loan to Hungary," *Transition*, December 1992–January 1993, p. 12.

[54]Statement by the Honorable David C. Mulford, p. 2.

Indeed, since the late 1980s, this "leveraging" principle has become a familiar Treasury Department refrain. In April 1988, then–Treasury secretary James A. Baker III implored Congress to support a $75-billion capital increase for the World Bank by touting "the level of World Bank support to countries who are very important to us but where there is the virtual absence of U.S. bilateral assistance."[55] According to Baker, in 1987 new World Bank loans to a group of 10 countries, including Mexico, Brazil, Argentina, and the Philippines, totaled $7.7 billion, compared to $1.1 billion in U.S. bilateral aid to the group.

Despite the fact that those nations had long been suffering from top-heavy government sectors—which stifled private-sector activity—the Bush Treasury, like the Reagan Treasury before it, could not seem to learn the lesson. The international financial institutions, as required by their charters, deal with and lend funds to governments and government agencies *only*. Of course, more loans to governments mean increasing the economic (and political) power of those governments.

In addition to the leveraging facilitated by Japan and the European nations joining the United States as major World Bank contributors, there is also a hyper-leveraging facilitated by the off-the-balance-sheet manner in which Congress funds U.S. contributions to the bank. As Baker noted in 1988, "The U.S. portion of the paid-in capital (which is actual budget authority) that supported this $7.7 billion lending program was [only] approximately $60 million."[56] To be sure, this appears quite a bargain, at least until one considers the direct parallel between how Congress funds the World Bank and how U.S. taxpayers unwittingly backed up the Federal Savings and Loan Insurance Corporation (FSLIC). In addition to the $60 million, Congress also authorized in 1988 (but did not appropriate) $1.94 billion in "callable capital"—that is, unfunded contingent liabilities of the U.S. budget.

As things are presently engineered, Congress annually contributes some $2.8 billion to the World Bank—3 percent in appropriated funds and 97 percent in unfunded pledges. The World Bank raises most of its loanable funds in international capital markets by annually borrowing, on a dollar-for-dollar basis, against these (97 percent) callable capital

---

[55]James A. Baker III, testimony before the Subcommittee on Operations of the Senate Committee on Appropriations, March 30, 1988, p. 4.

[56]Ibid.

pledges of the United States, Europe, and Japan. Thus, the World Bank is a major issuer of bonds in international capital markets, in fact, the largest single issuer. For fiscal year 1992, the World Bank issued some $11.7 billion in new bonds to fund its activities. Without the World Bank, part of this investment capital would gravitate to developing countries only to the extent that they offer dynamic and secure investment opportunities. Instead, the World Bank effects a *misalloca- tion* of nearly $12 billion in valuable investment capital annually— soaking it out of international markets and funneling it to state investment schemes throughout the developing world.

With the EBRD, 30 percent of member nations' shares are paid in. Thus, the U.S. contribution profile comprises $363 million in paid-in capital and $847 million in (unfunded) callable capital—or $73 million paid-in and $169 million callable over each of five years. Again, this sounds like quite a bargain until one considers the FSLIC bankruptcy and recipient governments' appetite for cheap funds to finance endless loss-making programs and schemes.

Addicting Eastern Europe

The heavily indebted developing nations, particularly those in Latin America, are now on a borrowing treadmill with the World Bank. Arrears in repayment of World Bank loans have grown in recent years. As of June 30, 1992, $3.1 billion in World Bank loans were on nonaccrual status. Although the seven nations in arrears are small economies, such as Syria, World Bank officials know that preservation of the bank's critical AAA credit rating requires that none of the mega-debtors (e.g., Mexico, Brazil, Argentina) fall into arrears with the World Bank. To head off any such possibility, the World Bank is annually extending ever-larger levels of new loans to the 17 most heavily indebted developing countries, which are primarily in Latin America, in an effort to keep them servicing their old World Bank loans.

Those borrower-nations can be expected to seek—and the World Bank to encourage—ever-larger levels of World Bank borrowing as their repayment requirements to the World Bank continue to grow. Latin American nations are effectively hooked on World Bank loans. As the World Bank now radically expands lending in Eastern Europe, together with the lending activity of the EBRD, the result can easily be one of hooking these nations on development bank loans—an effective Latin Americanization of Eastern Europe.

The bottom line is that the World Bank is fundamentally a money-moving institution. Its current level of new loan generation—about $23 billion annually—allows little room for discretion among potential borrowers or projects. In addition, the bank has no record of assisting any borrower-government through any sort of "critical stage" and then withdrawing. Nations that become World Bank borrowers remain borrowers for decades. A major 1987 internal report on the World Bank's experience with rural development lending, its lending fad from the mid-1970s through the mid-1980s, revealed some of the dynamics that may play out in the bank's rush to lend in Eastern Europe:

> Lending was supply-driven by funds and project slots and the need to meet arbitrary target criteria, rather than demand-driven by sound strategies and realistic, well-prepared project proposals. Moreover ... the Bank lost sight of the reality that the cost of failures ... would be borne by the borrower countries and not the Bank. . . . [The World Bank's] program divisions were usually allocated country lending quotas [that] determine the potential average loan size even before the requirements of individual projects are known.[57]

Conclusion

The World Bank's record throughout the developing world and in Eastern Europe overwhelmingly disqualifies it as a catalyst for radical change in the region. Similarly, the new EBRD is fundamentally a rearguard socialist undertaking. The last thing nations in transition need is multilateral development bank loans to politicize their economies. The new political structures in Eastern Europe are weak, and the inflow of massive, concessional credits can easily forestall the needed transition to market prices and private investment.

It is indeed a tragedy that the United States and its European allies are showering the new democracies of Eastern Europe with the same programs of subsidized, government-to-government loans that have financed big government throughout the developing world, while maintaining substantial barriers to key Eastern European exports in areas as diverse as agriculture and textiles. Although, as Czech prime

---

[57]"Rural Development Lending, 1964–1986: A Review of Experience," Washington, D.C., World Bank, Operations Evaluation Department, 1987, classified.

minister Vaclav Klaus points out, outside factors play a small role when it comes to domestic reform, some external factors do have a positive impact. Those identified by Klaus include

- "the rapidly growing *flow of visitors* (both tourists and business-men) from abroad, who bring into the country market-oriented attitudes, habits and experience;
- "the *international trade* of goods and services which undermines the long-prevailing atmosphere of semiautarchic centrally planned economies . . . and which brings into the transforming country real competition and previously nonavailable world standards"; and
- "*foreign real investment*, provided the country is in a situation where property rights are already clearly defined and reasonably protected."[58]

Klaus is not the only Eastern European calling for greater integration along free-market lines with the West. At the April 1991 opening of the EBRD in London, Eastern European officials repeatedly argued that their priority is freer access to European Community markets and that they hoped the EBRD would become an influential lobby in support of that goal.[59] One potential, hopeful scenario is that, once the Eastern European nations struggle through several years of the West's hypocrisy of aid-not-trade, they will sharpen their call for trade-not-aid.

[58]Vaclav Klaus, "The Relative Role of Domestic vs. External Factors in the Integration of Former Communist Lands into the World Economy," Speech before the Mont Pèlerin Society, August 31, 1992, Vancouver, Canada, mimeographed, p. 3. Emphasis in original.

[59]Anthony Robinson, "Czech Bank Chief Appeals," *Financial Times*, April 16, 1991, p. 2.

7. Aid for Black Elephants: How Foreign Assistance Has Failed Africa

George B. N. Ayittey

One of the charges African nationalists leveled against the colonial powers was that colonialism failed to promote credible social and economic development for Africans. And the critics were right. Colonial administrations were frugal and fiscally conservative. The colonies were expected to pay their own way instead of draining the finances of the mother country.

Yet the development of Africa required large capital outlays that the home administrations had not envisaged. Where investment was necessary—to lay down some minimal infrastructure for the exploitation of minerals and raw materials—the mother countries expected such expenditures to be financed by the colonies themselves. If the colonies borrowed any funds, the colonies were supposed to service their own debt.

In the British colonies, the only "aid" offered consisted of grants under the 1929 Colonial Development Act to meet the cost of repaying loans approved for capital projects. The French colonies obtained comparable assistance under Fonds d'Investissement pour le Développement Economique et Social. No such arrangements existed for the Belgian colonies.

After World War II, grudging contributions to colonial development were made by the British and the French in token appreciation of African soldiers who aided in the war effort. Although precise figures are difficult to come by, those contributions were small.

> In 1959, for example, British East Africa (Kenya, Uganda and Tanganyika) received 5 million pounds sterling (mps) in official grants; by 1962 that had risen to 23 mps. Nigeria received an official donation of 5 mps in 1960. These, of course, were in addition to commercial loans raised on the London money market. But these were quite modest. Nigeria, for example, raised only 6.8 mps in new loans between 1946 and 1955, Tanganyika 6.69 mps. Kenya was a heavy borrower: in these

years, it borrowed 18.7 mps; and in addition, the East African High Commission borrowed 31.5 mps, whose burden was spread between the three countries.[1]

Foreign Aid after Independence

After independence, African nationalists settled down to the task of developing Africa—in its own image. No more would Africa be relegated to the inferior status of "hewers of wood and drawers of water," producing raw materials to feed the industries of Europe. Colonialism was exploitive, and, since the colonialists declared themselves to be "capitalist," the nationalists believed, in one monumental syllogistic error, that capitalism, too, was exploitive. Thus, Africa was to be developed, not by capitalist or imperialist principles, but by a socialist ideology under which the state not only participated but captured the "commanding heights of the economy."

The nationalists' impatience to develop Africa grew as the gap between rich and poor nations widened. Only the state under the banner of socialism, they argued, possessed the necessary powers to mobilize the requisite resources to accelerate the pace of development. Many of these resources were to be secured domestically through increased savings, sacrifice, and belt-tightening. The remainder was to be sought through foreign aid requests.

Initially, foreign aid was expected to fill the gap between domestic savings and investment. The rationale was the banal "vicious circle of poverty." Savings or investable resources were low because of poverty and incomes were low because of low investment, which, in turn, was due to low savings. Foreign aid could supplement domestic savings, enable a higher rate of investment to be attained, and propel the economy out of its "low-level equilibrium trap."

Even if domestic savings were adequate, a more mundane rationale was used to justify aid. African countries lacked capital-producing sectors. Thus, they needed to import tractors, equipment, and machinery, as well as intermediate goods such as fuel, lubricants, and spare parts, which were necessary for development. But foreign exchange was required to import those critical goods. Since most African

---

[1]D. K. Fieldhouse, *Black Africa 1945–80* (London: Allen and Unwin, 1986), p. 244.

currencies are not freely convertible, a transfer of even ample domestic savings in *cedis* or *kwachas* to investors cannot be used to purchase tractors in Britain.

Instead, to be useful, such savings must be converted into foreign exchange through exports and the foreign exchange receipts used to import machinery and equipment. Thus, an African country's *effective savings* is the difference between its foreign income (export earnings) and imports of consumer goods. The country can obtain more foreign exchange to finance imports of capital goods if it earns more abroad or curtails its imports of such luxury items as caviar, pickled French sausages, or Mercedes-Benzes, for example.

In the 1960s, advocates of aid deemed an African country's capacity to earn more foreign exchange through exports limited by the following factors: an inelastic foreign demand for African exports, an unjust international economic system, protectionist policies of industrialized nations, and monopolistic as well as oligopolistic practices of multinational corporations. Therefore, even if imported consumer goods were reduced to the barest minimum (assuming African elites would consent to an abstemious diet), the foreign exchange earnings saved would still be insufficient to finance huge capital imports. Given those assumptions, foreign aid was expected to play a vital role in accelerating development by financing critical imports.[2]

Such theoretical arguments for greater foreign development assistance were buttressed by emotional invective. Colonialism raped and plundered Africa. Argued the newly independent states, it was the responsibility, in fact the moral duty, of the West to repair the damage, return the booty, and rectify the injustices perpetrated against black Africans. It is difficult to determine whether the West was persuaded by academic arguments or succumbed to its own collective guilt over the iniquities of colonialism and slavery. Nevertheless, the West responded to African appeals with generous contributions of aid, as Jennifer Whitaker noted:

> Even in 1965 almost 20 percent of the Western countries' development assistance went to Africa. In the 1980s, Africans, who are about 12 percent of the developing world's popula-

---

[2]For a summary of the "Two Gap Models of Development" and the role of foreign aid, see H. B. Chenery and A. M. Strout, "Foreign Assistance and Economic Development," *American Economic Review*, September 1966, pp. 679–733.

tion, were receiving about 22 percent of the total, and the share per person was higher than anywhere else in the Third World—amounting to about $20, versus about $7 for Latin America and $5 for Asia.[3]

Earlier, the World Bank had reached similar conclusions.

External capital flows to sub-Saharan Africa have been quite high. Between 1970 and 1982, official development assistance (ODA) per capita increased in real terms by 5 percent a year, much faster than for other developing countries. In 1982, ODA per capita was $19 for all sub-Saharan African countries and $46 per capita for low-income semiarid countries—compared, for example, with $4.80 per capita for South Asia. Aid finances 10 percent of gross domestic investment in Africa as a whole, but up to 80 percent for low-income semiarid countries and over 15 percent for other low-income countries. For some countries, ODA finances not only all investment, but also some consumption. During the 1980–82 period, however, ODA levels stagnated, even though sub-Saharan Africa's share in the total increased from 21 percent in 1980 to 24 percent in 1982.[4]

Changing Foreign Assistance Patterns

Africa's experience with aid programs can be divided into two phases. Phase I covers the period from independence to the beginning of the 1970s. During this period, bilateral aid was the main source of development assistance to Africa. Private foreign investment in Africa was not significant, largely as a result of the socialist rhetoric and policies of African nationalists. There was some recourse to private credit markets overseas but this was modest, and, where utilized, tended to be of high cost, as in the case of supplier's credit. Although the former colonial powers (Britain, France, and Belgium) provided the bulk of bilateral assistance, other countries such as Canada, Norway, Sweden, the Soviet Union, and the United States assumed an increasingly prominent role in aid disbursements to Africa.

Phase II began in the early 1970s when multilateral institutions, such as the World Bank, the International Monetary Fund (IMF), the European Development Bank, the Organization of Petroleum Exporting Countries Special Fund, the International Fund for Agricultural

---

[3]Jennifer S. Whitaker, *How Can Africa Survive?* (New York: Harper & Row, 1988), p. 60.
[4]World Bank, *Toward Sustained Development in Sub-Saharan Africa* (Washington, D.C.: World Bank, 1984), p. 13.

Development, the United Nations Development Program, the Arab Bank for Economic Development in Africa, the African Development Bank, and the Commonwealth Development Corporation, became increasingly important providers of development assistance. For example, in 1970, aid from multilateral sources accounted for only 13 percent of the total; by 1987, that figure had grown to 34 percent. Indeed, net official development assistance from multilateral sources rose from 1.1 percent of recipient gross domestic product in 1980 to 3.0 percent in 1989.[5] Table 7.1 illustrates the phenomenal growth of multilateral aid in the 1970s and 1980s.

Table 7.1
GROSS DISBURSEMENTS OF EXTERNAL LOANS TO SUB-SAHARAN AFRICA ($ Millions)

Disbursements	1970	1975	1980	1984	1987
Total concessional bilateral	432	1,405	2,954	3,354	4,687
Total multilateral	151	621	2,357	2,487	3,957
Total private	593	2,020	5,583	3,840	3,014
Total public and private	1,176	4,046	10,894	9,681	11,658

SOURCES: World Bank, *Financing Adjustment with Growth in Sub-Saharan Africa 1986–1990* (Washington, D.C.: World Bank, 1986), p. 82; and World Bank/United Nations Development Program, *African Economic and Financial Data* (Washington, D.C.: World Bank, 1989).

In contrast, private nonguaranteed credit from private commercial lending institutions as well as net foreign direct investment has been declining in sub-Saharan Africa. Net foreign investment in black Africa was a paltry $9 million in 1980. That figure rose to $1.2 billion in 1982 and fell sharply to $498 million by 1987.[6]

[5]World Bank/United Nations Development Program, *African Economic and Financial Data* (Washington, D.C.: World Bank, 1992).

[6]World Bank/United Nations Development Program, *African Economic and Financial Data* (Washington, D.C.: World Bank, 1989), p. 43.

As foreign bankers and investors have found black Africa an increasingly unattractive place to extend credit, the multilateral agencies and donor governments have felt compelled to give and lend more. That pressure would ease if the foreign private sector would allocate more resources to Africa. But that is unlikely to occur unless outside investors have confidence in African economies. The fanciful investment codes and array of interventionist policies undertaken by African governments do not restore such trust. Why, for instance, would a foreigner invest in African countries if Angolans, Ethiopians, or Kenyans themselves would not invest in their own economies? Indeed, how can foreign investment be expected when African ruling elites choose to place their own wealth in Switzerland?

The most effective way of attracting foreign investment is by attracting *domestic* investment. But currently, an assortment of burdensome regulations, arbitrary seizures of commercial properties, political instability, and civil conflict discourage domestic investment. Yet the World Bank has called for an increase in development assistance from the current level of $12.7 billion a year to $22 billion a year by the year 2000.[7]

Some idea of the magnitude of foreign aid to Africa since 1960 can be gleaned from Africa's foreign debt, which in 1992 totaled $282 billion, with repayments consuming 24 percent of export earnings.[8] For sub-Saharan Africa, the total amounts to $183 billion, including IMF and World Bank debt. However, as in Latin America, the debt is concentrated in a few African countries: Egypt, Nigeria, Sudan, Ivory Coast, Zaire, and Zambia. Unlike Latin America, where about 55 percent of the region's $431-billion debt is owed to private banks, a greater proportion of Africa's debt (about 40 percent) is owed to or guaranteed by Western governments and 36 percent is owed to multilateral financial institutions such as the IMF and the World Bank.[9] The bulk of the remainder, which is unsecured commercial debt, is accounted for by Nigeria, Ivory Coast, Congo, Gabon, and Zimbabwe. Nigeria alone is responsible for an estimated 50 percent of sub-Saharan Africa's total commercial debt.

[7]World Bank, *Sub-Saharan Africa: From Crisis to Self-Sustainable Growth* (Washington, D.C.: World Bank, 1989), p. 179.

[8]*Wall Street Journal*, April 26, 1992, p. A17.

[9]Peter Marsh, "IMF Urges Rate Cuts to Increase World Growth," *Financial Times*, April 27, 1993, p. 1.

The growth of sub-Saharan African debt was far more rapid than that of any other region. In the period 1978–83, its debt ratio (outstanding debt over export earnings) doubled to over 200 percent. For some individual countries, the debt ratios at the end of 1985 skyrocketed. Sudan's debt ratio reached 1,232 percent; Mozambique's, 1,518 percent; and Guinea-Bissau's, 1,042 percent.[10]

Not surprisingly then, the Paris Club, set up in 1956 to deal with government-to-government debt in Latin America, has in recent years negotiated far more reschedulings for African debtors. Between 1976 and 1987, 68 agreements were reached for sub-Saharan African countries compared to 25 for Latin American countries.

The Failure of Bilateral Aid to Black Africa

A general consensus has emerged that aid to Africa, both bilateral and multilateral, has been ineffective. But the results of bilateral projects have proved to be particularly poor. There is nothing to show for billions in assistance annually, except a multitude of "black elephants," economic collapse, social disintegration, and political chaos.

Sub-Saharan Africa alone received total aid of some $83 billion between 1980 and 1988. Yet all those funds failed to spur economic growth and arrest Africa's economic atrophy. The standard of living in black Africa fell by 1.2 percent a year during that time period. In the 1965–84 period, 18 black African countries had growth rates of less than 1 percent per annum. The worst performers were Benin, Burkina Faso, Chad, Ghana, Liberia, Somalia, Sudan, Uganda, and Zaire—all ruled by military dictators and supported by Western aid.

By the mid-1980s, even the United Nations was uncharacteristically displaying reservations about Africa's economic prospects in the light of the ineffectiveness of aid programs. In 1986, the world body adopted the Program of Action for African Economic Recovery and Development (UN-PAAERD). A midterm review report submitted by Secretary-General Javier Pérez de Cuéllar in September 1988 offered a grim assessment.

> The overall economic situation in Africa has worsened since UN-PAAERD was adopted. The continent's gross domestic

[10]International Monetary Fund, *World Economic Outlook* (Washington, D.C.: IMF, 1986).

product, in per capita terms, declined by 2.0 percent in 1986 and a further 2.2 percent in 1987, and is today lower than in 1980.[11]

Specific country experiences are horrifying. In Tanzania, much Western aid went to support an ill-conceived *ujaama* socialist experiment. The *New York Times* reported the outcome:

> At first, many Western aid donors, particularly in Scandinavia, gave enthusiastic backing to this socialist experiment, pouring an estimated $10 billion into Tanzania over 20 years. Yet, today as Mr. Nyerere [Tanzania's leader] leaves the stage, the country's largely agricultural economy is in ruins, with its 26 million people eking out their living on a per capita income of slightly more than $200 a year, one of the lowest in the world.[12]

The World Bank's *1990 World Development Report* noted that Tanzania's economy contracted on average by 0.5 percent per year between 1965 and 1988. Average personal consumption declined dramatically by 43 percent between 1973 and 1988. *The Economist* observed in 1990 that for all the aid poured into the country, Tanzania had only "pot-holed roads, decaying buildings, cracked pavements, demoralised clinics and universities, and a 1988 income per capita of $160 (lower than at independence in 1961)" to show for it.[13]

Under the late Alan Woods, the U.S. Agency for International Development (U.S. AID) acknowledged the scandalous failure of Western aid in a 1989 report. Noting that the United States had provided some $400 billion in aid to developing nations, U.S. AID admitted that no country receiving U.S. aid in the past 20 years had progressed from less developed to developed country status. Worse, "only a handful of countries that started receiving U.S. assistance in the 1950s and 1960s has ever graduated from dependent status."[14] A bipartisan congressional task force of the House Foreign Affairs Committee reached a similar conclusion in 1989: "Current aid

[11]Secretary-General Pérez de Cuéllar, *UN-PAAERD: Mid-Term Assessment* (New York: United Nations, 1988).

[12]Paul Lewis, "Nyerere and Tanzania: No Regret at Socialism," *New York Times*, October 24, 1990, p. A8.

[13]"A Teacher Retires," *The Economist*, June 2, 1990, p. 48.

[14]U.S. Agency for International Development, *Development in the National Interest: U.S. Economic Assistance into the 21st Century* (Washington, D.C.: U.S. AID, 1989), p. 112.

programs are so encrusted in red tape that they no longer either advance U.S. interests abroad or promote economic development."[15]

Harvard economist Nicholas Eberstadt provided an even more searing indictment regarding financial transfers to Africa.

> Western aid today may be compromising economic progress in Africa and retarding its development of human capital. Overseas development assistance (ODA), after all, provides a very substantial fraction of the operating budgets of virtually all governments in sub-Saharan Africa. In 1983, ODA accounted for two-fifths of Liberia's central government budget, for three-quarters of Ghana's, and four-fifths of Uganda's. Western aid directly underwrites current policies and practices; indeed, it may actually make possible some of the more injurious policies, which would be impossible to finance without external help.[16]

Sir William Ryrie, executive vice president of the International Finance Corporation, a World Bank subsidiary, concurred with that general conclusion when he declared that "the West's record of aid for Africa in the past decade [1980s] can only be characterised as one of failure."[17]

Several factors help explain the failure of Western aid programs in Africa. On the donor side, the machinery of aid was often sabotaged by bureaucratic dictates and distorted by partisan politics. A congressional task force, reported the *Wall Street Journal*, "skewered Congress and past administrations for piling 33 differing and often conflicting foreign-assistance objectives on top of each other. It noted that current programs are caught in a maze of 75 different statutory priorities and 288 separate congressionally mandated reports. Changes in any of 700 programs must be reported to Congress."[18]

The result has often been tardy responses to deadly crises. During the 1985 famine crisis in the Sudan, for example, there were several instances of food aid shipments arriving too late to be of help while thousands perished. Similarly, the slow response of the donor community to the famine crisis in Somalia in 1992 was widely criticized.

---

[15]Peter Montagnon, "Foreign Aid Failure," *Wall Street Journal*, March 2, 1989, p. A16.

[16]Nicholas Eberstadt, *Foreign Aid and American Purpose* (Washington, D.C.: American Enterprise Institute, 1988), p. 100.

[17]"Western Aid for Africa Seen as Failure," *Financial Times*, June 7, 1990, p. 7.

[18]Montagnon.

Poor planning also bedeviled many aid programs. In Senegal, the United States built 50 crop-storage depots but placed them in locations the peasants never visited. The depots, which cost about $2 million, now stand empty. A fifth of the Ivory Coast's foreign borrowing went to build two sugar mills that started production in 1981 and are now closed.[19]

Other donors were equally culpable. In 1974, the sugar the Soviets shipped under their aid program to Guinea-Bissau refused to melt in coffee. The Soviets rectified the situation. The next batch of sugar they sent melted at the port of entry!

> In Sudan, the Soviets also built a milk-bottling plant at Babanusa in 1965. But Babanusa's Baggara peasants drink their milk straight from the cow. Since there were no facilities to ship milk out of Babanusa, the 25-year-old plant has not produced a single bottle of milk.... In Uganda, a railroad expert discovered to his amazement that a repair shop built with foreign funds was 7 times as large as the one he ran in Germany.[20]

Whitaker reported other debacles:

> In Sudan, a plant for making tomato paste was placed in an area where the farmers cultivate date palms, not tomatoes. A milk dehydration plant was built in an area where there are no dairy cows.... In northern Kenya, Norwegian aid officials built a fish-freezing plant near a lake for the Turkana tribesmen. But the Turkana are pastoral people who survive by raising cattle, goats and camels. Worse, after the plant was built, it was discovered that freezing fish in the daily 100-degree temperatures would take more electricity than was available in the entire Turkana district.[21]

But even if the disbursement of aid were a relatively simple operation, government-to-government transfers lack accountability. One problem is that despite the rhetoric about encouraging private-sector initiatives, more than 90 percent of U.S. aid funds were distributed to governments in 1989. Moreover, much aid has been predicated upon ideological or geopolitical considerations. As a result, massive

---

[19]Steve Mufson, "Aid to Africa Is Widely Considered Ineffective but Continent Is More Dependent Than Ever," *Wall Street Journal*, July 29, 1985, p. 18.

[20]Ibid., p. 18.

[21]Whitaker, p. 74.

amounts of U.S. aid have underwritten—and continue to underwrite—some of the most improvident recipient programs.

The United States' $2.1-billion annual aid disbursement to Egypt, rewarded for its friendship with the United States, provides a perfect example. Audits of U.S. AID projects in Egypt revealed cases of appalling waste. Researcher Melanie Tammen recounted some of the findings:

> About 5,000 U.S.-made stoves were useless because they were designed for pipeline use rather than tanked gas used in Egypt. . . . Twenty-six irrigation pumping stations established as part of a $19 million U.S. AID project were not working, in part due to lack of electrical power at the sites; at the same time AID sponsored a separate $32 million renewable-energy project involving water pumping without linking it to the irrigation project. . . . A $108 million AID-financed grain-silo complex completed in 1987 was unable to operate for several years due to insufficient power. Of 400 AID vehicles inspected, 93 were found to have been diverted for the personal use of Egyptian government officials and U.S. and expatriate consultants.[22]

Even worse has been the result of U.S. aid to kleptocratic regimes in the Ivory Coast, Liberia, Malawi, Somalia, and Zaire because those states professed to be "pro-Western" and "capitalist." Despite posturing and ideological pronouncements, there was little real difference in political-economic philosophy among black African governments. Most reigned over one-party states and ran socialist "command" economies.

The Multilateral Aid Panacea

Those manifold problems, it has been argued, reflect the partisanship and lack of professionalism inherent to bilateral aid. However, multilateral lending, which began to rise sharply in the 1970s, was supposed to be different. But those transfers, too, were ill-used. During the 1970s, the international markets for African exports such as cocoa, coffee, tea, peanuts, sugar, sisal, phosphate, and uranium were enjoying a boom. That export bonanza enabled African governments to hike their expenditures. Expectations of continuing favorable export perfor-

---

[22]Melanie Tammen, *Wall Street Journal*, January 23, 1989, p. A19. Subsequent audits of U.S. AID revealed continuing poor performance; see, for example, *Washington Post*, April 15, 1991, p. A3.

mance further fueled expansion of government development programs. When the commodity markets collapsed and the first oil shock hit in 1973, African governments, reluctant to scale back on public expenditures, borrowed extensively from the multilaterals. Kathie Krumm described the situation:

> Much of the external borrowing went to finance directly large public investment projects which spanned the range of economic efficiency. . . . There are a number of examples of public investments in nonproductive categories whose external financing continues to be burdensome. Large-scale commercial borrowings were used to finance conference centers, administrative buildings, new capitals, and university centers.
>
> In the "productive" sectors, many of the externally financed projects proved to be economically unviable. Ill-conceived projects include luxury hotels, oil and sugar refineries, and steel mills. Certain major agricultural projects proved unviable because of the weak administrative framework. World price trends have also weakened the viability of many projects in both the agricultural and mining sectors. Ambitious infrastructure projects were often externally financed at terms much shorter than the profile of returns. These include hydroelectric projects, airports and highways.[23]

When the second oil price shock (1979–80) hit Africa, the region already faced precarious balance-of-payment problems. Its oil import bill rose from $1.4 billion in 1978 to $3.1 billion in 1980, and its current account deficit increased from $4.7 billion in 1978 to $6.5 billion in 1980.[24] Domestic prices and government expenditures soared as a result.

Even without the oil price hikes, African government budgets were in a disastrous state. Since 1960, virtually every government in sub-Saharan Africa has run persistently large budget deficits. Runaway expenditures reflected many factors, such as socialist ideology and excessive expansion in the state bureaucracy, particularly the use of government jobs to reward the party faithful. Moreover, social programs in the fields of education, health care, and social welfare, neglected by the colonial powers, were expanded enormously. Those expenses alone would have left most African regimes in the red.

---

[23]Kathie L. Krumm, "The External Debt of Sub-Saharan Africa: Origins, Magnitude and Implications for Actions," in *World Bank Staff Working Papers*, no. 741, 1985, p. 11.

[24]Ibid., p. 12.

Alas, such recurring costs were supplemented by excessive capital (or development) expenditures. Governments included any undertakings expected to spur development or any new one-time outlays in this catchall category. Some countries counted almost anything as a capital investment. In the case of Ghana, Tony Killick noted that the government lumped together an array of capital and development spending.

> The conventional classification of government spending into current and capital items, is only a poor indicator of the consumption and development contents of the budget. Ghana's Ministry of Finance classified all capital spending as being synonymous with development, but this is misleading. The current budget includes spending on the agricultural extension services, the educational system, community development and other items which might be more appropriately thought of as developmental, and the capital budget includes the building of government offices, the purchase of *military equipment* and a host of other things with few developmental returns.[25]

Thus, the construction of marble office buildings, show airports, basilicas, and other black elephants is treated as "development expenditures." A military government could acquire a huge arsenal of tanks, helicopter gunships, and bazookas, characterizing such outlays as "development expenditures."

To finance the resulting deficits, African governments resorted to increased taxation and requests for bilateral aid. Quite often, however, the deficits turned out to be much larger than anticipated. Revenue collection was low, in part because of rampant evasion by the wealthy ruling elites. More significant, peasant cash crop producers rebelled against increasingly heavy export duties and taxes implicit in low producer prices by smuggling their produce or curtailing production. The results were declining physical volumes of exports.

As a result, over the years, greater reliance was placed on foreign aid to close the budgetary gap. But donors' resources were limited and an increasing number of developing countries were competing for them; hence, the incessant lament of "inadequate aid."

When aid was insufficient to fund their desired spending plans, African leaders had to make a choice, which, more often than not, was dictated by political considerations. Obsessed with clinging to power,

---

[25]Tony Killick, *Development Economics in Action: A Study of Economic Policies in Ghana* (London: Heinemann, 1978), p. 149.

most African heads of state opted to use aid received to finance recurrent expenditures rather than genuine capital investments, since the basis of their political support was derived from state workers. Governments considered it politically expedient to secure the workers' loyalty, rather than their competence, with swift payment of salaries, cheaper urban prices (through the imposition of price controls), and other forms of patronage, such as refrigerator loans to government employees. When the aid received was not sufficient to cover even recurrent expenditures, African governments covered remaining expenditures by printing money—a policy that had devastating inflationary consequences.[26] Thus, although capital expenditures usually appeared in the budgets of African states, there were no funds available to finance development. Only with assistance from multilateral agencies such as the World Bank could such projects be undertaken.

Unfortunately, multilateral aid has failed to advance development even in this limited way. One problem is that the typical budgetary process of recipients is marred by much chicanery and fraud. Aid often effectively financed imports of military equipment, bombs, and construction of government-owned show buildings and conference halls—all considered "development expenditures." To the extent that aid money financed recurrent expenditures, which it frequently did, the loans were simply consumed, thus violating the cardinal principle of borrowing. In theory, loans were to be invested *productively*, generating enough income to be serviced. In practice, loans were frequently used to pay salaries, purchase consumer goods, and buy military equipment and other items that generated no such income.

Moreover, aid money, even where "tied" to particular projects or purchases, is fungible and often used for purposes not intended by the donor. Consider, for example, an African government that has budgeted $10 million for a $30-million road development project. It presents the project to various multilateral agencies for funding. The World Bank contributes $15 million and the United Nations' Development Program chips in $11 million instead of the $10 million in the

[26]Such was the case in Ghana, Sierra Leone, Somalia, Sudan, Uganda, Zaire, and Zambia. The currencies of those countries are now worthless. For example, Ghana's money supply increased at an average rate of 40 percent a year between 1981 and 1987. In Uganda, the money supply doubled every other year over the same period.

nation's budget for the project. The African government now has to make up only $4 million. The $6 million "saved" can be used to purchase, say, weapons to repress and slaughter the African people.[27] The regimes of the late Samuel Doe of Liberia, ex-president Siad Barre of Somalia, and President Mobutu Sese Seko of Zaire, longtime recipients of international aid, always found resources to spend on the military despite growing budgetary exigencies.

Most African "development projects," in any case, came to grief. Several factors accounted for the failure: construction delays, poor design, inadequate supervision, inappropriate technology (i.e., too capital-intensive), corruption, and pilfering. In its 1981 report, the European Economic Community noted the common elements of failed projects.

> Many development projects failed in Africa because they were on too large a scale and were not adapted to the population and the environment they were supposed to benefit. . . . The projects of most lasting value are generally those which are simplest and directly benefit the local community concerned.[28]

For a time, at least, the World Bank entertained a more optimistic view in an evaluation of its own projects.

> Despite the difficult economic environment, 85 percent of all projects reviewed in 1986 were characterized as having achieved satisfactory results. The percentage is lower, however, for projects in Sub-Saharan Africa. Of particular concern is the continuing disappointing performance of projects in Eastern Africa. . . . The Bank has made intensive efforts in recent years to respond to performance shortfalls in its Africa portfolio, especially in agriculture projects. This involved restructuring many projects and shifting the emphasis in new operations to macro and sector policy work, sector institutions and services, and investment rehabilitation.[29]

In a subsequent report on project performance in black Africa, however, the World Bank was more forthcoming:

[27]That anomaly was evident in U.S. dealings with the Soviet Union. During the Cold War, the United States sold the Soviets millions of dollars worth of cheap food. The unintended effect was that cheap food imports from the United States allowed the Soviets to spend *less* of their limited resources on agriculture and *more* on arms buildup.

[28]*West Africa*, January 18, 1982, p. 188.

[29]World Bank, *Project Performance Results for 1986* (Washington, D.C.: World Bank, 1988), p. xiii.

There are countless examples of badly chosen and poorly designed public investments, including some in which the World Bank participated. A 1987 evaluation revealed that half of the completed rural development projects financed by the World Bank in Africa had failed. A cement plant serving Côte d'Ivoire, Ghana, and Togo was closed in 1984 after only 4 years in operation. A state-run shoe factory in Tanzania has been operating at no more than 25 percent capacity and has remained open only thanks to a large government subsidy.[30]

Before 1980, much of the lending by the World Bank was project-specific and confined to the agricultural or rural sector, while IMF credit facilities had been restricted to the management of balance-of-payment crises as required by charter. However, following the oil price hike and mounting debt problems in the early 1980s, the composition of lending shifted. Loans for energy, urban development, water supply, and waste disposal increased while lending for agriculture declined. The bank also increased its nonproject operations in the form of IMF-style structural adjustment loans.

The bank took the latter step because it had become apparent that balance-of-payment disequilibria, domestic imbalance, and budgetary deficits were inextricably intertwined. For instance, since the consequences of budgetary incontinence were being felt in the trade sector, balance-of-payment difficulties could not be resolved without injecting some sanity into the budget process.

Thus, under a typical structural adjustment program (SAP), a country devalued its currency to make the exchange rate better reflect the currency's real value. Doing so was supposed to reduce imports and encourage exports, thereby alleviating the balance-of-trade deficit. The second major thrust of most SAPs was to trim the borrower's statist behemoth by reining in expenditures, removing price controls, eliminating public subsidies, selling off unprofitable state-owned enterprises, and generally "rationalizing" the public sector to make it more efficient. Substantial allocations of credit were made to African governments under structural adjustment programs. By 1989, 37 African countries had signed SAP agreements, but only 2 (Ghana and Tanzania) were deemed "successful performers" by the World Bank. In fact, the World Bank's own March 1990 internal report lamented,

---

[30]World Bank, *Sub-Saharan Africa: From Crisis to Self-Sustainable Growth*, p. 27.

"Adjustment lending appeared to have been relatively less successful in the highly-indebted countries and *Sub-Saharan Africa.*"[31]

There were several reasons SAPs failed in Africa. As designed by the World Bank, SAPs in Africa typically reorganized bankrupt companies and placed them, together with massive infusions of new capital, in the hands of the same incompetent managers who ruined them in the first place. Certainly, that arrangement would not be tolerated in the West. Why, then, should the World Bank impose such a "solution" on Africa?

Worse, there was often no input by Africans, the very people who would be most affected by World Bank decisions. Wayne Ellwood, a journalist, put it succinctly:

> Time and time again local communities are ignored. Misconceived, harmful development projects are dropped in their laps without consultation and the people of the industrialized countries, who bankroll most of the Bank's activities, are asked to pay the bill.[32]

The World Bank employs the services of management consultants. About 80,000 expatriate consultants work on Africa alone. Less than 0.1 percent are Africans. In 1988, the World Bank spent close to $1 billion on consultants. Characterizing that as the "great consultancy rip-off," *South* magazine noted:

> There is increasing concern (World Bank) advice is often overpriced, poorly researched and irrelevant. Although some management consultants give value for money, many simply recycle standard off-the-shelf reports, regardless of whether they are appropriate, say critics. Frequently, management firms send rookie staffers with little experience of Africa to advise on sensitive political issues there. Or they provide theoretical studies, full of high school economics, but with no practical applications.... One top World Bank man, who declined to be identified, says that of all the countries in Southern Africa, the only government which gets value for its money from management consultants is Botswana, which has rigorous bidding procedures for the work.[33]

Structural adjustment programs also assume that development takes place in a vacuum. The civil wars, environmental degradation, deteri-

---

[31]World Bank, *Report on Adjustment Lending II: Policies for the Recovery of Growth* (Washington D.C.: World Bank, March 1990), p. 21 (emphasis added).

[32]*New Internationalist*, December 1990, p. 6.

[33]*South*, February 1990, p. 42.

oration of infrastructure, and the general state of violence in many African countries are treated as unrelated to economic development. In Mozambique, for example, the 16-year civil war cost at least $8 billion and an estimated 900,000 civilian lives. Over a third of the country's population was displaced. Angola has suffered similarly. Yet Western donors and institutions seek to "restructure" those two nations' economies, unmindful of the raging civil wars. Perhaps the most ludicrous "restructuring programs," however, were implemented in Sudan and Somalia, where the World Bank sought to revamp economies that did not exist. In both countries, ongoing civil wars had devastated the nations by the time the World Bank attempted to implement its adjustment programs.

Another reason SAPs have failed is that economic reform without concomitant political reform is meaningless. Africa's experience suggests that economic reform under dictatorships is generally not sustainable. Black Africa is characterized by dictatorships or weak authoritarian regimes that maintain their authority through personalistic patron-client relations.[34] Those relationships are prone to sudden and erratic changes, which produce social instability. Africa's own history reveals that such instability impedes the correction of structural economic imbalances. It is no wonder that the region's record of reform has been dismal.

That is not to say that such governments never change their economic policies. But African governments generally restructure not to save their economies but to save their regimes. That motivation is evidenced by the cycles in which restructuring occurs: reforms are aborted when a crisis abates and reinstated upon reemergence of a new economic crisis. The governments of Sudan, Equatorial Guinea, Zaire, and Liberia have all followed that pattern. Even during restructuring, measures are often implemented perfunctorily without the conviction and the dedication needed to carry them through.[35] In many cases, government folly and dishonesty shatter public confidence in whatever reforms are undertaken. The government of Angola, for example,

---

[34]Of the 45 black African countries, only 13—Benin, Botswana, Cape Verde Islands, Congo, The Gambia, Madagascar, Mali, Mauritius, Namibia, Sao Tomé and Principe, Senegal, Seychelles, and Zambia—allow their people the right to vote and choose their leaders.

[35]George B. N. Ayittey, "The Political Economy of Reform in Africa," *Journal of Economic Growth*, Spring 1989.

drew up an investment code to attract foreign investors without also introducing other substantive economic reforms. Even *West Africa* magazine was perplexed: "Why should the foreign investor put money into agriculture, trade or manufacturing in war-torn Angola (or much less Ethiopia, Mozambique, Somalia, Sudan or Uganda) when a host of apparently stable, structurally adjusting African countries (or better yet, Asian and now Eastern European countries) offer opportunities in the same sector and more?"[36]

In Sierra Leone, President Momoh declared to parliament in 1989 that austerity and self-sacrifice must prevail—but not for his government. According to *West Africa* magazine, Momoh "explained that the government had continued to fund its activities by printing money, spending in excess of tax revenue, and borrowing from the Central Bank, while the nation's meagre resources were used for imports that were irrelevant to the needs of the economy."[37]

In Ghana, the military government declared its willingness to allow private-sector participation in the economy after decades of socialist management and ruin. But its actions contradicted its pronouncements. Through its economic liberalization measures, the government had sought to woo foreign investors by assuring them of the safety of their commercial properties and of the government's commitment to private-sector development. But no such assurances were forthcoming to *domestic* investors. In 1989 alone there were three reported cases of arbitrary seizures of the commercial properties of burgeoning indigenous entrepreneurs without due process of law.

The entire African aid program reeks of scandal. In the West, foreign assistance has become an "industry" whose workers are not interested in reforming the system—an outcome that could jeopardize their jobs. In Africa, governments are more interested in their political survival than in reforming their economies. To them, it is a game and the donors know it. The following account by Ambassador Frank Ruddy, former U.S. diplomat to Equatorial Guinea, is revealing.

> Equatorial Guinea, where I lived for a little more than 3 years, receives more than $30 million in foreign aid for a population of 300,000 people, making it one of the highest per capita recipients of aid in the world. The World Bank and IMF

[36] *West Africa*, March 13–19, 1989, p. 407.
[37] *West Africa*, June 12–18, 1989, p. 958.

officials would come to Malabo [the capital] looking very serious and would lay down very tough terms for the IMF agreement and structural adjustment loan. The government would pledge austerity, civil servant reductions, whatever was required, and go its merry way until the team turned up to measure progress; then the government would lie. At first I was shocked. Then I had to admit I was somewhat impressed that the Guineans played the game better than their visitors from Washington.

On one occasion, after pledging all kinds of austerity measures, including not spending any government funds on an annual Central African states meeting which Equatorial Guinea was to host in 1986, the government went ahead and built 5 villas for visiting heads of state and purchased 29 Mercedes for the participants' use, just as we knew they would. When the Bank and IMF people returned to check on the country's progress under the austerity program, the government denied doing any of these things. . . . When I asked the Bank and IMF people why they did not pursue this, since all of it was common knowledge, I was told the government had denied it, and that was the end of the matter. Of course, the Guineans knew all along it would be the end of the matter.

The infuriating part, of course, is that a small group of embezzlers were doing exactly what the international aid system encouraged them to do, for which they were being maintained in the style to which they had become accustomed, while the people and institutions of the country, which were supposed to benefit from the aid, never would.[38]

Most of those problems are known in the West. As *Le Monde*, a Paris newspaper, observed in March 1990, "Every franc we give impoverished Africa comes back to France, or is smuggled into Switzerland and even Japan." In light of those problems, the World Bank's call for increased development assistance to sub-Saharan Africa ($22 billion annually by the year 2000) seems risible. If foreign aid donors and multilateral agencies wish to throw away their money, they should not hold the African people responsible for that outcome.

Conclusion: African Aid Programs Fundamentally Flawed

One common fallacy about aid programs is that they benefit the African people. They do not. As can be expected, each foreign group

[38] *Foreign Service Journal*, March 1991, p. 24.

advances its own agenda. It is naive to believe that aid agencies pursue the interests of the African people. For far too long, outsiders have arrogantly assumed that role, and for far too long, average Africans (in contrast to the ruling elite) have been excluded from defending their own interests.

In fact, another problem is that foreign aid donors fail to distinguish between the African people and those ruling them. Aid programs in Africa have traditionally assumed that African governments will act to the benefit of the African people. But in fact, there are two classes in Africa: the peasants and the vampire elites. In the peasants' supposedly "backward and primitive" system, the African chief cannot borrow money or undertake any development project *without* the consent of the people. In 1908, for example, Taki Obli, the *mantse* (king) of the Ga people (of Ghana) was dethroned for his unauthorized attempt to sell town land and to appropriate for himself money and privileges that were not by native custom a *mantse's*. In contrast to the postcolonial governments, indigenous African institutions, long ignored by such governments, are characterized by participatory forms of democracy and provide the basis for a more free society in Africa.

Botswana provides an exceptional example of a country whose political system is based upon indigenous traditions. There, the people participate in the decisionmaking process through their *kgotlas*, or public forums, in which citizens freely express their views. One *Washington Post* staff writer reported on one such *kgotla* meeting in which the government's plans for a \$25-million river project were discussed:

> The idea seemed ingenious: Siphon a portion of water from Botswana's wildlife-rich Okavango Delta to irrigate new farmland and to supply badly needed water to thirsty northern towns and a particularly profitable diamond mine. . . .
>
> The public was invited by government officials to express opinions about the plan. Which they did with gusto. "You will dry the delta! We will have no more fish to eat! No more reeds to build our houses!" exclaimed an elderly villager at a recent public meeting in the northern city of Maun, where more than 700 citizens berated government leaders for 6 hours over the project.
>
> Days later, stunned by the public's opposition, the government of President Quett Masire announced that the Okavango project was postponed indefinitely pending further study and technical consultations. . . .

The Maun *kgotla* "was truly a revelation," according to a Western diplomat posted here. "One by one, these people—most of them illiterate herders—stood up and just let the government have it. I have been in Africa quite a long time, and I never saw anything quite like it."[39]

It has become apparent to most Africans that aid programs do not benefit them. David Karanja, a former member of parliament in Kenya, put it this way:

Foreign aid has done more harm to Africa than we care to admit. It has led to a situation where Africa has failed to set its own pace and direction of development free of external inter-ference. Today, Africa's development plans are drawn thousands of miles away in the corridors of the IMF and World Bank. What is sad is that the IMF and World Bank "experts" who draw these development plans are people completely out of touch with the local African reality.[40]

Africans have now realized that they have no say in decisions made on their behalf. Indeed the entire aid allocation business is shrouded in secrecy to the point that ordinary Africans often have no idea of how much aid has been granted them or how it has been utilized. That situation should change. At the very least, any African government receiving foreign aid should be required to explain to its people *how much* aid was received and *how* it was used. Ultimately, however, it is Africans who must solve their own problems. As long as the World Bank, the IMF, and other official aid agencies continue funding and counseling Africa's ruling elites, the day that the African people provide their own solutions will be postponed.

[39]Neil Young, *Washington Post*, March 21, 1991, p. A3.
[40]*New African*, June 1992, p. 20.

8. Development Planning in Latin America: The Lifeblood of the Mercantilist State

Paul Craig Roberts

In September 1987, I addressed a conference at Stanford University on the Latin American debt crisis. The participants from both North and South America were uniformly Marxist in their outlook, and my remarks, which stressed that development planning had undermined the role of private property in economic development and left Latin America mired in debt, were greeted with hostility. My audience believed that more aid was the only solution. Private trade would simply allow the Yankee imperialist to ravage Latin America. If left unprotected by planned policies of import substitution, consumer sovereignty would prevent indigenous industrialization and leave the region a colony with balance-of-trade deficits while foreign capital removed the economic surplus.

Those left-wing doctrines were pernicious, because they robbed Latin Americans of successful economic institutions and the confidence to build them. In a development as extraordinary as the collapse of communism, the psychology of the patrimonialist economy disappeared overnight in Latin America. Today, Mexico, Chile, and Argentina have the confidence to seek free-trade agreements with the United States, and the United States lacks the confidence to grant them.

Today, the protectionist doctrines of Raúl Prebisch are alive and well in North American policy circles funded by labor unions. In recent years a statist U.S. government has imposed massive regulatory, tax, and legal costs on all investments sited in the United States. Labor, being much less mobile internationally than capital, now fears global competition more than ever. U.S. labor unions such as the AFL-CIO, for example, have campaigned vigorously against the North American Free Trade Agreement, which would expand trade with Mexico. The intellectual left, which is far more numerous in the United States than the intellectual right, favors the anti-capitalist policies of the government. Economists know that anti-capital policies punish labor by reducing productivity and the growth of real wages. However, the old left sees such policies as egalitarian, and the new left sees them as pro-environment, because they stop economic growth.

As Latin Americans are now struggling to overthrow the historical rent-seeking institutions of a mercantilist, patrimonial society, the United States is falling more and more under the sway of rent-seekers. Open, dynamic societies fare better than societies run by an oligarchy or by government planning.[1] The tension in U.S. society moves between two extremes. U.S. citizens have to maintain enough commonality to hold together, but not so much as to come under the sway of fossilized elites, who are forever attempting to turn an entrepreneurial society into one that overpays privileged and protected interests.

Free Trade and Domestic Reforms

Trade liberalization can help erode the mercantilist tradition by eliminating the special privileges (high prices, little or no competition) elites have enjoyed from protectionism. Free-trade agreements can therefore promote greater welfare and economic reform in Latin America. However, there are two great dangers to Latin America of a free-trade agreement. The most important key to the economic development of Latin America is the continuation of the domestic reforms that make countries attractive to investment capital, both foreign and their own. If the value of a free-trade agreement is exaggerated, Latin Americans might accept conditions that would be counterproductive. Alternatively or additionally, governments with deep roots in the patrimonial economy could come to regard the benefits of a free-trade agreement as a subsidy that would compensate for the costs of maintaining inefficient institutions, and internal reforms could wither.

The success of Latin American countries depends on making domestic policy changes that establish a favorable business climate. Internal changes—not a free-trade agreement—have brought progress to Chile, Mexico, and Argentina. Success in stabilizing the currencies and advances in private property are transforming those once crisis-ridden countries into entrepreneurial societies. A few years ago,

---

[1]See Mancur Olson, *The Rise and Decline of Nations: Economic Growth, Stagflation, and Social Rigidities* (New Haven, Conn.: Yale University Press, 1982).

Mexico was a hopeless case, but in recent years it has enjoyed the best performing stock market in the world. The administration of President Carlos Salinas de Gortari has cut taxes, liberalized investment laws, and undertaken a privatization campaign. The government cut the maximum corporate income tax rate from 42 to 35 percent and cut the maximum individual rate from 60.5 to 35 percent. There is no tax on capital gains for publicly traded firms. Privatization is also far advanced. Out of the 1982 peak of 1,155 state-owned enterprises, fewer than 215 remained in the government's hands by mid-1993, and most of these were slated for divestment. In 1993, even subsidiaries of PEMEX, the sacrosanct national oil monopoly, were slated for auction.

Administrative reform began in the financial and economic bureaucracies. In 1993, it was extended into the fishing, education, and agriculture bureaucracies. By amending Mexico's constitution in 1992, President Salinas extended private ownership and market forces into the inefficient, collectivist *ejido* system of agriculture, traditionally a sacred cow.[2] In 1993, Salinas proposed to amend the constitution to create an independent central bank.

The new, streamlined bureaucracies are implementing automatic universal rules that leave no room for bureaucratic maneuver. The outcome is lower transaction costs for firms and individuals, and declining corruption, enhancing the Mexican business climate. Even if these reports were nothing but propaganda, there would be significance in the propaganda. The claims are being made for private property, not for socialism.

As a result of Mexico's unprecedented reorientation to a market economy, capital is flowing into Mexico. The favorable business climate has attracted over $40 billion in foreign capital since 1988 and $10 billion in foreign investment in 1992 alone. The Mexican-U.S. border region is the fastest growing region economically on earth.

The Argentine government has initiated a similar course. With the 1990 privatization of Entel, the state telephone company, the government began a privatization campaign that by 1993 was far advanced. Even the national oil company, Yacimientos Petrolíferos Fiscales, was scheduled to be sold. By June 1993, the government had received $5.4

[2]"The Legal Proposal for Mexico's Agricultural Reform," Embassy of Mexico briefing paper, November 1991; and Damian Fraser, "Salinas Sows Seeds for Economic Benefits," *Financial Times*, March 6, 1992, p. 30.

billion in cash and more than $12 billion in canceled government debt through the privatizations, which covered all major economic sectors. The benefits of privatization go beyond the directly financial. According to Juan Carlos Sánchez, privatization secretary in the Ministry of the Economy, the privatized companies were receiving an average of $2.1 billion annually in taxpayer subsidies between 1980 and 1989.[3]

In 1991, Finance Minister Domingo Cavallo announced a broad deregulation program to stimulate the economy. The measures, he avowed, would eliminate the bribes and special "Argentine cost" of doing business. Two years later, while much remained to be done, bureaucratic procedures had been streamlined in many areas, and universal rules began to operate. The level of corruption diminished, and transaction costs fell. Capital began to flow to Argentina in 1992, reversing more than a decade of capital flight.

Chile has virtually completed its transformation to a market society based upon the principles of private property and free enterprise. Begun by the military government of General Augusto Pinochet, since 1973 more than 350 state companies have been privatized and only a few remain in state hands, among them the state copper company, Codelco. Prices and interest rates were freed, labor markets were deregulated, the foreign exchange rate was stabilized, and fiscal deficits fell. Chile unilaterally liberalized foreign investment rules and in 1991 established a flat 11 percent tariff rate on virtually all imports.

Beginning in 1981, Chile privatized the inefficient social security system, creating a system of private pension funds, long-term life insurance policies, and private health care institutions, which is the envy of the hemisphere. Workers contribute a portion of their salaries to build their own pension fund, which they own and can pass on to their heirs. In the 1980s, the pension funds became major players in Chilean capital markets.

Since 1974, Chile has attracted more than $8.5 billion in foreign investment, a large achievement for a country with a market limited by a small population of 13.5 million inhabitants. In 1992, according to Chilean government figures, $1.2 billion in new foreign direct investment entered Chile.

Countries that create conditions conducive to business activity naturally attract investment capital, and incentives develop for trading

---

[3]Stephen Fidler, "Ownership Switches," *Financial Times*, May 27, 1993, p. 36.

partners to lower trade barriers on a piecemeal basis—a way of acquiring a free-trade agreement without a "grand bargain" that could bring more costs than benefits.

The demand for social welfare programs in all countries is high. Successful governments, such as those in Chile and Mexico, are shrinking government on the one hand and expanding social welfare spending on the other. The focus on long-neglected poor populations is commendable as is the shift to contracting with private providers for public services. However, governments that give in to demands for increased spending on social programs will again foster interests that become entrenched and demand further increases in spending. In March 1992, Mexican president Salinas decried the "new reactionaries" who "would like to see the return of the excessively proprietary, expansive state."[4]

Countries such as Mexico and Chile that are transforming themselves from mercantilist or patrimonialist societies to entrepreneurial societies must avoid importing U.S. labor, environmental, legal, and social policies as the price of a free-trade agreement. If U.S. tort liabilities and the U.S. bureaucratic approach to environmental protection (as opposed to market incentives) were imported to Mexico, Chile, and Argentina on the back of a free-trade agreement, they could greatly retard development. Indeed, holdovers from Mexican statism would look with favor on costly free-trade conditions that could cripple the emerging new society.

In countries where the institutions of development planning are fading—or, in the case of Chile, have been largely overcome—the last thing reformist governments could possibly want is for a free-trade agreement to resuscitate the old inefficiencies. President Salinas observed that Mexico still has unsavory elements whose

> ideology is the expression of 20 or 50 years ago, that of closing our borders and engaging in confrontations with other countries. They are waiting for the imaginary pendulum of history to swing back toward vindicating the bureaucratic, excessively proprietary state.[5]

[4]Address by President Carlos Salinas de Gortari on the 63rd anniversary of the Institutional Revolutionary Party (PRI), *La Jornada* (Mexico City), Supplement "Perfil de la Jornada," March 5, 1992, pp. I–III.

[5]Ibid.

Nationalist Myth and Protectionist Dogma

Today, the old economic myths have lost their power, and cutting-edge scholars in Latin America no longer believe that the region suffers from too much capitalism. It has dawned on Latin Americans that their societies have been blocked by the mercantilist system that was strengthened by development planning. Different authors call the incentive-sapping system by different names. For example, Argentine Jorge Bustamante prefers the term "corporativism," while Brazilian José Penna uses the term "patrimonialism," Peruvian Hernando de Soto uses "mercantilism," and Colombian Edgar Revéiz describes Colombia as the "co-opted society."[6] It does not matter what name is finally settled upon. It is a common condition—one that Latin America is growing out of and that the United States may be growing into.

The fact is the economic system they describe is the same. From the Rio Grande to Patagonia, the concentration of most profitable opportunities in the hands of government led all of society to coalesce into redistributive combines seeking special privileges and protection from the state. Nationalist myths and protectionist dogma became a veil for the parceling out of favors to protected interests.

Forty years of development planning, which substituted public debt and planning for private equity and the market, left the region with a $429-billion debt, a littered landscape of inefficient government-owned companies, and a more deeply entrenched mercantilism.

The Yankee imperialist blocked Latin American development not with his foreign investment, but with his socialist ideas imposed through his multilateral aid institutions. Left-wing Latin thinkers, by denouncing private investment, were complicit in the plot that kept potentially powerful countries relegated to the economic backwaters. Development planning prescribed exactly the wrong medicine for Latin America. Rather than breaking up the elites' economic stranglehold, the advice of Western academics and the loans from the international bureaucracies served to extend the elites' control over the economies of the Southern Hemisphere. The mercantilist tradition of government control and the interests of rent-seeking elites dovetailed

---

[6]Jorge Bustamante, *La República Corporativa* (Buenos Aires: Emecé Editores, 1988); José Osvaldo de Meira Penna, *O Dinossauro* (São Paulo: T. A. Queiroz, 1988); Hernando de Soto, *The Other Path* (New York: Harper & Row, 1989, first published 1986 in Spanish); and Edgar Revéiz, *Democratizar para Sobrevivir* (Bogotá: Edgar Revéiz, 1989).

with development planning. Chilean historian Claudio Véliz has observed that development planning merged with the well-established clientelistic traditions of *compadrazgo* and nepotism to increase the power of traditional elites.[7]

The policy benefited the few, while all of society was burdened for repayment of the loans. As a result, countries lost the growth opportunities of the post–World War II period and accumulated huge debts that brought them under virtual International Monetary Fund (IMF) suzerainty and further impoverished the poor with currency devaluations and higher taxes.

Resisting the Interventionist Impulse

In the 1990s, development planning is still present, although it is on the defensive. Countries that have not yet reduced the size of the state, such as Venezuela, Peru, Brazil, and Ecuador, are still mired in crisis. Moreover, illustrative of the die-hard nature of bureaucracies everywhere, the IMF, Inter-American Development Bank, World Bank, and the U.S. Agency for International Development are still lending Western taxpayer dollars to build up Latin American government bureaucracies to carry out infrastructure projects and build the institutions of the welfare state.

The statist "solutions" are still being offered to crisis-ridden countries. Peru is a case in point. The country confronts societal breakdown—economic, moral, and political collapse—as a result of the division of society into rent-seeking coalitions that encrust the interventionist state. Yet Harvard professor Jeffrey Sachs contends that Peru's crisis is due to the small size of the state. In their 1991 book, *Peru's Path to Recovery*, editors Jeffrey Sachs and Brookings Institution economist Carlos Paredes asked how more government could be financed, rather than how Peru could build a viable economy. The two economists contended that Peru's tax revenues were too low to finance the kind of massive welfare programs they believed were needed and urged the government of Alberto Fujimori to increase taxes as a proportion of gross domestic product (GDP) on a shrinking economy. In their view, an increase from about 5 to 18 percent was needed. Unfortunately, the Fujimori government tried to follow their recom-

[7]Claudio Véliz, *The Centralist Tradition of Latin America* (Princeton, N.J.: Princeton University Press, 1980), p. 262.

mendations and by 1993 had raised taxes to 9.7 percent of GDP, according to official reports. Finance Ministry officials believe revenues should rise to at least 17 percent of GDP.[8]

Just as George Bush's tax increase helped to bring about the longest postwar U.S. recession and increased the budget deficit, the Peruvian tax increase is not working. GDP fell in 1992, and the government predicts the budget deficit will amount to more than 2.9 percent of GDP in 1993.[9] Shrinking the reported tax base has never been known to raise revenues.

Boding better for the future, President Fujimori is trying to privatize the economy at breakneck speed. Between May 1992 and April 1993, 13 state enterprises were sold, generating $435 million for the government.[10] A further 80 state enterprises were preparing for divestment under an ambitious privatization schedule. The Peruvian government aims to divest all government-owned commercial ventures and services by 1995. Together with trade and financial reforms, the privatizations may mark the beginning of Peru's reorientation to the private sector.

Aid, Institutional Corruption, and Entrenched Interests

Four hundred billion dollars in Latin American development assistance[11] financed the growth of the unproductive institutions in Latin American societies. Economists, such as Douglass North, who study economic institutions contend that the kinds of institutions and the path of institutional change prevalent in a society determine the structure of property rights and, "together with the standard constraints of economic theory, determine the opportunities in a society."[12] Since societies are always characterized by a mix of institutions, some

[8]Comisión de Promoción de la Inversión Privada (Copri), Peruvian government commission, "The Turn of Peru," second edition, May 1993, p. 7.

[9]Ibid.

[10]Comisión de Promoción de la Inversión Privada, reports on the privatization process prepared April 1993 and January 1993.

[11]Gross aid flows from all sources since 1945.

[12]Douglass North, *Institutions, Institutional Change and Economic Performance* (Cambridge, England: Cambridge University Press, 1990), p. 7.

that foster economic development and others that do not, what matters is whether markets under the system are competitive and transaction costs are low.[13]

In Latin America, foreign development assistance did not help to open markets or lower transaction costs—quite the opposite. Western loans financed the growth of bureaucracy at the expense of the market economy. With the aid contingent upon the countries' adoption of a national development plan, planning ministries sprouted in the posh districts of Latin American capitals. Over the decades, bureaucratic employment exploded as government entities competed for foreign loans. In Mexico, by 1982 a total of 1,155 state-owned enterprises and entities under the federal government controlled 14 percent of GDP. In 1992, Brazil had more than 500 state companies and Peru at least 270. Moreover, in March 1992, Peruvian finance minister Carlos Boloña estimated that there were almost 1.2 million public employees in Peru and that one out of every six workers labored for the state.[14] In Argentina, in 1988 there were almost 2 million bureaucrats out of a working population of 11.5 million.[15]

It is not an exaggeration to say that the World Bank, IMF, Inter-American Development Bank, and other multilateral and bilateral aid agencies helped to shape the institutional development of Latin America. The similarities among the economic bureaucracies of the different countries are striking: Peru's PescaPeru (Peruvian state fishing company) and Banpesca in Mexico (the Mexican fishing development bank); Chile's Sendos (national sewerage company) and Peru's Seda-pal (the Peruvian equivalent); Brazil's Electrobras (national electricity company) and Peru's ElectroPeru and Chile's Chilectra (the Peruvian and Chilean national electricity companies, respectively). All of these state companies had one thing in common: a desperate hunger for multilateral development bank loans. Each state company had staffs appointed as liaisons to the multilateral development institutions and departments dedicated entirely to working on projects financed by the multilateral development institutions.

---

[13]Ibid., p. 95.

[14]Interview with Economy Minister Carlos Boloña Behr by Vidal Silva Navarrete, *La República* (Lima), February 16, 1992.

[15]Instituto de la Economía Social de Mercado study, published in *La Prensa* (Buenos Aires), March 19, 1989.

Dense layers of bureaucracy developed in part as a response to the fact that each aid agency has different rules and procedures that developing country bureaucracies must follow to receive aid. A 1986 study sponsored by the Organization for Economic Cooperation and Development found that "local officials have to deal with at least ten and sometimes twenty or thirty different procedures. Unless the government machine is well equipped to cope, departments become clogged with project documents."[16] The result, according to the study, is that large segments of developing country governments have been reoriented to serving the international aid bureaucracy, diminishing what little accountability they had to local populations.[17]

All of this activity did not constitute sustainable economic development. Instead, the expansion of the state wreaked havoc upon private property rights as governments confiscated private property to make way for state-supported ventures and otherwise loaded the productive sector with heavy burdens of high taxes, high inflation, and repressive regulation. Transaction costs rose as every transaction came to require bribes of public officials who had carved out personal fiefdoms. Entrepreneurial individuals were attracted by the opportunities in the governing bureaucracies or found themselves relegated to the black market.

Economic life took on aspects of the surreal. Since bureaucrats cannot possess the information required to make informed investment decisions, bribery emerged as the most efficient way to allocate government resources. Channeling foreign largesse through patronage-ridden, unaccountable governments served to institutionalize corruption and make political elites into an aristocracy similar to the communist "new class" that Milovan Djilas described in his classic book, *The New Class: An Analysis of the Communist System*.

From Mexico to Argentina, "kleptocrats" or "maharajahs," as they are known in Brazil, provisioned themselves with palatial estates, private zoos, multimillion-dollar collections of classic cars, and fat Swiss bank accounts. Latin presidents themselves were no slouches at feeding from the public trough. The Central Intelligence Agency estimates that former Mexican president José López Portillo suborned

---

[16]Bernard Lecomte, *Project Aid: Limitations and Alternatives* (Paris: Organization for Economic Cooperation and Development, 1986), p. 61.

[17]Ibid., p. 62.

$1 billion to $3 billion during his 1976–82 tenure.[18] Not since those ancient, heady days when the officers of the Spanish monarchy plundered the treasure at Potosí and the mines of New Spain had government officials so freely converted vast public resources to their own use. It cannot be surprising that placing large sums in unaccountable government hands enriched the few and did not produce the revenues to repay the loans.

The interests of the dominant governing class came to link "the public and private sectors in such an intricate web of interests, privileges, profits, and gains" that Brazilian economist Oliveiros Ferreira terms the prevailing system in Brazil a mafia.[19] Numerous accounts detail institutionalized corruption in Latin America that stemmed from the state-directed development approach.[20]

In Brazil, for example, legally designated recipients of government appropriations, even government agencies, have to pay bribes to receive their funding. Gumercindo Domingos, mayor of a city in the São Paulo area, complained that to receive its appropriated school funds from the Ministry of Education and Culture, the city had to hire the services of a bureaucratic go-between.[21]

The modus operandi of the Brazilian government is as unaccountable to the public as that in neighboring countries. In Peru, public officials apparently treat the national budget like their own bank account. Critics on the left and right decry the "immorality" of the practice. In June 1991, the Peruvian newspaper *El Comercio* reported that over the past two decades, tens of billions of dollars in public monies had disappeared without a trace.[22] In 1991, Peruvian senator

[18]Jack Anderson, "Politics Dilute Anti-Corruption Effort in Mexico," *Washington Post*, August 24, 1984, p. E11; and "Mexican Wheels Are Lubricated by Official Oil," *Washington Post*, May 14, 1984, p. B11.

[19]Oliveiros Ferreira in de Meira Penna, p. 147.

[20]A sample includes on Brazil: Mario Barros Junior, *A Fantástica Corrupção no Brasil* (São Paulo: Mario Barros Junior, 1982); de Meira Penna; on Argentina: Jorge Bustamante, *La República Corporativa*; on Venezuela: Carlos Ball, *Libertad, Democracia y Corrupción* (Caracas: Ediciones Libertas, reprinted 1984, first published 1983); on Peru: Hernando de Soto, *The Other Path*.

[21]"'Contrato de Risco' na Intermediação," *O Estado de São Paulo*, February 26, 1988.

[22]"Entrevista: Urge que administración pública incorpore modernos sistemas de control de gasto," interview with Senator Daniel Bocanegra Barreto, *El Comercio* (Lima), June 2, 1991.

Daniel Bocanegra Barreto, president of the Joint Review Commission of General Accounts, said his staff of nine was investigating the case of 10,564 fraudulent checks, totaling $1.3 billion, written by the Peruvian national bank (Banco de la Nación) in 1986.[23]

In January 1992, Ecuadorean vice-presidential candidate Alberto Dahik decried administrative corruption in Ecuador. He declared that "deburocratización" of the economy is necessary to overcome moral decline and public-sector obstacles that cause every transaction to require a bribe. He noted that corruption worsens as it "trickles down" from the top.

> If the minister himself steals, the undersecretaries will commit assaults and the departmental directors will engage in theft, extortion, robbery, and murder. When the perception is that corruption begins at the top, everything falls into decay.[24]

Some would correctly point out that U.S. government scandals and the congressional check-kiting episode show that the United States faces its share of corruption. In fact, wherever the level of government intervention in the economy is rising, so is the level of corruption.

Latin American bureaucrats long ago realized that planning was a failure, but a network of interests benefiting from the foreign largesse had become entrenched in the planning bureaucracies and government ministries. Likewise, as early as the 1960s, it was no secret in the international development community that planning was a failure.[25] Yet in the industrialized countries as in Latin America, strong interests were encrusted around the aid institutions, and they called for ever-increasing levels of development assistance. Those privileged by aid—ranging from private corporate aid contract winners and international bureaucrats in the West to the redistributive combines in the recipient countries—all faced incentives to cover up the reality and to keep the aid flowing.

[23]Ibid.

[24]Interview with Sixto Duran-Ballen, Republican Unity party presidential candidate and vice-presidential candidate Alberto Dahik, leader of the Conservative party of Ecuador, in *El Universo*, January 25, 1992.

[25]Studies acknowledging the failures of planning proliferated during the 1960s. A sample includes Albert Waterston, *Development Planning: Lessons of Experience* (Baltimore: Johns Hopkins Press, 1965); and Economic Commission on Latin America and the Caribbean, "General Administrative Aspects of Planning," in *Administrative Aspects of Planning* (New York: ECLAC, 1969).

Thus, in the final analysis, countries pretended to produce a comprehensive plan, and the international organizations went through the motions of basing their policy decisions upon the plans, which merely furnished lists of projects to finance. In 1974, after surveying over 200 planners, University of California at Berkeley economists Naomi Caiden and Aaron Wildavsky concluded:

> It didn't matter whether the plan worked; what did count was the ability to produce a document which looked like a plan, and that meant using economists and other technical personnel. If these skills were not available within the country, they had to be imported in the form of planners and foreign-aid advisors. A demand existed and an entirely new industry was created to fill the need. Thus national planning may be justified on a strict cash basis; planners may bring in more money from abroad than it costs to support them at home.[26]

A Lost Decade: The Price of Development Planning

During the 1980s, Latin Americans found themselves in the position of enforced poverty to pay for the mistakes of development planners. Heavily indebted governments were hard pressed to pay salaries of the bloated bureaucracy. They printed money, leading to high inflation, which the poor were least able to avoid. The austerity plans adopted under the advice and tutelage of the IMF have hurt the poor the most.

Typically, IMF programs have entailed cutting government spending and raising taxes to balance the budget; slowing monetary growth and freezing wages and prices to slow inflation; and devaluing the currency and raising taxes further to cut domestic demand. This mishmash of policies, designed to facilitate debt repayment in the short run, hurt the economy in the long run by instilling disincentives to production. The resulting climate of economic depression impoverished the struggling middle classes and worsened the condition of the poor.

After four decades of public investment, benefits have not "trickled down" to the poor. During the "lost decade" of the 1980s, living standards fell. In the 1990s, countries that have taken the fewest steps to dismantle the interventionist state are still in severe crisis and the number of the poor people in those countries is exploding. In Brazil,

---

[26]Naomi Caiden and Aaron Wildavsky, *Planning and Budgeting in Poor Countries* (1974; New York: Transaction Publishers, 1990), p. 286.

while some bureaucrats enjoy high salaries and government-subsidized mansions whether they even show up for work or not, the Brazilian news magazine *Veja* reported that never have so many people been living in the streets. *Veja* estimated that Brazil has 60 million homeless, a number that the magazine admits cannot be verified.[27]

Noting that even the United States has homeless people, *Veja* found a critical difference. In the United States the homeless tend to be disconnected persons suffering from alcoholism, drug addiction, or mental illness, while in Brazil the homeless tend to be employed. With even shacks renting for four times the minimum wage, families end up finding shelter under viaducts and bridges, or wherever they can.[28]

Western Imposition

The West is partly to blame for the economic, social, and political backwardness of Latin America—but not for the reasons usually given by leftists. Western intellectuals pushed the interventionist model on Latin America, making foreign aid contingent upon the adoption of national development plans. The West is culpable for squandering a historic opportunity in the post–World War II period to transmit the ideas of free markets and free enterprise conducive to economic success.

Latin Americans anxious for progress have been deterred by the extraordinary resources that the developed countries have committed to attacks on the values and institutions of a free society. A skeptical observer could come to the conclusion that development planning was a Machiavellian strategy by which the less developed countries were denied the ideas necessary for progress.

In the development literature, capitalism was redlined and most influential academics converged to recommend central planning for less developed countries. Stanford University professor Paul Baran concluded in his influential 1957 book, *The Political Economy of Growth*, that

> the dominant fact of our time is that the institution of private property in the means of production ... has now come into

[27]*Veja*, December 19, 1990, cover and "Carta ao Leitor."
[28]Ibid.

irreconcilable contradiction with the economic and social advancement of the people in the underdeveloped countries.[29]

As early as 1956, the extent of the faith in planning was so great that Nobel laureate Gunnar Myrdal was able to claim that

> all special advisors to underdeveloped countries who have taken the time and trouble to acquaint themselves with the problems, no matter who they are . . . recommend central planning as a first condition of progress.[30]

Marxist and Keynesian economics, British and French socialism, the New Deal in the United States, and the postwar Marshall Plan for Europe all played a role in convincing the West to impose development planning on the Third World. Above all else, however, academic claims for planning were buttressed by the alleged success of the Soviet planned economy—one of history's great frauds.

Academics were candid about their reliance on the Soviet model. In 1962, John Kenneth Galbraith explained that

> five-year plans are the invention of, and were once the exclusive possession of, the Soviet Union. Now Americans and Western Europeans assemble without thought to consider how they may help finance the five-year plans of India or Pakistan. The country which does not have goals, and a program for reaching these goals, is commonly assumed to be going nowhere.[31]

Today, the glowing words of praise for the Soviet economy expressed by development bigwigs, such as Jan Tinbergen, Gunnar Myrdal, Ragnar Nurkse, Walt Rostow, W. Arthur Lewis, and others, redound with silliness. A few examples reveal the mindset of development planners in their heyday. In 1956 Myrdal viewed the Soviet model *"as fundamentally a system for the development of underdeveloped countries. This particular point cannot be stressed too much."*[32] Not to be outdone, Rostow concluded in his influential 1960 book, *The Stages of Economic Growth*, that Stalin had completed the modernization of the

[29]Paul Baran, *The Political Economy of Growth* (New York: Monthly Review, 1957), p. xl.

[30]Gunnar Myrdal, *An International Economy: Problems and Prospects* (New York: Harper & Row, 1956), p. 201.

[31]John Kenneth Galbraith, *Economic Development in Perspective* (Cambridge, Mass.: Harvard University Press, 1962), p. 36.

[32]Myrdal, p. 144. Emphasis in the original.

Soviet Union.[33] American leftists, such as Robert Heilbroner, thought Soviet drabness was "more psychologically appealing, to the common man of the backward areas than the gaudy and fantastically removed way of life of the West."[34]

With such a low level of intellectual acuity prevailing in development thinking, it is no wonder that Latin American countries that most closely followed the model found themselves in severe crisis.

Breaking the Chains of Mercantilism

If so-called experts had researched the historical record, they would have learned that for 400 years Latin American economic progress was hindered by a mercantilist tradition that stimulated the growth of nonmarket institutions. The official economy was traditionally reserved for rent-seeking elites, and market activity was pushed into the unofficial economy.

Well documented by Escalona y Agüero, Solórzano, León Pinelo, Campillo, De Gálvez, Haring, and Vicens, the record shows that from the start, Latin American countries were at a disadvantage because the institutions that were strong—the government and the Catholic Church—were not economically productive ones. Property rights have historically been strong only in government and the Catholic Church, while private property in the productive sector has been subject to heavy and haphazard taxation, repressive regulation, and confiscation.

From the 18th century onward, the economic history of most of the countries of the region has consisted of the alternate strengthening and weakening of the old mercantilist institutions without ever breaking away from them. At times when economic controls were decreased, production and trade increased, the power of political elites declined and a middle class of merchants, artisans, and professionals emerged. At other times, during periods of widespread confiscation of private property, production collapsed, the middle class disappeared, and economic opportunities became concentrated in privileged sectors.

[33]W. W. Rostow, *The Stages of Economic Growth: A Non-Communist Manifesto* (1960; Cambridge, England: Cambridge University Press, 1962), p. 66.

[34]Robert Heilbroner, "The Struggle for Economic Development in Our Time," in *From Underdevelopment to Affluence: Western, Soviet and Chinese Views*, Harry G. Shaffer and Jan S. Prybyla, eds. (New York: Appleton-Century-Crofts, 1968), p. 43.

As early as 1743, enlightened reformers of the Spanish monarchy, such as Joseph del Campillo,[35] called for the strengthening of private property rights throughout the realm to revive the moribund empire. During the 19th century, classical liberal ideas penetrated many countries to varying degrees. Francisco Pimentel of Mexico and Juan Alberdi of Argentina were forthright in urging an overhaul of economies based upon a system of free enterprise.[36] It is unfortunate that the United States did not understand that Latin American development required the historic mercantilist bonds to be broken rather than strengthened. However, perhaps little could have been done prior to socialism's intellectual demise in the ninth decade of the 20th century.

Latin America has a newfound confidence. No longer afraid of the Yankee, the region wants to trade freely with him, because it is building the economic institutions that make competitive achievement possible. Indeed Chile, with its privatized social security and health care systems and a 1992 growth rate of 9.7 percent, can be said to have surpassed many of the achievements of the United States. Those of us north of the Rio Grande hope and pray that Latin Americans continue to create economic liberty. One day the immigration may reverse, as gringos flee to Latin America seeking opportunity.

[35]Joseph del Campillo y Cosío, *Nuevo Sistema de Gobierno Económico para la América* (Mérida, Venezuela: Universidad de los Andes, 1971, first published 1789, written in 1743).

[36]See D. Francisco Pimentel, *La Economía Política Aplicada a la Propiedad Territorial en México* (Mexico City: Ignacio Cumplido, 1866); and Juan Alberdi, *Bases y Puntos de Partida para la Organización Política de la República Argentina* (1858; Buenos Aires: Editorial Universitaria de Buenos Aires, 1966).

9. Mexico, Markets, and Multilateral Aid

Roberto Salinas León

Mexico has experienced dramatic changes in economic policy since President Carlos Salinas de Gortari assumed office in 1988. His broad-based modernization program has been characterized by substantial fiscal adjustment, aggressive deregulation of many sectors of society, large-scale privatization of inefficient state-run enterprises, and trade liberalization. That economic strategy stands in stark contrast to the country's crisis-ridden years of foreign indebtedness, import-substitution protectionism, and wholesale state interventionism in practically every sector of economic life. The North American Free Trade Agreement (NAFTA) is a vivid demonstration of Mexico's commitment to the challenges of open markets and globalization.[1]

The strides toward free trade and market-oriented reform undertaken in the past five years seem to confirm the popular expression that Mexico seeks "trade, not aid." Indeed, foreign capital investment has increased exponentially and public debt no longer represents a serious threat to stable and sustained economic growth. It is received wisdom among national and international analysts that the relative success of the Salinas program could not have occurred without the 1990 renegotiation of Mexico's massive $107-billion foreign debt under the so-called Brady plan—a scheme in which multilateral aid agencies subsidized the reduction of the government's commercial debt. It is important to note, however, that multilateral aid and debt accrual have not diminished in the wake of market-oriented reform. Foreign indebtedness is still a standard practice by the remaining inefficient state-owned ventures, particularly the vast oil concerns and the electricity

The author is grateful to José Enrique López, research assistant at the Centro de Investigaciones Sobre la Libre Empresa, for his valuable help in collecting material used in this chapter.

[1]For a more complete discussion of those points, see Roberto Salinas León, "Free Trade and Free Markets: A Mexican Perspective on the NAFTA," in *NAFTA and the Environment*, Terry Anderson, ed. (San Francisco: Pacific Research Institute, 1993).

sector. A critical question for future policymakers in Mexico is whether the reform process initiated under the Salinas administration is sufficient to attract the investment needed by an underdeveloped and severely undercapitalized society or whether a more profound transformation of existing economic structures, institutionalizing the shift to a free-market society, is required.

The adjustment process during the 1989–93 period yields two crucial lessons about the benefits of market reform and the perils of debt renegotiation. First, Mexico provides a prominent example of how market-oriented change generates sound fiscal and monetary policy. Similarly, the emphasis on open trade implies a shift from the earlier tradition of financing state projects via multilateral aid to the new practice of forging a superior investment climate based on private-sector growth. Second, the country represents a negative case study of the detrimental consequences of relying on government-to-government aid to sustain expensive state-run enterprises. A crucial strategic dimension of NAFTA is that the accord is bound to replace the 1980s statist practice of public indebtedness with private investment inflows and unrestricted multilateral trade as the principal mechanisms of economic growth.

The Salinas Program: A Clean Bill of Health

Mexico's success in balanced budgets, large-scale privatization, and trade liberalization is the outcome of overlapping efforts on the part of the Salinas administration to bolster investor confidence and build an economic climate of stability and growth. Although the 1990 Brady plan, which renegotiated the nation's $107-billion foreign debt, played a role in that process, the fundamental basis for Mexico's economic and financial recovery has been the consistent pursuit of fiscal discipline and strict austerity in managing the public balance sheet.

Restructuring public finances is an integral part of the modernization program, complemented by broad-based initiatives to divest unprofitable state-run concerns and deregulate international trade and the economy. The most notable accomplishment of those policies has been price stabilization. Whereas in 1987 Mexico recorded the highest inflation rate in its modern history (159 percent), by 1992 inflation had fallen to a respectable 11.5 percent. And although the government's current exchange-rate mechanism, which combines fixed and free-floating exchange rates, has been criticized as an untenable hybrid, the

drastically lower inflation has contributed to Mexico's exchange-rate stability. Moreover, Mexico has set a 7 percent rate of inflation target for 1993. If the country meets that target, it will be the first time in 22 years that Mexico has experienced single-digit inflation.

This progress is the outcome of strict monetary and fiscal discipline. For example, the government has put a very tight lid on the money supply (M1 has fallen from 109 percent to 19 percent in two years). In order to prevent the government from using the printing press to finance populist ventures, in 1993 President Salinas decreed the independence of monetary policy from the government. That dramatic move implies the full autonomy of Mexico's central bank, Banco de México, in managing inflation targets, exchange-rate stability, interest rates, and other matters of monetary policy. By formally severing the government's financial needs for cash from the social need to protect and strengthen the purchasing power of the local currency, the Salinas administration has made it much more difficult to abandon fiscal discipline and budget austerity. The government will no longer be able to rely on quick financing of populist programs through a policy of monetary expansion.

Moreover, contrary to the populist debt-ridden days of the 1980s, the government is no longer spending more than it takes in. In 1987, the federal budget recorded a highly unstable deficit of 17 percent of gross domestic product (GDP). That figure resulted from costly financing of foreign and domestic debt. Indeed, outlays for interest obligations alone absorbed approximately three-fourths of net government expenditures. However, by 1992 the deficit had been transformed into a surplus of 0.4 percent of GDP. In 1993, the government has targeted another surplus of 1.7 percent of GDP. Importantly, those examples of fiscal health do not include windfall revenues obtained through the sale of state-owned entities.

Mexico's impressive privatization program has helped improve the public fiscal balance. To date, the number of state-owned entities has fallen from a peak of 1,200 in 1982 to some 260 by the end of 1992.[2] Those nearly 1,000 sales represent 10 percent of the entire number of

---

[2]For an extensive analysis of the virtues and vices of Mexico's privatization program, see Roberto Salinas León, "Privatization in Mexico: Good but Not Enough," Heritage Foundation Backgrounder no. 797, November 15, 1990; and Salinas León, "Privatization in Mexico: Much Better but Still Not Enough," Heritage Foundation Backgrounder Update no. 172, January 20, 1992.

enterprises divested worldwide since 1979. They include hotels, airlines, ports, telecommunications, mining and steel mills, agriculture, the commercial bank system, insurance companies, airports and bridges, highway infrastructure, customs unions, radio and television concerns, and the fertilizer, coffee, and tobacco monopolies. Not only has that wave of privatizations generated $22 billion in revenues, it has also removed the source of much government red ink.

For example, the two steel holdings, AHMSA and SICARTSA, were sold for $1.5 billion in late 1991. They lost some $10.5 billion during a 12-year period and absorbed $700 million per year in federal subsidies. The number of productive jobs that could have been generated by channeling those outlays to the private sector virtually defies comment.

A significant (and understandable) concern that emerged at the outset of the Salinas privatization program was whether the monies obtained via privatization would be squandered in semipopulist programs of "social spending." That worry faded with the creation of a contingency fund—one of the most astute and creative mechanisms of fiscal policy in the nation's recent history. Since 1990, the government has deposited privatization-generated revenue in that special trust and used it to cancel outstanding foreign and domestic debt. So far, three-fourths of all windfall revenue have been used to retire debt, cutting interest rate obligations. In 1992, total public-sector principal was reduced by $14.5 billion: internal debt fell from $49 billion to $39 billion and sovereign foreign debt from $79 billion to $75 billion. All told, foreign debt service has fallen from 44.2 percent of GDP to 12.5 percent in the past five years. In net terms, total public-sector debt has plummeted from 80 percent of GDP at the end of 1987 to 28 percent of GDP.

The government plans to continue using privatization funds to cancel debt, with a total of 37 state companies currently slated for privatization and expected to generate another windfall revenue of $5 billion. That expected income has allowed the government to project another round of reductions in public-sector debt service, this time by 50 percent. The ventures to be privatized include basic foodstuffs distribution centers, a remaining percentage of the fertilizer monopoly, a media package, and the insurance conglomerate, ASEMEX. The Salinas administration has also developed a medium-term plan to privatize ports, airports, and secondary petrochemical concerns, which could produce another $15 billion to $20 billion in revenue. Officials believe that process will make the country "debt free" by the year 2000. However, as explained below, Mexico could be debt free in a matter of 6 to 12 months.

Mexico's experience with sound fiscal policy demonstrates that only domestic solutions can resolve the foreign debt problem. External factors, such as debt restructuring, bailouts, and further aid from creditor institutions, are not necessary to achieve economic growth. In fact, the main problem with the aid approach is that it tends to perpetuate a negligent attitude toward the requirements of fiscal balance and strict monetary policy. Unfortunately, notwithstanding Mexico's noteworthy reforms, the country remains addicted to foreign borrowing in crucial sectors of the economy.

Debt Restructuring and the Mexican State Sector: An Unfinished Agenda

The 1990 Brady plan was a landmark debt-reduction package, superior in many ways to its predecessors (e.g., the Baker plan) in that it emphasized debt relief rather than rescheduling. The deal was based on the notion that Mexico required relief of some $23 billion in outstanding debt obligations to fashion the program of economic reform within an atmosphere of relative financial stability.

The Brady plan reduced the debt burden by 20 percent, saving the country $3 billion to $4 billion in interest over five years. The plan gave the government fiscal space to implement structural reform in a society devastated by years of stagnation and a 47 percent loss in purchasing power. In that light, the Brady plan was an undisputed success. Foreign debt no longer causes acute concern as it once did.[3]

Nevertheless, the Brady plan was not without its problems. Three years have elapsed and the medium-term effects appear to confirm the worst fears of critics suspicious of conditioning domestic progress on foreign aid. The Brady plan appears to have suffered two major shortcomings: (1) an ill-founded assumption that foreign indebtedness was the cause, not the effect, of macroeconomic instability and economic underperformance during the 1980s crisis and (2) an inaccurate belief that debt reduction is a sufficient condition to enable full recovery from the factors responsible for economic instability.

[3]That orthodox view of the "benefits" of the Brady plan is succinctly summarized in an important note entitled "To Him That Hath Not," *The Economist*, April 20, 1989, p. 90.

Latin America's economic predicament during the 1980s seems to confirm those points. The region's experience demonstrates that debt-amelioration strategies (new lines of fresh credit, reduction of obligations or principal, etc.) postponed urgently needed reforms by supplying an artificial cushion of time and money to keep rotting structures in place. In Mexico, despite the reductions in debt obtained through the Brady plan, there has been a resurgence of external indebtedness. The debt-reduction initiative indeed diminished Mexico's sovereign debt to some $79 billion, but since 1989, Mexico has incurred an additional $10 billion in new debt from multilateral institutions and other creditor agencies. In nominal terms, Mexico has gone backwards.

A large portion of Mexico's total foreign debt (some $111 billion as of May 1993) has been incurred by domestic private sources in the form of commercial paper with medium-term maturities and stock placements in the international financial markets. Although the amount has skyrocketed from $6 billion in 1990 to more than $30 billion by mid-1993, as Finance Minister Pedro Aspe has observed, private debt is the business of the private sector. If the money is used to modernize companies, making them more competitive, then future revenues can be earmarked for debt amortization. That is "business as usual"—or so officials claim.

Nevertheless, the government has taken a variety of loans since 1989 to sustain politically motivated state projects. In 1992, the Ministry of Finance was authorized to contract foreign debt in excess of $2 billion to subsidize state-run concerns. In 1993, the amount authorized has been set at $3.5 billion. The Inter-American Development Bank recently authorized a controversial loan to offset the high differentials between exports and imports by stimulating the nation's external sector performance. The loan, however, revealed that debt dependence and debt restructuring are a symptom of the problem and not the problem per se. The main failing in the nation's ailing state sectors is not lack of credits, but fund mismanagement resulting from the political privileges and monopoly status enjoyed by many state companies. Other loans include ongoing programs to subsidize imports of U.S. foodstuffs and agricultural commodities. Unfortunately, programs such as Salinas's revolutionary initiative to liberalize agriculture risk being dragged down by growing debt dependency. An obvious danger is that further debt accumulation will delay urgently needed additional reform.[4]

According to the Economic Commission for Latin America and the Caribbean, Mexico's net foreign debt was equivalent to $106 billion by the end of 1992. And despite a $4.2-billion reduction in principal in 1992, outlays for total debt service during the Salinas administration have approached $58 billion. Moreover, while further internal and external cancellations are projected in 1993 at an amount equivalent to 10 percent of GDP, foreign debt rose by $1.6 billion in 1992 and, as already stated, is expected to jump by as much as $3.5 billion in 1993. It is estimated that $34 billion has gone to service foreign debt in the 1989–92 period. That is equivalent to 97 percent of total foreign investment in the same period. Today, interest obligations on principal of outstanding foreign debt absorb $7.5 billion per year. Those payments could obviously have found more productive uses elsewhere in the Mexican economy.

The Role of the Multilaterals

Growing debt even in the midst of a serious reform program reflects the immense social cost of not undertaking a privatization of inefficient state assets. The International Monetary Fund (IMF) played a major role in perpetuating the legacy of statism in Mexico during the 1980s—despite its conditioning of debt renegotiation on "market-oriented reform." That legacy was based on the erroneous assumption that chronic underdevelopment in Mexico was the result of a lack of credits and capital flight. Thus, the IMF encouraged bailouts, foreign debt reschedulings, and further expansion of debt. The principal source of the debt crisis in Mexico during the 1980s, however, was not negative capital flows per se, but rather the existence of a massively expensive state sector. The new credits, far from alleviating the crisis, helped prolong the existence of the economically devastating state entities.

---

[4]According to economist Rogelio Ramírez de la O, a future debt renegotiation in the context of NAFTA is something that cannot be ruled out. See Ramírez de la O, "A Mexican Vision of North American Economic Integration," in *Continental Accord: North American Economic Integration,* Steven Globerman, ed. (Vancouver: Fraser Institute, 1991), pp. 23–24.

As part of five rounds of debt renegotiations during the 1980s, the IMF conditioned new loans on the privatization of state entities. That process began in 1983, and by 1987 the state sector had divested some 750 companies, leaving about 450 government-owned enterprises by the beginning of 1988. Although that may seem impressive on the surface, the majority of those companies were small and represented only a small fraction in the growth of deficit spending. The main state entities (e.g., railroads, electricity, oil, steel) were kept under exclusive state control, sustained in large part by the new lines of cash made available by the IMF. As a result, real market reform was minimal and deficit spending reached all time highs (17 percent of GDP by 1987).

With the advent of the Brady plan, the World Bank, too, has continued in its role of creating a national dependence on foreign financing of costly state projects. In 1989, the bank issued nine loans to Mexico amounting to $2.7 billion for various state-run concerns in the electricity, water, and railroads sectors. In 1990, six loans for underwriting similar projects totaled $2.5 billion. Some $2 billion in emergency loans for the energy and electricity industries were authorized in 1991. Lately, the World Bank has also taken interest in "helping" the government with the nation's acute environmental problems in air and water quality. Mexico received $1.4 billion or one-fourth of all loans the World Bank made to Latin America in 1992. That brings the debt contracted from the bank since 1989 to more than $8 billion—most of which has been channeled to the electricity and energy-generating sector.

Despite its gross inefficiency, the electricity monopoly, CFE, has not been slated for privatization. The company is currently seeking private capital for joint projects in energy generation. However, ownership will remain exclusively with the government. As long as that is the case, that industry is likely to continue losing large sums of money. The state-run subsidiary, Compañía de Luz y Fuerza, for instance, registered an outrageous $800 million in red ink in 1992. On the other hand, sale of the state-run electricity and railroad monopolies, for example, would draw a considerable inflow of capital (an estimated $20 billion) and remove the cause of poor performance—overemployment, corruption, and transfer subsidies.

A similar situation afflicts the state-owned oil monopoly, PEMEX. PEMEX is the 10th largest company of its kind in the world, but also one of the least efficient. The government resists reform for purely political reasons. The 1938 expropriation of foreign petroleum assets has come to symbolize "national sovereignty," making PEMEX a cherished institution among large portions of Mexico's population. Mexico's intransigence on that issue was manifested during the NAFTA negotiations, in which Mexico agreed to liberalize almost everything but its most profitable commodity. Unfortunately, Mexico has incurred enormous costs in the name of sovereignty, and oil is no exception. Perhaps the most vivid expression of that legacy was the disastrous explosion of pipelines in Guadalajara in April 1992, which killed 200 citizens and devastated a portion of the city.

That tragic incident prompted the Salinas administration to "restructure" PEMEX into a holding company with four independent subsidiaries: production, refining, natural gas and primary petrochemicals, and secondary petrochemicals. Although that initiative was insufficient to fully unleash market forces, it has proved to be a catalyst for more radical reform. In 1993, for example, the government announced plans to sell the secondary petrochemical companies for a projected $6 billion.

Only wholesale privatization, however, can address the corruption, inefficiency, and red ink that continue to characterize PEMEX. Indeed, many independent studies show that without a massive influx of capital for exploration and exploitation, the oil monopoly will no longer be able to meet rising domestic demand in the first years of the 21st century. That means that Mexico, eighth in the world in proven oil reserves, could turn into a net importer of crude by the year 2005. The country is already importing up to some $2 billion annually in refined products, natural gas, and oxygenated gasoline.

A major reason for PEMEX's inability to improve its technological capabilities is the enormous fiscal burden imposed by the government. PEMEX's tax contribution in 1992 was $14 billion—equivalent to 75 percent of its total earnings—leaving little to reinvest in production and refining.

Thus, PEMEX has become dependent on foreign borrowing. Since 1990, it has issued a series of bonds in international markets and plans to raise $12 billion via such operations as part of an estimated $20-billion investment program for the 1990–95 period. In addition, the U.S. Export-Import Bank has approved a critical and apparently political loan for $5.6 billion to finance the ailing petroleum sector. So far, $1.6 billion has been issued. All this borrowing highlights a spectacular irony: a constitutionally defined "strategic" sector, considered a symbol of independence, requires foreign credit to sustain its financial status.

Despite the compelling case for sweeping privatization of the so-called strategic sectors, top government officials continue to resist introducing such measures. The standard argument is that constitutional provisions prohibit private participation. Finance Minister Pedro Aspe, for example, claims that the case for keeping "strategic" companies under state control is "cultural and historical." If those sectors are truly strategic, however, then it is even more important to open them to market forces and competition. The record of Mexico's state-owned enterprises provides convincing enough evidence about the inefficiency of government industries and their drain on the overall Mexican economy.

The Organization for Economic Cooperation and Development (OECD) reached a similar conclusion. In a special report, the OECD noted that despite Salinas's laudable efforts to privatize everything from cabarets and hotels to steel mills and telecommunications, the most important enterprises remain under exclusive government control. Moreover, the OECD deemed the constitutional arguments unconvincing. Mexico changed constitutional clauses in order to sell the bank system and implement its agricultural reform, for example.

The increase in foreign debt since 1989 illustrates the crucial conceptual flaw of the Brady plan: debt reduction alone will not remove the source of Mexico's economic problems, which are fundamentally domestic. Today, despite its achievements in economic reform and trade liberalization, Mexico continues to be categorized as a high-risk country by international investors. Extending the reform policy to the electricity and oil sectors would do much to remedy that situation. The state-owned petroleum assets alone have an estimated worth of $148 billion—enough to amortize all public-sector domestic and foreign debt, augment hard currency reserves, and generate an impressive permanent savings in interest payments. In addition, liberalization of oil would draw the sustained flow of capital investment required to modernize the sector and transform it into the highly productive industry it can and should be.[5]

---

[5]That estimate is made in Wesley Smith, "Oil and Prosperity: Reforming Mexico's Petroleum Monopoly," Heritage Foundation Backgrounder Update no. 923, December

Accounting for Mexico's Current Account

One of the most prominent anomalies brought about by debt is the resulting pressure on the current account balance. In Mexico, the current account deficit has grown exponentially in the past three years—from $4 billion in 1990 to an estimated $26 billion in 1993. Most of that is due to an expansion in the trade deficit, although some 15 percent of net expenditures in the current account have been absorbed by foreign debt service during the past four years.

Some observers worry that Mexico's growing trade deficit will require an exchange-rate devaluation that could lead to a financial crisis that, in turn, would lead to greater foreign indebtedness to bail out the economy. Other critics claim that Mexico is simply incurring new foreign debt (from private sources) to finance an intolerably expensive experiment with large trade deficits, commercial liberalization, and an allegedly overvalued rate of exchange. So far, the "price" has been on the order of $20.5 billion. The first worry typifies IMF fears concerning an "unfavorable" evolution in the balance of payments. The second concern is expressed by the democratic left.[6]

Mexico's economic reforms have generated an attractive investment regime. The once-unimaginable target of $24 billion in capital flows projected for the entire six-year term of the Salinas administration was met 18 months ahead of schedule and has since been surpassed. Capital flows amounted to $28.8 billion as of 1993 with projected inflows of an additional $22 billion before the conclusion of Salinas's term. A crucial issue confronting the administration is how to make those badly needed private capital flows permanent.

However, speculation about a domestic recession, a fragile exchange rate, and a high trade imbalance have led to the belief that a sharp devaluation of the peso is necessary to enable exporters to compete successfully in global markets. The critics cite the 1992 expansion of the exchange-rate ceiling from 20 to 40 centavos per day as a red alert of an

15, 1992, pp. 14–15. See Gary Hufbauer and Jeffrey Schott, *North American Free Trade: Issues and Recommendations* (Washington, D.C.: Institute for International Economics, 1992), chapter 10, for a detailed discussion of the various problems afflicting PEMEX and the Mexican oil industry.

[6]For an example of a view that combines elements from both claims about private indebtedness and a large current deficit, see Christopher Whalen, "Mexico's Government Creates Another Debt Crisis," *Wall Street Journal*, March 12, 1992, p. A13.

impending modification in the rate of exchange. However, the primary motivation for the daily microdepreciation of the currency was to neutralize a rapidly growing expectation that a devaluation was just around the corner. High interest rates (16 percent) have helped to temper a speculative onslaught against the peso's real monetary appreciation. Nevertheless, the exchange-rate expectations reflect a historical concern among most investors that the country is rapidly approaching a current account deficit similar in GDP terms to the one recorded in 1981 (some 7 percent of GDP) that initiated the vicious cycles of devaluation–high inflation–devaluation that characterized the "lost decade" of the 1980s.

There are fundamental differences between the current account deficit of the early 1980s and that of the early 1990s, however. A deficit in the current account means that net expenditures surpass net revenues. In the 1980s, the deficit was due to foreign debt accumulation and massive public-sector spending in state-run ventures. In 1970, Mexico had a meager foreign debt of $4 billion and some 300 state-owned companies in operation. By 1982, the number of state-owned enterprises reached 1,200 and the foreign debt escalated to $107 billion. In 1981 alone, for instance, oil-backed borrowing from abroad reached a staggering $40 billion. Thus, the current account deficit crisis was a result of years of poor government policy and mismanagement, much of which was supported by official foreign assistance.[7]

Because of Mexico's recent trade liberalizations and market-based reform, however, the current account deficit today means that the private sector is spending capital (i.e., private debt) that has flowed from abroad to finance profitable projects at home. In short, the deficit reflects an investment boom and confidence in the country's economic climate. Thus, while the current account deficit reached an historic nominal proportion in 1992—more than $21 billion, or some 6.5 percent of GDP—direct investment from foreign sources and capital repatriation generated a global inflow of $26 billion during the same period—also an historic amount.

[7]For more on the markedly different nature of Mexico's current deficit in 1981 and the one that developed after 1990, see Roberto Salinas León, "Don't Cry for Mexico's Current Account Deficit," *Wall Street Journal*, February 21, 1992, p. A13; and Salinas León, "Mexico's Stability Program Won't Weaken the Peso," *Wall Street Journal*, July 10, 1992, p. A13.

A pattern has become apparent since 1988: the widening of Mexico's current deficit has been accompanied by consistent growth in foreign investment flows and capital repatriation. Thus, capital account surpluses have been used to finance current account deficits. As such, total foreign investment during the Salinas administration stands at $28 billion—more than twice the amount of all existing foreign investment when Salinas assumed office.

The close relationship between the current and capital accounts reflects the positive impact of Mexico's growth-oriented economic policy. The crucial point is that the growth in Mexico's latest current deficits is not the outcome of government borrowing to finance inefficient public concerns. One result is that the government balanced its budget in 1992 and even realized a surplus of 0.4 percent of GDP. That is largely due to the fact that the current account deficit is being financed by private sources. As Aspe has explained, when there is a private-sector current account deficit, there is simultaneously a private-sector capital surplus. The differential between imports (28 percent growth in 1992) and exports (2 percent growth in 1992) is therefore necessarily covered by private flows of capital investment. The logical macroeconomic result is not hyperinflation and devaluation, but a resurgence of growth. Indeed, Mexico has grown at annual rates of 3 to 4 percent during the past five years, surpassing the rate of demographic growth every year.[8] Other examples of growing economies running current account deficits of up to 12 percent of GNP—nearly twice Mexico's level in 1993—in the early stages of trade liberalization are Japan, South Korea, and Spain.

Devaluation: The IMF's Bad Recipe

Advocates of devaluation ignore the fact that such a policy is not a viable option for the Salinas administration. First, it would not correct the alleged trade disadvantage represented by the $20-billion trade deficit in 1992. The policy objective of devaluation, of course, is to generate a trade advantage for exports, by adjusting relative prices between the United States and Mexico. That is a standard IMF recipe to ameliorate the deterioration of balance-of-payments conditions. Yet Mexico's experience of widespread economic instability concomitant

[8]See Pedro Aspe, "Mexico's Macroeconomic Adjustment and Growth Perspectives," in *Policy Implications of Trade and Currency Zones* (Kansas City: Federal Reserve Bank of Kansas City, 1992), pp. 156–58.

with devaluation between 1976 and 1987 shows that devaluation can lead to runaway inflation and massive capital flight while failing to improve the nation's balance of payments.[9]

Although in the short term, a substantial peso-dollar adjustment would improve Mexico's balance of payments, by making imported consumer goods and much-needed foreign intermediary durables and capital-intensive goods more expensive, devaluation would also lead to price instability and inflationary pressure. Higher domestic wages and prices then would cancel out the short-term benefits accrued to exporters. The resurgence of inflation would soon leave exporters in a far less competitive position.

Devaluation would pose another danger. Confidence in the economy has been bolstered by a 0.5 percent budget surplus relative to GDP in the first quarter of 1993 and by Salinas's announcement of an independent monetary policy. Observers widely believe that the annual 1.7 percent budget surplus target for 1993, four times the surplus in 1992, is feasible. A dramatic shift in the nominal exchange rate could destroy that climate of relative confidence.

Even though Mexican trade balances may remain a concern, the current supply-side strategy seeks to simultaneously reduce inflation through monetary and fiscal discipline and increase productivity through deregulation, thereby compensating for the loss of exchange-rate competitiveness. That strategy lies behind the numerous initiatives to foster direct private investment in housing, potable water distribution, mining, fishing, aquaculture, port and airport privatization, and secondary petrochemicals. In addition, forthcoming modifications in laws governing foreign investment will attract even more funds. The outdated 49 percent foreign ownership limitation has already disappeared for projects of $100 million or less. A new law will

[9]That argument has been developed at length by economist Alan Reynolds, who has cited the positive experiences of numerous countries with large current account deficits. See Alan Reynolds, "The IMF's Destructive Recipe of Devaluation and Austerity," Hudson Institute, May 1992. See also Reynolds and Jude Wanniski, *Mexico 2000* (Morristown, N.J.: Polyconomics, Inc., 1990), in particular the chapter entitled "The Theory behind Devaluation and Austerity." A similar point has been made by Melanie Tammen in her "Time to Retire the World Bank and the International Monetary Fund," in *Market Liberalism: A Paradigm for the 21st Century*, David Boaz and Edward H. Crane, eds. (Washington, D.C.: Cato Institute, 1993). As Tammen states, it is not "inherently sinful to remain debtor nations" if such expense is financed by "voluntary, private capital" (p. 320).

allow foreigners full investment access without quantitative restrictions in more than 30 sectors of the economy currently restricted to national ownership.[10]

The cause of Mexico's large trade deficits and investment flows—the need to guarantee access to competitive intermediary and capital imports, thereby helping to modernize the domestic productive plant—is certain to continue, especially in the framework of growing trade integration under NAFTA. NAFTA is expected to help institutionalize a highly favorable investment climate capable of attracting sufficient annual resources to finance Mexico's economic expansion. A study by the Ciemex-Wefa firm estimated that approval of NAFTA would lead to foreign investment of up to $17 billion per year, while a rejection of NAFTA would cause a loss of $4 billion in potential investment, higher inflation, and decelerated economic growth. In the latter case, the current deficit would shrink to $10 billion annually, but so would capital inflows—an undesirable prospect for an underdeveloped economy seeking to attract badly needed investment flows from world financial markets characterized by acute scarcity.[11]

Official sources estimate that Mexico will require $150 billion in new investment and savings during the next 10 years to grow at the rates (6 to 8 percent per year) needed to service a rapidly expanding workforce (1 million new workers per year). The focus of concern should therefore be less on how to restrain the predictably expanding trade

[10]NAFTA is expected to improve the climate for foreign as well as domestic investment. The investment chapter of the trade accord was crafted to foment greater private participation in the reconstruction of the productive plant. Two aspects stand out as major improvements over the current legislative framework: first, elimination of performance requirements (for example, export requirements, domestic content, technology transfers, and so on) and guaranteed full national treatment to foreign investors; and second, elimination of highly discriminatory practices in the assignment of investment projects. As economist Rogelio Ramírez de la O points out, high capital inflows spurred by this new framework mean that private-sector current deficits will remain high—in the area of 7 to 8 percent of GDP—in the first stages following the implementation of NAFTA. See Rogelio Ramírez de la O, "The North American Free Trade Agreement from a Mexican Perspective," in *Assessing NAFTA: A Trinational Analysis*, Steven Globerman and Michael Walker, eds. (Vancouver: Fraser Institute, 1993).

[11]See Hiram Ordoñez Morales, "Ocasionará Pérdidas Notables a la Economía Mexicana el Rechazo del TLC," *El Economista* (Mexico City), May 17, 1993, p. 32. The world capital shortage derives, of course, from such factors as the high costs of German reunification, the reconstruction of East European economies, and Latin America's newfound friendliness to private capital.

deficit and more on how to guarantee sufficient incoming capital and its use to finance productive domestic enterprises. For that, Mexico needs more liberal laws governing foreign investment, solid legal protection for private property rights, and more tax and regulatory incentives—all of which would help to stimulate Mexico's export potential. Domestic exporters will benefit far more from increased productivity, better high-technology equipment, and access to competitive private credit than from the artificial stimulus of a devaluation or official assistance.

Thus, Mexico should not deviate from its current monetary and exchange-rate policy but rather continue to liberalize its economy—such as an overly concentrated capital market, with a 30 percent limit on foreign ownership of nonvoting stock of the newly privatized banks. Mexico, in other words, needs trade, not aid.

Trade, Not Aid: The Role of NAFTA

The phrase "trade, not aid" represents one of the Salinas administration's principal selling points for NAFTA. The catchphrase is self-explanatory. NAFTA will enable Mexico to enjoy membership in the world's largest market made up of 360 million consumers with a total output of $6.2 trillion. The agreement offers Mexico the opportunity to diversify its trade structures, attain higher levels of domestic competitiveness, and create jobs for the country's rapidly expanding workforce.

Freer trade through NAFTA will help increase the efficiency of Mexican producers and maximize Mexico's comparative advantages in four ways. First, it frames long-term rules of commercial exchange, which Mexico needs for improved business organization. Second, it will enable small and medium-size businesses to gain from economies of scale. Third, it will foster specialization and more efficient production methods in order to service foreign markets. Finally, NAFTA guarantees access to a much larger market in which regulatory and bureaucratic burdens have been reduced—also crucial if domestic businesses are to offer higher quality goods at lower prices.

Although the average U.S. tariff to outside countries is only 4 percent, many U.S. trade barriers to Mexican products remain. Some 111 Mexican-made products face a tariff of at least 20 percent while goods such as tobacco, brandy, beer, footwear, textiles, and ballpoint pens face levies as high as 50 and 60 percent. Access to a U.S. market free of tariff barriers for those and other products will provide important sources of growth and opportunities to strengthen comparative advantages.

Under NAFTA, tariffs on 84 percent of Mexico's nonoil exports (7,300 goods) will be immediately phased out, thereby giving those products unrestricted access to the U.S. and Canadian markets by January 1, 1994. Moreover, such goods will no longer be hindered by quotas and other similar nontariff barriers. Although the Generalized System of Preferences—a trade arrangement whereby developed countries give preferential treatment to imports from developing countries—already gives many Mexican goods duty-free status in the U.S. market, nontariff barriers remain significant. In this respect, then, NAFTA will afford producers enormous benefits.

Similarly, under NAFTA tariffs on 40 percent of U.S. and Canadian goods will be eliminated on the same date. Most of those products are high technology and modern equipment. Thus, Mexico will reap the competitive advantages of importing sorely needed capital and intermediary goods free of tariff and nontariff barriers.

NAFTA may be less a trade accord for Mexico than an investment strategy needed to stimulate large flows of new capital investment. (In this way, of course, it represents an additional repudiation of the debt-backed public-sector strategy of the 1970s and 1980s in which the government stimulated aggregate demand by massively expanding the state sector.) At a time of considerable scarcity in global financial markets, NAFTA will help Mexico to continue to attract capital by consolidating its investment regime. The accord does so by offering investors long-term institutional guarantees so that the government, whatever its ideological orientation, will be bound to follow good public policy. In essence, NAFTA binds Mexico to the norms established within the trilateral trade framework.[12]

Unfinished Business

It is thus understandable that concern about the weight of Mexico's foreign debt for public undertakings has been replaced with concern

---

[12]For more on the strategic role of NAFTA, see Luis Rubio, "Mexico: Debt and Reform," in *In the Shadow of Debt* (New York: Twentieth Century Fund Press, 1992), pp. 119–23.

about attracting overseas capital to finance private-sector projects. The latter worry is provoked by the fact that the government is maintaining high-yield interest rates to attract world capital. As a result, an estimated 70 cents of every dollar in incoming investment is absorbed by short-term portfolio projects and treasury certificates. That type of investment, sometimes called "quicksilver capital," is highly volatile and particularly dependent on investor perception. The obvious danger of the government's high interest rate policy is that the speculative capital attracted both fails to expand productive employment opportunities and can flee overnight as a result of changes in investor expectations.[13]

Thus, as economist Rogelio Ramírez de la O pointed out, the financial requirements of sustaining the large and costly imports of machinery and materials, expected to be $70 billion in the first years following NAFTA implementation, mean that the government must relax restrictions in the energy and financial services sectors in order to avoid depleting international reserves and further expanding public-sector debt. Ramírez estimated that without such changes, public borrowing will escalate to $5 billion per annum.[14]

Mexico's inadequate investment strategy reflects the lack of attention to the need for profound institutional reform in the country's property rights regime. As economist Sergio Sarmiento has correctly observed, the current trade and economic liberalization program should have a "legal complement" based on reliable private property ownership.[15] The absence of legal security for rights, Sarmiento says, "represents a hidden tax that increases the cost of doing business in Mexico."

Sarmiento's claim understates the problem. The so-called economic chapter—articles 25 through 28—of Mexico's constitution severely undermines private property rights. The first two of those articles, for

[13]For an expanded discussion on the thesis that competitive forces drive the flow of today's capital, see Dwight Clark and Richard B. McKenzie, *Quicksilver Capital* (New York: Free Press, 1991).

[14]Ramírez de la O, "A Mexican Perspective," pp. 80–81.

[15]Sergio Sarmiento, "Seeking a Legal Complement to Mexico's Opening Market," *Wall Street Journal*, April 3, 1992, p. A13. For a more detailed assessment of Mexico's lack of property rights, fully secured by the rule of law, see Arturo Damm, *Liberalización en México* (Mexico City: Edomex, 1991), pp. 30–36; and Roberto Salinas León, "Legal Reform and Institutional Reliability," *El Financiero International*, June 12, 1991, p. 8.

example, establish the basis for state "rectorship" of economic affairs, while the second two define the criteria for government control of specific areas of the economy. All four articles are incompatible with the goal of ensuring a reliable and long-term climate of investor confidence.

Articles 25 and 26 state that the government has the legal right to "coordinate, conduct, orient, and direct" national economic activity and to frame a "national system of democratic planning." Similarly, article 27 declares that all land and water are the property of "the nation" and are to be distributed accordingly. The article also endows the executive with exclusive responsibility to determine how such resources will be managed and allocated. In practice, of course, that has meant that the ruling party, Partido Revolucionario Institucional, has had the final say on who owns what and for how long. Thus, economic authoritarianism in Mexico has become institutionalized.

Finally, article 28 defines the criteria for "strategic and primary" areas—that is, those sectors of the economy whose ownership is exclusively reserved for the state. The provision also gives the legislative branch authority to determine what sectors qualify as "strategic" and power to expropriate property on the grounds that it constitutes a "public utility." As such, article 28 allowed the Mexican government to national-ize, among other industries, the commercial banking system in 1982.

Mexico should declare a moratorium on the concept of state rector-ship, right to seize private property, and duty to run certain industries enshrined in the Mexican constitution. Although that would require a broad-based revision of current law and the constitution, such a revision would be among the most welcome changes in that Mexico could gain full advantage of NAFTA-based investment and trade growth.

Conclusion: Problems and Prospects for a Free-Market Mexico

The status of Mexico's debt problem is closely related to the government's implementation of market-oriented reform. Economist Luis Rubio summarizes that point:

> With economic reform, Mexico has managed to get a positive response from the banking community, and debt no longer looks insurmountable. With the success of Mexico's reform, the whole theory of development may have to be reconsidered. The traditional path to development was based on the assump-

tion that "infant-industry" protection and a strong government hand in the economy were keys to economic development. To the extent that liberalization, privatization, deregulation and freer markets work in Mexico, the development concept will have to look different in the future.[16]

Though barely emerging, Mexico's new development concept is based on the need for permanence of market reforms. Indeed, Mexico's underdeveloped and undercapitalized economy cannot afford inconsistent public policy.

Fortunately, establishing free trade not only benefits countries practicing free trade but also encourages additional market-oriented moves. Since 1986, trade liberalization in Mexico has forced the government to dramatically reform agriculture, privatize ports and airports, introduce private management of highway infrastructure, deregulate the provision of water, privatize telecommunications, and so on. Extant economic structures have also had to become more competitive.[17]

Indeed, Mexico's free-trade policy underpins an aggressive and continuing reform process. The Salinas program has resulted in budget surpluses, capital account surpluses, price stabilization, and exchange-rate stability to name a few achievements. The government's market-based direction contrasts sharply with the policies of the 1980s, which so often were subsidized by multilateral aid, guided by IMF advice, and resulted in desperate government bailouts to avoid default on massive public-sector debt. To be sure, essential reforms must still be implemented, particularly in the area of property rights, to consolidate the shift from aid to trade. But far-reaching changes, such as the 1992 agrarian reform that assigned rural workers full ownership rights to their lands, the 1990 reprivatization of the bank system, and the 1993 grant of independence to the central bank, provide solid evidence that Mexico is attempting to replace official debt dependence with private trade and investment.

There is good reason to believe, therefore, that Mexico's institutional reforms will ultimately seal the transition to a market economy. An

[16]Rubio, p. 123.

[17]The basis of that argument was developed by Lawrence H. Summers, "Regionalism and the World Trading System," *Policy Implications of Trade and Currency Zones*, pp. 299–300; see also Roberto Salinas León, "Free Trade and Free Markets" for a more complete application of that argument to Mexico's economic reform and trade liberalization process.

open trading policy, especially in the context of NAFTA, is strategically important in that it forces domestic changes in public policy that link economic growth to the institutional conditions of a prosperous economy. A free-trade regime such as NAFTA locks in market reform and thus produces a long-term, attractive investment climate.

Access to foreign markets, especially the U.S. market, is important to Mexico. More critical, however, is the country's need for an improved investment climate and continued trade liberalization, even if it is unilateral. Only then will the Mexican economy fully rid itself of the legacy of the previous regime of foreign aid dependence and achieve sustainable development.

From 1982, when Mexico announced that it would default on its interest payments, to the implementation of broad-based market reform a decade later, the Mexican state has squandered an incredible amount of money—$127.5 billion—to service its foreign debt. In interest obligations alone, Mexico has paid an amount equal to almost one-third of its annual GDP—$92.5 billion—during that period. Since market reforms were initiated, moreover, the government has continued to rely on more aid and new debt. Nevertheless, Mexicans have come to realize that what their country needs is trade, not more aid. It is hoped that the popular realization—that only Mexicans can develop a more global and competitive economy for themselves and that such an approach represents Mexico's only viable alternative for ensuring sustained economic growth—will be both reflected in the policy of future Mexican governments and respected by the World Bank, the IMF, and the numerous other international aid agencies. If that happens, Mexicans may finally have a chance to create a prosperous and free society.

10. Brazilian Hyperstagflation: The Case against Intervention

Paulo Rabello de Castro

Inflation is always and everywhere a monetary phenomenon.
—Milton Friedman, 1963

Brazilian rulers and their misguided counselors—both foreign and domestic—are solely responsible for the predicament of our national economy. Neither Brazil's history, nor its people, nor its external debt, nor even its tragic educational and health plight can be blamed for the country's unprecedented mixture of persistent stagnation (zero per capita growth) and extreme inflation (over 20 percent per month on average) experienced during the last 10 years. Nor can production factor shortages, whether capital or labor, or financial constraints—due to balance-of-payments deficits or lack of domestic savings—explain the extent of the slump of the Brazilian economy. The roots of such a pervasive phenomenon must be sought elsewhere.

Hyperstagflation flourishes on general mistrust. Only a dramatic misguidance of economic policies combined with overt political rent-seeking, populist practices, not the rational behavior of business-people and the public, could lead to such disarray in Brazil. Politicians have repeatedly made poor economic analyses and implemented hetero-dox plans that have interrupted domestic production and markets.

Meanwhile, bad advice from international agencies during the past decade—especially from the International Monetary Fund (IMF) and the World Bank—has compounded the Brazilian malady. The IMF's basic prescription, for example, remained its variant of fiscal austerity: the conventional wisdom to cut expenditures and raise taxes. The IMF has completely disregarded the main issue, namely, why Brazilian economic production tends to contract instead of expand, unresponsive to

The author is grateful to Marcio Ronci of the Getulio Vargas Foundation, whose coauthored paper on Brazilian hyperstagflation (unpublished, 1991) provided the basis for this chapter. Helpful assistance from research associates Sheila Gaul and Carlos Alexandre da Costa of R.C. Consultores is also acknowledged.

187

nominal stimuli but very sensitive to any perception of extra uncertainty in the macroeconomic environment. As a result, the fund's standard advice became meaningless in Brazil's hyperinflated environment.

Even if the IMF's adjustment programs had been better designed, the puzzle remains as to how to enforce them. The fund has failed repeatedly, agreeing to at least 10 letters of intent with various Brazilian administrations. In fact, if there are no solid institutional grounds— whether ethical, legal, or monetary—upon which to lay the foundations of a balanced budget as required by the IMF, it becomes virtually impossible to achieve any positive results from the IMF's assigned therapy.

Likewise, all of the adjustment programs funded by the World Bank in the recent past were doomed to failure since they assumed that the appropriate financial incentives (i.e., more loans) would convert the political logic of an interventionist government into a free-market champion. Alas, the World Bank had no such effect. The tendency of any populist-prone administration is always to intervene more and resist any legal-institutional development that might threaten the authority's ability to intervene.[1] Thus, World Bank adjustment credit tended to reinforce rather than curtail the government's leverage, increasing its role compared to alternative private sources as a long-term corporate lender. Enhancing the clout of public financial institutions (federal and state banks) in this way induced a substitution effect of public for private lending sources, severely weakening the Brazilian financial markets. In the current literature about foreign aid, not enough emphasis has been placed upon the critically negative side effects of public loans on the structure of a recipient country's financial system. In Brazil, private financial resources for private uses—especially in agriculture and small businesses—have dwindled in the face of uncompetitive concessional loans provided by public banks with foreign aid funding (see Figure 10.1). Such an adverse combination of foreign misguidance and domestic political mischief by the conservative classes has contributed to a very painful expansion of Brazil's hyperstagflationary experience.

---

[1] For a detailed discussion of the relationship between political populism and institutional backwardness, see Paulo Rabello de Castro and Marcio Ronci, "Sixty Years of Populism in Brazil," in *The Macroeconomics of Populism in Latin America*, Rudiger Dornbusch and Stanley Fischer, eds. (Chicago: University of Chicago Press, 1991).

Figure 10.1
LOANS IN BRAZIL BY BANKING GROUPS, 1991

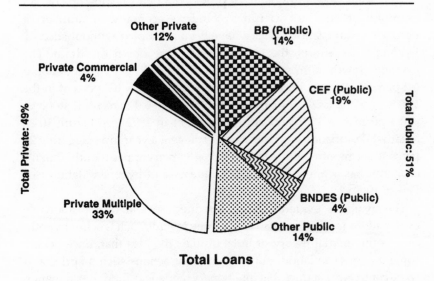

Total Loans

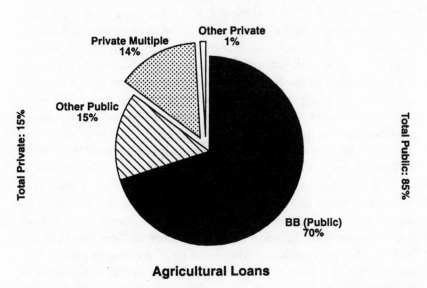

Agricultural Loans

NOTE: BB = Banco do Brasil, CEF = Caixa Econômica Federal, BNDES = Banco Nacional de Desenvolvimento Econômico e Social.

Brazilian Hyperstagflation

The recent years in Brazil have provided a rich kaleidoscope of bad examples of how not to run a country's economy. A number of heterodox stabilization policies have been attempted without success. Despite those efforts, the economy has gone down the drain. The average growth of gross domestic product (GDP) per capita of about 6.2 percent per year in the 1970s turned into a sorry 0.7 percent in the 1980s. In 1990, GDP per capita fell to about −6.0 percent; it stood at −0.3 percent in 1991 and at −2.2 percent in 1992 (see Figure 10.2). Meanwhile, inflation has risen from 20 percent a year to a staggering 20 percent per month, with peaks of up to 80 percent per month. Brazil's economy has actually become a unique case of hyperstagflation (see Figure 10.3).

The available evidence has discredited several once-fashionable explanations for the Brazilian crisis. They include such fanciful hypotheses as the inertial theory of inflation (i.e., the idea that, once people come to expect inflation, only government actions such as price and wage controls can reduce that inflationary tendency), the debt-stagnation hypothesis (i.e., the idea that the public debt represents such a burden on the economy that it is the primary cause of economic stagnation), and the disruption of public finances as the origin of growth stagnation. All of those explanations, nevertheless, have provided excuses for the government to intervene in the economy to perpetuate the status quo, while avoiding sorely needed institutional changes.

It is noteworthy that throughout the entire period, international agencies such as the IMF and the World Bank have been unable to diagnose the cause of Brazil's hyperinflation and develop a corresponding therapy. On the contrary, the international economic bureaucracy has flirted with most of the different Brazilian plans launched in the second half of the 1980s. The World Bank expressed sympathy for the inertial theory of inflation even before the stabilization scheme known as the first Cruzado plan was launched in 1986. The IMF also backed other interventionist schemes, such as the Bresser plan of 1987 and the Summer plan of 1989. (See Table 10.1 for more details about Brazil's various stabilization plans.) Those plans were based on the fallacy that government can instill market confidence through the

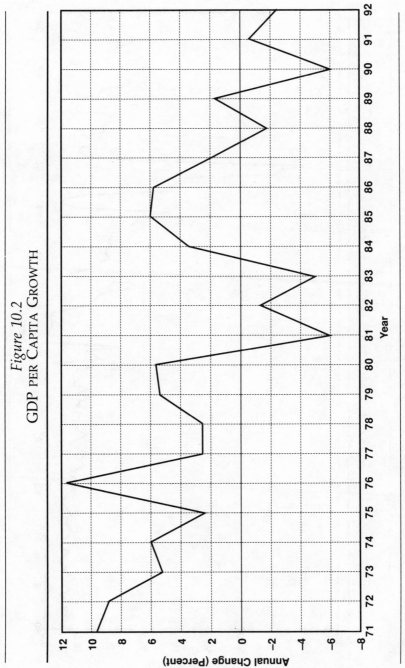

Figure 10.2
GDP PER CAPITA GROWTH

SOURCE: Fundação Instituto Brasileiro de Geografia e Estatística.

191

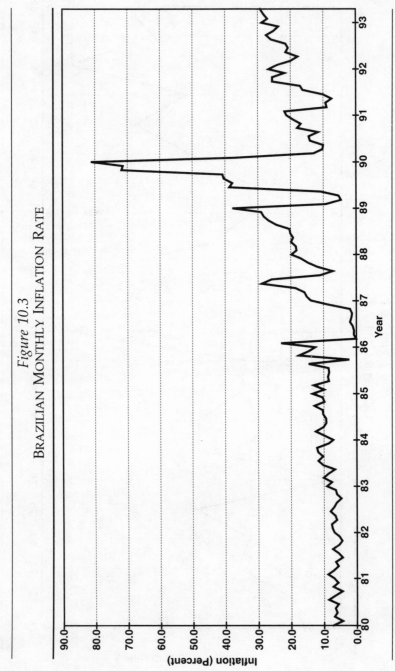

Figure 10.3
BRAZILIAN MONTHLY INFLATION RATE

SOURCE: Getúlio Vargas Foundation.

Table 10.1
COMPARISON OF FIVE ATTEMPTS TO STABILIZE THE BRAZILIAN ECONOMY

Plan	Goals	Results
Cruzado, Feb. 1986	Price and wage controls Loose fiscal and monetary policies No structural reform Full de-indexation New currency: cruzado	Prices, wages, and the exchange rate were held for six months only Accelerated growth but not sustainable Balance-of-payment crisis ensued
Bresser, June 1987	Price and wage controls Fiscal adjustment External debt reduction attempted No de-indexation No new currency	Prices and wages were held down for three months No fiscal adjustment performed Failure of external debt negotiations Loose monetary policy Recession Good trade balance performance
Summer, Jan. 1989	Price and wage controls High interest rates Fiscal adjustment Partial de-indexation New currency: cruzado novo	Prices and wages were held down for two months Monetary policy became loose No fiscal adjustment Default on external debt Daily indexation was introduced Hyperinflation threshold Falling external trade surplus

(Continued on next page)

Table 10.1—Continued
COMPARISON OF FIVE ATTEMPTS TO STABILIZE THE
BRAZILIAN ECONOMY

Plan	Goals	Results
Collor I, Mar. 1990	Price and wage controls Tight money Fiscal adjustment Free exchange rate New currency: cruzeiro Blockade of all financial assets Temporary external debt default Contractors' and bond market debt default No de-indexation, except for wages	Prices and wages were freed two months later Money supply highly unstable and increasingly loose Fiscal adjustment was short-lived Dirty floating of the exchange rate Pervasive uncertainty Productive sector disorganization, recession bias Poor trade balance performance
Collor II, Feb. 1991	Price and wage controls Full de-indexation Adjustment of public prices Reduction of import tariffs	Prices and wages were held down for three months A reference index rate was created and became an informal index used in most of the contracts Inflationary resurgence rapidly resulted in public prices falling in real terms

"visible hand" of price freezes, central planning, and bureaucratic controls. Such has been the rhetoric of populism in Latin America for decades.

But Brazil's domestic crisis stems from the interventionist model the country inherited from the authoritarian Vargas period of the 1930s.

Since then, state intervention in the goods and factors markets has become excessive and has led to growth stagnation. Such policies, especially those related to subsidized public lending, have had a devastating effect on savings and investment as well as on flows of private financing from abroad. The potential growth rate of the Brazilian economy has been severely curtailed as a result. The slump of fixed capital investment and the increase of capital flight are clear evidence (see Figures 10.4 and 10.5).

Devastating Effects

State economic intervention had shown its devastating effects even before the debt crisis of the late 1970s or the public finance crisis of the mid-1980s. The first signs of Brazilian economic stagnation can be traced to the mid-1970s when the productivity of physical capital and labor began to slow. The capital-output ratio grew significantly: it was about 2.1 in 1965–74, 4.0 in 1975–81, and 6.0 in 1981–89. In other words, the economy now requires as much as three times more capital to produce the same quantity of goods and services than it required in the 1960s.

Meanwhile, as a result of the country's lack of a well-functioning institutional framework (e.g., unresponsive democracy, unreliable legal system, pervasive corruption, and political instability), the central bank has covered the public deficit by printing unredeemable money. Politics has therefore always prevented the controller of currency from pursuing an independent monetary policy to fight inflation, which has been rising steadily since the early 1970s.

After the first unsuccessful IMF-backed attempts to control inflation from 1981 to 1984, an imaginative diagnosis of the Brazilian inflationary process emerged, based on the idea that there existed a certain degree of inertia in the course of rising prices and wages. That inertia would be produced by widespread indexation of wages and contracts, which meant that tomorrow's inflation would be significantly influenced by today's rates. According to that analysis, tight fiscal and monetary policies would have little effect upon inflation and would lead only to recession. The analysis would justify imposing a price freeze to curb the inflationary memory (that is, the so-called inertia) and to coordinate economic agents' decisions.

Ever since the failure of the Cruzado plan of 1986, which was based on the inertial hypothesis, more attention has been given to the

195

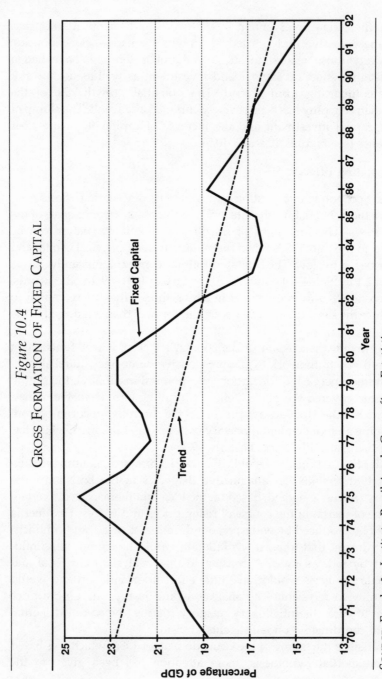

Figure 10.4
GROSS FORMATION OF FIXED CAPITAL

SOURCE: Fundação Instituto Brasileiro de Geografia e Estatística.
NOTE: Based on real 1980 prices.

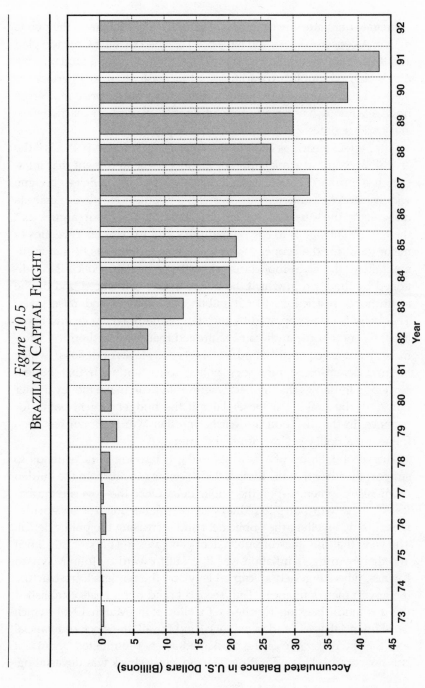

Figure 10.5
BRAZILIAN CAPITAL FLIGHT

aggregate demand side of the problem and, in particular, to the public deficit. A consensus seems to have been reached that the Cruzado plan and those plans that followed it backfired for lack of structural reforms that would cut public expenditure and increase taxes on a permanent basis. The government placed too much trust in the price and wage freezes without having effected substantial changes in its monetary and fiscal regimes.

After widespread rejection of the "inertial inflation hypothesis," the "fiscal" hypothesis explanation of inflation—the argument that inflation has primarily been caused by large budget deficits—became widely accepted and remains currently popular. However, analysts disagree on the causes of the deficits. The orthodox group argues that the main challenge is to cut expenditures and to raise tax revenues to make room for the proper monetary policy. Proponents of that argument share the fiscal-monetarist view that monetary policy is conditioned by the form in which the public deficit is financed and by the institutional restrictions to cut public expenditures and raise taxes. That view is also supported by the staff of the Brazilian central bank. More recently, some authors have argued that fiscal authorities determine an entire sequence of budget targets (surpluses or deficits), which in turn determine a monetary policy consistent with that budget sequence. It follows that monetary authorities can make money tighter now only by making it looser later if the budget targets point, for instance, in the direction of deficits. In other words, Brazil has been following a policy regime of fiscal dominance.

The second group of "fiscalists"—the heterodox bunch—tends to support the view that the budget deficit stems mainly from the burden of interest payments upon the public debt. Once the government has lost its creditworthiness, creditors charge higher interest on government bonds, swelling the public debt and increasing the public deficit. The view that the stock of public debt generates the bulk of the deficit and thereby triggers inflation was first put forward by John Maynard Keynes, who suggested a "capital levy" on the rentiers to restructure the government's finances. That second brand of fiscalists established the theoretical backing for the first Collor plan (March 1990), which froze financial assets and taxed, once and for all, the stock of financial wealth. The real value of the blockaded assets plummeted because it was not corrected by indexation. The monetary shock was devastating:

broad money (M4) shrank from 30 percent to 8 percent of GDP on the first day of the Collor plan.

The heterodox fiscal approach based on the idea of alleviating the burden of debt payments ultimately proved to be off-target. President Collor became disappointed with the team he had brought to his side to enact the Collor plan. Still, he let them try a second time in January 1991 with another price freeze and by redirecting savings toward a government fund (Fundo de Aplicações Financeiras). The government again failed to get the economy under control, thus leading the president to dismiss Finance Minister Zélia Cardoso and her team. Marcílio Marques Moreira, a former ambassador to the United States, replaced Cardoso. Through his links with the international community, he was encouraged to support the orthodox fiscal approach once more. Marques raised interest rates, attracted international hot money, constrained net internal credit through domestic recession, intensified a privatization program, and initiated discussions on a funds-raising tax reform.

Unfortunately, both views of the fiscal-crisis hypothesis, the orthodox (balanced budget) and the heterodox (interest burden), share the same emphasis on a policy regime of fiscal dominance. The only disagreement between the two groups involves the method of controlling the public deficit. In both cases, little attention has been paid to the institutional monetary setting, which, in fact, seems to provide a better explanation of the Brazilian economic crisis.

The Domestic Roots of Hyperstagflation

Brazil established a stable monetary regime in the 1964–67 period. During that time, Roberto Campos and Octavio Bulhoes, the minister of planning and the minister of the economy, respectively, conducted far-reaching fiscal and monetary reforms. They set up an independent central bank with enough power to carry on a reliable monetary policy. For instance, its board of directors could not be fired. To ensure coordination between the fiscal and monetary policies, the government created a monetary council. Although the finance minister presided over the council, the members of the central bank had a majority vote. In that way, the central bank had a strong say about policy.

However, soon after Campos and Bulhoes left office in 1967, the central bank had a confrontation with the military government, which

199

removed its president. Still, it was not until 1974 that the constitution of the monetary council was changed to give the Ministry of Finance decisive control over the central bank. Fortunately, as a result of the Campos-Bulhoes institutional reform, inflation had been kept down until the first oil shock of 1973. Indeed, as the budget deficits were small, they were easily financed without greatly expanding the monetary base.

Nevertheless, the regime of fiscal dominance established from 1967 onward was fraught with instability and prone to pork-barrel politics. In 1971, the government ordered the central bank to automatically finance the public deficit. The law did not require the government to include interest payments on the federal budget. Interest payments were financed either by issuing money or by contracting more public debt. That left the door open to reckless fiscal policies. The expansion of public investments during the late 1970s and the early 1980s, propelled by foreign aid money, made it extremely difficult to control federal and local expenditures. As a result, the federal government had to resort to printing money to finance its activities. The central bank became the lifeguard of bankrupt state banks. Once there was no monetary authority to discipline government, monetary policy followed fiscal policy passively. Thus, government finance became the art of manipulating monetary correction—a game in which short-term bonds issued to the public were sheltered from the inflationary corrosion provoked by the excessive money supply.

In fact, the monetary regime has increasingly operated with two currencies at the same time—the national currency (cruzeiros) and the interest-bearing treasury and central bank notes. The non-interest-bearing currency is mainly used by the poorest part of the population that has no access to the financial markets to hedge against inflation. The interest-bearing securities are used by business and the well-off part of the population. In effect, then, government securities are quasi money.

To avoid the "dollarization" of the economy and the consequent loss of seigniorage from issued currency, the Brazilian authorities have been accepting a gradual conversion of the non-interest-bearing currency into an interest-bearing one. (See Figure 10.6.) In real terms, however, the government has paid no interest. Those securities only

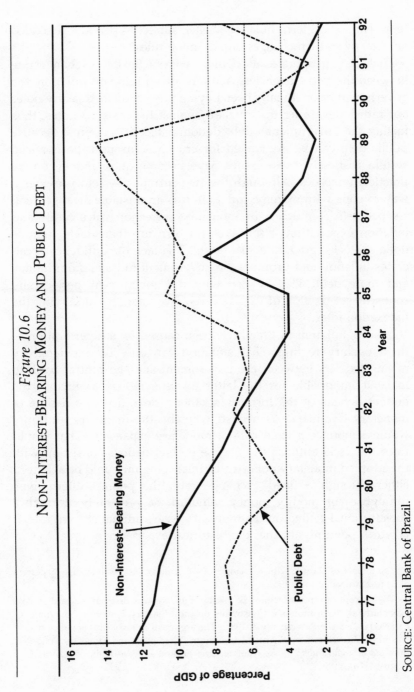

Figure 10.6
NON-INTEREST-BEARING MONEY AND PUBLIC DEBT

SOURCE: Central Bank of Brazil.

201

represent a short-term inflation shelter, subject to periodic concealed taxation by sudden changes of indexation rules.[2]

That system operates as if there were a flexible exchange rate between the two currencies. Actually, given rampant inflation, the government has not really been paying interest on its treasury notes but rather devaluing the cruzeiro against the treasury notes, thus raising the government's debt denominated in cruzeiros. Because public debt can be exchanged for cruzeiros through the financial system costlessly, those issues have become quasi money for all practical purposes. Although the two-currency system provides a way to cope with extreme inflation, it is an unstable arrangement. As people's confidence in monetary correction rules fades and inflation expectations rise, investors turn to other assets such as dollars, stocks, gold, and real estate. The lack of confidence accelerates inflation and prompts the government to issue more money and more debt. That is also why the government periodically confiscates a fraction of its securities' face value by modifying the indexation rates.

In sum, inflation in Brazil has been caused by a deterioration of the monetary regime. That situation can only be alleviated by raising barriers between the government and the central bank to make it impossible for the latter to issue money to finance the budget deficits of the former. In other words, a policy regime of monetary dominance is needed whereby the monetary authority would announce a fixed rule of monetary expansion. That would force the fiscal authority to choose budget deficits consistent with the adopted monetary policy rule.[3] Such a regime could be achieved either through a fixed exchange rate (the poorest alternative), through a commodity money standard, or, preferably, through a constitutional ceiling on the monetary base's annual growth rate. It is worth pointing out that the historical experience of great hyper-

[2]The actual loss of capital due to changes of indexation rules is estimated at 70 percent of its real face value since 1980.

[3]The concept of a policy regime of fiscal dominance was first put forward in Axel Leijonhufvud, "Constitutional Constraints on the Monetary Power of Government," *Economia delle Scelte Publiche*, no. 2 (1983.) The argument in favor of this policy regime was further developed by Bennet McCallum in "Credibility and Monetary Policy," in *Price Stability and Public Choice* (Kansas City: Federal Reserve Bank of Kansas City, August 1984).

inflations clearly shows that prices were controlled only when the power of issuing money was removed from the government.[4]

Hyperstagflation's Foreign Roots: Soft Money and Bad Advice

By condoning policies of fiscal dominance wherein the definition of hard currency plays only a minor role, the IMF has been displaying a persistent misperception about the actual source of hyperstagflation in Brazil. Although some have claimed that the IMF's advice theoretically derives from a "monetarist" viewpoint, the IMF's approach has had little monetary content in Brazil.

The IMF's perspective is basically financial: the agency is concerned about a country's ability to honor its foreign banking commitments. The IMF therefore targets a country's foreign reserves and its domestic net credit. No detailed IMF model exists, however, linking output to demand for money. The price level is not determined by the simultaneous equilibrium of such equations, but rather is determined from outside by a simple rule-of-thumb accommodation between the IMF negotiators and the country's representatives.

Such an approach is based on the conventional understanding that austerity (i.e., deep expenditure cuts coupled with a tax increase) would bring down the fiscal deficit and reduce the pressure to issue new money. Several agreements between the IMF and Brazil have tried this approach and none has succeeded.

That is not surprising since there can be no balancing of the budget if the currency regime is undisciplined. In other words, in a hyperinflated environment it is virtually impossible to bring the fiscal variables into line if the country has lost its standard of value. In such circumstances, the IMF's prescription has simply become bad advice.

It is quite odd, however, that the IMF has remained oblivious to the conceptual differences between standard inflation and hyperinflation. When we look back at the Brazilian experience in the past decade, it is evident that the IMF did not oppose any of the indexation rules that undermined the monetary regime and ultimately upset stabilization. In 1984, the IMF's letter of intent with Brazil introduced a target variable of "Public Sector Borrowing Requirement (PSBR) in real

---

[4]This last point is illustrated in Charles Maier, "Analogias e Diferenças: Ensinamentos das Inflações Europeias," International Conference on Hyperinflation, Fernand Braudel Institute of World Economy, São Paulo, August 1989.

terms." The so-called PSBR was introduced to facilitate reaching an agreement with the fund. In practice, that meant that the IMF authorized Brazil to ignore the effects of inflation on the public sector's balance sheet. In other words, "PSBR in real terms" means that everything goes on as if inflation no longer existed.

The "real PSBR" would apparently become neutral in terms of ongoing inflation, as if a significant price level variation simply did not matter with respect to its output and wealth effects in the domestic economy. The end result of that abstraction was to prevent the public from seeing the true targets of the IMF-Brazil agreements and so evaluate any actual progress regarding the announced goal of reducing inflation.

Condoning fallacious definitions might not be so damaging if the IMF were not also engaged in financing bad advice through both direct loans and collateral backing of creditor bank restructuring. The latter is particularly important because private banks, U.S. institutions in particular, have not actively searched for the true roots of hyperstagflation in Brazil. Such shortsightedness reflects how reliant private banks have become on the official IMF diagnosis of the Brazilian economy.

That behavior is partially understandable given the perceived transaction costs in evaluating the status of any proposed "stabilization" scheme. At the point when such a plan is proposed, and the IMF is called in to diagnose, prescribe, and collateralize, bad advice becomes another root—a foreign one—that perpetuates economic crisis in Brazil.

The IMF, myopic as it is about the institutional factors of currency stabilization in Latin America, and especially in Brazil, unfortunately has a counterpart—the World Bank. The two agencies' approaches admittedly differ: the World Bank is committed to fostering development, while the IMF has moved over the years from the more narrow goal of alleviating balance-of-payment problems to the broader goals of aiding the world's poorest countries and managing foreign debt "crises." Nevertheless, both agencies have had an overall negative effect on Brazil.

The World Bank's relationship with Brazil is quite old. It dates back to a first loan approved in 1949 (see Figure 10.7). Since then, the World Bank has approved about $19 billion in loans and disbursed $12.8 billion to Brazil. About $7.7 billion in debt is outstanding, to be paid back after the year 2000.

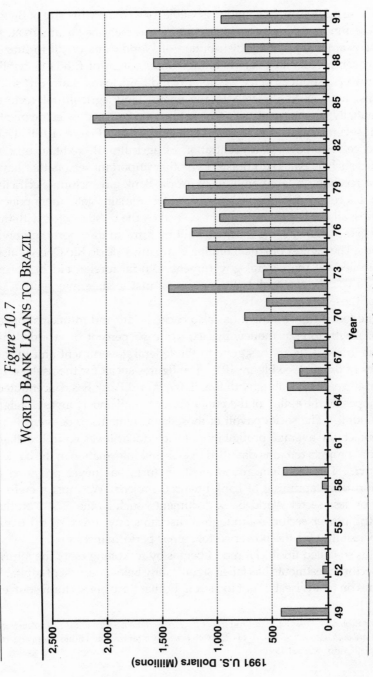

Figure 10.7
WORLD BANK LOANS TO BRAZIL

SOURCE: World Bank annual reports and international financial statistics.
NOTE: Values deflated by U.S. consumer price index.

Those figures might sound reasonable for a country the size of Brazil whose funding sources are scarce and investment needs are great. A close examination of the distribution of World Bank credit to Brazil, however, reveals an overwhelming concentration of funds to public borrowers. About 50 percent of total World Bank loans, many on "soft" terms, have been directed to the energy and agricultural sectors, essentially for the construction of publicly owned hydroelectric plants and several farm development programs (see Figure 10.8). That practice resulted in a concentration of agricultural credit in official banks such as Banco do Brasil. Two other important sectors that have been receiving a large amount of World Bank aid include electricity and telecommunications—both of which remain state monopolies. Almost all roads and railways are owned by the public sector, with the few exceptions of some railways built by firms to transport their own goods. The biggest Brazilian mining company, Vale do Rio Doce, is also controlled by the federal government. Official foreign aid has been unequivocally responsible for sustaining undue state intervention in all of those sectors.

The federal government has also backed state and municipal operations with foreign money. In fact, up to 50 percent of World Bank loans in recent years has gone to the federal government and to the states of Brazil. (See Figure 10.9.) The figures speak for themselves. In over 40 years of dealing with Brazil, the World Bank has concentrated its hopes on the ability of the public sector to judiciously invest foreign aid monies. The social payoff of those loans remains to be seen.

In fact, the average profitability of each dollar invested in Brazilian official projects remains classified (top secret) information in the bank's archives. The Brazilian government, in turn, has never provided a performance appraisal of bank-financed projects. We must therefore rely on less secret World Bank documents, such as the report on the electric power sector[5]—although it disclaims any direct World Bank responsibility for the power sector's poor performance.

This so-called unofficial report begins by reckoning that "the return on sector investments has fallen significantly below the cost of capital." It goes on to advise, but not too strongly, that "private-sector resources

[5]*The Evolution, Situation, and Prospects of the Electric Power Sector in the Latin American and Caribbean Countries*, vol. 1 of *Regional Report*, Organización Latinoamericana de Energía, Quito, August 1991.

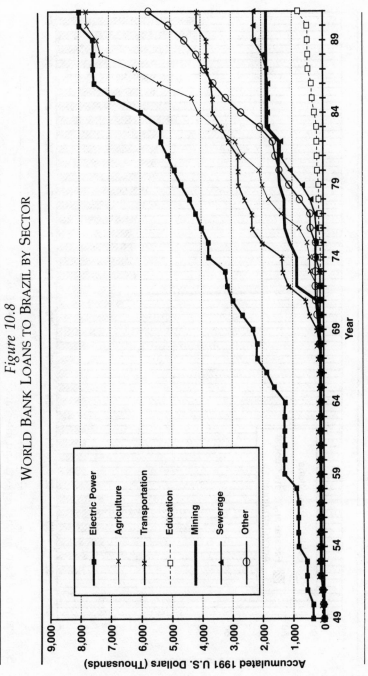

Figure 10.8
WORLD BANK LOANS TO BRAZIL BY SECTOR

SOURCES: World Bank, *Annual Reports* (1949–90); and Central Bank of Brazil.
NOTE: Values deflated by U.S. consumer price index.

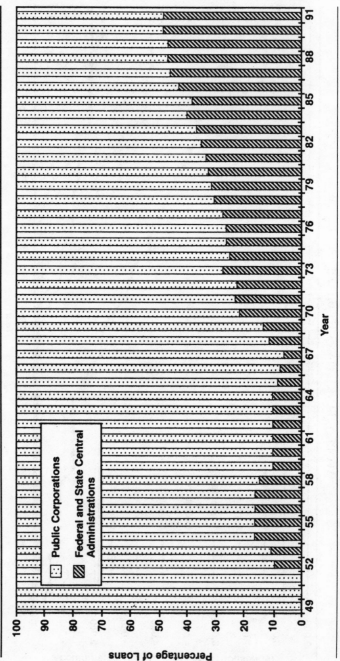

Figure 10.9
PERCENTAGE OF WORLD BANK LOANS TO BRAZILIAN BORROWERS

SOURCE: World Bank annual reports and international financial statistics.

NOTE: Public corporations include two private enterprises.

will be necessary to bridge the funding gap since future capital flows have to come as equity rather than as debt." Candidly, the report reminds the reader that, by 1950, "most of the LAC [Latin American and Caribbean] electric power sector was privately owned and served only the major population centers with very little effective regulation and little or no interconnection of systems." Good or bad? The reader cannot discern that from the report's statements until the very last page.

Despite some doubts expressed "about the ability of government-owned utilities to achieve such results"—i.e., overall efficiency—at the last minute the report introduces the dubious idea of corporate autonomy for public enterprises because "even if a utility is fully owned by the government it should be run on a commercial basis and regulated by a separate, autonomous branch of government." After 40 years of stimulating state monopolies in Latin America, the World Bank's recommendation does not represent much progress.

After all, it is no exaggeration to state that the World Bank has actively participated in the process of economic nationalization not only in Brazil, but in most Latin American and Caribbean countries. Through its support of soft governmental loans, foreign aid has prevented private businesses from expanding within the "national-ized" or state-dominated sectors and, worse still, has weakened private financial channels. That effect has been particularly impressive since public financial institutions in Brazil, supported by the federal government, have crowded out private lending sources from such sensitive sectors as agriculture and infrastructure. Foreign aid funding has become by far the most important source of long-term finance not only in agriculture (as shown in Figure 10.1), but also in areas such as water and sewerage, and roads and railways. Whatever role the private banking system might have played in providing long-term financing in those areas has been swept away by hyperinflation. The result has been a close interdependence between rent-seeking politi-cians and prospective borrowers (public or private) in agriculture, infrastructure, and capital goods.

Conclusion

Hyperstagflation is a curable disease. Milton Friedman has re-minded us of Irving Fisher's 1911 forewarning, quoted from the latter's *The Purchasing Power of Money*: "Irredeemable paper money has almost invariably proved a curse to the country employing it."[6] That simple truth has been repeatedly concealed by Brazilian rulers and their economic counselors.

National authorities are most responsible for perpetuating the status quo in Brazil. Populist attitudes have been maintained at the cost of institutional underdevelopment. Politicians, bureaucrats, and business-people in protected sectors of the Brazilian economy have all worked to prevent the public from clearly understanding the inflationary phenomenon. The price of such misguidance has been a dramatic impoverishment of the Brazilian people during the past decade.

Foreign aid has not helped to improve their situation. Instead of promoting the creation of a reliable monetary constitution, that is, a sustainable currency regime with at least an independent central bank, the IMF's prescriptions for Brazil have pertained mainly to financial issues. This fiscal approach, alas, has not advanced a better understanding of Brazil's hyperinflation.

The World Bank bears a fair share of the blame for creating the Brazilian crisis as well. The bank has extended soft credit to the Brazilian government for use to preserve inefficient state monopolies, resulting in economic stagnation. The expansion of foreign financial resources to the public sector, meanwhile, has dwarfed private-sector sources of finance.

If multilateral aid agencies now profess to back the private sector and market-oriented change, then they must redefine the macroeconomic policies their monies support. Even then, those agencies will probably not be instrumental in causing Brazil to implement a sound monetary regime and effective social policies.

[6]Irving Fisher, *The Purchasing Power of Money*, Reprints of Economic Classics (New York: Augustus M. Kelley, 1963).

11. Foreign Aid and India's Leviathan State

Shyam J. Kamath

With a debate now raging over whether further foreign aid programs financed by U.S. taxpayers are justified in the post–Cold War era, a review of the development experience of the recipient of the largest amount of foreign aid is instructive. India has received more foreign aid than any other developing nation—estimated at almost $55 billion since the beginning of its First Five-Year Plan in 1951.[1] It has long been an article of faith among development economists and policymakers that foreign aid is a necessary and central component of economic development, yet the record of Indian economic development since 1947 belies that view.

Foreign aid has directly financed and sustained India's centralized planning and control framework and thereby financed the growth of one of the noncommunist world's largest and most inefficient public sectors. In 1988–89, 101 of the country's 222 largest public-sector companies recorded losses and contributed to a federal deficit five times as large, in relative terms, as the U.S. budget deficit.[2]

India has had one of the lowest rates of growth of all developing countries and remains one of the poorest nations in the world. Today, after more than 45 years of planned economic development, India's annual per capita income remains around $300. Almost 40 percent of Indians live below the official poverty line, and the absolute number of Indians in that category increased sharply between the late 1950s and the mid-1980s. In short, India is a paradigmatic case of the failure of government-sponsored aid; it stands as a dramatic testimonial to why

[1]It is difficult, if not impossible, to get accurate totals of foreign aid when the number of donor countries and agencies and aid currencies exceeds 30. Data were compiled from various issues of the government of India's *Economic Survey*. (The $55-billion aggregate figure is historical-year, not current-year, dollars.)

[2]Steve Coll, "Budget Axe Endangers India's Socialist Icons: Massive Bureaucracy under Attack," *Washington Post*, February 26, 1991, p. A16.

such aid should go the way of the socialist development model it has bankrolled for decades.

A Brief Anatomy of India's Economic Failure

The centrally planned industrialization strategy of India's post-independence period has resulted in more than 60 percent of investment in the industrial sector going into public-sector enterprises. The private sector has been severely restricted by the banning of private-sector investment in major industries; a strict regime of industrial licensing; intrusive quantitative, price, and distribution controls; un-economic preferences for cottage, village, and other small industries; extensive labor-market and employment controls; and comprehensive external-sector controls.[3] Restrictions have included prohibitive tariffs, perhaps the developing world's most comprehensive and onerous set of quantitative controls and limits, an ever-expanding export control and subsidization scheme, and severe and often prohibitive restrictions on both direct and portfolio foreign investment.[4]

More than 20 million Indians are on the public payroll, and around 70 percent of all formal, above-ground employment is in the public sector. Confiscatory tax rates combined with a jungle of red tape—permission to open a hotel involves 45 applications and more than 25 different government agencies—have led to the growth of one of the largest and most thriving underground economies in the world, where an estimated 50 percent of India's economic activity is generated.[5]

From 1950 to 1985, per capita income in India grew at a meager average annual rate of 1.5 percent, compared with rates of 5.5 to 6.5 percent in the newly industrializing countries of Hong Kong, South Korea, Singapore, and Taiwan and 3 to 4 percent in the three Southeast Asian nations of Indonesia, Malaysia, and Thailand.

[3]Jagdish Bhagwati and Padma Desai, *India: Planning for Industrialization* (New Delhi: Oxford University Press, 1970) remains the classic reference on industrial planning (and plan implementation difficulties and failures) in India.

[4]See Jagdish Bhagwati and T. N. Srinivasan, *Foreign Trade Regimes and Economic Development: India* (New York: NBER and Columbia University Press, 1975).

[5]See Poonam Gupta and Sanjeev Gupta, "Estimates of the Unreported Economy in India," *Economic and Political Weekly*, January 16, 1982, pp. 69–75.

India's heavily centralized economic planning, its lack of openness to trade and investment, and its large accumulated inflow of foreign aid—mainly in the form of official development assistance—have set it apart from its neighbors.

Supporting Soviet-Style Planning in India

The interaction between a country's economic performance and official foreign economic assistance (hereafter referred to as foreign aid, in contrast to other voluntary, private foreign assistance) is difficult to isolate. Attempts to investigate the impact of foreign aid on economic development using statistical techniques have been inconclusive, although such evidence seems to indicate on balance that aid has had little or negative impact on development indicators such as savings, investment, and the growth of national income.[6] It is clear, however, that the majority of so-called developing nations that have received large amounts of foreign aid have failed to develop.

The history of official foreign aid to India is a classic example of the failure of foreign aid and its systematic facilitation of pervasive central planning. Foreign aid assumed a dominant role in India when a centrally directed heavy industrialization and "self-reliant" import-substitution strategy was adopted at the beginning of the Second Five-Year Plan in 1956–57. The plan's chief architects, Professor P. C. Mahalonobis and Prime Minister Nehru, patterned their socialist framework explicitly after the Soviet heavy-industry planning model. Nehru, India's prime minister for the first 17 years after independence, was heavily influenced by the ideals associated with the Bolshevik Revolution. In his 1936 presidential address to the Congress party, Nehru said that there was

> no way of ending the poverty, the vast unemployment, the degradation, and the subjection of the Indian people except

[6]See, for example, Keith Griffin and J. L. Enos, "Foreign Assistance: Objectives and Consequences," *Economic Development and Cultural Change*, no. 18 April 1970, pp. 313–17; V. Bornschier, C. Chase-Dunn, and R. Rubinson, "Cross-National Evidence on the Effects of Foreign Investment and Aid on Economic Growth and Inequality: A Survey of Findings and a Reanalysis," *American Journal of Sociology*, vol. 84, no. 3 (November 1978), pp. 651–83; Paul Mosley, "Aid, Savings and Growth Revisited," *Oxford Bulletin of Economics and Statistics*, no. 42, May 1980, pp. 79–85; and Donald Snyder, "Foreign Aid and Domestic Savings: A Spurious Correlation," *Economic Development and Cultural Change*, vol. 39, no. 1 (September 1990), pp. 175–81. The most comprehensive and detailed study of foreign aid emphasizing its negative impact is Paul Mosley, *Foreign Aid: Its Defense and Reform* (Lexington: University of Kentucky Press, 1987).

through socialism [and] the ending of private property, except in a restricted sense, and the replacement of the private profit system by a higher ideal of cooperative service.[7]

The underlying vision of Nehru and his associates that has molded India's economic policy since independence is further illustrated in his comments to a prominent Indian journalist in 1960:

We have accepted the socialist and cooperative approach . . . the planned and scientific approach to economic development in preference to the individual enterprise of the old *laissez faire* school. . . . Planning and development have become a sort of mathematical problem which may be worked out scientifically. . . . It is extraordinary how both Soviet and American experts agree on this. If a Russian planner comes here, studies our projects and advises us, it is really extraordinary how his conclusions are in agreement with those of, say, an American expert. . . . The moment the scientist or technologist comes to the scene, be he Russian or American, the conclusions are the same for the simple reason that planning and development today are almost a matter of mathematics.[8]

Aid Officially Promotes Comprehensive Planning

Indeed, in the 1960s India began to be heralded in the West as the epitome of rational, planned economic development. John P. Lewis, the dean of American foreign aid experts who had held prominent posts with the Council of Economic Advisers, the UN Reconstruction Agency, and the U.S. Agency for International Development's mission to India, argued thusly in his influential 1962 book, *Quiet Crisis in India:*

There is much less need now for [a] defense of the very concept of comprehensive economic planning in countries like India. . . . Today [such] planning is officially viewed as an essential concomitant of any national development that merits American assistance, and the United States government is urging such planning upon Latin American, African, and Asian governments that do not yet practice it.[9]

---

[7]Cited in V. B. Singh, ed., *Nehru on Socialism* (New Delhi: Government of India Publications Division, 1977), p. 67.

[8]Ibid., pp. 50–51.

[9]John P. Lewis, *Quiet Crisis in India* (Washington, D.C.: Brookings Institution, 1962), p. 115.

214

Lewis argued that India's planned development was the most feasible and desirable path for a country at an early juncture in the development process and that the decentralized market system was inappropriate, destined to fail, and had only led to the development of Great Britain and the United States because of "special circumstances." His book made an impassioned plea for vastly stepped-up levels of American aid to support the "rationally planned economic development" of India's Second Five-Year Plan.

Multilateral aid agencies such as the World Bank espoused a similar vision in their lending policies from the 1950s onward. The World Bank's *Fifth Annual Report (1949–50)* noted,

> The Bank would prefer to . . . base its financing on a national development program, provided that it is properly worked out in terms of projects by which the objectives of the program are to be attained.[10]

In the succeeding decades, the preference for national development programs made countries such as India, Tanzania, Indonesia, Ethiopia, and Mexico—which pursued centrally directed economic development plans—favored recipients of World Bank aid. But India received the most World Bank aid, an accumulated net amount of well over $20 billion in historical-year dollars (much more if measured in current dollars) from 1951 through 1989. Most of that $20 billion went to public-sector projects.

Although India has not become a communist or completely socialist country—its governments have always tolerated a substantial "private sector," which actively collaborates with the government to sustain monopolies and control the growth of competitors—India's comprehensive economic planning has been actively supported and reinforced by donor countries, international agencies, and the very nature of the aid-granting process. By requiring governments to undertake comprehensive development planning as a precondition for receiving foreign aid, donor nations and agencies actively abet the socialization of the developing world.

---

[10]World Bank, *Fifth Annual Report (1949–50)* (Washington, D.C.: World Bank, 1950), p. 8.

Banking on the Poor: The World Bank and India

India has been the World Bank's star patient and almost the raison d'être of its burgeoning growth. The bank's semiofficial historians, Edward Mason and Robert E. Asher, state:

> No country has been studied more by the World Bank than India.... India has influenced the Bank as much as the Bank has India.... This applies particularly to the Bank's conception of the development process—the role of government in the process [and] the need for grants, soft loans, and program assistance.... In the eyes of the Bank's management, India (because of its obvious needs and limited creditworthiness) offered the clearest justification for the creation [in 1961] of [the International Development Association] as its soft-loan affiliate [which makes zero-interest loans with 50-year maturities]; without IDA, the Bank could not have continued to be heavily involved with India.[11]

Indeed, India and the World Bank formed a lasting partnership that promoted centrally directed and coordinated nonmarket decisionmaking in the Third World. According to one commentator, that partnership made the World Bank "responsible for the rush to socialism in the Third World."[12]

The relationship between the World Bank and India illustrates all the characteristics of the foreign aid process that are emphasized by critics of such aid: a preference for national development plans, a bias toward large projects and unsuitable external models, greater government control over the economy, imposition of price and other economic controls, and the politicization of economic life.[13] That is clear in the following observation by Mason and Asher.

> The Bank conceived of its task as seeing that India's five-year plans got support, especially since India's needs for investment in infrastructure (railways, electric power, irrigation) matched the Bank's availabilities and expertise.[14]

[11]Edward Mason and Robert E. Asher, *The World Bank since Bretton Woods* (Washington, D.C.: Brookings Institution, 1973), pp. 675, 681–82.

[12]James Bovard, "The World Bank vs. the World's Poor," Cato Institute Policy Analysis no. 92, September 28, 1987, p. 1.

[13]See, for example, Peter T. Bauer, *Reality and Rhetoric: Studies in the Economics of Development* (Cambridge, Mass.: Harvard University Press, 1984), p. 46.

[14]Mason and Asher, p. 682.

India received its first World Bank loan on August 18, 1949, for development of the government-owned Indian Railways. That loan was followed by one for agricultural machinery for a large public-sector reclamation project and for the first stage of a large central government multipurpose project. With the establishment in 1960 of its "soft-loan" affiliate, the IDA, the bank began lending to India on highly concessional terms (zero interest and 50-year maturities—terms that in effect made those loans grants). The World Bank's commitments to India expanded rapidly thereafter.

Figure 11.1 shows the changing proportions of aid contributed by major donors at the end of selected years from 1961–62 to 1988–89. While the United States contributed 50 percent of total aid to India in 1961–62, the World Bank's share steadily increased through the years, and by 1988–89, it donated 69.3 percent of the total.

The majority of the funds received by India from the World Bank group, which includes three lending affiliates, has gone into the public sector. Government corporations that have been directly aided by World Bank funds include firms in the power, coal-mining, irrigation, oil, petrochemical, telecommunications, fertilizer, steel, mass transit, railway, airline, and cement sectors. Returns on concessional World Bank loans to projects in the power, coal-mining, fertilizer, steel, mass transit, railway, and cement sectors have been dismal; returns in the other industrial sectors have been positive only because of the nature of the product and the pricing policies of those industries (for example, oil and petrochemicals). The World Bank's continuing largesse to the Indian public sector is evidenced by the fact that currently some $16 billion in aid committed by the bank remains unused because the requisite rupee "matching funds" cannot be found either by the central government or by the state governments.

The effect of World Bank lending on one Indian town was described by the chairman of a private company there in a 1991 letter to Hoover Institution scholar Judy Shelton. That testimonial is worth quoting at length.

> [In response to] your comments on foreign aid on the CNN Crossfire show ... I would like to give you the following information on how the World Bank has ruined India by giving loans. In fact, it has given loans to bring structural change in the negative direction of going from [the] private sector to [the] public sector.

Figure 11.1
SOURCES OF EXTERNAL ASSISTANCE TO INDIA
(MILLIONS OF U.S. DOLLARS)

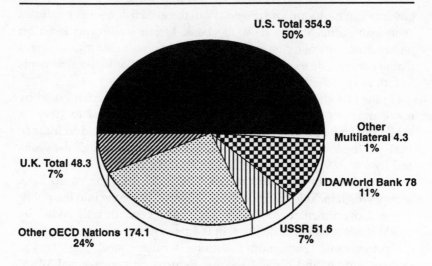

U.S. Total 354.9
50%

Other Multilateral 4.3
1%

IDA/World Bank 78
11%

USSR 51.6
7%

Other OECD Nations 174.1
24%

U.K. Total 48.3
7%

1961-62

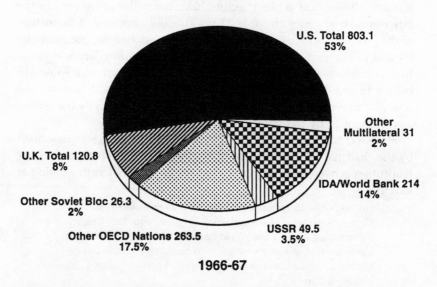

U.S. Total 803.1
53%

Other Multilateral 31
2%

IDA/World Bank 214
14%

USSR 49.5
3.5%

Other OECD Nations 263.5
17.5%

Other Soviet Bloc 26.3
2%

U.K. Total 120.8
8%

1966-67

NOTE: Percentages may not add to 100 because of rounding.

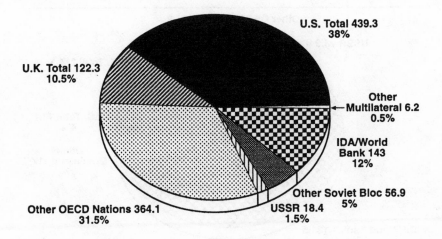

1971-72

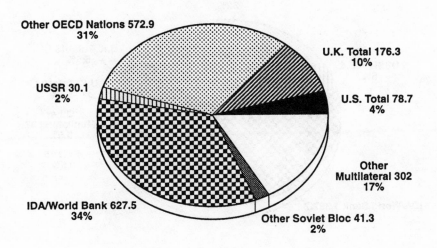

1976-77

(Continued on next page)

Figure 11.1—Continued
SOURCES OF EXTERNAL ASSISTANCE TO INDIA
(MILLIONS OF U.S. DOLLARS)

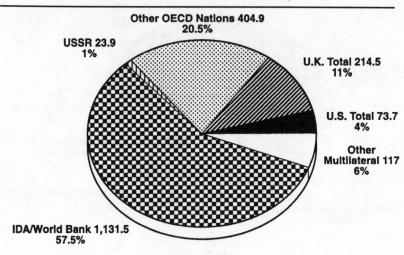

Other OECD Nations 404.9
20.5%

USSR 23.9
1%

U.K. Total 214.5
11%

U.S. Total 73.7
4%

**Other
Multilateral 117
6%**

IDA/World Bank 1,131.5
57.5%

1981-82

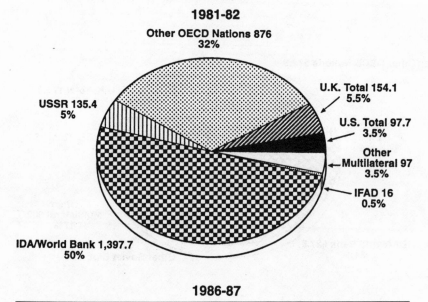

Other OECD Nations 876
32%

USSR 135.4
5%

U.K. Total 154.1
5.5%

U.S. Total 97.7
3.5%

**Other
Multilateral 97
3.5%**

**IFAD 16
0.5%**

IDA/World Bank 1,397.7
50%

1986-87

NOTE: IFAD = International Fund for Agricultural Development.

220

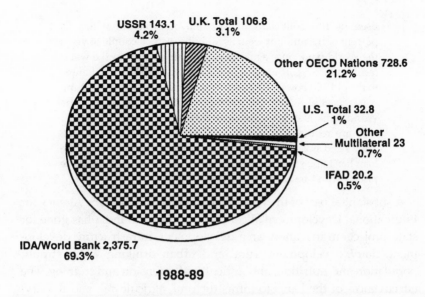

USSR 143.1
4.2%

U.K. Total 106.8
3.1%

Other OECD Nations 728.6
21.2%

U.S. Total 32.8
1%

Other
Multilateral 23
0.7%

IFAD 20.2
0.5%

IDA/World Bank 2,375.7
69.3%

1988-89

This town, Madurai had an excellent network of private busses giving efficient, good and punctual service. It was taken over by the government with [a] World Bank loan. Now we have nationalized transport which is continuously running in loss and giving extremely poor service. When the public sector company runs in loss, the World Bank insists on [an] increase in the fares until they get 15 percent return on investment as a condition for them to get [a] further loan. Then the public sector companies increase the fares. In reality, more than 15 percent return on investment could be obtained from these companies even after reducing the fares by 10 percent, if only the rampant corruption and inefficiency is removed.

The whole state of Tamil Nadu had several private busses running profitably and efficiently and they were all nationalized with World Bank loans and all the state-run transport corporations are running in loss. . . . Interestingly, the World Bank loans [were] used only to take over busses from [the] private sector and not to add new services where [the] private sector was not operating. In the same way, the World Bank is giving loans to [the government's] inefficient Railways, Telecomm system, etc. which can be run more efficiently by the private sector.

The World Bank has given [a] loan to this Madurai town to improve the water supply. Within a month the money was

221

used by the politicians to sink 100 borewells of which 50 percent of the amount went as [a] bribe. After a couple of years the World Bank once again gave [a] loan to improve the water facility. Once again, another 100 borewells were sunk right next to the old 100 borewells which were not in use. The same thing was repeated again. The corrupt politicians always use the World Bank loan since they can take up any project, whether they are required or not, just to get bribes from the project. They need not raise the tax to meet the project expense. The loan has to be repaid only by future taxes by which time these rascals won't be there.[15]

A substantial part of the World Bank's (as well as the U.S. Agency for International Development's) concessional loans to India has gone for state projects in irrigation, area development, infrastructure development, dairy development, rural and urban drinking water supply, population and nutrition, and agricultural extension and training. The effectiveness of the loans to infrastructural, agricultural, and tertiary-sector projects can be judged by examining an internal review by the World Bank Operations Evaluation Department of the bank's experience with rural development projects from 1965 through 1986. According to that review:

The most conspicuous project failures were in the large group of area development projects. . . . The audits to date of half of the area development projects judged them to have failed. . . . That form of area development project that came to be known as "integrated rural development" [performed] so poorly as to raise questions about the utility of that approach in many situations.[16]

Although a majority of those failed area development projects were in sub-Saharan Africa, the World Bank also provided aid to a number of large area development—especially integrated rural development—projects in India.

[15]Letter of August 21, 1991, to Judy Shelton from the chairman and managing director of a private company in Thenur, Madurai, India; the Cato Institute is holding the author's name in confidence in consideration of the political and economic climate in which he must continue to operate.

[16]World Bank, Operations Evaluation Department, "World Bank Experience with Rural Development, 1965–1986," Internal Report, 1987, p. viii.

Drowning in Aid—World Bank Loans for Public Irrigation

The major portion of the World Bank's lending to India for rural development has been for state-run irrigation systems. From 1971 through 1989, the bank provided concessional credits totaling some $3.8 billion to large-scale public irrigation projects in India. Worldwide, the bank currently devotes about 25 to 30 percent of its total lending program for agriculture to such projects, yet the real costs and returns of such endeavors have been widely criticized. One assessment, by Robert Repetto, reported:

> Public irrigation is heavily subsidized in the Third World as well as in the United States, and has become an enormous fiscal drain. Revenues collected from farmers in most countries cover barely 10 to 20 percent of the costs of building and operating the systems—less in many countries than the costs of operation and maintenance alone.... Neither farm beneficiaries, irrigation agencies, nor international banks are financially at risk for the success of irrigation investment, and so pressures for new capacity lead to a proliferation of projects, many of dubious worth. Benefit-cost analysis of such long-term investments is inherently speculative, and easily becomes overly optimistic when the political pressures of the pork barrel come into play.[17]

Public-sector irrigation systems everywhere are typically plagued with cost and time overruns, endemic inefficiency, chronic excess demands, and widespread corruption and rent-seeking. In India, government functionaries and system operators—who control the allocation of water supplies—routinely extort high rents from farmers. In spite of the web of problems associated with public irrigation systems, the World Bank continues to bankroll those wasteful projects in India and in many other nations. By 1986, large and medium-sized surface-water public irrigation schemes supplied about 40 percent of India's total irrigated acreage. The balance—60 percent—was supplied mainly by private (but heavily subsidized) groundwater irrigation and minor local surface irrigation schemes. The Indian Planning Commission itself has admitted the projects' fiscal failure.

---

[17]Robert Repetto, "Skimming the Water: Rent-Seeking and the Performance of Public Sector Irrigation Systems," World Resources Institute Research Report no. 4, December 1986, p. 1.

> In spite of large investments made in the irrigation sector and the phenomenal growth during the past 30 years, the returns from the investment, both in terms of yield as well as finance, are very disappointing. [And] the states are losing more than rupees 427 crores [1 crore = 10 million] per year on these irrigation projects.[18]

The huge amounts of World Bank aid to the irrigation sector in India led to a proliferation of projects far beyond the implementation capability of the government or the absorptive capacity of that sector. Despite the dismal performance of Indian irrigation and the large inefficiencies and waste involved, loan-maximization pressures at the bank and burgeoning demand on the part of Indian planners and administrators led to a cornucopia of lending that threatened to drown the Indian masses in corruption, rent-seeking, and displacement costs.

Private Irrigation Puts World Bank–Supported Projects to Shame

Private irrigation has a good track record of efficiently providing farmers with water, which translates into higher private returns. Even though private tubewell irrigation costs more than public irrigation, farmers are willing to pay the higher prices because of the higher returns they can get by using a reliable private source of irrigation. According to a U.S. Agency for International Development study on irrigation systems in India:

> Farmers in some areas with water control provided by private irrigation are willing to pay 6 to 9 times the water charges levied for [state-run] canal supplies. Millions of private tube wells, some equipped with piped distribution systems serving graded fields, are evidence of this.[19]

The greater efficiency of private tubewells is reflected in higher agricultural production, income, and cropping intensity.[20] In fact, farmers in public irrigation "command areas" fail to invest as much in land leveling, field channels, and crop configurations as do farmers

[18]Quoted in N. D. Jayal, "Emerging Pattern of the Crisis in Water Conservation," in *Indian Environment: Crises and Responses,* J. Bandyopadhyay et al., eds. (Dehra Dun: Natraj, 1985), p. 86.

[19]U.S. Agency for International Development, "Irrigation Development Options and Investment Strategies for the 1980s: India," Water Management Synthesis Project Report no. 6, July 1981; quoted in Repetto, p. 7.

[20]J. Thakur and P. Kumar, "A Comparative Study of Different Irrigation Systems in Western Uttar Pradesh," *Indian Journal of Agricultural Economics;* summarized in Repetto.

who are served by private or communal irrigation systems. As a result, output of food grains per hectare averages only 2 to 3 tons on canal-irrigated land and 5 to 6 tons per hectare on land irrigated by private tubewells.[21]

By 1985, the proliferation of new public irrigation projects—while existing ones in the process of completion, modernization, or rehabilitation were suffering gross time delays and cost overruns—led the Indian government to take the unprecedented and drastic action of proscribing all new starts during the Seventh Five-Year Plan (1985–90). In fact, at the end of the Sixth Five-Year Plan, 150 major and 400 medium-sized irrigation projects with an estimated cost to completion of more than $10 billion remained unfinished. The World Bank attributed the problem largely to "the proliferation of projects under construction, as [Indian] state governments succumbed to pressures to take up new projects whenever possible."[22] According to a brief prepared by the Environmental Defense Fund, India's

> large-scale irrigation projects have a poor record. In 1986, out of 246 large-scale irrigation projects that were started since 1951, 181 were still incomplete. In a speech in 1986 to state irrigation ministers concerning large-scale irrigation projects started after 1970, then Prime Minister Rajiv Gandhi stated "perhaps we can safely say that almost no benefit has come to the people. . . . For 16 years we have poured money out. The people have got nothing back, no irrigation, no increase in production, no help in their daily life."[23]

World Bank's Deadly Narmada Dam Project

Despite the impressive record of failure of public irrigation projects in India, the World Bank approved more than $1.2 billion in new irrigation credits for New Delhi between 1985 and 1990, including $150 million (of a total credit of $450 million) for the Narmada dam and river valley project. That dam project—budgeted at $3.2 billion—is the

---

[21]B. S. Dhawan, "Irrigation's Impact on the Farm Economy," *Economic and Political Weekly*, September 28, 1985, pp. 124–28.

[22]Leslie Abbie et al., "Economic Returns to Irrigation Investments in India," World Bank Staff Working Paper; cited in Repetto, p. 4.

[23]Environmental Defense Fund, "Environmental, Social and Economic Concerns Related to the World Bank–Financed Sardar Sarovar Dam and Power Project, and Sardar Sarovar Water Delivery and Drainage Project," Memorandum to Barber Conable, president of the World Bank, March 1991, p. 3.

single largest project of any type undertaken in India since independence. The threat of environmental damage, flooding of valuable agricultural and forest lands, destruction of critical ecosystems, and displacement of thousands of tribal and other communities has made the Narmada project (especially the component called the Sardar Sarovar project) one of the most hotly debated World Bank (and Indian) projects of all time. It is estimated that the project will flood around 1,000 square kilometers of forest and other land, destroy around 35,000 hectares of the country's meager forest cover, and displace more than 2 million people. An Indian government study has estimated that the dam will sharply increase the incidence of cholera, malaria, encephalitis, and other waterborne diseases.

The project was conceived in 1946, and the foundation stone was laid by Prime Minister Nehru in the early 1960s. Ever since, the project has been mired in controversy over the displacement of thousands of tribal people and farmers; the extent and distribution of benefits; and, more recently, the impact on the environment. The dam site has been the venue of demonstrations by hundreds of thousands of people. Indeed, the Environmental Defense Fund has estimated that the Sardar Sarovar part of the Narmada project alone will forcibly displace more than 100,000 tribal and rural people and lead to the submersion of around 14,000 hectares of valuable forest land and around 11,500 hectares of fertile agricultural land.[24]

In spite of a World Bank policy on involuntary resettlement, which requires that a resettlement plan be established *before* a project is approved, no comprehensive resettlement plan had been established for the Sardar Sarovar project; even the number of people to be displaced had not been determined. Only after intense public protests did the World Bank commission an independent report on the project, which criticized the "bank's appraisal of the project, the borrower's implementation and the bank's supervision work," forcing World Bank president Lewis Preston to admit that "it is clear that performance under these projects has fallen short of what is called for under Bank policies and guidelines."[25] Nevertheless, the World Bank did not withdraw its support of the project and actually proposed continuing

[24]Environmental Defense Fund, p. 1.

[25]Stephanie Gray and K. K. Sharma, "World Bank Admits Indian Dam Flawed," *Financial Times*, June 20–21, 1992, p. 4.

work on the dam while the recommended resettlement plans were being drawn up. In the end, the Indian government, unable to come up with the required resettlement plans, rejected further World Bank loans for the dam construction and pledged to continue the work on its own.

The Sardar Sarovar project would not have been the first World Bank undertaking to displace Indian villagers. One bank-financed project in Singrauli has forcibly relocated 200,000 to 300,000 of the rural poor two or three times, and in some cases even four or five times, over the past 25 years (each time with little or no compensation).[26] One specialist at the Environmental Defense Fund summed up the situation succinctly:

> The gap between the World Bank's stated goals and reality on the ground is growing. . . . The World Bank, rather than consistently aiding in alleviating Third World poverty, in reality has contributed to the marginalization and devastation of hundreds of thousands of tribal and indigenous people and rural poor in India, Indonesia, and Brazil. . . . *Worldwide, out of approximately 56 projects that the World Bank is financing involving resettlement, the Bank cannot document one single case where the population that has been resettled is better off than before or has reached the standard of living which they had before.*[27]

The International Monetary Fund: India's Perennial "Temporary" Reprieve

India was one of the first recipients of an emergency International Monetary Fund (IMF) loan after the IMF's founding in 1944, and (except for short periods of time) it has been on one or another IMF program ever since—that is, for more than four and a half decades. Several times in the 1970s India received short-term loans from the IMF for balance-of-payments support. Its biggest borrowing from the IMF was negotiated in 1980, when the combination of the oil shock of 1979 and a disastrous harvest led India to seek a $5.8-billion loan under the IMF's relatively new Extended Fund Facility. The loan's early repayment, due to a set of fortunate circumstances, caused India to be

---

[26]Statement of Bruce Rich during Hearing on Environmental Performance of the Multilateral Development Banks before the House Subcommittee on International Development Institutions and Finance, April 8, 1987; cited in Bovard, p. 6.

[27]Statement of Lori Udall on behalf of the Environmental Defense Fund concerning the social impact of forced resettlement in World Bank–financed development projects before the Congressional Human Rights Caucus, September 27, 1989, p. 4. Emphasis in original.

heralded as a developing nation that had matured and transcended the vicissitudes of uneven development. The fortunate circumstances included a string of good harvests, increasing remittances from Indians working in the Middle East, a surge of exports after the global recovery from the U.S.-led recession of 1981–83, and the tapping of the international credit market—then flush with recycled petrodollars—by Indian public- and private-sector companies.

During the mid and late 1980s, India borrowed extensively abroad—commercial borrowing as well as concessionary loans from such agencies as the World Bank—to finance its growing budget deficits. (In 1986, officials of India's central bank reported that new foreign commercial borrowing during the nation's seventh plan would total about $8.8 billion—in contrast, they noted, to the $20 billion in new commercial loans that the World Bank was "pressuring" India to accept during that period.)[28] By 1991, the consolidated budget deficit of the central and state governments totaled more than 10 percent of India's gross domestic product, and India's total foreign debt reached $70 billion that year.

The major portion of the government's fiscal deficit is due to its inability to check the growth of spending on expanding public-sector employment, expenditures on subsidies, interest payments on government debt, and other nonproductive expenditures. The government's annual borrowing to finance its own consumption rose 55-fold from 1981–82 through 1989–90. The figure reached approximately $10 billion in 1991.

In early January 1991, foreign exchange reserves fell to the equivalent of the value of two weeks of imports, and India came close to defaulting on its commercial borrowing as well as on loans from the World Bank and the IMF. In late January, the IMF hurriedly approved a $1.8-billion loan for India, which staved off the impending default. That initial loan was followed in October 1991 by another IMF loan of $2.3 billion. The terms of that loan committed India to negotiate a further structural adjustment loan of from $5 billion to $7 billion with the IMF.

In February 1991, a political crisis ensued when Prime Minister Chandrashekhar resigned under considerable pressure from Rajiv

[28]Narendra Reddy, "India to Scale Down Borrowing," *Indian Express*, October 14, 1986, p. 1.

Gandhi's Congress party. Chandrashekhar's resignation left his government as a caretaker because new elections would not take place until May. In March, another financial crisis developed as India's hard currency reserves fell to $2.1 billion—less than the value of six weeks of imports—and $1.5 billion in payments to the multilateral financial institutions was due at the end of March. India's central bank responded by initiating a classic IMF "austerity" contraction: it devalued the rupee to boost exports and imposed severe credit restrictions on imports.[29] To do the latter, the central bank substantially raised—to 133 percent—the cash deposit that importers of raw materials, components, and capital goods are required to pay before opening letters of credit. The aim was to cut India's imports in succeeding months by 10 to 15 percent by making them prohibitively expensive.[30] The objectives were to attempt a "quick fix" of the external payments crisis, please the IMF with which India was negotiating for another emergency loan, and make the nation appear more creditworthy.

Ten months later, in January 1992, the government released figures showing that India's trade deficit had declined sharply to $1.34 billion between April and September 1991 (compared with $3.04 billion in the same period of the previous year). But behind that seeming improvement lay another picture: Imports fell by 17.5 percent, but exports also fell—by 6 percent. The export falloff was chiefly the result of the import restrictions, which made raw materials, components, and capital goods scarce. Some Indian economists were saying that the economy was in the grip of an import-cut-induced recession.[31]

As those trade figures revealed, no amount of cosmetic manipulation of the economy in the name of "austerity" or "necessary devaluation" can help as long as the microeconomic and institutional fundamentals are not drastically altered. Without enforceable private property rights, the establishment of the rule of law, across-the-board scrapping of all internal and external regulations, dismantlement of the public sector, and restoration of a voluntary exchange market economy, any

[29]K. K. Sharma, "India Places Severe Import Credit Limits," *Financial Times*, March 22, 1991, p. 20.

[30]David Housego, "India Seeks Emergency Funding to Stave Off Payments Default," *Financial Times*, March 26, 1991, p. 1.

[31]K. K. Sharma, "Big Fall in India's Trade Deficit," *Financial Times*, January 15, 1992, p. 4.

efforts to solve the crisis will produce mislabeled "successes" such as trade deficit reductions in the midst of a policy-induced recession.

The IMF's focus on balance-of-payments difficulties ignores the fundamental institutional and microeconomic factors that underlie the current Indian crisis. As long as the funds obtained through the IMF, the World Bank, and other external assistance programs continue to be channeled into the resuscitation of India's moribund public sector, such crises will recur. The continued allocation of funds to unproductive public-sector undertakings will only cause the budgetary and external deficits to grow, the external debt to balloon, and the foreign exchange crisis to persist.

In fact, foreign aid has had another perverse trade effect: feeding India's appetite for public-sector imports. Before the heavy-industry-oriented Second Five-Year Plan, India had normally run a current account surplus and had built up substantial reserves of foreign exchange. By 1960–61, at the end of the second plan, the current account deficit had grown to around 2 percent of net national product; it was around 4 percent in 1970–71. Over the same period, foreign exchange reserves declined by almost 95 percent from their 1950–51 level, in spite of huge infusions of foreign aid.

India ran a large current account deficit throughout the 1970s and 1980s. Private remittances from abroad, especially from the Middle East and Europe as a result of increased labor migration to supply labor shortages in the newly rich members of the Organization of Petroleum Exporting Countries, and the government decision to allow nonresident Indians to open interest-bearing foreign exchange accounts prevented the situation from being worse.

Throughout that period, the account balance on private accounts was generally positive (with the exception of a few years), which meant that the current account deficits were due solely to the steeply rising imports and lack of export growth of the government sector. Given the decline in foreign exchange reserves, prohibitive restraints on foreign investment, and stagnant exports, the high level of government imports was made possible only by large capital inflows in the form of foreign aid. Yet those aid-financed imports were both largely ineffectual in increasing India's rate of growth and responsible for bloating the inefficient public sector.

American Aid Underwrites Government Enterprises

The multilaterals are not the only organizations to blame for subsidizing Indian socialism. Their negative impact has been reinforced by bilateral donors. The United States, for instance, has been the single largest donor of foreign aid generally and to India in particular in the postwar period. The bulk of American aid to India was disbursed from 1955 to 1971, when the Indian economy was being nationalized and national economic planning focused on heavy industry was being institutionalized. As a result, most of the American aid went to the Indian public sector. (Less than 5 percent of U.S. aid went to India's private sector between 1951 and 1985.) Washington's aid, like multilateral credits, was used to finance government fertilizer and industrial plants, large-scale irrigation projects, state-owned power and rural electrification projects, dairy development, highway construction, locomotives and rolling stock for the government-owned railway system, airplanes for the state-owned international airline, agricultural extension and the establishment of agricultural universities, and technical assistance and equipment for large state-owned institutions of higher education.

American aid to the public sector actively fostered the growth of that sector at the expense of the private sector. Leonard Tansky concluded in a 1967 book that

> such aid has increased the resources of the public sector relative to the private sector and has enabled the government to pursue policies which have tended to restrict the activities of private investment and have tended to discourage a larger inflow of foreign capital.[32]

Many of the projects that received American aid had low or negative rates of return, particularly the many fertilizer plants and electrical power projects that have always operated at a loss. In the agricultural sector, where a large portion of U.S. aid was directed, restrictions on prices and production, compulsory government procurement schemes, a ban on private wholesale trade in grain, and an inefficient public distribution network skewed the incentives of both suppliers and consumers of agricultural products. A ban on futures trading and speculation further hobbled the workings of private markets. The

---

[32]Leonard Tansky, *U.S. and U.S.S.R. Aid to Developing Countries* (New York: Praeger, 1967), p. 113.

result was perpetual shortages and rationing during most of the postindependence period and widespread food shortages during the 1960s. All the while, Washington continued to funnel American aid and "agricultural know-how" to the Indian government without requiring the removal of those distortions.

Another significant component of American aid to India was food aid, under the Food for Peace Program (Public Law 480), which was given directly to the Indian government. Although tracing the economic effects of P.L. 480 food imports is a complex task, a number of serious negative effects have been identified.[33] One major result was to lower domestic prices of wheat and other commodities, causing farmers to reduce the acreage planted in both wheat and competing cereals. In fact, the large and escalating shipments of P.L. 480 food aid between 1955 and 1965 bankrupted large numbers of Indian farmers. Another negative effect stemmed from the fact that, under P.L. 480, the Indian government appeared to receive the U.S. food grains free, and it could garner substantial rupee receipts upon resale of the grain in Indian markets—money used to finance its public development schemes.

U.S. and other Western aid to India is often applauded for the central role it has played in financing research on high-yielding varieties (HYVs) of cereals, particularly wheat, which ushered in India's so-called Green Revolution of the 1960s. It is estimated that without HYVs, Indian cereal output would have been about 15 to 20 percent less than it was during the late 1960s and the 1970s. HYV research was supported in large part by Western aid to international centers under the auspices of the Consultative Group for International Agricultural Research to which the United States was a significant donor.

Nevertheless, the development and introduction of HYVs accounted for less than 2 percent of the foreign aid that India received during those years. Any effect HYVs may have had on Indian yields and output merely reveals the potential of small investments in private agriculture. In any case, it is not universally agreed that the Green Revolution had any real impact on Indian agricultural development. For example, a number of studies have revealed that in spite of impressive gains in wheat yields and output since 1967, the overall rate of growth of agricultural output did not accelerate after the Green

---

[33]The analysis that follows relies heavily on B. R. Shenoy, *P.L. 480 Aid and India's Food Problem* (New Delhi: Affiliated East-West Press, 1974).

Revolution.[34] Thus, even in the agricultural sector the effects of foreign aid are ambiguous at best.

The Rest of the Aid Cabal

From 1960 through 1985, aid from the Aid India Consortium—comprising the United States, 13 other countries with developed market economies, and certain multilateral aid institutions such as the World Bank—accounted for 85 to 90 percent of total aid to India. As can be seen in Figure 11.1, from the period 1961–62 to 1988–89, Soviet bloc aid never made up more than 8 percent of the total. As the World Bank's share of contributions increased over the years (to 69.3 percent in 1988–89), the U.S. share declined to 1 percent of the total by 1988–89—less than the Soviet share. The changing proportions clearly indicate that, when it comes to bankrolling Indian socialism, the World Bank is filling the shoes vacated by the United States.

The other members of the consortium also made significant contributions to the socialization of the Indian economy, however. The British provided aid to build a large steel plant, a paper mill, a heavy electrical machinery plant, and a fertilizer plant—all in the public sector. The West German government funded another government steel plant and public-sector area development programs in the agricultural sector. The Japanese provided aid for large public-sector fertilizer and iron ore projects and agricultural extension programs. Switzerland, Denmark, the Netherlands, New Zealand, and Australia provided assistance for dairy development, animal husbandry, and the processing of animal products. Norway and Sweden primarily aided the forestry and fisheries industries. Most of those funds were channeled through the public sector (in a few cases the ultimate beneficiaries were in the private sector).

Although the Soviet Union and Eastern Europe never contributed more than 8 to 10 percent of the total aid received by India, they played a significant role in shaping India's development strategy. Soviet and Eastern bloc aid went predominantly into supporting public-sector heavy industry—such as steel, heavy machine building, coal-mining

---

[34]See, for example, U. N. Srinivasan, "Trends in Agriculture in India, 1949–50 to 1977–78," *Economic and Political Weekly*, Annual Number, August 1979; and P. K. Bardhan, *The Political Economy of Development in India* (New Delhi: Oxford University Press, 1984), p. 11.

machinery, heavy electrical equipment, oil refineries, and thermal power stations—and antibiotics and surgical instruments. The participation of those countries in the metals and minerals sectors was also significant; they provided aid, machinery, and technical assistance.

Since about 80 percent of the cumulative investment in public-sector manufacturing enterprises in the postwar period was in four major industrial sectors—metals and minerals, steel, chemicals and pharmaceuticals, and petroleum—the influence of Soviet and other Eastern bloc aid on the growth of public-sector enterprises was disproportionately large. Thus, both Western and Eastern bloc nations collaborated directly in the diminution of the role of the private sector in the Indian economy and the increased hold of the government over the private lives of the citizens of India. Given that the return on that public-sector investment was low or negative, foreign aid from those countries helped directly impoverish the Indian masses.

Liberalization and the Dismantling of the Public Sector: A Project Far from Complete

In 1980–81, the top 157 of India's 250 public-sector companies (including the always-profitable oil companies but excluding firms that by virtue of large cumulative losses had negative total capital employed) sustained an overall loss of more than $160 million on total capital of around $20 billion.[35] In 1984–85, India's public-sector companies (except oil) sustained a similar collective loss of around $160 million; the most disastrously unprofitable concerns were the coal-mining and textile corporations. By 1984–85, the public-sector National Textile Corporation, set up in 1974, had accumulated losses of $480 million, which were all absorbed by the central government. By 1989–90, the accumulated losses had risen to $860 million, compared with that year's sales of $685 million.[36]

India's state-owned electricity boards (SEBs), which were and remain large recipients of foreign aid (mainly from the United States and the World Bank), have been some of the most unprofitable undertakings in the Indian public sector. The cumulative losses of 17 SEBs in

[35]Hannan Ezekiel, ed., *Corporate Sector in India* (New Delhi: Vikas, 1984), Table 7.2.

[36]*India Today*, October 15, 1990, p. 64.

March 1990 stood at $186 million.[37] State road transport operations are also highly inefficient and overstaffed; they accumulated losses of more than $625 million from 1985 through 1990.[38] Yet they continue to be the recipients of foreign aid from a number of countries and multilateral institutions.

Fortunately, Prime Minister Narasimha Rao, elected in May 1991, promised to "restructure ... privatize ... and reduce the overmanning" of India's public-sector industries. Rao further reinforced those reforms through the 1993–94 budget, which introduced fundamental institutional changes that are moving India closer to a market-driven and open economy. Under Rao's program, India's industrial licensing system was all but scrapped, except for 18 "critical" industries, including (absurdly) sugar, automobiles, and pharmaceuticals. Price controls on a number of items such as steel were removed. Rules on foreign investment have been relaxed; foreign companies may now purchase property, use their own brand names, open branch offices, and accept deposits with minimal extradomestic requirements. Quantitative import controls, which excluded most goods unless large bribes were paid, have been almost completely eliminated (except for consumer goods). Tariffs, however, remain, though at a lower level. For example, the top tariff rate for consumer goods has come down from 150 percent in mid-1991 to 80 percent in mid-1993. Additionally, in its 1993–94 budget, the government made the rupee partially convertible.

The problem with those reforms is that, even though they are radical when compared to the policies of the last 45 years, they are neither comprehensive nor complete. They represent a significant rejection of the ideology of central planning and Nehruvian socialism. But they have failed to effect the necessary radical institutional surgery. They have been relatively easy politically since they have not threatened the special interests created by the postindependence "permit-licence raj." Rents continue to accrue to influential interest groups—politicians, bureaucrats, union leaders and members, public-sector employees, selected business groups, and farmers. Most fundamentally, private property rights are still not protected from government, which continues to regulate the sale of private homes and commercial property; purchase and sale of land; ownership of many kinds of private

---

[37]*India Today*, September 30, 1990, p. 67.
[38]Ibid.

property; price and distribution of some basic commodities; and distribution of critical commodities such as steel, fertilizers, and food grains.

Despite talk of privatization, moreover, not a single major state or central public-sector undertaking has been divested. The government has considerably watered down its much-heralded plan to privatize the nation's two state-owned airlines, proposing to make the government the majority shareholder with the right to appoint the chairman of the board, fix fares, decide on personnel and union policies, and control expansion plans. The government only envisages partial privatization of other public enterprises, even though a recent survey of 233 of the better run state firms found that their return on equity in 1989–90 averaged just 0.9 percent.[39] Furthermore, despite the abolition of the licensing and foreign-trade controls, not a single bureaucrat or public-sector employee has been fired. The most inefficient government enterprises and departments have maintained or increased the number of employees.

Thus, the Indian public sector continues to be a black hole—sucking in huge amounts of foreign taxpayers' money and sinking it into inefficient, loss-producing public-sector enterprises and projects. Foreign aid, then, represents a huge transfer of potentially productive financial resources to unproductive uses, which seriously diminishes the rates of economic growth and the growth of income in both the donor nations and India.

Conclusion

Except for a few instances of possible foreign aid success—such as critical food relief when millions were on the verge of starvation in the early 1950s and again during the mid-1960s—foreign aid to India has been an unmitigated disaster. It has acted as both a catalyst and an incentive for the politicization of the Indian economy. It has supported central planning and facilitated the growth of the public sector at the expense of the private sector and the establishment of a private-property-oriented market system. It has also encouraged corruption, rent-seeking, and graft in the Indian economy. Foreign aid has been—and continues to be—predicated on an outdated and false theory of development economics that assumes that only capital and access to

[39]*The Economist*, May 23–29, 1992.

technology are needed for economic development.

No amount of future foreign aid will provide the means for India to break the vise of its current underdevelopment. Fundamental changes in policy are required to restore a functioning market order. In India's case, such changes would include scrapping all remaining domestic and external-sector controls and regulations, dismantling the overbearing planning system, drastically reducing the centralized bureaucratic edifice, privatizing central government and state companies, restoring absolute rights to private property and voluntary exchange, and relying on market forces. In particular, the government needs to establish completely free trade as an immediate step toward achieving economic and political freedom.

Rao's recent limited economic liberalizations show the potential for growth from freeing the economy, but they will not suffice. Indian policymakers must adopt much more radical reforms. Officials should not fear the consequences of such a change, since they would be journeying down a well-traveled and successful path, particularly by the Western nations and the countries of East and Southeast Asia. The multilateral aid institutions, as well as the United States and other Western nations, should begin to wean India and their other clients off foreign aid. It is time for donors to stop encouraging the impoverishment of nations.

12. Philippine Development and the Foreign Assistance Trap

William McGurn

The year was 1983, Philippine president Ferdinand Marcos was still in power, and U.S. Agency for International Development (U.S. AID) officials were upset—not at Marcos, mind you, but at one of his cabinet officers, Placido Mapa. Although U.S. AID and other lending institutions had succeeded in rewriting the Philippine constitution to include a state mandate to "achieve and maintain population levels," their programs were highly unpopular and Mapa was proving a stumbling block to wider implementation. In no time at all he was yanked out of the cabinet and shunted off to the Philippine National Bank.

During the years of martial law, U.S. AID paid for a quarter to half of the Philippines' campaign to reduce population growth; among the foreign-aid brigade it remains an unquestioned article of faith that development is but another billion dollars or a billion condoms away. But the birth rate remained largely unaffected and the promised economic growth never came. After Mapa's ouster from the cabinet, however, one tiny area did show explosive growth: the Population Commission's budget, resources, and personnel. In the last five years of the Marcos regime alone the commission spent at least $94.5 million, a staggering sum in a country as poor as the Philippines.[1]

It is hardly surprising that in return for lucrative foreign aid, Marcos did not hesitate to allow foreigners to tell his people how many babies they should have or how many Filipinos there ought to be. But Cory Aquino outdid her predecessor here. In 1991, her cash-strapped government, with more help from Uncle Sam, endorsed a new,

---

[1]These numbers were given to me in 1988 by a former member of the Population Commission, Sonny de los Reyes, from a report by the National Economic Development Authority. The total expenditure for each of the years was as follows: P190,307,000 (1981); P181,552,000 (1982); P204,552,000 (1983); P255,376,000 (1984); P287,400,000 (1985); P328,585,000 (1986). The $94.5-million figure was arrived at by dividing each year's total by the average dollar exchange rate for that year and adding up the total.

$250-million program to help bring the country toward the Holy Grail of zero population growth, which became an official government target, showing that those who write the checks still call the tune. Today, President Fidel Ramos promises to go further (his sister, Leticia Shahami, has been one of the vocal supporters of population control in the Senate). The belief is that the president will have a freer hand because he is not Catholic. The World Bank and virtually every foreign-aid organization continue to push the population issue.

In another example of what development assistance can achieve, the Philippine government in 1975 moved to combine 4 cities and 13 municipalities around the capital into a new urban behemoth called Metro Manila. The move was supported by the World Bank. It was thought that one large entity rather than a number of smaller ones would facilitate lending and operations; the idea is that development trickles down from centrally directed multilateral lending agencies to the public. Soon after Metro Manila was created, Marcos appointed his wife, Imelda, governor.

Today, Imelda Marcos's extravagance is well known. But it would not be fair to the former Philippine first lady to suggest that she was thinking solely of herself. In October 1976, as part of an effort to beautify Manila in time for the International Monetary Fund (IMF)–World Bank conference there, some 60,000 squatters were relocated to areas far from their jobs and former homes. Marcos simply had tall white fences constructed around other slums, lest foreign loan officers have to endure the unsightly impoverished Filipinos they were pre- sumably there to help.[2]

Washington has by no means been alone in perverting political and economic incentives through aid. In the late 1980s, Japan surpassed the United States as the largest single contributor of aid to the Philippines (in part because of the rise of the yen and the depreciated dollar), in many ways more successfully integrating that economy via assistance into a Greater Co-Prosperity Sphere than it did via conquest in World War II. Japanese aid has especially targeted industrial projects and infrastructure that yield fat contracts for Japanese construction firms.

The Japanese, too, benefited from the Marcos dictatorship. Just before martial law was imposed, the Philippine senate refused to ratify

---

[2]Harvey Stockwin, "Fiesta, the Martial Law Way," *Far Eastern Economic Review*, October 15, 1976, pp. 20–21.

a Japan-Philippines Treaty of Amity, Commerce, and Navigation, but once martial law was declared Marcos simply pushed the treaty through. Although the Philippine public would undoubtedly benefit from more open trade with Japan, Marcos apparently had his eye on other, more personal benefits.

Japan's Overseas Economic Cooperation Fund (OECF) made it particularly easy for the Philippine president to line his pockets because it allowed him to choose his own contracts without bidding. This arrangement enabled him to pad costs of such projects as the Friendship Highway by as much as 10 to 15 percent, happily picked up by the Japanese trading firms handling the work and then funneled back to Marcos and his cronies as kickbacks. While it lasted it was a nice arrangement for both: Marcos got rich and in exchange allowed the Japanese to bind his country to aid projects that were essentially marketing ploys for Japan, Inc.

The Centralization of Economic and Political Power

Marcos has been out of power for almost eight years, but he remains a symbol of the Philippines' wrong turn. Although that is as it should be, it has been for the wrong reasons. It was not Marcos's undeniable avarice that did the Philippines in but his centralization of economic and political power in Manila. Debt figures hint at the magnitude of the shift. In 1966, when Marcos was first elected president (and when the Philippines was, after Japan, the most prosperous nation in Asia), the country's foreign debt was roughly $500 million. In 1972, the figure was still a relatively modest $1.9 billion, according to the World Bank. That was the same year Marcos imposed martial law, a move that greatly encouraged the lending agencies. Not coincidentally the Philippine debt ballooned, reaching $28.1 billion by the time Marcos was booted out in 1986.[3] The crime was not the figure itself. The crime was that there was absolutely nothing to show for it.

The tendency again is to attribute that reckless improvidence to Marcos's cupidity, as illustrated perhaps by the former first lady's vast shoe collection or the late president's commissioning of a Philippine Mount Rushmore in his own likeness. But waste and plunder explain only what happened. They do not explain *how* it happened—a

[3]World Bank, *World Debt Tables: External Debt of Developing Countries 1987–1988 Edition* (Washington, D.C.: World Bank, 1988), p. 302.

question best directed at members of the international aid brigade who happily rained dollars down on the Philippine first couple: U.S. AID, Japan's OECF, the IMF, the Asian Development Bank (ADB), the World Bank, and a host of smaller entities. Of all those groups, only one—the ADB—ever cut Marcos off, and even that did not come until 1985.

In fact, one of the big problems those on the receiving end have traditionally had was keeping up with all the money flowing into the country. Because much of it was contingent on coming up with matching local funding, there has long been a backlog of aid committed but never spent. For the same reason, Philippine officials were kept busy dreaming up ever-new projects so they would have something in the "pipeline" whenever one of the aid agencies came around. The project would then be approved, with little or no followup about whether it was ever finished.

Today, the individual stories of aborted aid projects are legion: there is even a city where foreign aid built a shell of a building, toilets and all, but no walls, and nothing else. Yet despite the overwhelming evidence, the multilateral and bilateral aid groups have emerged unscathed (not to mention unbowed) by their disastrous failure in the Philippines.

Logically, however, there are only two explanations, neither of them flattering to the development community. Either they knew what was going on in the Philippines and said nothing, or they had no idea that hundreds of millions of dollars were being ripped off right under their noses. The former would make them accessories; the latter criminally negligent. So why are they still in business?

Products of Aid: Criticism and Privilege

Ironically, such attacks as there have been on the lending follies of the international aid organizations have come largely from the left. A 1982 book called *Development Debacle* correctly savaged the World Bank for the abstractions it forced on the Philippine people, such as the reclamation of the Tondo Foreshore area, a strip just off Manila Bay.[4] When the World Bank decided in 1976 to clean up the area—one of the worst slums in Asia—it evicted thousands of people, many of whom

---

[4]Walden F. Bello, *Development Debacle: The World Bank in the Philippines* (San Francisco: Institute for Food and Development, 1982).

had title to their plots of land. The land was reclaimed all right, but most of those displaced could not afford the middle-class housing that went up and many were forced to live much farther from their jobs. An aptly named "Imelda Street" is today one of the roads that goes through the area.

Where the authors of the tome go wrong, however, is in seeing this use of force as the vanguard of international capitalism, a charge that would doubtless be greeted with great astonishment at, say, the *Wall Street Journal*, which makes the World Bank a favorite target. In its secret reports, the World Bank continues to stump for higher taxes, more austerity, and a halt to the growth of the Philippine birth rate. In 1992, for example, a World Bank report—noting that at 11 percent of gross domestic product Philippine tax revenue is less than that of its more prosperous neighbors—zeroed in on poor tax collection as the problem, arguing that it is "generally less than what is required to fund development expenditures." The bank report neither complained about rates nor warned about the disincentives aggressive tax collection might pose for development.[5]

That position could not be more different from the one presented in the so-called Woods report, named after a former U.S. AID chief. In 1989 that study (its formal title is *Development and the National Interest: U.S. Economic Assistance into the 21st Century*) went further than most by questioning the basic assumptions of the development-through-aid theory. As the report noted, not one of the less developed nations that the United States targeted for assistance for the previous two decades had moved up to developed status, despite the transfusion of billions of dollars on exceptionally generous terms.[6] Today's cruel irony is that most of the advice on how to pay off the crushing debt resulting from this huge spending spree now comes from those responsible for much of the debt in the first place.

Within the Philippines itself, perhaps the greater irony is the different standards imposed by nationalists on multinational corporations and multilateral lending agencies. For years, most nationalist ire has been expended on the former, raising fears that big multinational

[5]Rigoberto Tiglao, "Big Fish, Small Net," *Far Eastern Economic Review*, March 26, 1992, p. 50.

[6]U.S. Agency for International Development, *Development and the National Interest: U.S. Economic Assistance into the 21st Century* (Washington, D.C.: U.S. AID, 1989), p. 112.

243

firms would simply seize control of the country if they were allowed in. That happens to fit in nicely with what Philippine big-business interests want, since their monopoly-driven profits would be threatened if their products actually had to compete with similar imports on the basis of price and quality. At several points in Aquino's administration, those protectionist pressures kept her from lowering tariffs. Although she finally did reduce the barriers somewhat, the reduction was clearly a case of too little too late. Thus, both left-wing nationalists and fat-cat businesspeople meet on the common ground of keeping out foreign competition.

The Aquino administration's treatment of a proposed Taiwanese petrochemical plant is a case in point. In 1987, the Board of Investment approved a $200-million project for the Taiwanese company, but it soon became bogged down in government hearings and a supreme court suit until the permit was revoked in 1990. By that time the value of the potential investment had risen to $500 million, which would have made it the largest single investment since Marcos was ousted. The Taiwanese experience was taken as a sign by the foreign community that despite lip service about opening up to foreign investment, the political elites in the Philippines still hope to wall off their country from outside competition. Not surprisingly, foreigners have been hesitant about investing.

How different that is from the path chosen by nearby Hong Kong. With no natural resources, one of the most densely packed populations on earth (5,948 people per square kilometer versus 225 for the Philippines), and a total dependence for even such basics as food and water, Hong Kong probably would have remained a Chinese backwater had the World Bank and the IMF been around when the British flag was raised. In sharp contrast to the Philippines, multinational corporations in Hong Kong are free to do business—a good many of them make it their base for the region—and Hong Kong has prospered mightily as a result, even achieving higher per capita productivity than the United Kingdom in 1993. Taxes remain low, incorporation is easy and relatively cheap, and the government contents itself largely with maintaining law and order. By making Hong Kong a hospitable place for investment, the inhabitants were spared the presence of the IMF, World Bank, U.S. AID, and other aid institutions that are now more or less permanent landmarks in Manila (the ADB having recently built a palatial marble and wood headquarters). Among the more bitter twists of fate has been the complete reversal in the labor market for domestics: whereas 20 years ago Chinese maids were common in the Philippines, today Hong Kong has an increasing number of Filipinas—more than 90,000 working as domestics.

Conditionality, Half Measures, and Dependence

In fairness to the IMF and the World Bank, they have indeed both argued for lowering the Philippines' protectionist barriers for some time. But their own role in continuing to pump in money has allowed the government to either postpone reform completely or indulge in half measures. One reason the multilaterals kept the money tap open during the Marcos years was that it gave them more leverage over policy. In fact, since 1974 the real Philippine budget has been set not by the president of the country, the congress, or the cabinet, but by the Consultative Group. The group, made up of the Philippines' largest donors (now expanded into something called the Multilateral Assistance Initiative) and chaired by the World Bank, meets annually to decide aid levels and what policies they want in return, with implications for everything from government spending to tariffs and interest rates. Using an inherently top-down approach, the Consultative Group deals with development the way the federal government in the United States deals with housing.

For example, on February 25–26, 1991, the Consultative Group meeting was held in Hong Kong. Just days before, the IMF had approved a new transfusion of cash tied to commitments by the Philippine government to liberalize trade and lower its budget deficit. Among those were tax measures that had not managed to get through the Philippine Congress; instead, Philippine finance secretary Jesus Estanislao pushed through a 9 percent import levy. But the IMF still required Estanislao to stick to his promise that the levy would be phased out and replaced with tax measures. As the *Far Eastern Economic Review* reported at the time, "By the time [the Philippine] Congress knew what was happening, Manila was committed to introducing reforms."[7] In 1992, the IMF again conditioned new loans (to pay off the Philippine foreign debt) on monetary targets it set.

---

[7]Rigoberto Tiglao, "Economic Monitor: Philippines—Back to Square One," *Far Eastern Economic Review,* October 3, 1991, p. 46.

Development Assistance as Political Payment

Development assistance for the Philippines has not been without its political price. Washington and Manila were at loggerheads for years over the future of six U.S. military bases in the Philippines. Throughout the frustrating negotiations, Malacañang Palace made it abundantly clear that the debate over those bases had nothing to do with the defense of the Philippines or Southeast Asia, the Philippines' foreign policy, or the Philippines' place in the world. The only issue was the price at which the Philippines might be bought and the price that America was willing to pay. At one point during the negotiations the U.S. representative, Richard Armitage, told Philippine foreign secretary Raul Manglapus: "I am not an accountant and I do not stand next to a cash register when conducting foreign relations. Nor do I put a price tag on Philippine honor and sovereignty."[8]

That statement was not quite accurate. Although the Bush administration took a fairly tough negotiating line—the reduced Soviet threat, after all, left the Aquino administration with a depreciating asset—in practice America has relied on the cash register to get its way. Just days before the negotiations over the bases began, for example, U.S. AID suddenly came through with a $40-million grant for a pet population-control project for Philippine secretary Alran Bengzon's Department of Health. Bengzon, an old and ambitious anti-American leftist, happened also to be the vice chairman of the bases negotiating team. Almost all the promotional literature the U.S. Embassy in Manila used to distribute, moreover, devoted considerable space to the amount of money the bases poured into the Philippine economy, in terms of both outright assistance and local spending. In fact, next to the Philippine government, the bases made the U.S. government the Philippines' second largest employer.

Even the Multilateral Assistance Initiative was not without its political price. The initiative was first proposed back in 1987, when Senators Alan Cranston (D-Calif.) and Richard Lugar (R-Ind.) and Representatives Stephen Solarz (D-N.Y.) and Jack Kemp (R-N.Y.) wrote to Ronald Reagan urging a $5-billion to $10-billion multinational aid effort to shore up Aquino's fledgling democracy. In 1991, a group of 17

---

[8]John McBeth, "Danger Money," *Far Eastern Economic Review*, May 31, 1990, p. 28.

countries and five multilateral institutions pledged $3.3 billion in grants and soft loans to the Philippines at their meeting in Hong Kong. Although the money was not officially tied to anything political, it was well understood in Washington and every Asian capital that should the U.S. bases be forced out, the Philippines would never see the money. It was no coincidence, then, that the finance secretary usurped the role of the foreign secretary in these negotiations. In any event, the bases agreement that finally did emerge was rejected by the Philippine Senate. In response, the U.S. State Department slashed its request for aid to the Philippines by almost two-thirds, from $567.9 million for 1991–92 to $219.1 million in 1992–93.[9]

In the end, of course, the failure of the negotiations demonstrated that aid-based policies serve neither defense nor development. As the United States restructures its defense policies to meet a changing world situation, it would do well to note that of the 12 nations around the world that play host to American forces, the healthiest and most faithful allies—Germany, Japan, and South Korea—actually make contributions to the United States for the upkeep of the bases; after all, they are getting security in return. When the U.S. Navy pulled out of Subic Bay for the last time, prosperous Singapore offered to let them base part of their operations there. By contrast, the Greeces and the Philippines of the world continue to try to shake down Washington for ever more aid in periodic bouts of extortion. Certainly that kind of relationship does not foster goodwill.

In the Dark on Reform

The more fundamental problem with the offer of aid has to do not with its historical relationship to a bases agreement but with the nature of aid itself. Time and again aid officials promise that "things will be different": better controls, more lending to private citizens rather than to public entities, no Marcos. Yet for all the concern that aid programs be continued, not one Philippine official—not from the National Economic Development Authority, the central bank, nor the congress—has any clear idea how much money came in under Marcos or where it all went and why. On half a dozen separate visits to the Philippines, I visited all those institutions in search of some figure, *any*

---

[9]"Out of Pocket," *Far Eastern Economic Review*, February 6, 1992, p. 17.

figure, for the total amount of aid that came into the Philippines during the Marcos years. No one could tell me, except to point to the foreign debt as a rough indicator.

Perhaps the most heartening result of the closing of the U.S. bases is that it will at least force the Philippines to face up to its problems. To be sure, there has been some modest progress. Philippine Airlines has been privatized. President Ramos says that the government will no longer provide loans to companies that get into trouble. There have been tentative moves to open up the economy in other areas. The most refreshing sign of change was the August 1992 decision to lift virtually all restrictions on the flow of foreign exchange.

Unfortunately, the Philippines still has far to go in lifting those restrictions, and again, that largely has to do with the way it discourages foreign investment. It continues to have a huge bureaucracy—the National Economic and Development Authority—that sets out its glorious five-year plans. The lowering of tariffs, say some U.S. businesspeople, is simply going to be replaced by quotas and other regulations that make the economy not only less closed but less transparent. Philippine senator Blas Ople has cited the case of an assistant secretary for trade who documented that it took no less than 167 signatures for the release of an imported car from the Bureau of Customs; later, a customs officer proudly announced that the number had been reduced to 50.

The Philippines' $29-billion foreign debt remains a huge obstacle, not simply in financial terms but also in terms of economic policy, not least because half of that debt is held by the multilateral and bilateral lending institutions. That means that those lending institutions usually get what they want, whether it is setting deficit targets or devaluing the currency. Right now what they want is to squeeze every last peso from the Philippines to pay off the debt, thus creating a national form of debtor's prison in the 20th century.

In fact, often overlooked in the crisis of the underdeveloped world is that aid organizations such as the IMF, the World Bank, and the ADB are not disinterested players; their share of the debt makes them partisans. Naturally, then, the ledger line comes before incentives, which may explain why the World Bank thinks that the overriding problem with the Philippines is tax collection. The upshot is that while Manila continues to come up with enough fresh loans every few months to make payments on the old ones, the change promised by advocates of "People Power," who in 1986 vowed to get the govern-ment off the people's backs, has not come. In the end, more than half of the 300 or so state-controlled firms slated for privatization remain in government hands, including the San Miguel Brewery, the Manila Hotel, and the Petron subsidiary of the Philippine National Oil Corporation.

That centralized and exploitive system remains the real Marcos legacy. In terms of government spending, for example, until recent years, between 85 and 91 percent of all state expenditures (and consequently services) came from the national government, which means that national congressmen sitting in Manila have more of a say in local projects than local officials on the scene.[10] (The mayor of Olongapo City, former site of a U.S. Navy base, is a notable exception and is now fighting desperately to transform that base into a major export zone.)

More disturbing still is the government's role in energy prices. The Oil Price Stabilization Fund is, after the interest payments on the debt, the largest line item in the Philippine budget. The stabilization fund almost brought the government down during the Persian Gulf War, when the market price for oil initially surged. Coming on top of other woes, the volatility of oil prices almost literally put the Philippines out of business, since the government was forced to choose between allowing prices to rise in accord with the market or continuing to subsidize prices at considerable cost to a government already strapped for cash. Since the devaluation of the peso made subsidization even less affordable and because the IMF was unhappy about any continued subsidies for oil, the government raised fuel prices three times in six days in December 1990. Since then, the drop in oil prices from their end-of-1990 peaks has relieved pressure on the government, but the problem remains, ready to flare up in the next crisis.

Perhaps the largest problem the Philippines has is a monster entirely of its own making: its 80-page 1987 constitution. The most debilitating sections of the document deal with what is called "the National Economy and Patrimony." Almost all provisions begin with the words

---

[10]John McBeth, "Remote Control," *Far Eastern Economic Review,* November 23, 1989, pp. 32–33.

"The State shall. . . . " Throughout is a pronounced bias against both markets and foreign investment. The following are a few excerpts:

> Sec. 2. All lands of the public domain, waters, minerals, coal, petroleum, and other mineral oils, all forces of potential energy, fisheries, forests or timber, wildlife, flora and fauna, and other natural resources are owned by the State. With the exception of agricultural lands, all other natural resources shall not be alienated. The exploration, development and utilization of natural resources shall be under the full control and supervision of the State. The State may directly undertake such activities, or it may enter into co-production, joint venture, or production-sharing agreements with Filipino citizens, or corporations or associations at least sixty *per centum* of whose capital is owned by such citizens.

> Sec. 6. The use of property bears a social function, and all economic agents shall contribute to the common good. Individuals and private groups, including corporations, cooperatives, and similar collective organizations, shall have the right to own, establish and operate economic enterprises, subject to the duty of the State to promote distributive justice and to intervene when the common good so demands.

> Sec. 11. No franchise, certificate, or any other form of authorization for the operation of a public utility shall be granted except to citizens of the Philippines or to corporations or associations organized under the laws of the Philippines at least sixty *per centum* of whose capital is owned by such citizens, nor shall such franchise, certificate or authorization be exclusive in character or for a longer period than fifty years. . . . The participation of foreign investors in the governing body of any public utility shall be limited to their proportionate share in its capital, and all the executive and managing officers of such corporation or association must be citizens of the Philippines.

> Sec. 12. The State shall promote the preferential use of Filipino labor, domestic materials and locally produced goods, and adopt measure that make them competitive.

> Sec. 14. . . . The practice of all professions in the Philippines shall be limited to Filipino citizens, save in cases prescribed by law.[11]

---

[11]Albert Blaustein and Gisbert H. Flanz, "Constitution of the Republic of the Philippines—Article XII," in *Constitutions of the World* (Dobbs Ferry, N.Y.: Oceana Publications, 1993), pp. 204–9.

And on it goes, a virtual blueprint for underdevelopment. Not surprisingly, one area where the constitution has helped cripple Philippine chances for recovery is utilities. The limits on foreign capital, plus the growth of an environmentalist movement and corruption in the Philippine National Power Corporation, have left the country literally in the dark. When she first came to power, Aquino shut down a 600-megawatt nuclear power plant in Bataan built by Westinghouse. Although the plant represents some 10 percent of the Philippine foreign debt, it has not produced a single watt of electricity.

Worse still, when the government shut down the power plant, it took no steps to replace the electricity that it would have provided. The result, in addition to all its other woes, is that the Philippines now suffers from 8 to 10 hours of blackouts every day. A story in *The Economist* quoted industrialist Raúl Conception's estimate that the power shortages cost the Philippines some $800 million in the first quarter of 1993 alone. President Ramos was ultimately given emergency powers to tackle the situation. But the government's insistence on controlling energy prices has prevented it from getting necessary loans. Investors reason correctly that in the absence of free pricing, any money will simply be wasted in subsidies. Although several fast-track projects are nevertheless in the works, foreign observers doubt that the Philippines will make up its electricity shortfall any time in the next three to four years.

Development Begins at Home

Those domestic constraints are all problems no aid program can address. And to the extent that the aid measures do have an effect, it by and large has been to exacerbate the problem by distorting the incentives inherent in an open market. The emphasis today among the lending agencies on making loans to private rather than government enterprises is a move in the right direction, but it begs the question: why have these lending agencies at all, if the money is going into private hands?

The old answer was that developing countries do not have enough capital to work with. There are a number of problems with that sort of reasoning. In the first place, the idea that development, at least at its initial stages, requires huge amounts of capital is simply false. Benjamin Montemayor, the executive director of a nongovernmental credit organization, Tulay sa Gap-unlad (Bridge to Progress), reports that his

251

organization has managed to create a job for every $1,200 invested, a rate several times lower than the $9,600 average reported by large firms registered with the Philippine Board of Investment or even the $2,000 average reported by smaller firms registered with the Department of Labor and Employment. All that is done on the basis of small loans that may range as low as $20 to $80. What is the difference? For one thing, Tulay sa Gap-unlad charges market rates. For another, Montemayor's groups are self-administered, so creditors have a great incentive to carefully select where their money goes as well as to get the recipients to pay up.

In a world economy, moreover, even the larger amounts of cash required for infrastructure projects are generally available so long as the economy is open. In fact, where countries like the Philippines really have problems is in coming up with the amounts of capital for the required local participation and local commitments of most aid projects. Lifting the constitutionally required 40 percent cap on foreign equity and control would work wonders; after all, few investors are prepared to sink in substantial amounts of money if they will not have control over it. The government likes to point out that it has waived the 40 percent cap in a number of sectors where there is no indigenous enterprise, but this only confirms the gist of the problem: the multinational corporations are allowed in, but not to the point where they might actually do something for the Filipino worker by challenging a domestic monopoly.

That situation may be beginning to change. In the fall of 1992, Singapore senior minister Lee Kuan Yew traveled to Manila to deliver a blunt assessment of the economy. The first priority, he said, was restoring law and order and eliminating corruption in the government, which has risen to epidemic proportions first under Marcos, then under Aquino, and now under Ramos. The next priority was to take on the monopolies. Lee cited Aquino's backing down on tariffs, the survival of monopolies on concessional loans, access to licenses, and so forth. He cited the success stories of Indonesia, Malaysia, and Thailand as places that had opened up their economies to attract foreign capital. According to Lee, it was essential that the Philippines similarly open its economy by no less than 100 percent. Lee also noted that the presence of foreign concerns would put pressure on the government to privatize and clean up its act.[12]

That would have been strong medicine on its own. However, Lee went further, pointing to the Philippine Long Distance Telephone Company (PLDT) as an egregious example of a monopoly. Today the Philippines has less than two phone lines for every 100 people, and the PLDT enjoys great control through laws that restrict access to the phone market by other firms and force those who want phone lines to buy PLDT shares. It is not uncommon for families to have to wait more than a decade for a phone line. Stung by the criticism, President Ramos has now moved to dismantle some of the PLDT's protection. Nevertheless, many other forms of protectionism remain, as do the monopolies they sustain.

Time for a Turnabout

Today there are signs that the president at least knows what is at stake. During the six years of Aquino's rule, the Philippines squandered an opportunity to shuck off corruption and regain its rightful place among the developing countries of Asia. Certainly the talent and willingness to work hard are there. Every Manila street corner has its Filipino hawkers in shorts and flip-flops, small-time entrepreneurs who stand all day in the Southeast Asian sun peddling everything from newspapers and rags to single cigarettes. Fruit markets open early and close late. Taxi drivers work all day in the snarled traffic, clearing only a few pesos more than their petrol costs. And in places like the Middle East—home to a vast Filipino diaspora of guest workers—the word "Filipino" is synonymous with the capacity to do hard work.

Indeed, tens of thousands of young Filipinos with college degrees go abroad as domestics each year because there simply is no opportunity at home for them to earn enough to feed their families. Yet instead of opening up the economy, Philippine politicians have introduced a bill that ultimately seeks to prohibit women from taking such jobs abroad. According to the legislation, although domestic workers account for only a fifth of all Philippine workers abroad, they account for more

---

[12]Editorial, *Far Eastern Economic Review*, December 10, 1992, p. 4.

than 90 percent of the associated welfare problems (e.g., sexual abuse), which they say "distort the image of the Philippines worldwide."

In fact, the legions of Filipinos who go abroad each year to provide for their families—many of whom have college degrees, some of whom leave husbands and children behind, and others who bring their aged mothers to work with them in exile—project an accurate image of a nation whose leaders would rather have that happen than to open the economy to the foreign investment and competition that would create decent jobs at home. Those women are indeed the heroes of the Philippines, literally keeping their homeland from bankruptcy with the foreign exchange they send home. The women's industriousness abroad suggests that the Philippines would not be immune to the general dynamism of Southeast Asia today were all Filipinos' skills allowed to blossom in a free economy. If there is fault to be found, it lies with a political system that continues to rely on top-down aid projects and rigs the economy against competition for the benefit of a well-connected few. In the Philippines "People Power" has not failed. It has not yet even been tried.

PART IV

DEVELOPMENT WITHOUT AID

13. America's Iron Trade Curtain against Eastern Europe and the Former Soviet Union

James Bovard

While President Clinton has proclaimed his desire to help the nations of Eastern Europe and the former Soviet Union and has proposed increased transfers of government-to-government aid, Washington continues to maintain an array of trade barriers that stifle those nations' exports to the United States. Unfortunately, that protectionist trade policy makes a mockery of the aid that the United States is simultaneously providing to former communist countries that are struggling to convert to a market economy. Although American politicians receive ample, and positive, publicity for their promises to help Eastern Europe and the former Soviet Union, their support for barriers to those countries' exports has received little attention.

Textiles and Clothing

As a 1991 U.S. International Trade Commission (ITC) report observed, Eastern European "exports to Western countries were generally dominated by clothing and raw materials, reflecting in part the poor performance of consumer goods and more technologically advanced merchandise in Western markets."[1]

The United States has imposed a stranglehold on clothing and textile imports from most Eastern European countries. For instance, wool clothing is one of Poland's strongest industries. In 1993, the U.S. government is permitting Poland to export only 145,440 women's and

---

[1]"Eastern Europe: An Overview of Economic Reform, Industrial Structure, and Trade," draft report, U.S. International Trade Commission, Washington, D.C., February 1991, p. 68.

girls' wool coats and 212,100 men's and boys' wool suits[2]—a fraction of what Poland would be able to export without such restrictions. Yet Andrzej Olechowski, Poland's secretary of state in the Ministry of Foreign Economic Relations, said two years ago that textiles and food-processing industries are Poland's two most likely "engines" for his country's economic recovery.[3]

Czechoslovakia was forced to sign an agreement in 1989 restricting its clothing exports to the United States—even though Czechoslovak exports have amounted to far less than 1 percent of the U.S. clothing market.[4] Wool clothing is a traditional Czechoslovak specialty, but Washington currently allows the Czech and Slovak republics to ship to the United States only 199,980 men's and boys' wool suit coats and 161,600 men's and boys' wool suits each year.[5]

Romania's exports are restricted by quotas that limit annual exports to the United States to 62,784 women's and girls' wool coats, 102,183 men's and boys' wool suits, and 33,321 women's and girls' suits.[6] Hungary is allowed to export only 27,770 women's and girls' wool suits and only 1,533,311 pounds of sacks and bags to the United States each year.[7]

America's anti-textile import policy reduced the credibility of U.S. humanitarian efforts towards the nations of former Yugoslavia. On September 3, 1991, the Commerce Department unilaterally restricted the amount of textiles that Bosnia, Croatia, and Slovenia are allowed to export to the United States. Those nations, all suffering in varying degrees from the disruptions caused by military conflict, are permitted to export only 98,640 men's and boys' wool suits, 135,600 wool skirts, and 94,854 women's and girls' wool suits to the United States each year.[8]

U.S. textile import quotas presume that foreign governments strictly control their factories' export shipments. It is bizarre to expect a government mired in a devastating civil war to drop everything else

[2]*Federal Register*, October 21, 1992, p. 48022.

[3]Richard Lawrence, "U.S. Apparel Moves Fail to Satisfy Poland," *Journal of Commerce*, September 27, 1991.

[4]*Federal Register*, June 2, 1989, p. 23682.

[5]*Federal Register*, January 12, 1993, p. 3936.

[6]*Federal Register*, November 13, 1992, p. 53884.

[7]*Federal Register*, June 4, 1991, p. 25413.

[8]*Federal Register*, September 3, 1992, p. 40436.

and send officials around the countryside to count coats and skirts intended for export. In any case, it is difficult to understand why the United States would take a protectionist cheap shot at Bosnia when that country poses little threat of exports at this time. According to Clint Stack, a former Commerce Department textile official, the United States has "implemented something to please the domestic textile industry, which does not think that quotas can be dropped simply because countries disintegrate."[9]

Unfortunately, the unilateral quota on Bosnia is not unique. On July 24, 1991, the Commerce Department announced that it was imposing import quotas on cotton printcloth and sheeting from Armenia, Azerbaijan, Belarus, Georgia, Kazakhstan, Kyrgyzstan, Moldova, Russia, Tajikistan, Turkmenistan, Ukraine, and Uzbekistan.[10] Several of those nations face serious internal strife and external threats.

Even when import quotas do not close the borders to Eastern European clothing, the U.S. tariff code often does. For instance, a 22.3 percent tariff must be paid on women's wool suit jackets; men's wool overcoats are hit with a 24.3 percent levy; women's overcoats and cloaks, 22.65 percent; men's wool trousers, 21.5 percent; and women's blouses, 24.1 percent.[11] The 1989 *Economic Report of the President* concluded that tariffs and quota restrictions produced an average effective tariff charge of over 50 percent for apparel imports.[12]

It is not just foreign citizens who lose because of Washington's protectionist policies. William Cline of the Institute for International Economics estimates the combined costs to American consumers of textile tariffs and quotas under the Multifiber Arrangement to be $20.3 billion on the wholesale level and as much as $40 billion on the retail level.[13]

[9]Interview with Clint Stack, September 9, 1992.

[10]*Federal Register*, July 29, 1992, p. 33494.

[11]Office of the U.S. Trade Representative, *U.S. Proposal for Uruguay Round Market Access Negotiations* (Washington, D.C.: USTR, 1990), p. 208. (This document is labeled on the cover as "secret.")

[12]The White House, *Economic Report of the President* (Washington, D.C.: Government Printing Office, 1989), p. 172.

[13]William R. Cline, *The Future of World Trade in Textiles and Apparel* (Washington, D.C.: Institute for International Economics, 1990). p. 193.

Agriculture

Eighty years ago, Romania was the world's fourth largest exporter of corn and wheat, and Hungary and Poland were also leading agricultural exporters. Communism wrecked those industries and, unfortunately, trade barriers in the United States and the European Community are thwarting the natural revival of agriculture in Eastern Europe.

Poland and Hungary have good potential as dairy exporters—but the U.S. government prohibits Eastern European nations from selling a single pound of butter, dry milk, or ice cream in America. The U.S. quota on beef imports may also hinder the Eastern European countries. Restrictions on those goods are so high that the U.S. Department of Agriculture estimates dairy import quotas cost Americans between $5 billion and $7 billion a year,[14] while the beef import quota costs consumers $873 million in 1987.[15]

Bulgaria is another victim of protectionism. The ITC reported in early 1991, "Bulgaria ranks as the world's fourth largest exporter of tobacco and the world's largest exporter of cigarettes."[16] But the United States maintains high tariffs on both tobacco and cigarettes: 458.3 percent on tobacco stems, 34.9 percent on tobacco, and 32 percent on cigarettes.[17]

Steel

In 1989, the Bush administration announced its decision to extend steel import quotas through March 1992. U.S. quotas dictated that Poland could export only 350 tons of alloy tool steel; Czechoslovakia, 100 tons of stainless steel bars; and Hungary, 200 tons of stainless steel

[14]U.S. Department of Agriculture, *Estimates of Producer and Consumer Subsidy Equivalents, Government Intervention in Agriculture, 1982–87* (Washington, D.C.: U.S. Department of Agriculture, 1990), p. 310. The consumer costs per year ranged from a low of $5.1 billion in 1983 to a high of $7.025 billion in 1984.

[15]Ibid., p. 298.

[16]U.S. International Trade Commission, "Eastern Europe: An Overview of Economic Reform, Industrial Structure, and Trade," p. 72.

[17]Office of the U.S. Trade Representative, *U.S. Proposal for Uruguay Round Market Access Negotiations*, p. 57.

rod to the United States each year.[18] Those quotas provided a powerful disincentive for foreign investment in Eastern European industry that could help retool those nations' inefficient manufacturing sectors. The Bush administration quotas expired in March 1992, but the Clinton administration has reimposed steel import quotas on foreign nations, many of which face eviction from the U.S. market because of the U.S. dumping law.

Indeed, only three months after the steel quotas expired, U.S. steel companies filed anti-dumping petitions against foreign steel producers, alleging that their steel was being sold in the United States at unfairly low prices. Poland and Romania were both hit with lockout steel dumping margins (i.e., tariff surcharges set by the Commerce Department); Romania was assigned a dumping margin of 75 percent and Poland, 62 percent. The Commerce Department, in its June 1993 ruling on this case, effectively declared that Poland must be judged and penalized as if it were still a communist country. To make that ruling, Commerce officials compared Poland's export prices to the United States with the alleged costs of production in Thailand, South Africa, and Malaysia. The Commerce Department also made the duties it imposed on Poland retroactive, claiming that the Poles had been guilty of a "massive increase" in their steel exports after the dumping investigation began. But Polish steel exports amounted to less than 0.5 percent of U.S. steel consumption and were down sharply from previous years.

Similarly, Romanian exports have been effectively barred from the United States solely on the basis of unverified allegations made about them by American steel producers. The Commerce Department had no proof that Romanians were trading unfairly in steel and refused to accept evidence that the Romanians submitted to them. Nevertheless, after reviewing those cases, the ITC concluded that imports from Poland and Romania had somehow injured their American competition—even though they represented minute quantities of the steel imported into the United States. The ITC's decision amounts to an embargo on steel imports from those two countries yet will likely

[18]See, for instance, Office of the U.S. Trade Representative, "Arrangement Concerning Trade in Certain Steel Products between the Government of the Polish People's Republic and the Government of the United States of America," 1985, p. 3. The 1989 agreement extended the 1985 quota levels.

provide no benefit to U.S. companies, since Eastern European steel is of much lower quality than U.S. steel and does not compete with American steel.

Miscellaneous Products

Hungary and Romania are also handicapped by high U.S. tariffs on chemicals and pharmaceuticals. The ITC reported: "The chemical and pharmaceutical sector, with 20 percent of the country's industrial output, is a major growth area for Hungary and its largest industrial exporter, with one-fifth of total exports. It accounted for 5 percent of the world market in pharmaceuticals."[19] Yet the American Association of Exporters and Importers reports that the United States hits hundreds of chemicals with tariff rates of 20 percent or higher.[20] Eastern European nations are also victimized by other U.S. restrictions. Aspirin carries a 10.2 percent tariff; anti-depressants and tranquilizers, 16.6 percent; and sulfathiazole, an anti-infective agent, 15 percent.

Anti-Dumping Fines

One of the least known U.S. barriers to Eastern European exports is the American anti-dumping law, theoretically intended to prevent below-cost sale of foreign goods. U.S. law penalizes most nations if their exports are priced lower here than at home or if the foreign goods are priced lower than the cost of production plus an 8 percent profit. But American bureaucrats cannot find an easy way to judge the export prices of nonmarket economies, so these nations' prices are, in general, automatically assumed to be unfair. And, despite major reforms in Eastern Europe, the Commerce Department has no present plans to change how it judges Eastern European product prices.

Prices in nonmarket economies are set by administrative fiat, rather than by market competition, thus making international price comparisons difficult. The Commerce Department, which administers the anti-dumping law, "solves" this dilemma by randomly selecting other nations as surrogates and guesstimating how much it would cost the

[19]U.S. International Trade Commission, "Eastern Europe: An Overview of Economic Reform, Industrial Structure, and Trade," p. 75.

[20]American Association of Exporters and Importers, Submission to the Trade Policy Staff Committee, October 18, 1989.

second country to produce the product being exported by the Eastern European country. Commerce then compares this contrived price to the export price.

Thus, "fairness" of Eastern European prices depends almost entirely on which nation Commerce arbitrarily chooses as a surrogate. An Eastern European company can never know what country Commerce will choose for comparison of prices and production costs, so it is impossible for a company to set its own prices to avoid violating U.S. trade law. Nor could any American, in or out of government, predict which country would be a good model. Gary Horlick, deputy assistant secretary of commerce for import administration from 1981 to 1983, described the process to the Senate Finance Committee: "I can tell horror stories about how one goes about choosing a surrogate; it is usually done about 10 at night when one has run out of any reasonable alternative. Just to take an example, for Chinese shop towels we went through, in order: Pakistan, Thailand, Malaysia, Hong Kong, the Dominican Republic, Colombia, and wound up with a hypothetical Chinese factory in India. It just doesn't make any sense."[21] Former ITC commissioner Ron Cass and lawyer Stephen Narkin observed in November 1990, "Selection of the surrogate country provides boundless opportunity for biasing the outcome, and there is more than a little evidence that Commerce has availed itself of this opportunity on several occasions."[22]

Yet Eastern European exports are considered "fair" or "unfair" solely on the basis of how their prices compare to the contrived price that Commerce creates for a surrogate country. Anti-dumping orders are currently in place against Czech steel wire rod, Hungarian roller bearings, Romanian urea and ball bearings, and, as already cited, Romanian and Polish steel.

Uranium: A Case Study of the Anti-Dumping Maze

On May 29, 1992, the Commerce Department announced it was imposing a 115.82 percent dumping penalty on uranium imported

[21]U.S. Congress, Senate Committee on Finance, *Nonmarket Economy Imports Legislation* (Washington, D.C.: Government Printing Office, 1984), p. 18.

[22]Ronald A. Cass and Stephen J. Narkin, "Antidumping and Countervailing Duty Law: The United States and the GATT," Conference on the Commerce Department's Administration of the Trade Remedy Laws, Brookings Institution, November 29, 1990, p. 22.

from six of the nations created by the shattering of the Soviet Union—
Russia, Ukraine, Kazakhstan, Tajikistan, Uzbekistan, and Kyrgyzstan.[23]
Uranium had been the Soviet Union's fourth largest export, and the
Commerce Department's decision—which effectively bans imports—
devastated one of the Commonwealth of Independent States' (CIS) most
competitive industries.[24]

Domestic uranium producers and a labor union filed their com-
plaints against Soviet imports on November 8, 1991. The Soviet Union
officially dissolved on December 25, 1991, and was replaced by the CIS.
Under U.S. anti-dumping law, the period of investigation of a foreign
producer's prices is the six months *prior* to the filing of an anti-
dumping petition and investigations must focus on the *country* from
which allegedly unfair imports are coming.

The Commerce Department investigated whether Russia, Ukraine,
and other CIS countries charged fair prices on uranium exports from
June 1991 through October 1991—although none of the CIS governments existed at that time. Commerce deputy assistant secretary
Francis Sailer declared in a March 24, 1992, memo that "the dissolution
of the former Soviet Union after the initiation of an anti-dumping
investigation is not relevant. . . ." Yet, Commerce was preparing to
penalize new governments for the pricing behavior of a previous
regime's politically controlled industry over which they had no
control. Blaming the new CIS governments for the policies of the
deceased Soviet Union was like holding George Washington liable for
the crimes of King George III.

Nevertheless, Commerce sent representatives of CIS governments a
66-page questionnaire demanding detailed information on their uranium operations; but Commerce, in violation of U.S. law, failed to
provide CIS governments with copies of the full petitions filed by U.S.
industry against them. Two uranium-importing firms tried to gather
information for the Commerce Department but were denounced as
criminals in Kyrgyzstan for their questions about local uranium
production. One CIS official declared in Moscow in March that Com-

---

[23]*Federal Register*, June 3, 1992, p. 23380 et seq. (The *Federal Register* notice on dumping
cases is published a few days after the Commerce Department officially releases its
results.)

[24]James Bovard, "U.S. Protectionists Claim a Russian Victim," *Wall Street Journal*,
June 8, 1992, p. A10.

merce's questionnaire appeared to have been issued by the U.S. Central Intelligence Agency to obtain highly confidential information.

Indeed, uranium production, because of its military applications, is considered a top-secret activity by most nations. The General Agreement on Tariffs and Trade (GATT) Code specifically exempts governments from being required to provide information "contrary to [their] essential security interest," such as information "relating to fissionable materials or the materials from which they are derived." If foreign governments demanded detailed information on U.S. uranium production, the U.S. government would probably scorn their demand.

Commerce, however, convicted CIS governments for not providing thousands of pages of documentation on operations controlled by the Soviet Ministry of Atomic Power and Industry. That ministry was abolished in January 1992, and most CIS governments had only limited access to information on uranium operations in their territories during 1991. (Washington, in its May 29 ruling, rotely declared, "In a non-market economy case, the Commerce Department presumes central control of all production and exporting facilities.") The Commerce Department arbitrarily made the 115 percent anti-dumping duty retroactive to March 3, 1992. This meant that U.S. importers of uranium from the countries of the former Soviet Union—including a firm owned by its employees—faced millions of dollars of penalties that they had no means of paying.

As explained earlier, in most dumping cases, Commerce compares a foreign company's home market prices with U.S. prices. But for nonmarket economies such as the Soviet Union's, which lack realistic price systems, Commerce officials randomly select third countries and surmise third-country production costs to compare with the export prices. (Commerce, in violation of U.S. law, has refused to even consider whether any of the new CIS nations should be classified as market economies.)

How did Commerce decide that Soviet uranium prices were unfairly low? Commerce took the unproven assertions it received from U.S. uranium producers, juggled the numbers, and then announced that, if Soviet uranium had been mined with Canadian efficiency, Portuguese electricity, and Namibian labor costs, it should have cost 115 percent more than it actually did. Because the U.S. uranium industry asserted that Canadian uranium miners are four times as productive as Czech uranium miners, and Czechoslovakia was a nonmarket economy,

Commerce assumed that Canadian miners are also four times more productive than CIS miners. So Commerce boosted the dumping margins by assuming that CIS mines required four times as much labor as Canadian mines. Commerce's method gives new meaning to the old phrase, "close enough for government work."

Commerce used the most punitive method available in this case. Instead of the concoct-an-imaginary-uranium-producer test, Commerce officials could have judged Soviet export prices simply by comparing them to the prices of other major uranium exporters, such as Canada and Australia. This test might still have found small dumping margins, but it would not have destroyed the CIS's exports. Instead, Commerce officials chose the method that maximized their arbitrary power over imports.

In most dumping cases, a key issue is whether imports have injured an American industry. But every year since 1984 the U.S. Department of Energy (DOE) has publicly declared that the U.S. uranium industry is not commercially viable. U.S. uranium ore is of far lower quality than that of Canada, and the U.S. industry has been hemorrhaging losses and slashing operations for years. Thus, the question in this case is whether blocking CIS uranium imports can miraculously resurrect a dead industry.

Perhaps the strongest force pushing for anti-dumping penalties was the DOE, which paid $3.3 million to a Washington law firm to fight uranium imports. DOE owns and operates the only plants in the United States producing enriched uranium—a staple for nuclear power plants. DOE's uranium enrichment plants are technological dinosaurs; DOE uses an older technique to enrich uranium that requires 20 times more electricity than the Soviets used. The only way that DOE can remain "competitive" in the United States is by crippling the foreign competition.

DOE's victory was a disaster for America's public utilities and the 50 million Americans who rely on nuclear power. Commerce's 115 percent dumping duty on CIS imports could mean as much as $300 million in higher utility bills. New York Power, Virginia Power, and other utility companies loudly protested the dumping investigation.

The U.S. anti-dumping penalties provoked harsh reaction from Russian officials as well. Russia's minister of atomic energy, Victor Mikhailov, declared in a September 1992 speech in London:

When we hear talk of support for perestroika and for the changes under way in Russia but see no action, this bothers me a great deal. We believe efforts to limit or reduce our exports are unfair and unfortunate. Last year we exported uranium worth $500 million. You must understand that our mines and factories can produce much more—we have a high level of technological efficiency in this field and produce a high quality product. We can increase production four or five times to bring in two billion dollars. We are not asking for help from the West—we can earn the currency we need. We understand that increasing our exports of nuclear products and services has affected producers of these same products and services in the West, but such are the laws of supply and demand and the nature of competition. The nuclear fuel industry is one of the few industries in Russia with a high level of scientific and technical potential, state-of-the-art technology and a high efficiency which allows it to be competitive in the world market and provide hard currency revenues which Russia needs to implement various economic programmes.[25]

U.S. pressure eventually compelled the CIS nations to agree to restrictive import quotas in lieu of being totally excluded from the U.S. market by the Commerce Department's outlandish dumping margins.[26] Under the agreement, finalized in October 1992, the United States imposed quotas on uranium imports from Russia and other former Soviet nations. Kazakhstan, Kyrgyzstan, Tajikistan, and Uzbekistan have been banned from exporting uranium to the United States until the world uranium price rises at least 30 percent.[27]

Countervailing Duties

At least nonmarket economies are exempt from the U.S. countervailing duty law—yet another protectionist restriction that penalizes foreign companies for alleged government subsidies. Once Eastern European nations make a transition to market-oriented economies, however, their exports will be sitting ducks for Washington's counter-

[25]Judith Perera, "Energy: No Stopping Uranium Exports, Says Russian Minister," Inter Press Service, September 11, 1992.

[26]Keith Bradsher, "U.S. Initials Import Pact on Uranium," *New York Times*, September 18, 1992, p. D6.

[27]James Bovard, "Free Trade, 1990s-Style, Is Anything But," *Wall Street Journal*, November 10, 1992, p. A24.

vailing duty regime. Even if Eastern European nations adopt laissez-faire policies, Commerce can still penalize their companies for subsidies received from defunct communist regimes up to 15 years before. Commerce announced in the *Federal Register* a ruling penalizing German steel imports:

> The Department preliminarily determines that subsidies to government-owned companies are not extinguished by the subsequent privatization of those companies. The amount we countervail is the value of the benefit received by the company allocated over time under the Department's standard methodology. The only event that the Department would recognize as extinguishing a countervailable subsidy would be the repayment to the government by a recipient company of the remaining value of that subsidy in accordance with the Department's methodology.[28]

With the current methodology, Commerce investigators will likely be able to justify imposing countervailing duties on the products of almost any factory built in Eastern Europe during the 1980s.

Conclusion

Washington's trade barriers on Eastern European products are protecting Americans from a threat that does not exist. Eastern European nations cannot engage in predatory pricing because their coffers are empty, most of their products are inferior, and their market share in the United States is minimal. Yet while we lecture Eastern Europeans on "the miracle of the marketplace," all we have offered them is a mirage of a marketplace.

The disruption to American industry from allowing unlimited imports from Eastern Europe would be slight and temporary. The impact would be greatest on the U.S. apparel industry—an industry that has been one of the nation's laggards for over 200 years. On the other hand, if the United States impedes Eastern Europe from achieving self-sufficiency, the result will be pressure for permanent foreign aid payments and a consequently heavy burden on American taxpayers.

The United States should declare a unilateral end to all trade barriers to Eastern European exports. This—an opportunity to work rather

---

[28]*Federal Register*, December 7, 1992, p. 57772.

than receive a handout—would be the best gift the American people could give to the millions of people struggling to rebuild their lives and nations. Indeed, we must speedily reform our trade policies to avoid "strangling in the crib" the struggling entrepreneurs of the former Eastern bloc. The West should take seriously the words that Jack Saryusz-Wolski, Poland's undersecretary of state for European integration, spoke two years ago: "Access to Western markets is the broadest form of assistance the West can give us. . . . For us, this is a question of life or death."[29] (Eastern European governments are admittedly more concerned at this time about the trade barriers they face in the European Community than in the United States.)

By lowering its trade barriers, the United States could create a level playing field between itself and at least one Eastern European country. Poland currently has fewer trade barriers than does the United States. As the *Financial Times* reported in 1991: "Poland now boasts an open economy that would do credit to many industrial countries. There are no import quotas . . . and tariffs have been slashed to an average of 8 per cent, with some raw materials allowed in duty free."[30] (By contrast, more than 3,000 of the 8,753 tariff categories of the U.S. tariff code are restricted by import quotas.)[31] Polish politicians have shown vastly more vision in trade policy than have American politicians; Vice President Al Gore, during an April 1993 visit to Warsaw, rhapsodized about the "green shoots of free enterprise springing up in cities and on the land" in Poland.[32] The least that the United States could do is to equal the courage of a nation that American politicians and officials are busy lecturing on the proper road to development and democracy.

If the United States did abolish its trade barriers to Eastern European imports, it could establish clear rules of origin to ensure that only products substantially produced in Eastern Europe are granted duty-free entry into the United States. (Rules of origin are the federal regulations that determine the national origin of an imported good.)

---

[29]*International Trade Reporter*, June 12, 1991, p. 893.

[30]"The Squeeze That Made Them Export," *Financial Times*, November 20, 1990.

[31]James Bovard, "Customs Service's Fickle Philosophers," *Wall Street Journal*, July 31, 1991, p. A10. For more details, see James Bovard, *The Fair Trade Fraud* (New York: St. Martin's, 1991).

[32]Paul Richter, "Poland Viewed as Model for East Europe, Gore Says," *Los Angeles Times*, April 21, 1993.

The rules of origin for Eastern European products could be modeled after similar provisions in the U.S. agreements with Canada and Israel and the Caribbean Basin Initiative.[33]

The psychological benefits of unilaterally offering free trade to Eastern European nations cannot be overestimated. During the dark years of communism, the United States stood as the symbol of freedom for many beleaguered Poles, Hungarians, Romanians, and others. Now, we have the opportunity to make this ideal a living reality in the daily lives of Eastern Europeans.

Rather than donating food to the Poles and Romanians, perhaps we should instead send them a few planes full of Washington lawyers to help them navigate U.S. trade policy. After all, the current policy of aid rather than trade is little more than a complex scheme to launder U.S. tax dollars through Eastern European government treasuries and into the pockets of Washington trade lawyers.

Are we rich enough that we can afford to give Eastern Europeans shiploads of handouts—yet so poor and fragile that we cannot allow them a chance to earn a few dollars honestly? Charity is no substitute for opportunity.

---

[33]It would be preferable simply to abolish all rules of origin at the same time that we abolish our trade barriers for products from all nations. But it does not appear likely that Congress will do this in the near future. Unfortunately, rules of origin have frequently been abused by politicians and bureaucrats to create nontariff barriers to trade. As Washington lawyer David Palmeter observed, "Customs' more recent country of origin determinations smack more of protectionism than of consumer protection, as the agency contorts, gyrates, and twists its way to one restrictive ruling after another." N. David Palmeter, "The U.S. Rules of Origin Proposal to GATT: Monotheism or Polytheism?" *Journal of World Trade*, April 1990, p. 28 et seq.

14. The Liberating Potential of Multinational Corporations

David Osterfeld

The multinational corporation (MNC) is one of the most thoroughly misunderstood and criticized institutions in the contemporary world. MNCs are criticized for, among other things, exporting jobs to the less developed countries to exploit workers there by paying them low wages.[1] They are also blamed for upsetting wage rates in the less developed countries by paying higher than prevailing rates.[2] They are criticized for using the less developed countries as dumping grounds for outdated technologies,[3] as well as for introducing the most modern, capital-intensive, and often inappropriate technologies, which are then blamed for causing unemployment, hunger, and poverty.[4] They are accused of charging both above-market prices, thereby reaping monopoly profits,[5] and below-market prices, thereby driving local com-

---

[1]Richard Barnet and Ronald Muller, *Global Reach* (New York: Simon & Schuster, 1974), p. 298; Robert Cox, "Labor and the Multinationals," in *Transnational Corporations and World Order*, George Modelski, ed. (San Francisco: W. H. Freeman, 1979), p. 416; and Sanjay Lall, "The Rise of Multinationals from the Third World," *Third World Quarterly*, July 1983, pp. 621–22.

[2]Adeoye Akinsanya, "Multinationals in a Changing Environment," in *World Politics Debated*, Herbert Levine, ed. (New York: McGraw-Hill, 1989), p. 58; and Wayne Nafziger, *The Economics of Developing Countries* (Belmont, Calif.: Wadsworth, 1984), p. 242.

[3]Barnet and Muller, pp. 164–65; and Graham Hancock, *The Lords of Poverty* (New York: Atlantic Monthly Press, 1989), pp. 162–69.

[4]Akinsanya, pp. 56–58; Barnet and Muller, pp. 166–72; Ronald Muller, "Poverty Is the Product," in *Transnational Corporations and World Order*, pp. 249–500; and United Nations, "Report of the Group of Eminent Persons to Study the Impact of Multinational Corporations on Development and on International Relations," in *Transnational Corporations and World Order*, p. 312.

[5]Barnet and Muller, pp. 158–59; Isaiah Frank, *Foreign Enterprises in Developing Countries* (Baltimore: Johns Hopkins University Press, 1981), p. 73; and Joan Edleman Spero, "Managing the Multinational Corporation," in *At Issue: Politics in the World Arena*, Stephen Speigel, ed. (New York: St. Martin's, 1984), p. 471.

271

petitors out of business.[6] But in fact, the MNC is perhaps the principal mechanism for the transfer of prosperity to the Third World.

The multinational corporation, as its name implies, is nothing more than a species of the corporation. What distinguishes the corporation from the MNC are not economic but political criteria. To illustrate, assume that in 1964 the "Malaya Company" had two plants, one located in Kuala Lumpur, the other in Singapore. Since both were within Malaysia, the Malaya Company would be a purely domestic operation. However, after Singapore's separation from the rest of Malaysia the following year, the Malaya Company would be regarded as a multinational corporation. Thus, the transformation of a domestic firm into a multinational corporation was a result not of any *economic* change on the part of the corporation but solely of a change in *political* boundaries. The MNC crosses at least one political boundary. That distinction is important.

Criticisms of the MNC can be divided into two categories: political and economic. The solution for those who criticize MNCs on political grounds is straightforward: the separation of economics entirely from politics, thereby permitting the MNC to allocate resources and produce goods and services unimpeded by political interference. However, the criticism of the second group, which is by far the more numerous of the two, is of an entirely different character. The criticism of MNCs for their economic activities is that MNCs concentrate corporate power, and, by their nature and the nature of the market process, are able to dictate prices and wages, exploit masses of people, undermine the sovereignty of less developed countries, make less developed countries dependent on the more developed countries, and perpetuate poverty and economic backwardness in the host countries for their own gain. That is, in fact, not just criticism of MNCs but an attack on the existence of the firms themselves.

The Functions of the MNC

"The key institution in the world economy facilitating the transfer of prosperity from the industrialized countries to the developing ones," wrote Melvyn Krauss, "is the multinational corporation."[7] To understand how the process of prosperity transfer takes place and the role of

---

[6]Akinsanya, p. 55; and Frank, pp. 29–30.

[7]Melvyn Krauss, *Development without Aid* (New York: McGraw-Hill, 1984), p. 126.

the MNC in it, it is necessary to assume, for analytical purposes, a world characterized by private property and its corollaries, freedom of trade and migration, and thus a world in which states either do not exist or, if they do, exist as nothing more than administrative units. In such a hypothetical situation, the world becomes a single customs area and thus "the distinction between foreign investment and domestic investment disappears."[8] That assumption is necessary to examine the purely economic functions of the "multinational." Only after that is done can the impact of government interference with MNCs and the international economy be understood.

In such an order, capitalists and entrepreneurs, anxious to maximize profits, would transfer capital from areas where it was more plentiful relative to other factors, and thus where returns to capital were low, to areas where capital, and related resources such as technology and management and marketing skills, were scarce relative to labor and returns to them were correspondingly higher. Similarly, workers anxious to maximize their earnings would migrate from those areas where wages were low to those where wages were higher. This process would end only when both wage rates and returns to capital were equalized between areas.

The process of capital and labor migration is just what served to transform the Western world in the 19th century. Since Great Britain began to save and invest earlier than other nations, it had a higher standard of living than all other European countries. But "something happened which caused the headstart of Great Britain to disappear." That something was the internationalization of capital. Wrote Ludwig von Mises, in 1817:

> The great British economist Ricardo still took it for granted that . . . capitalists would not try to invest abroad. But a few decades later, capital investment abroad began to play a most important role in world affairs. . . . Foreign investment meant that British capitalists invested in those European countries which, from the point of view of Great Britain, were short of capital and backward in their development. It is a well known fact that the railroads of most European countries . . . were built with the aid of British capital. The gas companies in all the cities of

[8]Robert Aliber, "A Theory of Direct Foreign Investment," in *The International Corporation*, Charles Kindleberger, ed. (Cambridge, Mass.: MIT Press, 1970), p. 21.

Europe were also British. . . . In the same way British capital developed railroads and many branches of industry in the United States.[9]

Occurring at the same time was the "great migration" from Europe, which was relatively overpopulated and where wages were therefore low, to America, which was underpopulated and, accordingly, where wages were higher. This dual process of capital and labor migration would be expected to continue until equilibrium was reached, that is, until the marginal utilities of both capital and labor were equalized. This is essentially what occurred in the Western world although to the extent that tariff and migration barriers were present complete equalization was prevented.[10] But this dual migration played a vitally important role in transforming, within the space of just a couple of centuries, a stagnant and economically backward continent into the most vibrant and economically productive continent in history. There is no reason to suppose that the peoples of America and the West are inherently different from the people in other parts of the world. Therefore, other things being equal, this is also what one would expect to occur throughout the world. And it has, in fact, begun if not already occurred in such places as Japan, Hong Kong, Taiwan, and South Korea, to name but a few.[11]

In brief, the process of capital and labor migration is, in fact, the process through which prosperity is created and diffused. For expansion of the scope of the market order results in a deepening of the division of labor and increased specialization, and therefore a more efficient allocation of factors, labor as well as capital. Increasing productivity and thus expanding world output are the result. That is tremendously beneficial to the less developed countries, because they can least afford the squandering of scarce resources.

What function does the firm have in this process? Assume that a firm generates a new product or a new method of production for an established product. Given uncertainties—such as the demand for the product, reactions of competitors whose market the new product is

[9]Ludwig von Mises, *Economic Policy* (South Bend, Ind.: Regnery, 1979), pp. 78–80.

[10]See, for example, Ludwig von Mises, *Nation, State and Economy* (1919; New York: New York University Press, 1983), pp. 65–72, and *Liberalism*, (1927; Irvington-on-Hudson, N.Y.: Foundation for Economic Education and Cobden Press, 1985), pp. 136–42.

[11]See Krauss or Alvin Rabushka, *The New China: Comparative Economic Development in Mainland China, Taiwan and Hong Kong* (Boulder, Colo.: Westview, 1987).

jeopardizing, the possible need to adjust input mixes or to modify the product itself—it is usually vital at the early stage of what Raymond Vernon calls the "product cycle" for the firm to be located close to its intended market. "In the choice of location, flexibility and swift response were given more weight than capital and labor cost."[12] As demand for the product grows, the firm's initial response is to satisfy this demand through exports. Eventually the more distant markets may reach a size at which it becomes more economical to service them through new production facilities in those markets rather than through exports from the central site. That may be especially the case when competitors begin imitating the new product, thereby making price considerations a more urgent concern than product differentiation. The firm may, in fact, have no alternative to establishing production facilities in distant markets since, if it does not, competitors surely will, thereby driving the firm out of those particular markets. As Raymond Vernon summarized it:

> The enterprise, having lost its oligopoly advantage, finds that it can no longer claim any cost or other advantage over its imitators, local and foreign; even its overseas subsidiaries, operating in an economic environment no different from their competitors, begin to feel the pressure. At this stage, diseconomies associated with large size and an elaborate apparatus threatened to outweigh the economies.[13]

Thus, at this point the enterprise stops growing and may begin to retrench. It is clear that many if not most of the additional operating facilities would be located in administrative units—states—different from that of the parent firm, thereby transforming the domestic corporation into a multinational.

What makes the MNCs so important in the transfer of prosperity is precisely the fact that they link the less developed countries with the more developed countries through international trade. As already noted, the vast extension of the market that this linkage entails facilitates the efficient use of resources, thereby increasing world output. But other advantages follow. The MNC can, because of its function as a miniature capital market in which transaction costs are reduced or eliminated, facilitate the transfer of capital and technology

---

[12]Raymond Vernon, "The Product Cycle Model," in *Transnational Corporations and World Order*, p. 109.

[13]Ibid., p. 103.

to less developed countries at cheaper costs than they could otherwise be obtained. Moreover, the tremendous advantage the transfer of capital through MNCs or capital markets has over its acquisition through foreign aid is that it is far more likely to be productively used. Just as foreign aid is, by its nature, inefficient, foreign direct investment is, by its nature, efficient. As Peter Bauer and Basil Yamey point out, while mistakes will be made, "those providing the capital have a continuing interest in minimizing the chances of error and in taking remedial action when necessary. Their direct interest in the success of the investment and their power to control the use of their capital persist after the initial transfer of capital has been made."[14]

This leads to another, vitally important function of the MNC, that of serving as a buffer, or risk-reducing vehicle for less developed countries. The oil price shock of 1973–74 resulted in a massive surplus of savings in the oil-exporting countries that were recycled to banks in developed nations. Since the recession caused by the oil price shock reduced the demand in the developed nations for investment capital, interest rates declined (see Figure 14.1). And since the 1974 United Nations Resolution on the Establishment of a New International Economic Order deliberately discouraged foreign direct investment and applauded nationalizations of MNCs as the means to liberate less developed countries from dependence on the more developed countries, the result was a massive increase in commercial lending to less developed countries. Significantly, "loans to central governments and state owned enterprises were especially favored by commercial banks. Because of their sovereign status these entities were considered to be low risk. Developing countries were happy to take advantage of this unaccustomed access to cheap loans with few strings attached."[15] The result of the confluence of these two factors was to reinforce the decline of foreign direct investment's share of total foreign capital flows to the less developed countries. The problem was that the borrowing and investment decisions were "often imprudent and resulted in excessive indebtedness in a number of countries. And in a number of countries borrowing fueled a flight of capital that drained the pool of resources

[14]Peter Bauer and Basil Yamey, *The Economics of Under-Developed Countries* (Chicago: University of Chicago Press, 1957), p. 143.

[15]World Bank, *World Development Report* (New York: Oxford University Press, 1988), pp. 28–29.

Figure 14.1
INTEREST RATES ON EXTERNAL BORROWINGS OF DEVELOPING COUNTRIES, 1976–87

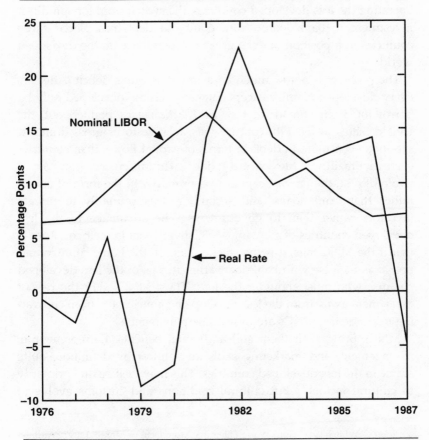

SOURCE: World Bank, *World Development Report 1988* (New York: Oxford University Press, 1988), Figure 1.9, p. 29. Reprinted by permission.

NOTE: LIBOR = London interbank offered rate. The nominal rate is the average six-month dollar LIBOR during each year; the real rate is the nominal LIBOR deflated by the change in the export price index for developing countries.

for investment even as the burdens of foreign debt mounted."[16] (See Figure 14.2.) The burden of debt repayment is now being shouldered by the citizens of the less developed countries in the form of both higher taxes and cutbacks in services. The irony is that far from liberating the less developed countries, the switch from foreign direct investment to bank loans, from equity to debt, has placed those countries in a position of even greater dependence on the developed world.

The problem is not so much an external accounts deficit. After all, every developed country except England became developed only by borrowing from abroad. In fact, as *The Economist* pointed out, the United States in the 19th century was, relative to its gross domestic product, even more in debt, in terms of capital flows, than countries such as Brazil and Mexico are today.[17] The difference, however, is twofold: first, the flow of capital was primarily in the form of equity rather than bank loans; and second, it was primarily to private investors rather than to governments. The advantage to the less developed countries of allowing MNC investment in their countries is that if the MNC fails, it is the stockholders in the home country, and not, as is the case with bank loans, the citizens of the less developed country, who must shoulder the loss. Thus, MNCs shift the risk of investment away from the less developed countries. Far from cultivating dependence, MNCs are in fact liberating agents.

MNCs bring with them still additional benefits. Entrepreneurial, management, and marketing skills are, almost by definition, quite scarce in the less developed countries. This may well be due primarily to cultural factors.[18] But cultural traditions and customs evolve to

[16]John C. Whitehead, "Third World Dilemma: More Debt or More Equity?" Address to the Council on Foreign Relations, New York City, October 1987. See also World Bank, p. 29.

[17]"Beggaring the Poor," *The Economist*, February 18, 1984, pp. 15–16.

[18]See, for example, Mark Casson, "General Theories of Multinational Enterprise: Their Relevance to Business History," in *Multinationals: Theory and History*, Peter Hertner and Jeoffrey Jones, eds. (Aldershot, England: Glower, 1987), pp. 56–57; Lawrence Harrison, *Underdevelopment Is a State of Mind* (Lanham, Md: Center for International Affairs and University Press of America, 1985); Michael Novak, "Why Latin America Is Poor," *Atlantic Monthly*, March 1982; and Richard Richardson and Osman Ahmend, "Challenge for Africa's Private Sector," *Challenge*, January–February 1987, pp. 16–25.

Figure 14.2
NET RESOURCE TRANSFERS TO DEVELOPING COUNTRIES,
1973–87

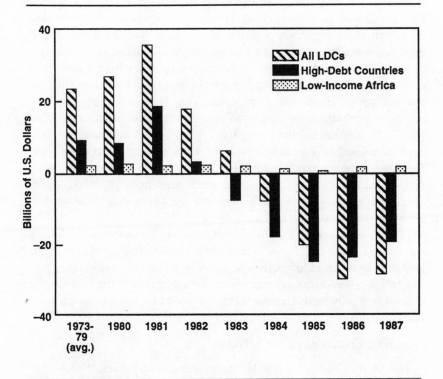

SOURCE: World Bank, *World Development Report 1988,* Figure 1.10, p. 30.
Reprinted by permission.
NOTE: Net resource transfers are defined as disbursements of medium and
long-term loans minus interest and amortization payments on medium
and long-term external debt.

adjust themselves to changing situations. Once the political environment ceases to suppress such skills, once it begins to reward rather
than punish innovation and entrepreneurial and management talents,
these skills will, in time, be developed. In fact, as studies by Hernando
de Soto and others who have studied the underground economy or the

informal sector have shown, there is a great deal more entrepreneurial activity in the developing world than traditionally thought.[19]

Moreover, the MNCs are the prime vehicles, directly as well as indirectly, not only for the transfer but, even more important, for the local development of these skills. The foreign firm is a principal means by which the indigenous population is able to acquire training and experience before striking out independently. And the very existence of the MNC, which means the concentration of rather large numbers of employees, creates a demand for certain goods and services that are seldom supplied by the firm itself. This demand stimulates the emergence of numerous stores and shops in the areas surrounding the MNC. The result is that the MNC, whether intentionally or not, contributes not only to developing local entrepreneurship but also to the development of such qualities as perception of economic opportunity, administrative skill, industry, discipline, frugality, and endurance.[20] Those qualities are indispensable for self-sustaining economic growth.

Finally, it should be pointed out that, as is the case with any corporation, the MNC is not inherently beneficial. It is good only so far as it is able to provide goods and services to people less expensively than they can be acquired elsewhere. Whether that is the case can be determined only through a market unimpeded by government restrictions.

Economic Criticisms of the MNC

The MNC has been subjected to numerous criticisms. These criticisms relate in one way or another to the belief that MNCs, in and of themselves, retard or even prevent economic growth and development in the less developed countries. An examination of the major criticisms of the MNC on purely economic grounds will help to shed further light on its operation in and impact upon the less developed countries. Criticisms include the following: (1) the MNCs transfer technology that

[19]Hernando de Soto, "Constraints on People: The Origins of Underground Economies and Limits to Their Growth," in *Beyond the Informal Sector*, Jerry Jenkins, ed. (San Francisco: ICS Press, 1988), and *The Other Path* (New York: Harper and Row, 1989); Gregory Grossman, "The Second Economy of the USSR," *Problems of Communism*, September–October 1972, pp. 25–40; and Wojtek Zafanolli, "A Brief Outline of China's Second Economy," *Asian Survey*, July 1985, pp. 715–36.

[20]Bauer and Yamey, pp. 108–10.

is too capital intensive and thus inappropriate for the economic situation of the less developed countries; (2) the MNCs are major components of an international economic system that holds down prices and thus wages in the less developed countries, thereby causing the terms of trade for the less developed countries to deteriorate; (3) MNCs pay higher salaries than domestic competitors can, thereby widening the income gap between the haves and have-nots; (4) MNCs retard the development of local entrepreneurship by driving local firms out of business; (5) MNCs do not transfer much capital to the less developed countries but instead acquire most of it through local borrowing, thereby raising interest rates, squeezing local enterprises out of business, and retarding development by transferring more profits out of the less developed countries than they put in through investments; and (6) the MNCs jeopardize the sovereignty and independence of the less developed countries and impede development by creating dependence on the MNCs, which impedes or prevents the development of local enterprises.

Inappropriate Technology

A common complaint against MNCs is that their investments in the less developed countries are "inappropriate" because while those countries have rapidly growing labor forces, MNC investment, it is claimed, is capital rather than labor intensive and thus does little or nothing to relieve the severe unemployment problems that plague these countries.[21] The reason usually cited is that the MNCs put profits before people.

First, the charge is not borne out by the available data. A study of more than 200 manufacturing firms indicated, in fact, that MNCs had a lower capital-labor ratio than their domestic counterparts.[22] And another study revealed that either there were no differences between foreign and domestic firms on this point or "where differences are present it is the MNCs that typically show more adaptation of technology."[23]

[21]Akinsanya, p. 58; Barnet and Muller, pp. 166–70; Frank, p. 73; and Spero, p. 471.

[22]Wilson Schmidt, "The Role of Private Capital in Developing the Third World," in *The Third World*, Scott Thompson, ed. (San Francisco: ICS, 1983), p. 274.

[23]Howard Pack, "Appropriate Industrial Technology: Benefits and Obstacles," *Annals of the American Academy of Political and Social Science*, November 1981, p. 34.

But even if the data are incomplete or the charge were to become true at some point in the future, one must ask why a company concerned solely with profits would employ expensive and sophisticated capital-intensive technologies, thereby deliberately passing up the gains to be made from introducing labor-intensive technologies that take advantage of cheap labor. The answer is not hard to find. Many governments in less developed countries have imposed minimum wage laws, prohibited the layoff of domestic workers during slack periods, or adopted other policies that increase the price of labor relative to that of capital. On the other hand, government restrictions on the importation of used machinery coupled with host country pressures on the MNCs to employ the most modern and sophisticated technologies are common in the less developed countries, as are overvalued exchange rates, ceilings on interest rates, and subsidies and tax breaks for the importation of capital equipment. The result is a systematic and substantial reduction in the cost of using capital. The net effect of such policies, which artificially increase the cost of labor while reducing the cost of capital, is to distort the price structure in such a way as to encourage firms operating in the less developed countries, foreign as well as domestic, to employ unnecessarily complex, capital-intensive technologies.[24]

For example, policies introduced in Peru by the government of Velasco Alvarado in the late 1960s, some of which remain in effect to this day, have significantly distorted factor prices to the detriment of labor. Policies such as minimum wage rates and taxes on wages raised the real cost of labor while other policies, including interest rate subsidies, tax exemptions on import duties, and overvalued exchange rates, reduced the cost of capital importation. As a result, the price of labor rose by 102 percent relative to the price of capital. The effect was to encourage the substitution of capital for labor, thereby reducing employment in the formal sector by nearly 40 percent. And this figure, according to the World Bank, "is probably an underestimate" since the effect of these distortions did not "take into account lost opportunities for exports of labor-intensive products. High labor costs reduced

[24]See Frank, pp. 76–77; Krauss, pp. 134–38; Nafziger, pp. 242–43; Pack, pp. 34–37; and Gustav Ranis, "Technology Choice and the Distribution of Income," *Annals of the American Academy of Political and Social Science*, November 1981, p. 51.

Peru's natural comparative advantage in these commodities."[25] A recent World Bank study has noted that tax breaks for the importation of capital equipment, subsidized credit policies, and overvalued exchange rates artificially reduce the price of capital.[26] This, coupled with minimum wages, job security laws, social security, and other "pro-labor" policies, has increased the price of labor relative to capital by as much as 50 percent in Argentina, Brazil, and Ivory Coast; 90 percent in Tunisia; and as much as 300 percent in Pakistan. The result was an increase in the capital intensity of production and a reduction in the relative demand for labor. For example, studies of job security regulations have indicated that the regulations reduced the demand for labor during the decade of the 1980s by 18 percent in India and by 25 percent in Zimbabwe. To quote the World Bank, "By trying to improve the welfare of workers there, governments reduced formal sector employment, increased the supply of labor to the rural and urban informal sectors, and thus depressed labor incomes where most of the poor are found."[27]

But government-spawned "inappropriate technology" is not solely a matter of foreign investment. Government-created factor distortions will likewise affect the investment of domestic capital. Through its policy of permitting fixed investments to be fully depreciated in the first year and then to be depreciated as much as six times over, Brazil has encouraged excessive capital investment in land. Brazil's tax policy, according to the World Bank, "encourages excessive mechanization, . . . reducing the demand for unskilled labor. . . . Opportunities for unskilled workers to acquire skills by becoming long-term workers have been substantially reduced by subsidized mechanization."[28]

Inappropriate technology is therefore not an example of so-called market failure. It is a result of government failure. Misdiagnosing the problem as one of market failure has had significant ramifications. It has resulted in, or at least has been used to justify, increased regulation of MNCs by many less developed country governments. Both the

---

[25]World Bank, *World Development Report 1987* (New York: Oxford University Press, 1987), p. 126.

[26]World Bank, *World Development Report 1990* (New York: Oxford University Press, 1990), pp. 62–63.

[27]Ibid., p. 63.

[28]Ibid., p. 59.

United Nations' Code of Conduct on the Transfer of Technology, adopted in the early 1980s, and the Brandt Commission report not only applaud these policies but call for increased international regulation of the MNCs to reduce "market imperfection."[29] The tragedy is that since the basic cause of such "market imperfections" as "inappropriate technology" and the resulting high unemployment rates experienced by many less developed countries is too much government interference in the market, additional regulation can only aggravate the very problems it was designed to solve. The only way to discover which technology is appropriate for any given less developed country is for the governments of less developed countries to cease distorting the price structures in their countries by abandoning their interventionist measures and permitting the price mechanism of the market to perform its function of indicating relative scarcities.

Deteriorating Terms of Trade

Another common complaint is that the less developed countries face deteriorating terms of trade, that is, that the prices of primary products fall relative to manufactured goods and since less developed countries are exporters of the former and importers of the latter, they must constantly produce more and more simply to remain where they are. Richard Barnet and Ronald Muller have written that the industrialized nations

> have used their technological and marketing superiority to obtain terms of trade which, not surprisingly, favor them at the expense of their weaker trading partners in the underdeveloped world. Thus, over the past twenty-five years, until the 1970s, because of the falling relative price of certain essential raw materials the countries of the underdeveloped world have had to exchange an ever increasing amount of such raw materials to get the finished goods and technological expertise they need. This steady worsening of the terms of trade between the rich countries and the poor is an important reason why the "gap" between them has continued to grow.[30]

[29]See, for example, Rachel McCulloch, "Technology Transfer to Developing Countries: Implications of International Regulation," *Annals of the American Academy of Political and Social Science*, November 1981, pp. 121–22; and Willy Brandt et al., *North-South: A Program for Survival* (Cambridge, Mass.: MIT Press, 1980), pp. 195–98.

[30]Barnet and Muller, p. 136.

MNCs are important components in this process since they "control many of the most important export commodities of developing countries."[31]

The argument dates from the works of economists Raúl Prebisch and Hans Singer in 1950. Those studies showed that the ratio of the prices of primary commodities relative to manufactured goods declined from 100 for the period 1876–80 to 64.1 for the period 1936–38.[32]

There are numerous problems, statistical as well as theoretical, that call into serious question any inherent tendency of the terms of trade for the less developed countries to deteriorate. First, Prebisch's findings were generalized from data restricted to the United Kingdom, and the validity of his findings depends, therefore, on whether the British data are representative of all industrialized countries. Estimates by Charles Kindleberger, which show a modest 19 percent improvement in the terms of trade for the industrial European countries between 1900 and 1938 in contrast to Prebisch's 34 percent improvement for the United Kingdom during the same period, suggest that they are not.[33] Second, the available data, although scanty, show that the British terms of trade steadily declined throughout the first half of the 19th century and reached their nadir in the 1860–80 period, precisely the period Prebisch chose as the base years for his study. Thus, the choice of the base years biased the results against the primary commodity exporting countries. And third, "the basic British export price index is on a F.O.B. (free on board) basis, while import prices are measured C.I.F. (cost, insurance and freight), that is, including transportation charges." Since freight rates declined by 50 percent between 1870 and 1913, this alone accounts for much and perhaps *all* of the decline in British import prices during the period. In fact, concluded Cole, "since the prices of British manufactured exports declined by 15 percent, the terms of trade of primary producing countries," far from declining, "may well have improved over that period."[34]

There are further difficulties. The quality of primary goods like copper, iron ore, and cotton remains about the same. But that of such manufac-

[31]Akinsanya, p. 56.

[32]Julio Cole, "The False Promise of Protectionism for Latin America," *Journal of Economic Growth*, Fourth Quarter 1986, p. 32, Table 1.

[33]Ibid., p. 32.

[34]Ibid., p. 33.

tured goods as tractors, automobiles, and computers has undergone tremendous improvement over the years. Failure to account for new products and quality improvements in existing manufactured goods introduces a serious upward statistical bias in the reporting of the prices of manufactured goods.[35]

Further, it should be noted that while an improvement in the commodity terms of trade can be interpreted as an improvement in national welfare, the reverse is not necessarily true. It is quite possible for national welfare to improve simultaneously with a deterioration in the terms of trade. What is crucial is not the price of a good exported relative to the price of a good imported. Rather, it is the *cost* of the good exported, that is, the sum of the factor prices, relative to the price of the good imported. Thus, since the price of copper declined from $1.10 per pound in 1975 to $0.76 per pound in 1985, the commodity terms of trade for copper exporters have, assuming stable import prices, deteriorated by more than 25 percent. But if the cost of manufacturing that copper has fallen from, say, $1.00 to $0.50 per pound, the profit or foreign exchange a less developed country would earn from the sale of the same amount of copper would be much higher in 1985 than it was a decade earlier ($0.10 per pound in 1975; $0.26 per pound in 1985). It is obvious that a less developed country could import more goods in 1985 than in 1975 even with deteriorating terms of trade.

That is just what has happened in much of the Third World. Because of improvements in transportation and the introduction of newer production techniques, usually through the MNCs, the cost of producing such goods as cocoa, sugar, rubber, and many other primary products has dramatically declined.[36] And since the same line of reasoning applies to wage rates, deteriorating terms of trade are also consistent with rising real wages. The key fact is that nearly *everyone* pays less for food, shelter, and clothing today than in, say, 1900. That is because the economic pie has been increasing more rapidly than population. True, the improvement has tended to be less rapid for the less developed countries than for the more

[35]Peter Bauer, *Dissent on Development* (Cambridge, Mass.: Harvard University Press, 1972), p. 242.

[36] Bauer, p. 241; Gottfried Haberler, "Terms of Trade and Economic Development," in *Economics of Trade and Development*, James Theberge, ed. (New York: John Wiley, 1968), p. 329; Arthur Lewis, "A Review of Economic Development," *American Economic Review*, May 1965, pp. 1–16; and Raymond Vernon, *Storm over the Multinationals* (Cambridge, Mass.: Harvard University Press, 1977), pp. 2–3.

developed countries. But, of course, that is what is meant by the term "less developed countries."

Moreover, the thesis is based on the assumption that less developed countries are solely exporters of primary products, while developed countries are solely exporters of manufactured goods. That may have been largely true in the first half of this century but it certainly no longer holds. Singapore, Hong Kong, Taiwan, South Korea, and Brazil have all become major exporters of electronic equipment such as televisions and radios. And automobile production has recently been increasing at a yearly rate of 14 percent in Brazil and nearly 10 percent in Mexico, compared to only 4.4 percent in the United States and 3.4 percent in Britain. The Philippines, South Korea, and Malaysia are also quietly becoming major producers of automobiles.[37] In fact, as Nathaniel Leff has observed, "Multinational corporations with 'sourcing' subsidiaries located in the Third World have had a large role in this expansion of manufactured exports from developing countries."[38] Conversely, more developed countries, such as the United States, are major exporters of agricultural products and, in the case of Canada, major exporters of raw materials.

Finally, even if the Prebisch-Singer thesis were logically valid, it is difficult to see how it could account for the poverty of the poorest of the less developed countries, since they have so little trade with other countries that changes in the terms of trade, regardless of direction, would have a negligible impact.

Given the statistical and theoretical problems of the Prebisch-Singer thesis one would not expect it to "explain" the data. It does not. As Table 14.1 shows, the commodity terms of trade for the less developed countries improved by 23 percent during the period 1937–59. As for the post-1959 period (Table 14.2), the terms of trade for both Latin American exports as a whole and Latin American exports of primary products were stable up to 1970. They showed significant fluctuations

---

[37]Geoffrey Godsell, "Tomorrow's Big Powers: Confucian Work Ethic Thrusts Small Nations into Big League," in *World Politics 80/81*, Chau T. Phan, ed. (Guilford, Conn.: Dushkin, 1988); John Kimball, "The Trade Debate: Patterns of U.S. Trade," in *World Politics 80/81*; Lall, pp. 618–26; Barbara Samuels, *Managing Risk in Developing Countries* (Princeton, N.J.: Princeton University Press, 1990), p. 6; and John Spanier, *Games Nations Play* (New York: Holt, Rinehart and Winston, 1981), p. 372.

[38]Nathaniel Leff, "Beyond the New International Economic Order," in *The Third World*, Scott Thompson, ed. (San Francisco: ICS, 1983), p. 246.

Table 14.1
TERMS OF TRADE, 1937–59 (1937 = 100)

Year	Underdeveloped Countries	Latin America
1937	100	100
1948	108	123
1951	160	138
1954	128	139
1957	127	128
1959	123	110

SOURCE: Cole, p. 33. Reprinted by permission.

during the 1970s and early 1980s, due no doubt to the oil crisis. But overall the data show no indication of systematic, long-term deterioration. That is especially the case because the data have not been adjusted for quality changes and other biases.[39]

Despite its shortcomings, the Prebisch-Singer thesis is regarded by many as true. That is tragic, since if trade with the more developed countries is harmful to the less developed countries as the thesis suggests, then it follows that the less developed countries would be better off severing their ties with the more developed countries. Thus the Prebisch-Singer thesis leads logically to a policy of protectionism and economic autarky. But protectionism most harms the countries practicing it. Withdrawing from the world market means that a country must produce what it needs within its own borders. That, in turn, means that it must divert factors from where they were being employed so they can now be used in the production of goods that were previously imported. But since the only reason they were not produced domestically in the first place was because they could be purchased more cheaply from abroad, factors are diverted from areas where they were used more productively into areas where they are utilized less productively. The basic problem is that "the use of protection to promote substitution of local for foreign production does nothing to reduce the comparative disadvantage of local as contrasted with foreign entrepreneurship."[40] For example, since it is often the

[39]Cole, pp. 13–14.

[40]Harry Johnson, "Tariffs and Economic Development: Some Theoretical Issues," in *Economics of Trade and Development*, pp. 371–75.

Table 14.2

TERMS OF TRADE FOR LATIN AMERICA, 1959–83 (1970 = 100)

Year	Total	Nonoil	Primary Products
1959	102	–	108
1960	102	–	106
1961	100	–	101
1962	94	–	98
1963	95	–	105
1964	97	–	109
1965	93	–	105
1966	95	–	105
1967	93	–	98
1968	95	–	98
1969	96	–	102
1970	100	100	100
1971	97	–	90
1972	100	–	93
1973	113	–	124
1974	131	–	130
1975	114	82	95
1976	119	–	105
1977	126	98	117
1978	113	–	98
1979	117	82	100
1980	121	–	98
1981	110	66	88
1982	101	–	80
1983	94	–	88

SOURCE: Cole, p. 33. Reprinted by permission.

case, especially in the less developed countries, that the domestic market for a good is too small to permit the exploitation of economies of scale, the costs of production are inordinately high.

Thus, although protection may artificially stimulate industrialization, industrialization should not be confused with development. It usually correlates with development because on the free market new technologies are introduced only when they reduce costs by increasing output per unit of input. But such is not the case with protectionism. Since what occurs is a shifting of resources from more to less productive uses, the result is that everyone, except perhaps the domestic producers of the good, is less well off. Moreover, a policy of protectionism or import substitution requires a great deal of governmental interference. And as the domestic economy becomes politicized, effort is diverted from the production of wealth to its transfer. The reduction in output means that the country is now poorer than it otherwise would have been.

This argument is consistent with the data. Figures 14.3 and 14.4 show that those less developed countries having the least trade with such developed countries as the United States have had the most difficulty generating economic growth and development. On the other hand, those that have had the most trade with the developed countries have also been the most successful at stimulating consistent, self-sustaining economic growth.

That, of course, is the exact reverse of what one would expect to find if the Prebisch-Singer thesis were correct.

Finally, the reduction in foreign trade is likely to be accompanied by increased dependence on foreign capital. That is, goods that were previously obtained via imports must now be produced locally. And if the country is not able to do that on its own, it must entice foreign firms to construct plants there. But that must mean a misallocation of resources, since otherwise the MNC would have constructed such plants even before the tariff. It is likely that the foreign firm will demand a compensating advantage in the form of guarantees by the host country to keep out competitors, domestic or foreign, thereby enabling the MNC to obtain monopoly profits.

As Peter Drucker has written:

> The multinational's capacity to allocate production across national boundary lines and according to the logic of the world market should ... be a major ally of the developing countries. The more rationally and the more "globally" production is being allocated, the more they stand to gain. ... Thus, the most advantageous strategy for the developing countries would seem to be to replace—or at least supplement—the policy of "domestic content" by a policy that uses the multinationals'

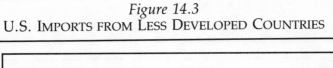

Figure 14.3
U.S. IMPORTS FROM LESS DEVELOPED COUNTRIES

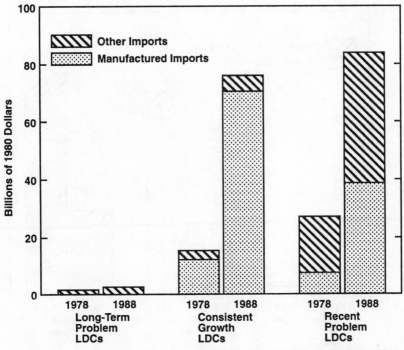

SOURCE: U.S. Agency for International Development, *Development and the National Interest* (Washington, D.C.: Government Printing Office, 1989), p. 76. Reprinted by permission.

integrating ability to develop large production facilities with access to markets in the developed world.... As Taiwan and Singapore have demonstrated, it can make much more sense to become the most efficient large supplier worldwide of one model or one component than to be a high-cost small producer of the entire product or line. This would create more jobs and provide the final product at lower prices to the country's own consumers. And it would result in large foreign-exchange earnings.[41]

[41]Peter Drucker, "Multinationals and Developing Countries," *Foreign Affairs*, October 1974, pp. 128–29.

Figure 14.4
U.S. EXPORTS TO LESS DEVELOPED COUNTRIES

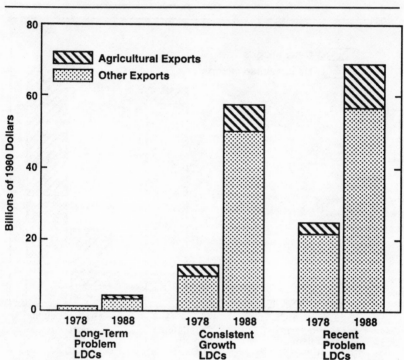

SOURCE: U.S. Agency for International Development, p. 76. Reprinted by permission.

MNCs and High Wage Rates

It is true that in the less developed countries the wage rates paid by the MNCs tend to be higher than those of domestic firms. That, argue critics of the MNCs, widens the income gap between the elite and the masses, thereby creating polarization and social conflict between economic classes in the less developed countries.[42]

In direct contrast with the terms of trade critique, which maintains that MNCs exploit workers by holding prices and wages down, this argument criticizes the MNCs for paying above domestic market

---

[42]Akinsanya, p. 58; and Nafziger, p. 242.

levels. But so long as the higher incomes of the MNC employees are a result of wealth creation rather than redistribution of existing wealth, the presence of the MNC, *even by the logic of the critique,* constitutes a welfare gain for the domestic economy: some are made better off while no one is made worse off. It is hard to understand why anyone would oppose such a phenomenon except on the grounds of envy.

But, of course, the process does not stop there. The higher incomes of those working for the MNC increase their purchasing power, which thereby generates additional demand for goods and services, many of which can be supplied, sometimes *only* be supplied, locally. This additional local demand therefore opens up wealth opportunities for other segments of the indigenous population. This is precisely what Krauss meant by the transfer of prosperity. The creation of new wealth sets in motion a self-sustaining process by which additional wealth is created and diffused throughout the society. The MNCs play a vital role in this process. To focus solely on its initial phase is to misrepresent entirely the nature of the market process.

MNCs and Local Businesses

Another criticism is that MNCs are so large and powerful that local firms cannot compete and are either driven out of business or bought out by the MNCs.[43] This, it is alleged, not only results in foreign-owned monopolies but also impedes or prevents economic growth in the less developed countries by retarding the acquisition of entrepreneurial and other skills needed for self-sustaining economic growth.

It is true that local businesses are sometimes "smothered" by the entry of an MNC. But the conclusions usually drawn from that do not follow. If a foreign-owned enterprise is able to offer enough to buy out a locally owned firm, it means that both parties believe that the MNC is able to use those assets more productively than the local firm. If they are correct, then resources are transferred from those using them less productively to those who are able to use them more productively. That is clearly a benefit to the local economy. The same is no less true for local firms driven into bankruptcy. For the government to "stimu-

---

[43] Akinsanya, p. 55; Barnet and Muller, p. 139; Frank, pp. 43–44; and Stephen Hymer, "The Efficiency (Contradictions) of Multinational Corporations," *American Economic Review*, May 1970, pp. 444–45.

late" local businesses by "protecting" them from competition rewards inefficiency and harms the local consumers who must pay higher prices, either directly or indirectly in the form of subsidies, for the products they buy.

Moreover, insulating inefficient firms from competition is hardly the way to foster entrepreneurial and other business skills. As already mentioned, far from inhibiting the development of local entrepreneurship it is precisely through the foreign-owned firm that such skills are best developed. Isaiah Frank has noted that the data show that a "substantial majority of managerial positions in subsidiaries are held by nationals."[44] That is because "it is very costly to transport and maintain foreign managers and their families. Moreover, foreign assignments may take an executive out of the mainstream of career development." Where "indigenous personnel are not experienced enough to run the operation," the MNCs will have no choice but to send in foreign executives at least on a temporary basis. Frank quotes one executive as saying, "When we send in a foreign manager, we hope he will do himself out of a job."

Finally, it is not true that local businesses cannot compete with MNCs. Local businesses often have advantages, such as a better knowledge of the market or lower overhead costs, that will enable them to be quite competitive. Ghanaian economist George Ayittey has observed that "many native [African] businessmen, despite their lack of capital and managerial skills, competed successfully with European firms."[45] But even where the MNC does achieve a monopoly by buying up or bankrupting local firms, it may still not harm the local consumers. Not only do "excessive profits" correct themselves by attracting new entrants, domestic or foreign (if allowed by the host government), but

> while direct investment may gobble up competitors and exploit its monopolistic advantages, its main impact is in widening the area of competition. Domestic markets are protected, if not by tariffs, at least by distance, ignorance, lethargy. The small, inefficient domestic producer is typically more of a monopolist than the large, monopolistically competitive wide-ranging firm. Such a domestic market thrives on high prices

[44]Frank, pp. 87–88.

[45]George Ayittey, "Who Ruined Africa? Don't Blame the Colonialists," *Herald Examiner*, September 9, 1988.

and low volume. . . . The cost advantages of the intruder are so
great, even when its conduct is not aggressively competitive,
that prices are reduced, volumes expanded, and the monopolistic phenomenon extends the area of competition.[46]

In brief, the presence of the MNC increases rather than reduces
competition and the efficient use of local resources. It also stimulates
rather than retards the acquisition of entrepreneurial and other business skills by the indigenous population.

MNCs and Local Capital

Yet another criticism is that much of the capital used by the MNCs
is obtained locally, thereby providing little if any additional capital. In
fact, since much of the profit obtained by the MNCs is "taken out" of
the country, the result is that the MNCs actually drain the less
developed countries of their wealth. Barnet and Muller, for example,
contend that the activity of the multinationals is little more than

a process of wealth depletion which has resulted inevitably in
lower consumption for the local population. The net outflow of
finance capital from the underdeveloped societies weakened
their capacity to develop the knowledge to produce wealth,
and thus further decreased their bargaining power.[47]

That, like many of the other criticisms of the MNCs, misunderstands
the nature of the economic process. First, it should be noted that the
inhospitable environment, especially the ever-present possibility of
nationalization by the governments of less developed countries, deters
the inflow of capital from abroad. One estimate has placed the
uncompensated losses from expropriation at $6 billion in the postwar
period.[48] Obviously, MNCs do not like to have their assets nationalized, and their losses are significantly reduced if the expropriated
factory was built with funds borrowed locally.

Second, and more important, the real issue is not whether the capital
used by the MNCs was imported from abroad or borrowed locally. The
real issue is whether it is efficiently used. As Bauer and Yamey have
noted, often one of the essential problems in the less developed
countries is not the shortage of capital but the inefficiency with which

[46]Charles Kindleberger, "The Monopolistic Theory of Direct Foreign Investment," in
Transnational Corporations and World Order, p. 104.

[47]Barnet and Muller, p. 135.

[48]Schmidt, p. 276.

a large part of the available capital is used.[49] If foreign investors borrow capital locally, it means that they believe that they are able to use that capital more productively than local borrowers. Once again, if they are correct, the result is an expansion of local output and a rising local standard of living. If they are wrong, their firms go bankrupt and the capital is again available to local borrowers. As William Glade has observed, the common complaint that "in some given period the outward flow of interest and profit exceeds the current inward capital flows," like the related criticism that "a portion of the interest or profits eventually remitted to the home office constitutes a foreign exchange 'drain' for which no offsetting initial inflow of capital was ever received," simply ignores "what exactly is done with the capital in between inflow and outflow: that is, the use of investment to expand productive capacity, with a possible saving on imports or an increase in exports."[50]

Finally, far from squeezing out local investors, the use of local capital by the MNCs has actually had the opposite effect—for two reasons. First, the increased demand for local capital causes interest rates to rise. That, in turn, stimulates increased local saving. And second, once the profitability of an investment has been demonstrated, and the environment has been shown to be a relatively safe one for saving and investment, additional entrepreneurs in need of additional capital will be attracted. As a result, not only would foreign capital begin to flow into the country, but capital flight, which plagues so many less developed countries, would cease to be a problem.[51]

MNCs and Sovereignty

According to many of their critics, perhaps the most serious problem with the MNCs is that they undermine national sovereignty. Akinsanya says that "MNCs are beyond national control; they constitute *imperium in imperio* and thus undermine the territorial nation state."[52] And Stephen Hymer refers to the "great disparity between the bargaining power of the corporation and the bargaining power of the

---

[49]Bauer and Yamey, p. 114.

[50]William Glade, "Multinationals and the Third World," *Journal of Economic Issues*, December 1987, p. 1900.

[51]Bauer and Yamey, pp. 133–34; Glade, pp. 1900–1901; and Krauss, p. 129.

[52]Akinsanya, p. 58.

government." He believes that one of the most "serious problems" of the MNCs is that "they reduce the ability of the government to control the economy."[53]

First of all, it is doubtful that MNCs have seriously undermined the sovereignty of the nation-state. Much, of course, depends on the bargaining positions of the two parties, and that will vary from case to case. However, the scenario commonly used to demonstrate the inferior bargaining position of the state vis-à-vis the MNC is that of a single state with few or even no options and an MNC with numerous options. Thus the MNC is presented as being in a position to present the state with a take-it-or-leave-it proposition.[54] But this is hardly the typical situation. There are now approximately 187 sovereign nations; the number of MNCs has been placed at 10,000.[55] If anything, the bargaining strength would seem to lie with the nation-state rather than the MNC.

But more important, one must ask just what is wrong with undermining the ability of the government to control the economy. Government control of the economy is probably the principal obstacle to economic development in today's world. Therefore, as Krauss has put it, "To the extent that the multinationals help control governments by inducing competition between them, they render the public a valuable service."[56] Probably the only reason that is not more widely recognized is the common failure to distinguish between the freedom of a nation-state and the freedom of its people. The two are not necessarily connected, as the situation in Africa should make evident. As Ayittey has made clear, the political independence of black Africa went hand in hand with the subjection of large numbers of black Africans. As the countries of Africa became "free," many of the new leaders used their newfound freedom to enslave their subjects.[57] In view of the politically

---

[53]Hymer, pp. 446–47.

[54]See, for example, Hymer, p. 447.

[55]Barry Hughes, *Continuity and Change in World Politics* (Englewood Cliffs, N.J.: Prentice-Hall, 1991), p. 362.

[56]Krauss, p. 129.

[57]See George Ayittey, "A Double Standard in Black and White," *Wall Street Journal*, July 22, 1985, and "African Freedom of Speech," *Index on Censorship*, January 1987.

and economically inhibiting role governments have played in the developing world, one can only hope that the critics are correct about the impact of MNCs.

Government and the MNC

A method often used by critics to illustrate the "economic power" of the MNCs is to compare their gross incomes with the gross national products (GNPs) of various countries. One list shows that the gross sales of British Petroleum are equal to the GNP of Algeria, that the income of Volvo is about the same size as the GNP of Bangladesh, and that Standard Oil's income is roughly equal to the size of the economy of Malaysia.[58] But just what do those figures mean?

PepsiCo operates in well over 100 countries. Does it really make any sense to compare the total value of all economic activity inside one country with the gross sales from a single, often very narrow, type of activity—say the production of one brand of soft drink—in a multitude of countries scattered around the world? Comparing the GNP of a country with the gross income of an MNC makes about as much sense as comparing apples with kangaroos. The two are so different that any comparison is meaningless.

But the point of such comparisons is to show that the MNCs are too powerful, that they have become so large that governments can no longer control them. Gustav Ranis, for example, referred to the "undoubtedly correct accusation that the MNC . . . has unprecedented power, unchallenged by either the [less developed country] governments or developed country governments."[59] And Hymer has bluntly stated that "in a word, the multinational corporation reveals the power of size and the danger of leaving it uncontrolled."[60] This argument is based on three major, but highly dubious, assumptions: (1) all MNCs are large; (2) *regardless of the nature of the institution*, size confers power; and (3) the market is not an effective mechanism for regulating the

[58]Charles Kegley, Eugene Wittkopf, and Lucia Rawls, "The Multinational Corporation: Curse or Cure?" in *The Global Agenda*, Charles Kegley and Eugene Wittkopf, eds. (New York: Random House, 1984), pp. 275–77.

[59]Gustav Ranis, "The Multinational Corporation as an Instrument of Development," in *The Multinational Corporation and Social Change*, David Apter and Louis Goodman, eds. (New York: Praeger, 1976), p. 106.

[60]Hymer, p. 448.

activities of MNCs, and thus, government control is needed to keep them in line. None of these assumptions hold.

MNCs and Size

First, the prevalent view of the MNC as a giant monster corporation is not borne out by the data. According to a 1988 United Nations report, only 600 companies have annual sales in excess of $1 billion and half of all multinationals are in fact small to medium-sized operations.[61] Twenty-three percent of all Japanese MNCs employ fewer than 300 people; nearly 80 percent of all British multinationals have fewer than 500 employees.

MNCs and Power

Second, governments are centers of power. Many obtain labor services through conscription; all obtain revenue through taxation. But firms are purely *voluntary* institutions. They can neither conscript nor tax. They can merely offer their goods and services for sale. This applies not just to consumers but to laborers and factor suppliers as well. Any firm that fails to produce what consumers want to buy at prices they are willing to pay will lose its customers to other firms. Any firm trying to underpay its employees or factor suppliers will lose them to other firms. The MNC is nothing more than a firm. The fact that it does business in more than one country does not alter the nature of the process. It is a mistake to assume that on the free market ownership confers power. It is not the owners but the consumers, by their buying and abstention from buying, who really control the activities of the firm.

A common criticism of MNCs is that their often close relationship with the governments of the world does, in fact, enable them to acquire monopolistic positions by influencing governments to pass laws or adopt policies insulating them from competition. They are then able to exploit workers by paying below-free-market wages and to exploit consumers by charging above-free-market prices.

There is a good deal of truth to that charge. The relationship between governments and MNCs is a complicated one. And that relationship may alter the very nature of the MNC investment by changing it from a positive to a zero-sum operation. First, an MNC may attempt to

---

[61]"Come Back Multinationals," *The Economist*, November 26, 1988, p. 73.

pressure the host government to get special privileges, such as tax exemptions and subsidies, or licensing restrictions and tariffs, thereby protecting it from competition. It may do this through either lobbying, bribery, or veiled threats to locate elsewhere. That should hardly be surprising. Contrary to the usual chamber of commerce rhetoric regarding the glories of free enterprise, businesses are not particularly fond of competition. Far from favoring open entry, businesses have often been at the forefront of attempts to get the government to "rationalize" the economy through the imposition of regulations restricting entry and thus competition.[62] That does not change merely because a firm crosses a political boundary.

But there is no reason that such questionable practices have to originate with the MNC. It would be surprising if there were not at least some highly placed host-country government officials who had used their positions to obtain special advantages for themselves, that is, to extort MNCs for their own benefit.

There is a variety of questionable payments. One can distinguish between two types of payments originating from the MNC intended to influence public officials in the host country: "grease" and bribery. Grease is so named because its purpose is to "lubricate" or facilitate certain government activities. Grease payments normally go to low-level government employees and are typically small bribes—gratuities—intended to get the government employees either to perform their duties or at least to perform them expeditiously. Those duties include such things as providing work permits, visas, licenses, customs clearances, police protection, hotel accommodations, appointments with public officials, and a host of other services. But grease may also be used to get local officials to look the other way, to shirk their duties, to ignore certain regulations, thereby enabling the MNC to conduct certain types of business operations or at least to conduct them at a lower cost. Examples include payments by the MNC to allow it to evade customs duties or to circumvent various tariff restrictions on imports. Thomas Gladwin and Ingo Walter reported that while grease

---

[62]See, for example, Gabriel Kolko, *The Triumph of Conservatism* (New York: Free Press, 1977); and Ronald Radosh and Murray Rothbard, eds., *A New History of Leviathan* (New York: E. P. Dutton, 1972).

accounts for about 95 percent of all questionable payments made by the MNCs, the dollar amount is probably less than 25 percent of the total.[63]

Bribery is the payment of large sums of money, or its equivalent, to high-ranking government officials. The purpose is to obtain benefits that lower level officials are not in a position to grant. These include such things as the acquisition of contracts, tax concessions, import as well as export exemptions, and changes in the laws and policies of the host country.[64] While cash payments are the most common form of payment, other forms are not unheard of. They might include a gift of a Mercedes-Benz, jobs for the official's relatives or friends, or free vacations on the Riviera, to name but a few.

Finally, there is blackmail or extortion, where the questionable practice originates at the receiving end. Blackmail would include such things as threats to renege on existing or potential contracts, to nationalize or expropriate the company, or even to harm or kill MNC officials if the demands are not met.[65]

Since both bribery and extortion are illegal, it is probably impossible to determine just how common such practices are. However, the available information suggests that those activities are fairly common.

Investigations of MNC activities in such countries as the United States, Canada, Venezuela, Spain, West Germany, Switzerland, Greece, Iran, and Egypt have resulted in massive revelations about the illegal activities of the MNCs. They have led to the arrest and trial of former prime minister of Japan Kakuei Tanaka; the resignation of Giovanni Leone, president of Italy; and the overthrow of the leader of Honduras, General Oswaldo López Arella. They have also resulted in the demotion or dismissal of over 100 corporate officials as well as the suicide of a few top executives such as Eli Black, chairman of the board of United Brands.[66] A 1974 United Nations report indicated that "more than 100 United States MNCs have engaged in these practices [large-scale bribery such as the paying of large commissions or giving gifts to governmental leaders or their families] to the tune of millions of

---

[63]Thomas Gladwin and Ingo Walter, *Multinationals under Fire* (New York: John Wiley, 1980), p. 299.

[64]Ibid.

[65]Ibid., p. 300.

[66]Ibid., p. 297.

dollars a year."[67] And investigations by the U.S. Securities and Exchange Commission disclosed that American-based MNCs had made in excess of $1 billion in "questionable payments."[68] As investigations in other countries show, such activities are not limited to MNCs based in the United States.[69]

There is also clear evidence that government officials have used their positions to extract benefits for themselves from the MNCs. Consequences for refusing to pay range from outright expropriation to physical harm and even death. For example, Ashland Oil was forced to pay $190,000 to two government officials in Gabon to satisfy "two outstanding obligations" of highly questionable validity. Haitian government officials attempted to extort $250,000 from Translinear, Inc., following the firm's $3-million investment in a port facility there. When the firm refused, the project was terminated. And Gulf Oil was forced to pay $4 million to the Democratic Republican party of South Korea. The party's finance chairman, S. K. Kim, subjected Gulf's chairman, Bob Dorsey, to "severe personal abuse" and, according to Dorsey, "left little to the imagination if the company would choose to turn its back on this request."[70] On a far less dramatic scale, "grease" payments may often be more in the nature of extortion than bribery. Most low-level government officials in the Third World are poorly paid. The expectation is that they will use their positions to augment their incomes. Thus, bribes are often a sine qua non to get them to perform their duties. Although it is difficult to prove, the same is probably true of many tariffs, licensing restrictions, and other interferences with the market process: they are created to elicit bribes for their circumvention.

Not surprisingly, studies by, for example, Freedom House, show that bribes and extortion payments are concentrated in those countries with the most centralized and authoritarian political structures. According to Gladwin and Walter:

> In "less free" settings MNEs [multinational enterprises] confront governments that hold essentially unlimited power. Civil

[67]Werner Feld, *Multinational Corporations and U.N. Politics* (New York: Pergamon Press, 1980), p. 32.

[68]Gladwin and Walter, pp. 297, 299.

[69]Feld, p. 32.

[70]Gladwin and Walter, p. 300.

servants are vested with discretionary authority to grant or withhold permits for almost any kind of commercial activity. Those at the seat of power see themselves as dispensers of privileges and exceptions, and the ordinary workings of political processes or free market cannot be relied upon to safeguard legitimate business interests. Constantly threatened with governmental interference in business affairs or afraid of worse things to come, MNEs are moved to dispense "good will" or yield to extortion to protect themselves. And on top of this are the inevitable grease or whitemail payments, based on political and social connections necessary to obtain favorable treatment.[71]

What can be said of these questionable practices? Where the economy is rigidly controlled and changes in government personnel or policies can mean the difference between continued operation and bankruptcy or even expropriation, access to those determining policy is merely prudent business practice. And, by facilitating the flow of resources, such practices can serve to stimulate economic growth and development. However, when access is used to go beyond that and enters the realm of extracting such special privileges as tariffs or licensing restrictions, it impedes rather than facilitates the operation of the free market and therefore becomes an obstacle to economic development.

There is also a more subtle, and for that reason a more pernicious, method by which MNCs manage to use the political process to secure huge profits at the expense of the less developed countries. Many MNCs have, for example, become ardent proponents of foreign aid. That is because much of foreign aid is "tied," which means that the recipient country must use the money to purchase products from companies in the donor country. That enables the MNCs to raise their prices for recipient-country purchasers well above market prices. Markups of 30 percent are common and even 50 percent is not unheard of.[72] But not only are products overpriced, they also are often of poor quality or simply unsuited to the needs of the recipient country. For example, the United Kingdom extended nearly £2 million in aid to Zambia to improve its transportation system. Since the aid was "tied," Zambia had to use it to purchase 50 buses from British manufacturers. British Leyland provided the chassis parts, and Willowbrook Interna-

---

[71]Ibid., p. 308.

[72]Hancock, p. 162.

tional supplied the bodies. Within a few months, the bodywork had deteriorated beyond repair, and shortly after that, the same thing happened with the chassis. While the two British companies benefited handsomely, the losers were both the taxpayers in the United Kingdom, who paid for the aid, and the taxpayers in Zambia, who had to pay for expensive maintenance and repairs in a futile attempt to keep the buses going.[73] Similarly, a £10-million subsidy was extended to Egypt by the United Kingdom's aid agencies to help out Rolls-Royce. Rolls-Royce was eventually paid £28 million to supply Egypt with gas turbines for generating electricity. The turbines have proven very expensive to operate and, according to one commentator, "represent a real and on-going burden to Egypt."[74] Cheaper and more appropriate alternatives were available but were not even considered by the aid authorities, which is hardly surprising since the proposal originated with Rolls-Royce.

These examples could be multiplied many times. They certainly help explain the animosity so many in the less developed countries have toward the MNCs. What needs to be pointed out, however, is that the only reason the MNCs have been able to get away with providing such shoddy products and services is that the nature of the foreign aid process systematically excludes any direct connection between the company and the "customer," which is necessary to keep the firm responsive to the needs of its clients. The projects are worked out between the aid agencies in the donor countries, the rulers in the recipient countries, and the MNCs. The "official" beneficiaries in the recipient countries are seldom even consulted on the projects, nor are those footing much of the bill for the projects (the taxpayers in the donor countries). Can there be any doubt about the response of the citizens of Peru if asked if they would voluntarily pay for the construction of a road, if they knew that the policy of the contractors was, when meeting an obstacle such as a river, simply to stop at one side and begin again on the other?[75] And how many Ghanaians would have voluntarily supported the construction of a mango-canning plant with a capacity that exceeds the entire world trade in mangoes?[76]

[73]Ibid., p. 164.

[74]Ibid., p. 163.

[75]Ibid., p. 148.

[76]George Ayittey, "Economic Atrophy in Black Africa," *Cato Journal*, vol. 7, no. 1 (Spring–Summer 1987), p. 212.

The coalition of the MNCs, the less developed country governments, and the aid agencies in the developed countries enables all three to benefit. The MNCs can make huge profits at little risk since they are paid by the taxpayers in both the less developed countries and the donor countries; the elites in the less developed countries benefit since the normal "leakage" (official jargon for theft by high-level government officials) tends to run at between 10 and 20 percent of the total aid package.[77] And the aid agency officials in the donor countries benefit since the more aid they dispense, the faster they are promoted. Ironically, the only losers, it seems, are the official beneficiaries in the less developed countries, that is, the customers of the MNCs, and the tax-paying citizens in the developed countries who shoulder a large part of the cost.

Finally, there is the relationship between the MNC and the government of the home country. Harry Magdoff, for example, believes that "the pervasive military presence of the United States around the globe, the strength of this military power, and the design of the imperial world order under U.S. leadership" have benefited the MNCs by opening "doors in advanced as well as underdeveloped countries" and by inspiring "confidence in foreign investors—most especially, of course, in U.S. business interests—about the security of their overseas investments."[78] There is more than a kernel of truth in this statement. Major General Smedley Butler of the U.S. Marine Corps made a very famous comment in 1931:

> I helped make Mexico safe for American oil interests in 1914. I helped make Haiti and Cuba a decent place for the National Bank boys to collect revenue in. I helped purify Nicaragua for the international banking house of Brown Brothers. . . . I brought light to the Dominican Republic for American sugar interests in 1916. I helped make Honduras "right" for American fruit companies in 1903. Looking back on it I might have given Al Capone a few hints.[79]

---

[77]Hancock, pp. 174–83.

[78]Harry Magdoff, *The Age of Imperialism* (New York: Modern Reader, 1968), p. 207.

[79]Sheldon Richman, "Multinationals: Peacemakers or Exploiters?" *Reason*, December 1982, p. 21.

More recently, the interventions by the Central Intelligence Agency (CIA) or the American military have benefited U.S. MNCs. In 1954, for example, the CIA engineered the overthrow of the recently elected Guatemalan government of Jacobo Arbenz Guzman, who had expropriated 160,000 acres of land belonging to United Fruit. Arbenz was replaced by Colonel Castillo Armas, who quickly restored the land to United Fruit. Interestingly, Allen Dulles, the head of the CIA, was a former president of United Fruit; his brother, Secretary of State John Foster Dulles, was not only a stockholder in the company but his law firm had handled United Fruit's legal affairs. And the assistant secretary of state, John Moors Cabot, was also a major stockholder.[80]

The 1965 intervention in the Dominican Republic bears striking similarities to that in Guatemala. A new constitution prohibited large landholdings, required landowners to sell all land in excess of the legal maximum, and restricted the amount of land foreigners could acquire. In May 1965 the Organization of American States, an inter-American security association, sent a 23,000-man military into the Dominican Republic. The force was dominated by the United States and was ordered in at the insistence of U.S. president Lyndon Johnson with the objective of removing President Juan Bosch, one of the principal architects of the constitution. It was probably more than a coincidence that several of Johnson's closest advisors had significant economic interests in the Dominican Republic. They included Abe Fortas, who had been on the board of directors of Sucrest, a large sugar refinery heavily dependent upon sugar from the Dominican Republic; Adolf Berle, formerly the chairman of the board of Sucrest; Ellsworth Bunker, the former president of the National Sugar Refining Corporation; and "molasses magnate" J. M. Kaplan.[81]

But undoubtedly the best known is the role of the CIA and International Telephone and Telegraph (ITT) in undermining the government of Salvador Allende in Chile in the early 1970s. Allende, a self-proclaimed Marxist who made no secret of his intentions to nationalize Chilteco, a subsidiary of ITT, was the favorite to win the November 1970 presidential election. John McCone, a director of ITT and a former director of the CIA who was still a consultant to that

---

[80]Walter LaFeber, *The American Age* (New York: Norton, 1989), pp. 517–20; and John Swomley, *American Empire* (New York: Macmillan, 1970), pp. 153–57.

[81]Swomley, pp. 157–65.

agency, expressed his concern about Allende to the head of the CIA, Richard Helms, and later to the special assistant to the president for national security affairs, Henry Kissinger. What followed was a systematic and massive attempt first to prevent the election of Allende and, when that failed, to undermine Allende's presidency by generating "economic chaos." In its report on its investigation of the affair, the U.S. Senate acknowledged that the "company's concern was perfectly understandable," as was "its desire to communicate that concern to the appropriate officials of the U.S. Government and to seek their judgment as to how the United States would view the possible eventuality of a seizure of company property without adequate compensation." But, it continued: "What is not to be condoned is that the highest officials of the ITT sought to engage the CIA in a plan covertly to manipulate the outcome of the Chilean presidential election. In so doing the company overstepped the line of acceptable corporate behavior."[82] These strictures seem reasonable. For, as the Senate report later noted, morality aside, activities such as ITT's "are incompatible with the long-term existence of multinational corporations" since "no sovereign nation would be willing to accept" the "specter of foreign intervention" in any dispute between an MNC and the host government "as the price of permitting foreign corporations to invest in its territory."[83]

Home-government interventions on behalf of MNCs are the exception rather than the rule. Numerous companies have been expropriated by many different countries. The vast majority have not precipitated home-government intervention.[84] Intervention has occurred only when additional, special considerations have been present. That is, intervention has only occurred when, to cite the two most common examples, the nationalized company has had major stockholders in key positions in the home-country government or when nationalization has been, accurately or not, perceived by the intervening government as part of a communist takeover or a threat to national security. That does not justify the interventions, but they have been the

[82]U.S. Senate, Subcommittee on Multinational Corporations, "The International Telephone and Telegraph Company and Chile, 1970–71," in *Transnational Corporations and World Order*, p. 242.

[83]Ibid.; for a very different assessment of ITT's activities, see Krauss, pp. 133–34.

[84]Spanier, pp. 411–12.

exception rather than the rule and have occurred only when factors other than simple nationalization have been present.

MNCs are commonly criticized for exploitation of, and retarding development in, the less developed countries. Much of that criticism is misdirected and stems from a misunderstanding of the nature of the free-market process. But part of it is legitimate. One must then ask, how is it that a voluntary organization such as the MNC is able to engage in exploitation? The answer is that too often it is able to acquire what may be termed secondhand power. While the MNC has no intrinsic power, it is quiet often able to obtain power from government in the home and/or host country or both. It is then able to use that power to exclude competitors, obtain subsidies, hold down wages, charge exorbitant prices, and foist its products on people who neither need nor want them.

MNCs and the Market

The answer to that problem, however, lies not in additional government regulation. Rather it lies in the complete separation of the economy and the government by creating a wall between the two in both the less developed countries and the more developed countries. The data show, in fact, that the notion of consumer sovereignty, so derided by critics of the MNC, is an effective method of regulating the multinationals. "As one reads Hobson's *Imperialism*, published in 1902 or Lenin's book by the same name," wrote Vernon, "a striking aspect of both works is the archaic nature of their illustrations, the repeated references to cases that no longer exist."[85] Today, foreign-owned companies in nearly every area mentioned by Lenin and Hobson— mining, agriculture, banking, railroads, textiles, and utilities[86]—are, noted Vernon, "gone," having been pushed out by local competitors.

For example, in the approximately quarter century of Fulgencio Batista's rule in Cuba (1933–44 and 1952–59), a period of friendly relations between the United States and Cuba, the share of Cuba's industry owned by U.S.-based MNCs fell from 65 percent to 40 percent. The reason, according to Vernon, was the learning and

[85]Vernon, *Storm over the Multinationals*, p. 99.

[86]J. A. Hobson, *Imperialism* (London: George Allen and Unwin, 1954), pp. 226–27, 240, 247–49.

adoption of the technology by native Cubans.[87] It was not an isolated occurrence in terms of geography, sector, or time. The United Nations Center on Transnational Corporations has noted,

> The complete hegemony of the transnational corporations in developing country minerals that prevailed until about 1960 had been reduced by 1980 to a situation where the corporations have ceded a large part of their ownership positions to other agents, and where their financial contributions towards expansion constituted only a minor proportion of the total.[88]

Perhaps surprisingly, trends in the manufacturing area parallel those in the primary goods sector. Between 1968 and 1974, Vernon noted, U.S. multinationals sold 717 (or more than 10 percent) of their 6,500 foreign-based subsidiaries.[89]

What, perhaps, is even more important is the growth in the Third World manufacturing sector, something that, according to Lenin, Hobson, and the dependency theorists, could not happen. Figure 14.5 shows that between 1963 and 1985 the percentage of world exports supplied by the less developed countries increased from 4.3 to 12.4 percent. Figure 14.6 shows that in every category of manufactured goods, less developed country exports are growing at a faster rate than those from more developed countries. It ought to be pointed out, however, that some of this industrialization was a result of attempts by MNCs to circumvent less developed country tariffs and nontariff barriers. Such "tariff jumping" artificially stimulates industrialization. It therefore entails some factor distortion and thus exaggerates the amount of industrialization in less developed countries that would have occurred in a free market. But it should also be noted that tariffs and nontariff barriers imposed by the developed countries constitute a serious impediment to Third World industrialization. Estimates are that the cost to the Third World of more developed country trade restrictions is "worth several billion dollars a year."[90] Significantly, since developed nations typically allow primary products to be imported duty free, not only do more developed country trade policies

---

[87]Vernon, *Storm over the Multinationals*, pp. 99–100.

[88]United Nations Center on Transnational Corporations, *Trends and Issues in Foreign Direct Investment and Related Flows* (New York: United Nations, 1985), p. 64.

[89]Vernon, *Storm over the Multinationals*, p. 100.

[90]World Bank, *World Development Report 1987*, p. 148.

Figure 14.5
WORLD EXPORTS OF MANUFACTURERS, 1963–85
(PERCENTAGE SHARES)

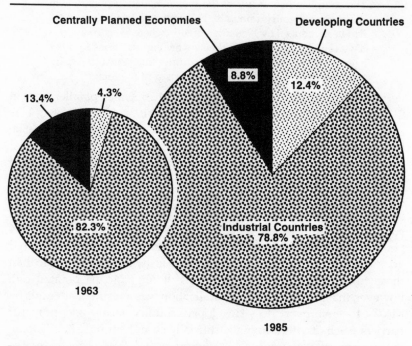

Centrally Planned Economies   **Developing Countries**

8.8%

12.4%

13.4%   4.3%

82.3%

Industrial Countries
78.8%

1963

1985

SOURCE: World Bank, *World Development Report 1987* (New York: Oxford University Press, 1987), Figure 8.3, p. 147. Reprinted by permission.

impede Third World industrialization, they also hamper attempts at economic diversification.

While the international picture has changed drastically during the 20th century—MNCs no longer dominate sectors such as the mineral extraction industries, having been pushed out by a variety of market and government actions—the question is still open of whether the market is sufficient to control the MNC. Table 14.3 strongly suggests that is the case. In every instance, the reason given by U.S. parent companies for establishing overseas subsidiaries was to deal with local competitive threats.

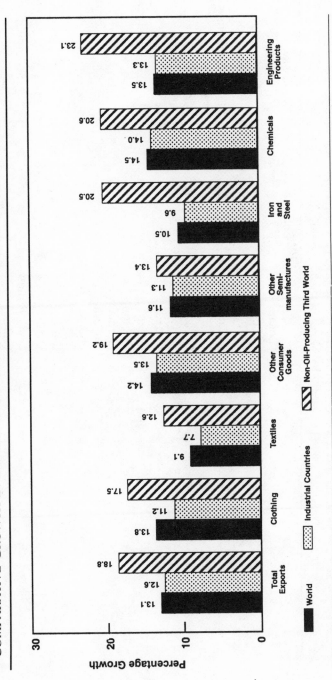

Figure 14.6

COMPARATIVE GROWTH IN EXPORT RATES BY CATEGORY OF EXPORTS AND COMMODITY, 1973–82

SOURCE: Walter Jones, *The Logic of International Relations* (Glenview, Ill.: Scott-Foresman and Company, 1988), p. 207. Reprinted by permission.

Table 14.3

CHARACTERISTICS OF FOREIGN MANUFACTURING PLANTS ESTABLISHED
BEFORE 1900 BY SPECIFIED U.S. PARENTS

U.S. Parent	Principal Products	Location of Foreign Plants	Substantial U.S. Exports before Foreign Investment?	Asserted Reasons for Foreign Investment
Colt	Firearms	Great Britain	Yes	Local competitive threat
Singer	Sewing machines	Great Britain Austria Canada	Yes	Local competitive threat, lower costs
ITT	Communications	Great Britain Belgium Germany Austria France Italy Russia Japan	Yes	Local competitive threat, lower costs
General Electric and its predecessors	Electrical products and equipment	Great Britain France Germany Canada	Yes	Local competitive threat, lower costs, national pressures

Company	Product	Countries		Reasons
Westinghouse Air Brake	Air brakes and signal equipment	Great Britain France Germany Russia	Yes	Local competitive threat, lower costs, national pressures
Westinghouse Electric	Electrical products and equipment	Great Britain France Russia	Yes	Local competitive threat, lower costs
Eastman Kodak	Photographic goods	Great Britain	Yes	Local competitive threat, lower costs
United Shoe Machinery	Shoe machinery	Great Britain France Germany Switzerland	Yes	Not determined
Parke, Davis	Pharmaceuticals	Canada	Yes	Lower costs
American Radiator and Standard Sanitary's predecessor	Radiators	France	Yes	Lower costs, larger demand

SOURCE: Table from Raymond Vernon, *Sovereignty at Bay: The Multinational Spread of U.S. Enterprises* (New York: Basic Books, 1971). Reprinted by permission.

> The decision to set up manufacturing facilities abroad has commonly been triggered by the perception of a threat to an established export market.... In the case of nine petrochemicals, for example, the original producers did not set up a plant outside their domestic market without first being threatened by the appearance of some uncontrolled competitor. More generally, unlicensed imitators or parallel innovators have commonly provided the immediate threat that has led to the initial overseas investment.... The decisions of innovators to try to prolong their hold on overseas markets by direct investment has induced not only their rivals but also their suppliers to take similar action.[91]

Looked at from the other end, the data similarly suggest that the market is an effective means to regulate the MNC. Standard Oil was able to obtain a large share of the domestic U.S. market in the late 19th century only by reducing prices from 26 cents to 8 cents per gallon of kerosene. Yet despite the price cuts, its market share began to decline, and well before the court ordered Standard Oil's dissolution in 1911, it declined rapidly. There have also been repeated attempts by petroleum producers to control prices through voluntary cartelization. Yet none lasted more than a very short time because of "cheating" by cartel members and the actions of independents, leading the American Petroleum Institute in the early 1930s to plead for government-imposed mandatory controls to hold prices up. The numerous attempts to establish international oil cartels met with the same fate. It is doubtful that even the Organization of Petroleum Exporting Countries (OPEC), the best-known oil cartel, has had any significant impact on oil prices. It was founded in 1959, fully 14 years before the first oil "price shock" and has had virtually no impact on prices since the late 1970s. OPEC's "control" of oil prices during that brief period was more apparent than real. U.S. oil production peaked in the early 1970s and was declining by 1973, creating an oil shortage. Oil prices began to rise as early as February 1971, more than two years before the October 1973 price shock. While OPEC may have had an impact on the timing of the price increases, it probably had little influence on their ultimate size.[92] As conditions changed, the pre-1973 government-regulated prices

---

[91]Vernon, "The Product Cycle Model," pp. 111–13.

[92]David Osterfeld, "Voluntary and Coercive Cartels: The Case of Oil," *The Freeman*, November 1987.

were far too low to be maintained much longer. And the 1973 price controls only played into the hands of OPEC by reducing oil production in the United States.

Further, while admittedly somewhat speculative "due to the poor quality of much of the data on direct investment," a 1985 International Monetary Fund study on foreign direct investment in less developed countries between 1974 and 1982 did show that average rates of return on foreign direct investment (1) are not "excessive," ranging between a low of just under 10 percent in 1980 and 1982 and a high of just under 13 percent in 1974, and (2) are positively correlated with annual rates of growth of less developed country economies.[93]

Finally, a look at the *Fortune* 500, practically all of whom are MNCs, clearly illustrates the tenuous hold of even the largest corporations. Over the past several years, the number of corporations on the *Fortune* 500 list that are losing money has averaged over 50 per year, or more than 10 percent of the list. Some, such as the Dallas-based steel company LTV, acknowledged bankruptcy by filing for chapter 11. And the turnover rate on the list is also high, with about 44 companies displaced from the list each year.

The simple fact is that it is neither necessary nor desirable for governments to regulate the activities of the MNCs. The free market is a much more effective and less costly method of regulation. It is also far more conducive to the maintenance of a free and prosperous society than reliance on ever-larger and more powerful governments. Similarly, while one can sympathize with the expropriated MNC, military intervention and other types of home-government pressure are unacceptable. The free market means that individuals must shoulder the risks of their own decisions. That should apply to both the economic and the political realms. Moreover, nationalizations are self-defeating, at least in the long run. If less developed countries truly desire foreign investment, they will have to provide a secure environment. They must provide a secure environment in which there is little or no fear of expropriation. In such an environment, the MNCs will be able to live up to their potential as engines for development.[94]

---

[93]International Monetary Fund, *Foreign Private Investment in Developing Countries* (Washington, D.C.: IMF, 1985), pp. 38–39.

[94]Ibid.

15. The High Cost of Trade Protectionism to the Third World

J. Michael Finger

If aid does not work, then what? The answer is increased *trade* to boost the economies of developing countries. That is, admittedly, not a new idea. What has not yet received sufficient attention is the magnitude of the effect of trade.

Of particular note are the following points: developed countries' import restrictions reduce developing countries' national income by about twice as much as developing countries receive in aid; departures from multilateral treatment (i.e., preferences, especially within Western Europe) on the whole work *against* developing countries' export interests; *developing* countries' import restrictions contain the same biases against developing countries as do the restrictions of developed countries.[1]

Although the conclusions of this chapter are based on trade restriction figures from the early to mid-1980s, the findings remain relevant in the 1990s and, given more recent developments in the trade policies of industrialized nations, may understate the negative effects of the trade barriers of developed countries on developing countries. For example, the industrialized countries' tariffs have generally not decreased in any meaningful way in recent years; indeed, those countries' use of nontariff measures has significantly increased.[2] That shift

---

[1]The results summarized in this chapter are drawn from three studies I have done with three different colleagues: J. Michael Finger and Samuel Laird, "Protection in Developed and Developing Countries: An Overview," *Journal of World Trade Law* (Geneva, December 1987), pp. 9–23; Finger and Patrick A. Messerlin, "The Effects of Industrial Countries' Policies on Developing Countries," World Bank, Policy and Research Series no. PRS 3, Washington, D.C., 1989; and Finger and Andrzej Olechowski, "Trade Barriers: Who Does What to Whom," in *Free Trade in the World Economy*, Herbert Giersch, ed. (Tubingen, Germany: Mohr, 1987).

[2]The number of anti-dumping and countervailing duty cases filed in the United States against developing countries rose more than threefold from the 1980–81 period to the

317

toward aggressive trade retaliation has been accompanied by the inability to draw to a successful conclusion the latest round of multilateral tariff reduction negotiations under the General Agreement on Tariffs and Trade (GATT). In contrast, many developing countries, particularly in Latin America, have dramatically reduced their trade barriers in recent years, but those developments do not detract from the general conclusions of this chapter.

Effects of Developed Countries' Restrictions on Developing Countries

There are a number of recent examinations of industrial-country trade restrictions, but most of them concentrate on own-country effects.[3] There have been few studies of the effects on exporting countries. Particularly rare are estimates of the effects on the efficiency of suppliers in developing countries—that is, the cost to those economies of the inability to exploit their comparative advantage and use their resources in sectors that are, by world standards, the most effective.

Efficiency or "Welfare" Gains

Table 15.1 presents estimates of the welfare gain from elimination of all industrial-country tariffs and nontariff barriers.[4] Those estimates are from simulations on one of the few global general-equilibrium models that have been used to examine complete trade liberalization and do not cover the effects of nonborder measures. The welfare gain takes into account the increase of real output that results from "allocative efficiency"—shifting resources toward sectors in which a country has a comparative advantage—and the gain (or loss) of purchasing power that results from terms-of-trade changes. The figures measure only the

1988–89 period. See Anne O. Krueger, *Economic Policies at Cross-Purposes: The United States and Developing Countries* (Washington, D.C.: Brookings Institution, 1993), p. 112.

[3]To look first at how much a country's trade restrictions affect someone else risks reinforcing the incorrect view that a country's imposition of trade restrictions is a *victimless crime* within that nation. In fact, nine-tenths of the impact of a trade restriction is the shift of money from one person's pocket to another's within the country that imposes the restriction. Most of the beggaring done by a trade restriction is at the expense of fellow citizens, not foreign citizens.

[4]The estimates are from John Whalley, *Trade Liberalization among Major World Trading Areas* (Cambridge, Mass.: MIT Press, 1985).

Table 15.1
EFFICIENCY GAINS TO DEVELOPING COUNTRIES FROM
REMOVAL OF INDUSTRIAL COUNTRIES' TRADE BARRIERS

Type of Removal	As a Percentage of Developing Countries' GNP	As a Percentage of Industrial Countries' GNP
Unilateral removal by		
European Community	1.1	0.7
United States	0.8	0.4
Japan	0.7	0.0
Multilateral removal by		
all industrial countries	2.9	0.6

SOURCE: Based on estimates by Whalley, p. 181.

NOTE: Estimates of the effects of the complete removal of all tariffs and nontariff barriers in place in 1977. The estimates assume no change in the level of resource utilization.

static increase in real national income; they do not take into account possible improvements in efficiency that might occur in a more open trading system. Finally, the simulations assume that macroeconomic management maintained a given level of resource utilization in each country.

The estimated efficiency effect comes to about 3 percent of all developing countries' gross national product (GNP). In other words, because of industrial countries' trade restrictions, the developing countries' GNP is about 3 percent less each year than it otherwise would be. That cost comes to 0.6 percent of industrial countries' income, or about twice the 0.3 percent that the Organization for Economic Cooperation and Development (OECD) countries devote to official development assistance.

An alternative estimate by Jan Haaland and Victor Norman came to the same overall figure but separated the effects on the major exporters of manufactured goods from the effects on other developing countries.[5] As one might expect, the impact on the major exporters of manufactured goods is larger—about 4 percent of GNP compared with 2 to 2.5 percent for other developing countries.

[5]Jan I. Haaland and Victor D. Norman, "EFTA and the World Economy: Comparative Advantage and Trade Policy," EFTA Occasional Paper no. 19, October 14, 1987.

The real losses are almost certainly greater. The models are built on a 1979 database, and in 1979 trade restrictions were less extensive than they are now. Further, the models exclude the many dynamic impacts of policy changes and so do not incorporate the trade effects of nonborder measures.

Effect on Export Receipts

Estimates of effects on export earnings tend to take a shorter term view, focusing on increased exports as a matter of putting idle resources to use or of switching resources from producing for the domestic market, where they do not earn foreign exchange, to producing for the export market, where they do. A United Nations Conference on Trade and Development study has estimated that elimination of all trade restrictions of industrial countries would lead to more than a 10 percent increase in exports from developing countries. More than 40 percent of that increase would be exports of clothing, and another 10 percent would be exports of food and food products.[6] Refik Erzan and Guy Karsenty found that the gains from reducing the highest tariffs of the industrial countries to a maximum 10 percent would be even more concentrated on clothing and textiles, products that bear the highest tariffs and most restrictive nontariff barriers.[7]

Viewed from a longer term perspective, the concentration of the trade effects of protection has had a significant effect on resource allocation. Naheed Kirmani concluded that the removal of tariff and nontariff barriers in the main OECD countries could increase developing countries' exports of textiles by 82 percent and of clothing by 93 percent.[8] Alan Deardorff and Robert Stern, in an analysis focused particularly on the allocative effects of industrial countries' protectionism, estimated that employment in the apparel industry would in-

[6]United Nations Conference on Trade and Development (UNCTAD), "Protectionism and Structural Adjustment, Introduction and Part I," TD/B/1081 (Part I), Geneva, January 1986.

[7]Refik Erzan and Guy Karsenty, "Products Facing High Tariffs in Major Developed Market Economy Countries: An Area of Priority for Developing Countries in the Uruguay Round?" UNCTAD Discussion Paper no. 22, 1987.

[8]Naheed Kirmani et al., "Effects of Increased Market Access on Exports of Developing Countries," Staff Paper, International Monetary Fund, Washington, D.C., 1984.

crease by more than 20 percent in 7 of the 16 developing countries studied.[9]

Patterns of Protectionism in Developed Countries

Local production can be supported and import competition disadvantaged through subsidies as well as through import restrictions. Subsidies to industry expanded widely after the first oil shock and grew rapidly through the early 1980s. The expansion was particularly marked in Northern Europe, but there was a substantial rise in subsidies even where such aid was traditionally low, such as in the United States and Switzerland.

Much of the rise was assistance to help industry and transport adjust to increased petroleum prices and took such forms as financial aid or tax incentives to save energy or switch to fuels produced domestically, particularly electricity, gas, and coal. Other assistance tended to focus on a small number of sectors in difficulty: shipbuilding and steel and, to a lesser extent, electronics, aircraft, and autos.

Subsidies, however, have a direct impact on public budgets, and that caused the shift toward direct support in the late 1970s and early 1980s to be temporary. Although agriculture and transportation are still heavily subsidized in developed countries, most industry is aided primarily by import restrictions. While direct support of production and prices makes necessary complementary trade restrictions in agriculture, trade restrictions substitute for direct support in manufacturing.

For instance, data prepared by the Australian Industries Assistance Commission indicate that import restrictions provide more than 95 percent of governmental assistance to the manufacturing sector.[10] Among industrial countries, Australia tends to have relatively high tariffs, extensive nontariff barriers, and low subsidies, but the figure is broadly indicative of the "mix" of border versus nonborder protection for industrial countries.[11]

[9]Alan V. Deardorff and Robert M. Stern, "Alternative Scenarios for Trade Liberalization," Paper prepared for the 10th annual Middlebury Conference on Economic Issues, Middlebury, Vermont, April 7–9, 1988.

[10]Industries Assistance Commission, *Assistance of Manufacturing Industries: 1977–78 to 1982–83*, Information Paper (Canberra: Australian Government Publishing Service, 1985).

[11]Compared to figures for all industrial countries, the average Australian tariff rate is 1.8 times as high; see Finger and Laird. Australian nontariff barriers cover 1.3 times as large a fraction of imports, and Australian subsidies (as a share of GNP) are 0.9 times as

Tariffs

After the seven rounds of multilateral GATT negotiations since 1947, tariffs in the industrial countries are now on average quite low. In the Kennedy Round of the 1960s, tariffs on all but key sensitive products, such as textiles and steel, were reduced some 50 percent. As a result of the 1970s Tokyo Round, the trade-weighted average most-favored-nation (MFN) rate on industrial products was estimated to have been reduced from 7.0 percent to 4.7 percent for the industrial countries.[12] The Generalized System of Preferences (GSP), introduced in the 1970s, has provided imports from developing countries preferential access to the industrial countries.

Still, several characteristics of tariff schedules create significant market access problems for developing countries.

- MFN rates are, on average, higher on goods imported from developing countries.
- Departures from MFN rates sometimes favor other industrial countries rather than developing countries. Various preferential arrangements among industrial countries often outweigh the impact of the GSP.
- Tariff peaks tend to be concentrated on products exported by developing countries.
- The escalation of tariffs from raw materials to processed products both generates relatively high effective rates of protection for primary products and retards the movement of Third World exporters into manufacturing.

---

large; see Julio Nogués, Andrzej Olechowski, and L. Alan Winters, "The Extent of Nontariff Barriers to Industrial Countries' Imports," *World Bank Economic Review*, vol. 1, no. 1 (September 1986) pp. 181–99. Imports as a share of GNP are approximately the same for Australia as for the industrial countries as a group, 18 percent; see OECD, *National Accounts*, vol. 1, Paris, 1986. If, in calculations for the industrial countries, we use the same elasticities as were used in the Australia calculation, take nonborder assistance to be twice as high as in Australia, and border protection to be one-half as high, we would still conclude that $8 of every $10 of assistance would be provided through the price effects of import restrictions; see World Bank, *1987 World Development Report*, (Oxford: Oxford University Press, 1987).

[12]GATT, "The Tokyo Round of Multilateral Trade Negotiations—II Supplementary Report," Geneva, January 1980.

MFN Rates

MFN rates are the standard rates in industrial countries' tariff schedules. That is, each country promises to charge import duties (on goods from any other GATT contracting party) no higher than the posted MFN rates. As Table 15.2 shows, the MFN rates on products from developing countries are generally higher. That may reflect the

Table 15.2

INDUSTRIAL COUNTRIES' TARIFF AVERAGES ON
MANUFACTURES (IMPORT-WEIGHTED AVERAGES OF
POST–TOKYO ROUND MFN RATES AND APPLIED RATES
AS OF 1983)

Importing Country and Origin of Imports	MFN Rate	Applied Rate
Australia		
Industrial countries	15.2	10.0
Developing countries	18.4	9.8
Canada		
Industrial countries	7.7	4.6
Developing countries	13.8	10.3
European Community		
Industrial countries	5.6	3.3
Developing countries	6.0	4.5
Finland		
Industrial countries	6.7	0.8
Developing countries	11.1	6.7
Japan		
Industrial countries	4.2	3.9
Developing countries	5.2	2.9
New Zealand		
Industrial countries	16.9	13.5
Developing countries	21.6	14.7
Norway		
Industrial countries	5.7	0.8
Developing countries	5.1	4.6
Sweden		
Industrial countries	5.0	0.8
Developing countries	7.2	5.7

(Continued on next page)

Table 15.2—Continued
INDUSTRIAL COUNTRIES' TARIFF AVERAGES ON
MANUFACTURES (IMPORT-WEIGHTED AVERAGES OF
POST-TOKYO ROUND MFN RATES AND APPLIED RATES
AS OF 1983)

Importing Country and Origin of Imports	MFN Rate	Applied Rate
Switzerland		
Industrial countries	2.7	0.2
Developing countries	2.8	2.6
United States		
Industrial countries	3.9	3.9
Developing countries	7.9	7.6

SOURCE: World Bank.

NOTES: Applied rates are calculated from information on customs collections by tariff line, by country of origin.

In the case of EC member states, trade-weighted rates against industrial countries are based on imports from outside the community, that is, intra-EC trade is excluded—not treated as a departure from MFN rates.

In computing applied rates, account is taken of volume limitations on the application of GSP rates.

limited participation of developing countries in earlier trade negotiations. In any case, such differences are part of the reason the rates actually applied to imports from developing countries are higher than the rates on imports from other industrial countries. In addition, rates actually applied are more often discounted below the MFN rate on imports from other industrial countries than on imports from developing countries.

Departures from MFN Rates

The tariff rates that industrial countries actually apply are often lower than the GATT's MFN rates. As is well known, preferred treatment of exports of the developing countries that are under the GSP, the least developed countries, and even certain developing countries (for instance, those covered by the Caribbean Basin Initiative and the Lomé Convention) reduces effective tariffs. What may not be so well known is that industrial countries offer substantial preferences to each other, including those between the European Free Trade Association (EFTA) and the European Community (EC); between Australia and New Zealand; and between the United States and Canada. (See Table 15.2 for comparisons between MFN rates and the rates actually applied.)

The GSP and other tariff preferences for developing countries are reflected in the differences between MFN and applied rates on imports from developing countries. But reductions from MFN rates on imports from industrial countries are often larger. Most EFTA countries have applied rates that are three to four times higher on goods from developing countries, reflecting the duty-free treatment of most manufactured goods traded between the European Economic Community and EFTA.

Tariff Peaks

Despite industrial countries' generally low tariffs, 20 percent of EC tariffs on manufactured imports have MFN rates above 10 percent, as do 18 percent of American and 13 percent of Japanese tariffs on manufactured goods. Most of the higher rates protect textiles, clothing, and miscellaneous manufactured goods—categories in which developing countries tend to have significant export positions. The high-rate sectors have a higher incidence of nontariff barriers, such as quotas, as well. Because products of which developing countries are strong exporters tend to be excluded from tariff preference systems, those exports are usually subject to the high MFN rates.[13]

Tariff Escalation

Tariffs are a considerable barrier to processed exports. For example, jute enters most industrial countries duty free, but Austria's 3 percent duty on jute fabrics provides 7 percent effective protection for Austrian processors of jute fabrics. Similarly, Australia imports hides and skins duty free, but its 20 percent duty on leather manufactured goods provides 36 percent effective protection for those manufacturers. Effective rates of protection for oilseed processing exceed 50 percent in the EC and in Japan.

Table 15.3 shows the escalating tariff and nontariff barriers faced by a variety of exports from developing countries. The high rates on

---

[13]This section draws on information from Erzan and Karsenty and on unpublished material supplied by the authors.

Table 15.3
ESCALATION OF INDUSTRIAL COUNTRY PROTECTION

Processing Chain and Stage	Average Tariff[a]	NTB Coverage Ratio[b]
Meat		
Fresh and frozen	6.2	34.0
Prepared	8.4	41.3
Fish		
Fresh and frozen	4.3	56.9
Prepared	4.1	7.0
Vegetables		
Fresh and frozen	6.9	42.6
Prepared	13.2	16.4
Fruits		
Fresh and frozen	7.4	24.0
Prepared	17.1	15.0
Tobacco		
Unmanufactured	1.2	12.0
Manufactures	18.1	25.0
Sugar		
Sugar and honey	1.0	51.0
Preparations	20.0	19.0
Cocoa		
Beans, powder, paste	1.0	0.0
Chocolate and products	3.0	1.0
Rubber		
Crude	0.0	0.0
Manufactures	3.9	3.3
Leather		
Hides and skins	0.1	0.0
Leather	2.9	1.7
Manufactures	7.2	11.7
Wood		
Rough	0.0	0.0
Shaped	0.2	0.2
Veneer and plywood	1.7	6.6
Manufactures	3.5	2.7
Cotton		
Raw	0.0	0.0

Processing Chain and Stage	Average Tariff[a]	NTB Coverage Ratio[b]
Yarn	3.0	2.2
Fabrics	5.8	62.1
Iron		
Ore	0.0	4.9
Pig iron	2.2	8.7
Ingots and shapes	2.2	8.7
Bars and plates	3.4	18.7
Other metallic ores		
Nonferrous ores	0.0	4.9
Wrought and unwrought metals	2.4	1.0
Phosphates		
Natural	0.0	0.0
Fertilizer	3.2	13.7
Vegetable oils		
Oilseeds	0.0	1.9
Oils	4.4	15.8

SOURCE: Alexander Yeats, "The Escalation of Trade Barriers," in *The Uruguay Round: A Handbook for the Multilateral Trade Negotiations,* J. Michael Finger and Andrzej Olechowski, eds. (Washington, D.C.: World Bank, 1987), Table 15.1.
[a]The tariff rates are trade-weighted averages of rates actually applied by Australia, Austria, the European Community, Japan, New Zealand, Norway, Sweden, Switzerland, and the United States.
[b]Percentage of industrial countries' import value that is subject to nontariff barriers.

processed goods shield domestic processors from import competition and encourage imports of raw materials. Table 15.4 shows the result: exports from developing countries are heavily concentrated in products at lower stages of production.

That tariff escalation has negative effects on primary production as well as on processing. Tariffs on any stage raise the price of the final good and hence tend to reduce consumption. Internal taxes have a similar effect. Germany imposes a consumption tax of DM3.60 a kilogram on unroasted coffee, DM4.30 a kilogram on

Table 15.4
DISTRIBUTION OF IMPORTS OF SELECTED INDUSTRIAL
COUNTRIES BY STAGE OF PROCESSING

Level of Processing	Distribution of Imports from Developing Countries (percentage)	Imports from Developing Countries as a Percentage of Imports from All Countries
Stage 1	72	41
Stage 2	25	30
Stage 3	2	29
Stage 4	1	11
All stages	100	36

NOTES: Australia, Austria, European Community (10 countries), Finland, Japan, New Zealand, Norway, Sweden, Switzerland, and the United States.

Product coverage is the same as in Table 15.3; stages are as listed there.

roasted coffee, and DM9.35 a kilogram on soluble coffee. Such internal taxes on tropical beverages are widespread in Western European countries.[14] Without that tax and tariff burden, consumption of final products—and therefore demand for primary products—would be higher.

Especially important for the poorer countries are measures that would increase demand for primary products and facilitate primary producing countries' advance to first-stage processing activities. Higher stage processing requires many of the same skills and factor inputs as manufacturing, and expansion of higher stage exports tends to be dominated by industrial and advanced developing countries. There is, however, considerable room for processing in lower income countries.

Tariff escalation often protects very simple processes. For example, the U.S. tariff on pineapples in bulk is 64 cents a kilogram. Based on 1984 import-unit values, that comes to 8.4 percent ad valorem. On crated or packaged pineapples, the rate is 1.3 cents a kilogram. If packaging and crating increase the value of a shipment of pineapples by 20 percent, then the effective rate of protection

[14]GATT, "Tropical Products: Background Material for Negotiations" (MTN. GNG/NG6/W/6 REV1), January 18, 1988.

those nominal rates provide for packaging and crating is 5.2 times higher than the rate of protection provided to pineapple growers. The EC duty is 9 percent ad valorem on pineapples, 20 percent on unsugared pineapple juice. The EC allows a GSP rate of 17 percent on unsugared pineapple juice. On sugared juice, the rate is 19 to 42 percent, depending on density, plus an additional charge on the sugar content. Again, the effective protection provided the juicing process is proportionally higher. Imports of pineapple juice from Lomé Agreement countries enter duty free, but that source, which accounted for less than 6 percent of EC consumption in 1983, is not a serious threat to EC processors.

Nontariff Barriers

While the momentum of past GATT negotiations continued to reduce tariffs of industrial countries (the tranche of cuts agreed to at the Tokyo Round went into effect January 1, 1987), the 1980s saw a slow but continuous increase in the use of nontariff barriers, which now affect about one-fifth of overall imports by industrial countries (see Table 15.5). Those restrictions take many different forms. Hard-core nontariff barrriers are made up of quantitative import restraints, including discretionary import licensing, especially voluntary export restraints and measures to enforce decreed prices. Other nontariff barriers include quotas, anti-dumping and countervailing duties, price investigations and other price and volume monitoring measures, and nondiscretionary or automatic import licensing. Government procurement, health, sanitation, and technical regulations may also discriminate in favor of domestic suppliers, but information about them is lacking.

The expansion of hard-core nontariff barriers reflects several widely reported actions:

- Voluntary export restraints on steel and steel products imported by the United States and the EC from all major suppliers;
- Voluntary export restraints on automobiles imported by Canada and the United States;
- Voluntary export restraints on television receivers, videocassette recorders, and other consumer electronic products imported by the EC from Japan and South Korea;

Table 15.5
INDICES OF NTB COVERAGE APPLIED BY SELECTED
INDUSTRIAL COUNTRIES, 1981–87 (1981 = 100)

	1981	1982	1983	1984	1985	1986	1987
All products except fuels							
All NTBs	100	103	104	106	112	119	120
Hard-core NTBs	100	101	99	104	106	106	105
Hard-core NTBs							
On all products	100	101	99	103	104	104	104
On manufactured products	100	99	101	101	112	111	109

SOURCE: United Nations Conference on Trade and Development, "Problems of Protectionism and Structural Adjustment: Introduction and Part I; Restrictions on Trade and Structural Adjustment," TD/B/1081 (Part I), Geneva.

NOTE: The index is constructed as follows: (1) Each importing country's "NTB schedule" for each year is applied to its import values as of 1984. (The intent is to isolate the expansion of NTBs, hence the changing schedule of NTBs applied to a given pattern of trade.) (2) The proportion of total import value covered by each year's NTB schedule is converted to an index number, with 1981 set at 100.

- Expansion of the product and country coverage of the Multifibre Arrangement and additional restraints on textile imports outside the agreement.

Less often noted in the media but equally threatening to an international trading system was the simultaneous expansion of various kinds of import surveillance and import price discipline measures, particularly anti-dumping measures. From 1980 to 1986, there were 1,605 anti-dumping or countervailing duty cases in the industrial countries. Sixty percent (981) led to formal import restrictions; many others were part of a process that led to voluntary export restraints.

Analysis of anti-dumping cases in Australia, the United States, and the EC—three of the most frequent users of anti-dumping measures—have found that anti-dumping enforcement is often a form of protection for domestic industries. It imposes limits on foreign sellers that antitrust regulations do not apply to domestic firms. The Australian study recommended that Australia "reduce the discrepancy between the concept of 'unfair trading practices' as it is applied within Australia and as it is applied by Australia to its imports."[15] Apart from formal import restrictions and voluntary export restrictions, the frequency with which such cases are filed against successful exporters creates considerable uncertainty that their performance can be maintained, given the domestic politics of administered protection. That has a chilling effect on developing countries' efforts to make the efficiency gains and investments necessary for export-led growth.

And barriers are spreading. Some nontariff barriers were removed in the 1980s, for instance on American and Canadian imports of footwear. Among soft-core nontariff barriers, the major change was the elimination by the United States of an automatic licensing requirement for imports of petroleum. But on the whole, approximately $4 of industrial countries' imports have come under hard-core import controls for each $1 on which such controls have been removed. New voluntary export restrictions fell relatively heavily on developing countries' exports. For example, of 124 such arrangements listed by GATT, 77 were with developing countries.[16]

Nontariff barriers cover approximately the same percentage of industrial countries' total imports from developing countries as from industrial countries. But beneath that overall equality lie considerable sectoral differences. Since many tropical products, fuels, and raw materials tend to be noncompetitive, they face fewer nontariff barriers than more competitive food and raw materials imported from industrial (often temperate-climate) countries. In manufactured goods, where they do compete head-on, however, developing countries' exports face 50 percent more nontariff barriers than industrial countries' exports. Nearly a third of industrial countries' imports of manufactured goods from major developing countries are subject to nontariff barriers— more than two-thirds of textiles and clothing imports, more than half of steel imports.

---

[15]J. Michael Finger, "Antidumping and Antisubsidy Measures," in *The Uruguay Round: A Handbook for the Multilateral Trade Negotiations*, J. Michael Finger and Andrzej Olechowski, eds. (Washington, D.C.: World Bank, 1987), p. 158.

[16]GATT, *Developments in the Trading System: April–September 1987*, GATT Document no. C/W/528, October 28, 1987.

Developing Countries' Trade Restrictions

Information on trade restrictions of developing countries is not as systematic as data on industrial countries' restrictions, but it is nevertheless sufficient to conclude that developing countries have tended to have more, higher, and more volatile trade restrictions. Reductions in trade restrictions among many developing nations during recent years may reflect the fact that those countries have realized the harm they have inflicted upon themselves by not liberalizing trade.

Tariffs

Tariffs in developing countries have been very high (see Table 15.6). Trade-weighted, ad valorem, average custom duties and charges for a large number of developing countries amount to about 10 percent, two to three times the rate estimated for industrialized countries. There are, of course, large differences among individual countries. For example,

Table 15.6
AVERAGE AD VALOREM IMPORT CHARGES OF SELECTED DEVELOPING COUNTRIES, 1982 (DUTIES COLLECTED AS A PERCENTAGE OF C.I.F. IMPORT VALUE)

Countries	Customs Duties	Other Charges
Low income	26	2
Lower middle income	10	2
Upper middle income	6	1
High income oil exporting	1	0
All	9	1

SOURCE: IMF, *Government Finance Statistics Yearbook* (Washington, D.C.: IMF, 1986).

NOTE: Developing countries included in the survey: Argentina, Bahrain, Barbados, Belize, Botswana, Brazil, Burkina Faso, Burma, Cameroon, Costa Rica, Cyprus, Dominican Republic, Egypt, El Salvador, Fiji, Ghana, Guatemala, Guyana, India, Iran, Israel, Jordan, Kenya, Kuwait, Liberia, Madagascar, Malawi, Malaysia, Mali, Malta, Mauritius, Mexico, Morocco, Nepal, Nicaragua, Oman, Pakistan, Panama, Papua New Guinea, Paraguay, Peru, Philippines, Senegal, Sierra Leone, Singapore, South Korea, Sri Lanka, Sudan, Swaziland, Thailand, Togo, Tunisia, Venezuela, Yemen (Arab Republic), Zaire, Zambia, Zimbabwe. C.I.F. stands for cost, insurance, and freight.

the rate for Cyprus is 69 percent; for Zaire, 49 percent; for Burma, 41 percent; and for India, 36 percent. At the other extreme is Kuwait at 0 percent, Singapore at 1 percent, and Oman at 2 percent. In general, tariff rates appear to be strongly and negatively related to national income, perhaps reflecting the changing importance of customs as a source of government revenue at different stages of countries' fiscal and economic development[17] and the correlation of protectionism with statist economic policies.

The average also conceals large differences across individual products. As a result of their fiscal role, tariff structures in developing countries reflect the priorities and objectives of overall economic policies. Thus, almost universally, the rates have tended to be very high (often prohibitively so) on food and nonessential luxury products, moderately high on goods for mass consumption (a basic source of revenue), low on consumer products and industrial inputs, and very low on capital goods and equipment. That pattern results in a bias against products of export interest to other developing countries: the average tariff facing those goods has been estimated to be about 5.5 percentage points higher than that facing products exported by industrial countries. It also produces a structure of production incentives biased strongly against agriculture. The 1986 *World Development Report* tabulated such relative incentives for 13 developing countries and found that in only 2 of them (South Korea and Malaysia) was the incentive for agriculture as high as the incentive for manufacturing. For the remaining 11 countries, the incentive for agricultural production ranged from one-third to three-quarters of that for manufacturing.

Nontariff Barriers

Table 15.7 contains results of a survey of developing countries' import regimes as reported by the International Monetary Fund. Some 108 countries were grouped in four categories: those where all or most import transactions require an authorization and those where such control pertains to a large number of products, only some products,

[17]In 1979, duties on foreign transactions accounted for 21.3 percent of central government revenue in countries with GNP per capita under U.S. $1,000, for 9.6 percent in other developing countries, and 1.7 percent in industrial countries. See United Nations Conference on Trade and Development, "Non-Tariff Barriers Affecting the Trade of Developing Countries and Transparency in World Trading Conditions," TD/B940, Geneva, 1983, p. 8.

Table 15.7
THE EXTENT OF DIRECT GOVERNMENT CONTROL OF IMPORTS
IN SELECTED DEVELOPING COUNTRIES (1984)

Countries	Percentage of Countries Where Control Extends to			
	All or Most Products	Large Number of Products	Some Products	No Products
Low income	63	26	11	–
Lower middle income	46	26	24	4
Upper middle income	37	21	37	5
High income oil exporting	20	–	40	40
All	48	24	23	5

SOURCE: IMF, *Exchange Arrangements and Exchange Restrictions* (Washington, D.C.: IMF, 1986).

NOTE: Developing countries included in the survey: Afghanistan, Algeria, Antigua and Barbuda, Argentina, Bahamas, Bahrain, Bangladesh, Barbados, Belize, Benin, Bhutan, Bolivia, Botswana, Brazil, Burma, Burundi, Cameroon, Central African Republic, Chad, Chile, China, Colombia, Congo, Costa Rica, Cyprus, Dominican Republic, Ecuador, Egypt, El Salvador, Equatorial Guinea, Ethiopia, Fiji, Gabon, Gambia, Ghana, Grenada, Guatemala, Guinea-Bissau, Guyana, Haiti, Honduras, Hong Kong, India, Indonesia, Iran, Iraq, Israel, Ivory Coast, Jamaica, Jordan, Kenya, South Korea, Kuwait, Laos, Lebanon, Lesotho, Libya, Madagascar, Malawi, Maldives, Mali, Malta, Mauritania, Mauritius, Mexico, Morocco, Mozambique, Nepal, Netherlands Antilles, Nicaragua, Niger, Nigeria, Pakistan, Papua New Guinea, Paraguay, Peru, Philippines, Rwanda, Saudi Arabia, Senegal, Sierra Leone, Singapore, Solomon Islands, Somalia, Sri Lanka, Sudan, Surinam, Swaziland, Syria, Tanzania, Thailand, Togo, Trinidad and Tobago, Tunisia, Turkey, Uganda, United Arab Emirates, Uruguay, Venezuela, Vietnam, Western Samoa, Yemen (Arab Republic), Yemen (People's Democratic Republic), Zaire, Zambia, Zimbabwe.

and none at all. Although the classification was to some degree judgmental, each of the industrial countries reviewed in the preceding section would have been included in the "some" category.

In almost half of developing countries, all or almost all import transactions require prior government authorization. One of four covers only a limited number of products in this way and 5 percent do not so regulate imports. Here, too, the extent of government control appears to be related to the level of income and economic development. That relationship reflects the changing role that governments play in their economies as well as their use of trade policy to manage balance-of-payments difficulties. In many countries, for instance, imports are allowed only to the extent that they complement rather than compete with local production.

Developing countries tend to impose different forms of trade barriers than do industrial nations. The latter typically restrict imports to assist selected domestic producers, but developing countries' actions are more limited (e.g., restrictions on fruit, vegetables, and honey in South Korea; tiles and sacks in the Ivory Coast; batik sarongs in Malaysia; and textiles in Egypt). Much broader measures, often of short duration, are more typical of developing countries. Thus, GATT reported increases between 1983 and 1985 in import charges in the Philippines, Malawi, Zambia, Ghana, and Israel; bans on large ranges of products by Zaire, Argentina, Guyana, and Colombia; introduction of licensing for wide groups of goods by Brazil, Colombia, Trinidad and Tobago, Burkina Faso, and Gabon; and temporary suspension of certain imports by Jamaica, Ghana (for one month!), and Israel.

Those measures appear to be directed more at managing balance-of-payments problems (particularly foreign exchange shortages) than at helping selected industries meet their international competitors. That suggests that even though developing countries might formally adopt an import substitution trade strategy, other concerns often dominate its implementation.

Effects on Developing Countries

The costs developing countries' trade restrictions impose on themselves are large. Bela Balassa and C. Michalopoulos estimated the immediate costs to range between 2.5 and 9.5 percent of GNP.[18] Such short-run costs might be acceptable as part of the development process if trade restrictions accelerated the economy's growth, bringing even larger benefits in the future. But that is not the case. Trade restrictions impose both short- and long-run costs considerably in excess of their

[18]Bela Belassa and C. Michalopoulos, "Trade Policy Issues, Protectionism and Development," Development Committee Paper, World Bank, Washington, D.C., March 19, 1985.

benefits on the citizens of developing as well as industrialized states. In contrast, countries that have avoided the short-run costs of trade restrictions have enjoyed the long-run benefits of growth.

Conclusion and Cautions

Trade restrictions are disproportionately imposed both against the exports of developing countries and by developing countries. They therefore suffer on both accounts—probably more on the latter than the former.

While agriculture and transportation tend to be heavily subsidized in developed countries, import restrictions are the primary form of aid to industry on the whole. Industrial countries' tariffs tend to be considerably higher on manufactured imports from developing countries than on those from industrial countries for two reasons: MFN rates tend to be higher on products exported by developing countries, and reductions of MFN rates on imports of manufactured goods from industrial countries, particularly among Western European countries, are larger than reductions or preferences on imports from developing countries. Moreover, developing countries' exports of manufactured goods to industrial countries face 50 percent more nontariff barriers than do products from industrial countries.

Industrial countries' protection reduces developing countries' national income by roughly twice the amount provided by official development assistance. There is still a theoretical *potential* for aid's helping poorer nations—but institutional structures and human frailties often reduce the results to a fraction (maybe a negative fraction) of that potential. Similarly, institutional problems and human frailties can compromise the potential of trade liberalization, not because trade liberalization is unable to deliver the economic goods (and services), but because the system will not deliver trade liberalization. For Americans, the immediately relevant institution is the U.S. Congress. Trade liberalization, like charity, begins at home.

16. Self-Determination through Unilateral Free Trade

by Jim Powell

For much of this century, one country after another has pursued economic nationalism, attempting to gain control of its destiny by closing its borders. The aim has been to carry out national plans, achieve self-sufficiency, prevent foreigners from taking over supposedly vital industries, protect local jobs from outside competition, and avoid having local culture overrun by foreign ideas.

Yet everywhere economic nationalism has been tried, it has backfired. To the degree that countries have closed their borders, they have suffered from chronic stagnation, decline, backwardness, and corruption. The countries that have done the most to cut themselves off from the outside world have not only suffered through worse economic crises than those that have remained relatively open, but have also thus aggravated a host of other problems.

20th-Century Experiments with Closed Economies

The Russian Revolution launched the most ambitious effort in human history to make a closed society work. Never before had so much police power been directed at so many millions of people in such a large country, one that spanned 11 time zones and was endowed with more natural resources than any other country on earth.

For decades, that dramatic experiment was heralded as a success for reportedly transforming the Soviet Union into a world-class industrial nation and a military superpower. Western visitors such as George Bernard Shaw, Harold Laski, and Sidney and Beatrice Webb marveled at Stalin's seeming successes. During the 1950s, Soviet economic growth rates seemed to be faster than those in the United States, inspiring Soviet leader Nikita Khrushchev to boast that "we will bury you."

Since then, of course, the Soviet Union has collapsed, revealing the great experiment as a catastrophic failure. As it turned out, almost all the reports about Soviet economic success were overblown. Such progress as occurred in a few sectors came at the expense of most other sectors. From the standpoint of living standards, the Soviet closed system never worked.

Massive human suffering in the Soviet Union did not occur because the government had too little power or too few competent managers. Rather, suffering was an inevitable consequence of the closed system itself. When Soviet commissars created shortages, closed borders prevented people from protecting their interests by seeking alternative suppliers abroad. The problems of the commissars were thereby spread to innocent people, victimizing Soviet citizens.

Similarly, the communist vision of a closed society was supposed to usher China into the modern age. In 1949, the charismatic Mao Zedong triumphantly seized power after more than two decades of struggle. He had much going for him. China was richly endowed with natural resources such as oil, coal, iron, tin, lead, zinc, and gold. China had some of the world's most fertile agricultural lands, which made it a top producer of wheat, rice, tea, cotton, and beef. As heirs of the oldest continuous civilization, the Chinese traditionally had great respect for learning and so had a capacity to develop valuable knowledge.

Mao claimed to be a revolutionary, but that was true only in the sense that power changed hands violently. The closed regime he imposed on China—the "Bamboo Curtain" as it became known in the West—harked back to the xenophobic Ming dynasty, which, reacting against previous Mongol emperors, sealed off China from the outside world and set the stage for three centuries of stagnation. During that time, the West went through a peaceful capitalist revolution that lifted living standards to unprecedented heights and left the Chinese economically far behind.

Under communism, the Chinese have not fared any better than under the Ming dynasty. Mao's most memorable legacies have been violence, stagnation, and famine. In many respects, China's living standards are comparable to some of the most backward regions of Africa.[1] Nevertheless, even China has realized that it cannot shut itself off from the world if it is to maintain a level of sustainable economic growth. Under the guidance of Deng Xiaoping, the country's para-

---

[1]See, for example, Steven W. Mosher, *Broken Earth: The Rural Chinese* (New York: Free Press, 1983).

mount leader, trade liberalization and the introduction of "special economic zones" in China's southern provinces in recent years have led to an explosion of commerce and productivity. Indeed, in 1992 China's growth rate was 12.8 percent—the world's highest—and was expected to reach 13 percent in 1993.[2]

Among noncommunist nations, none pursued the dream of a closed society with more determination than India after it gained independence in 1947. The world's largest democracy, it seemed full of promise. India had an extensive rail network built by British investors, a reasonably well-trained civil service, and a vast, low-cost labor force. Its political leaders were determined that India would become a global power by embracing autarky.

Mahatma Gandhi, India's first postindependence leader, believed in autarky with religious fervor. "If not an article of commerce had been brought from outside India, she would be today, a land flowing with milk and honey," he declared. "Foreign goods and goods made by means of complicated machinery are, therefore, tabooed."[3]

Gandhi's most famous follower, Cambridge-educated Jawaharlal Nehru, shared the hatred of open markets. He had visited the Soviet Union in 1927 and been impressed with Soviet theories of forced industrialization through central planning, which required closed borders. India's socialists adapted their notorious import licensing system from that of British colonial administrators. To import practically anything required some kind of license, such as an advance license, a capital goods license, an import passbook license, a special imprest import passbook license, an imprest license, a supplementary license, or an import replenishment license. Import licenses were available only for end users, thus making it difficult for wholesalers to store goods in anticipation of possible shortages. Applying for a license could easily involve assembling a dozen documents, such as a no-objection certificate and a verification certificate. In hundreds, perhaps thousands, of cases, officials have taken more than *five years* to process

[2]Lena H. Sun, "China's Output Growing at World's Fastest Rate," *Washington Post*, April 25, 1993, p. A25.

[3]"Mahatma Gandhi on Swadeshi," in S. R. Vakil, *Revival of Swadeshi Spirit—An Answer to Smuggling* (Bombay: Forum of Free Enterprise, 1974), p. 19. That is consistent with other Gandhi utterances, such as those quoted in Francine R. Frankel, *India's Political Economy, 1947–1977* (Princeton, N.J.: Princeton University Press, 1978), pp. 8–13.

a license application.[4] India scholar Francine Frankel outlined obstacles the private sector has faced.

> The new bureaucratic apparatus for control of the private sector was formidable. Applications for licenses by larger industrial houses and foreign firms had to pass through multiple checkpoints on a long journey toward clearance. An interministerial licensing committee, with members of all concerned ministries, including industrial development, company affairs, finance, and the Planning Commission had to be satisfied before any application could be forwarded to the Ministry of Industrial Development for final approval. Those applications that were considered problematical, moreover, could be referred for advice to the Monopolies Commission and/or the Economic Affairs Committee of the Cabinet, a procedure that in the last analysis required the larger business houses to get personal approval of the prime minister and her [Indira Gandhi's] closest advisors for new ventures.[5]

India further closed its borders with government monopolies, exchange controls, and tariffs, which—often well over 100 percent—have been among the world's highest.[6]

Moreover, the government has not even permitted people to benefit from India's large internal market. Licenses effectively divide the country into myriad small autarkies. Although many Indian factories are small by world standards, they often dominate their restricted markets. No one was permitted to start a new industrial enterprise—or expand an existing operation—without explicit approval from New Delhi. Officials determined who could start a business, where it would locate, how much financial support it would get, what its labor policies would be, and much more. Since officials considered consumer goods relatively unimportant, they simply denied consumer goods companies allocations of coal, credit, imported machinery, and other essentials. They forced consumer goods companies out of business or into the realm that Indians call "black money."

The results have been the opposite of what was intended. The government sector commands about 75 percent of India's industrial

---

[4]For a description of India's licensing system, see *India, An Industrializing Country in Transition* (Washington, D.C.: World Bank, 1989), pp. 28–31, 94–95.

[5]Frankel, p. 438.

[6]U.S. Trade Representative, *1993 National Trade Estimate Report on Foreign Trade Barriers* (Washington, D.C.: Government Printing Office, 1993), p. 120.

assets, yet accounts for less than a third of the country's industrial production. Cut off from the outside world, India's economy became dependent on foreign aid handouts from prosperous open-market economies.[7] Unable to sustain such an irrational system, Prime Minister Narasimha Rao introduced economic reforms in 1993 that reduced India's top tariff rate to 80 percent, eliminated much of the industrial licensing system, and relaxed some foreign investment laws.[8] To be sure, India remains largely a closed society, but seems to be taking its first steps toward opening up.

Autarky has also caused injustice on a massive scale by denying freedom of choice to millions of ordinary people, subjecting them to the capricious whims of government monopolies and protected private companies. Injustice is perhaps most obvious in India where the government has used its power to transfer resources away from rural areas, where an estimated 80 percent of the poorest people live, to subsidize city dwellers who tend to be better off. Probably the biggest beneficiaries of rural exploitation are middle-class professionals who operate the government's industrial monopolies.

Closed-border policies have yielded dismal results in industrialized countries, too. The most heavily protected and subsidized sectors in Japan have been the worst performers—agriculture, retail distribution, railroads, petrochemicals, and steel, for instance.[9] Europe's policy of protecting and subsidizing "national champions" has resulted in national laggards, like most of the computer, electronics, airline, and automobile companies.[10] In the United States, the standard account of tariff history found that tariffs generally did not help nurture competitive companies, and the Commerce Department acknowledged that import restrictions have failed to make the textile, apparel, footwear, steel, and automobile companies more competitive; on the contrary,

[7]Rajni Bonnie Sohri, "The Free Market Works in India," *Journal of Economic Growth*, Second Quarter 1987, p. 42.

[8]Shyam J. Kamath, "The Promise and Perils of India's Economic Reforms," *Policy* (Australia), Autumn 1993.

[9]Katsuro Sakoh, "Japanese Economic Success: Industrial Policy or Free Market?" *Cato Journal*, vol. 4, no. 2 (Fall 1984) pp. 521–44.

[10]See Kenneth Flamm, *Targeting the Computer* (Washington, D.C.: Brookings Institution, 1987), as well as reports such as Stephen Greenhouse, "Europe Stumbles in Computers," *New York Times*, April 22, 1991, p. D1; and Guy de Jonquieres and Alan Cane, "National Champions Become Laggards," *Financial Times*, April, 29, 1991, p. 17.

those sectors seem to have become addicted to continued protection that depresses living standards for millions. It is past time to acknowledge that closed-border policies are a principal cause of stagnation, decline, and backwardness.[11]

Foreign Influence and Increased Prosperity through the Millennia

Ironically, it has been the case for more than 5,000 years that the more borders are open and the more seemingly vulnerable a country is to foreign influence, the greater the degree of prosperity for ordinary people. Private, commercial contact with the outside world has proven to be perhaps the most powerful, persistent stimulus for human progress.

The first people known to have traded widely by sea were the Minoans, who created a civilization on Crete 5,000 years ago. They prospered by trading primarily in wine, olives, and figs. The Minoans did not erect colossal statues of kings like the brutal Egyptians or modern Stalinists. Rather, Minoan art depicted scenes of everyday life. Merchants had seals with a great deal of individuality. That commercial civilization, which appears to have been relatively peaceful, lasted for more than 600 years.[12]

In prosperous mercantile Athens, the birthplace of democracy, most businesses—including the largest businesses—were owned by foreigners.[13] Athenians created cultural marvels with papyrus imported from Egypt and an alphabet based on the one first developed by Phoenician traders.[14] Similarly, the Roman Empire thrived by import-

[11]Frank W. Taussig, *The Tariff History of the United States* (New York: Putnam's Sons, 1932); and Congressional Budget Office, *Has Trade Protection Revitalized Domestic Industries?* (Washington, D.C.: Government Printing Office, 1986).

[12]Herbert J. Muller, *Freedom in the Ancient World* (New York: Harper & Brothers, 1961), pp. 76–79.

[13]Will Durant, *The Life of Greece* (New York: Simon & Schuster, 1966), pp. 276–77; Michael Grant, *The Ancient Mediterranean* (New York: New American Library, 1969), p. 210; and Harry Elmer Barnes, *An Economic History of the Western World* (New York: Harcourt, Brace & Co., 1937), pp. 48–49.

[14]Donald Jackson, *The Story of Writing* (New York: Taplinger Publishing, 1981), pp. 26–37.

ing daily necessities such as grain. Rome's trade was handled almost entirely by foreigners who brought with them invaluable knowledge of Greek civilization.[15]

The commerce of Byzantium, or Istanbul, was in the hands of foreigners, including Venetians, Pisans, Genoese, Spaniards, Greeks, Russians, Bulgars, Turks, Syrians, Arabs, and Jews—and Byzantium thrived for a thousand years after the Fall of Rome[16] In the Ottoman Empire, which covered a larger territory than did the Roman during its heyday, most commerce was carried on by foreigners.[17]

Commerce, dominated by Arabs and Jews, brought cloistered Europe out of the Dark Ages. Those traders introduced backward societies to sophisticated mathematical techniques, new technology, and long-lost learning from the ancient world.[18] Likewise, for more than 200 years during the late medieval period, the German Hanseatic League handled the commerce of Northern Europe from Novgorod to London, and people prospered.[19]

The Dutch provided an estimated one-quarter of the capital needed to finance the British industrial revolution in the 18th century, and the British provided a big chunk of investment capital for Argentina, the United States, and other countries in the 19th century.[20]

Japan emerged from two centuries of isolation and stagnation by importing Western free-market ideas and technology. During that era,

[15]Will Durant, *Caesar and Christ* (New York: Simon & Schuster, 1944), pp. 78, 139; Grant, pp. 272, 298–99; and Barnes, pp. 68–70.

[16]Charles Diehl, *Byzantium: Greatness and Decline* (New Brunswick, N.J.: Rutgers University Press, 1957), pp. 80–83; and Barnes, pp. 104–11.

[17]Paul Kennedy, *The Rise and Fall of the Great Powers* (New York: Random House, 1987), p. 12.

[18]Albert Hourani, *A History of the Arab Peoples* (Cambridge, Mass.: Harvard University Press, 1991), pp. 109–13; Paul Johnson, *A History of the Jews* (New York: Harper & Row, 1977), pp. 174–77, 184; Barnes, pp. 111–17; and Fernand Braudel, *The Wheels of Commerce* (New York: Harper & Row, 1979), pp. 154–60.

[19] Johannes Schildhauer, *The Hansa* (Leipzig: Dorset Press, 1988); and Philip Dollinger, *The German Hansa* (Stanford, Calif.: Stanford University Press, 1964), pp. 210–77.

[20]On Dutch capital for Britain, see T. S. Ashton, *The Industrial Revolution, 1760–1830* (London: Oxford University Press, 1961), p. 103; and Charles P. Kindleberger, *A Financial History of Western Europe* (London: George Allen & Unwin, 1984), p. 215. On British capital for the United States, see Kindleberger, pp. 224–25; and Ron Chernow, *The House of Morgan* (New York: Atlantic Monthly Press, 1990), pp. 7–12, 24–25, 43–44. On British capital for Argentina, see A. G. Ford, "British Investment and Argentine Economic

Japan abolished feudal restrictions on freedom of movement, freedom of trade, freedom to enter professions, and freedom to buy land. Soon the Japanese were importing foreign crops, railroads, telegraph systems, cotton-spinning machinery, and educational techniques. Foreigners handled the bulk of those transactions. As it developed into an industrial power, Japan incurred substantial trade deficits.[21]

Russia became a world power in the late 19th and early 20th centuries, thanks very much to foreign investment. French investors, for instance, were instrumental in developing Russia's vital rail network.[22] By 1914, foreign investors owned 28 percent of the Russian textile industry, 40 percent of the metallurgical industry, 90 percent of mining operations, and 100 percent of the oil business. Prospects for economic progress were good until Russia entered World War I, which brought the country chaos and communism.[23]

Throughout much of Asia, a disproportionate volume of commerce has been carried on by immigrant Chinese. Overseas Chinese have contributed mightily to prosperity in Hong Kong, Taiwan, Indonesia, Malaysia, and Australia.

American companies likewise expanded aggressively in Europe during the 1960s, providing fresh capital, new technology, and improved management skills—all of which contributed to Europe's boom.

In the 1980s, the United States imported a tremendous amount of capital—approximately $630 billion[24]—while Europe and Japan exported capital. During that period, the United States created more jobs than Europe and Japan combined.

The United States has absorbed more foreign influence than any other country in history. The nation has opened its doors to more than 50 million immigrants—more than the rest of the world combined—and immigrants have brought their languages, religions, food, music,

---

Development," in *Argentina in the Twentieth Century*, David Rock, ed. (Pittsburgh: University of Pittsburgh Press, 1975), pp. 12–40.

[21]G. C. Allen, *A Short Economic History of Modern Japan* (London: Macmillan, 1983), pp. 34–39; and Johannes Hirschmeier and Tsunehiko Yui, *The Development of Japanese Business* (London: George Allen & Unwin, 1981), pp. 120–32.

[22]Kindleberger, pp. 226–27.

[23]Kennedy, p. 234.

[24]Calculation made from figures in *Economic Report of the President* (Washington, D.C.: Government Printing Office, 1993), p. 463.

literature, architecture, and other aspects of their culture to the United States, much of which have become part of American culture.[25]

For thousands of years, the most prosperous regions of the world have thrived to the degree they have been open to the outside world. The time has come to recognize that foreign influence is a source of prosperity because it means people are free to gain the advantages of ideas, products, capital, and talent that may not be available at home. Opening an economy to foreign competition forces companies to give people what they want or see them protect their vital interests by shopping elsewhere.

Self-Determination through Unilateral Free Trade

In one country after another, farsighted leaders have recognized that they themselves have the means to reinvigorate their economies by opening their borders. That does not require agreement with, or financial aid from, other countries. Borders can be opened unilaterally, through bold independent action, because the primary benefits go to those who do so.

Thus, the revival of Europe after World War II was led by West Germany. While the French, British, and others dithered behind a maze of self-inflicted central economic plans and border restrictions, West Germany unilaterally began eliminating price controls, exchange controls, and many trade restrictions in June 1948. That was the beginning of what many people called the West German "miracle."[26]

Germany's unilateral liberalization forced the French to admit the failure of their interventionist policies, which had produced only inflation and stagnation. Unable to keep Germany down, the French proposed forming a customs union, the European Coal and Steel Community, which led to free trade in those commodities among member countries, and helped spark the economic revival of postwar Europe.

With perhaps the world's most open borders, Hong Kong has taken in millions of immigrants first from mainland China, then from Southeast Asia. Hong Kong has welcomed dozens of foreign banks

---

[25]U.S. Department of Commerce, *Statistical Abstract of the United States* (Washington, D.C.: Government Printing Office, 1990), p. 9.

[26]Sidney Dell, *Trade Blocs and Common Markets* (New York: Alfred A. Knopf, 1963), p. 94; and Jean Monnet, *Memoirs* (Garden City, N.Y.: Doubleday, 1978), pp. 291–96.

and investments from countries around the world, and its per capita income is about 27 times higher than mainland China's.[27]

In Chile, the economy was wrecked by Salvador Allende, who nationalized industries and imposed tight border restrictions, price controls, and rationing, all of which led to runaway inflation. As economic chaos often does, Allende's policies precipitated a military takeover in 1973, and General Augusto Pinochet came to power. Although he suppressed political opponents, he unilaterally liberalized the economy, cutting taxes, privatizing enterprises, and abolishing restrictions on trade and foreign investment. Because of such policies, Chile's economy has become the healthiest in Latin America, generating pressures that led to its return to democracy in 1990.[28]

On several occasions during the past three decades, South Korea pursued industrial policies with subsidies and steep trade restrictions for heavy industries such as steel, chemicals, machinery, transportation equipment, and electrical power. The result was costly excess capacity in heavy industries and shortages in light industries, which South Korea's planners had neglected. South Korea began unilaterally liberalizing its policies in 1978 and followed up with a broad liberalization effort in 1983. Since then, the South Korean government has eliminated 95 percent of its import licensing restrictions, which had applied to more than 7,900 products. Tariffs, gradually being reduced, are now about 10 percent.[29]

In Britain, after World War II, the new Labor government intensified trade restrictions and nationalized so-called key industries such as coal, steel, electricity, gas mining, and health insurance. But the results were poor. Britain's postwar recovery lagged far behind Germany's and that of other European countries. By the 1970s, the "British

[27]World Bank, *World Development Report 1990* (New York: Oxford University Press, 1990), p. 179.

[28]Roger Cohen, "All Latins Should Try Chile's Homemade Growth Recipe," *Wall Street Journal*, September 30, 1989, p. A27; Peter Hakim and Richard Feinberg, "The Lessons from Chile and Peru," *Financial Times*, November 30, 1988, p. 25; and Robert Graham, "Recovering a Lost Democracy," *Financial Times*, October 7, 1988, p. 22.

[29]Tibor Scitovsky, "Economic Development in Taiwan and South Korea, 1965-1981," in *Models of Development*, Lawrence J. Lau, ed. (San Francisco: Institute for Contemporary Studies, 1986), pp. 188–90; Soo-Gil Young, "Korean Trade Policy and the Implications for Korea/US Cooperation," *Korea's Economy*, May 1988, p. 8; and U.S. Trade Representative, p. 171.

disease" had become a common term of derision, referring to stagnation, inflation, and chronic labor strife.

In 1979, the new government led by Margaret Thatcher began unilaterally liberalizing the British economy. Thatcher privatized industries, significantly reducing business subsidies and turning government deficits into surpluses, and unilaterally abolished exchange controls, thereby exposing British entrepreneurs to global markets.

Equally remarkable was Thatcher's bold deregulation of services. She deregulated airlines, extending vigorous competition not only throughout Britain but to continental Europe as well. The deregulation of British telecommunications led to sharp rate reductions that forced stubborn European telecommunications monopolies to cut their rates or lose business to newly invigorated British competitors.[30] Thatcher's deregulation of capital markets helped London expand its role in global finance: after the 1986 "big bang," brokerage commission rates fell 20 percent. As the cheapest and easiest place to raise funds on the Continent, London handles about a fifth of the world's international banking business, half of foreign equity trading, half of foreign exchange trading, three-quarters of the Eurobond volume, and a substantial share of international fund management.

Like so many other Third World countries, Turkey pursued economic nationalism in the post–World War II era and suffered the consequences. Stagnation, inflation, and violence triggered a military takeover in 1980. Three years later, with order restored, elections were held, and economist Turgot Ozal, a founder of the new Motherland party, became prime minister.

Ozal unilaterally liberalized import restrictions and abolished most price controls. He eliminated many investment restrictions, such as limits on the percentage of foreign ownership and the ability of an investor to repatriate profits. Foreign investment increased tenfold. Benefits were most apparent in tourism, chemicals, plastics, paper, textiles, fertilizers, transportation equipment, and banking. Economic growth was substantially higher than before liberalization.[31]

---

[30]Patrick A. Messerlin, "Liberalization in Services: The Experience and Challenge of the European Community," World Bank, Washington, D.C., September 30, 1989, pp. 3–4, 11, 13.

[31]"On the Banks of the Bosphorus, Another Korea," *Business Month*, November 1988, pp. 26–27; "A Survey of Turkey: Half Inside, Half Out," *The Economist*, June 18, 1988; and "Turkey Opts for Free Enterprise," *Forbes*, August 26, 1985, pp. 46–47.

For years, Australia stagnated behind protectionist walls. To resolve the crisis, Robert Hawke, elected prime minister in 1983, supported liberalization of the economy. His treasurer, Paul Keating, was the guiding light behind that effort. Australia deregulated the banking system to introduce competition with nonbank institutions. Barriers against foreign banks were eliminated. Australia abolished foreign exchange controls, thus allowing funds to move freely in and out of the country. The Hawke government cut expenditures, abolished foreign investment restrictions, deregulated financial markets, and lowered many tariffs.[32] Keating, elected prime minister in 1993, has continued to move his country along the path of unilateral liberalization.

Like Australia, New Zealand had stagnated for a long time. *The Economist* called it "the developed world's most protected, over-regulated and distorted economy." In 1984, after the Labor party ousted the protectionist National party, Finance Minister Roger Douglas began to liberalize the economy. The top income tax rate was cut in half to 33 percent. Tariffs were scheduled to be reduced below 10 percent by 1996 on all goods except textiles. Import quotas, price controls, and agricultural subsidies were abolished—an extraordinary feat considering the inability of the United States and Europe to curb the greed of their special-interest lobbies. The New Zealand government privatized banking, oil, steel, telecommunications, and more. New Zealand's long-protected financial markets are now among the most open in the world.

Indonesia faced a crisis when oil and gas prices plunged during the mid-1980s. Impressed by the sustained success of East Asia's market-oriented economies, President Suharto started unilaterally liberalizing Indonesia's economy in 1985. He cut government spending for the first time in more than 20 years. The tax system was simplified from 58 different rates to just 3, and the top rate was cut to 35 percent. Overall tariffs have come down dramatically. Suharto curtailed import monopolies and abolished import restrictions for export-oriented manufactures. Indonesia unilaterally liberalized foreign investment restrictions,

---

[32]"Hawke Swoops, the Worm Turns," *The Economist,* September 23, 1989, pp. 36–37; "Financial Times Survey: Australia," *Financial Times,* June 14, 1989; and "Australia: Renaissance Down Under," *The Economist,* May 6, 1989, survey, p. 5.

and the number of companies willing to risk their capital in that country has surged.[33]

In Mexico, decades of expropriation, inflation, and trade restrictions brought nothing but crisis. The Mexican economy was a wreck by the 1970s. Nationalized enterprises incurred huge losses, the protected private sector was a notorious laggard, and overregulation brought massive corruption. Mexico could put off the day of reckoning only until oil prices collapsed in 1982.

Since then, Mexico has unilaterally opened itself to the outside world. In December 1987, President Carlos Salinas de Gortari abolished most import quotas and cut tariffs to an average 10 percent. Imports jumped 50 percent in 1988. Better quality products became readily available to large numbers of Mexicans. Prices fell. Salinas cut tariffs further and privatized the government telephone monopoly, steel companies, banks, and hundreds of other state-owned enterprises. The reforms have allowed Mexico to experience average growth rates of 3.5 percent (outpacing population growth) since 1989. Mexico's enthusiasm for liberalized trade has further been reflected in its desire to enter into the North American Free Trade Agreement with the United States and Canada.

Argentina, too, has stopped runaway inflation, privatized government monopolies, and liberalized trade restrictions in recognition that its closed economy has been responsible for the country's depressing stagnation and massive corruption of recent decades. As Argentina's minister of the economy, Domingo F. Cavallo, declared: "We have to be integrated to the world, not isolated like we were for six decades. We want to be neighbors and partners with the winners of the world. We need capital, so we need to open to foreign capital, and capital that comes from abroad is as good as capital that comes from inside the country."[34]

During the past three decades, the European Community talked a lot about abolishing internal restrictions, but little was done. Then

---

[33]Geoffrey B. Hainsworth, "Indonesia's Economic Downswing and Political Reforms," *Current History*, April 1987, p. 172; Steven Erlanger, "Indonesia Moving Quietly toward a More Private Economy," *New York Times*, October 11, 1989, p. A13; and David Clark Scott, "Indonesia Aims for Spot as Asian Tiger," *Christian Science Monitor*, March 27, 1990, p. 5.

[34]Nathaniel C. Nash, "Plan by New Argentine Economy Chief Raises Cautious Hope for Recovery," *New York Times*, April 28, 1991, p. A3.

during the 1980s, the buoyant U.S. economy created almost 20 million jobs, and the market-oriented East Asian economies experienced a dramatic boom while Europe stagnated. European countries protected their industries behind myriad restrictions, so those industries remained small and inefficient. Milk, telephones, insurance, trucking, and thousands of other products and services cost substantially more in Europe than on the world market. Unemployment was stuck at around 10 percent. European Commissioner Jacques Delors acknowledged that Western Europeans were spurred to draw up their internal market liberalization agenda for 1992 by the fear of falling further behind.[35]

As restrictions were abolished, growth picked up in the European Community, intensifying pressure on Eastern Europe where the stagnation and backwardness were far worse. On their television sets or shortwave radios, Eastern Europeans were reminded daily that the future was leaving without them, which helped to set the stage for tearing down the Berlin Wall.[36]

Other formerly highly statist countries such as Vietnam, Mongolia, and Peru have taken steps to liberalize their economies.

Those and other countries are not liberalizing their economies mainly to please others. They are liberalizing to please themselves. The future belongs to countries that take their destiny in their own hands, open their borders, force their companies to be more competitive, and make purchasing goods and services easier and cheaper for millions of working people who deserve nothing less than complete freedom of choice.

---

[35]Stephen Greenhouse, "On to 1992: The World Watches Europe, the Power That Will Be," *New York Times*, July 31, 1988, sec. 4, p. 1; and James M. Markham, "Europeans, East and West, Are Indulging in Revival," *New York Times*, July 17, 1988, sec. 4, p. 1.

[36]"Perestroika: And Now for the Hard Part," *The Economist*, April 28, 1990, survey, p. 5.

Index

Contributors

George B. N. Ayittey is an associate professor of economics at the American University, president of the Free Africa Foundation, and author of *Africa Betrayed*.

Doug Bandow is a senior fellow of the Cato Institute and a former special assistant to President Reagan. He is author of *The Politics of Plunder* and editor of *U.S. Aid to the Developing World*.

James Bovard is an associate policy analyst of the Cato Institute and author of *The Fair Trade Fraud*.

James B. Burnham is the Murrin Professor of Global Competitiveness at the School of Business at Duquesne University and a former U.S. executive director at the World Bank (1982–85).

Nicholas Eberstadt is a visiting fellow at Harvard University's Center for Population Studies, a visiting scholar at the American Enterprise Institute, and author of *Foreign Aid and American Purpose*.

J. Michael Finger is the lead economist for trade policy at the World Bank and former director of the Office of Trade Research at the U.S. Department of the Treasury.

Shyam J. Kamath is a professor of economics and Asian studies at California State University at Hayward and author of *The Political Economy of Suppressed Markets*.

William McGurn is senior editor of the *Far Eastern Economic Review*.

David Osterfeld (1949–93) was a professor of political science at St. Joseph's College and author of *Prosperity versus Planning: How Government Stifles Economic Growth*.

Jim Powell is a senior fellow of the Cato Institute and author of *The Gnomes of Tokyo: Why Foreign Investment Is Good for Us*.

Paulo Rabello de Castro is vice president of the Instituto Atlântico and director and managing partner of R. C. Consultores in Rio de Janeiro, Brazil.

361

Paul Craig Roberts is president of the Institute for Political Economy and a distinguished fellow of the Cato Institute.

Roberto Salinas León is executive director of the Centro de Investigaciones Sobre la Libre Empresa in Mexico City.

Melanie S. Tammen is an adjunct scholar of the Cato Institute.

Ian Vásquez is assistant director of the Cato Institute's Project on Global Economic Liberty. His articles on foreign policy have appeared in newspapers in the United States and Latin America.

Roland Vaubel is a professor of economics at the University of Mannheim in Germany and coeditor of *The Political Economy of International Organizations: A Public Choice Approach.*

Cato Institute

Founded in 1977, the Cato Institute is a public policy research foundation dedicated to broadening the parameters of policy debate to allow consideration of more options that are consistent with the traditional American principles of limited government, individual liberty, and peace. To that end, the Institute strives to achieve greater involvement of the intelligent, concerned lay public in questions of policy and the proper role of government.

The Institute is named for *Cato's Letters*, libertarian pamphlets that were widely read in the American Colonies in the early 18th century and played a major role in laying the philosophical foundation for the American Revolution.

Despite the achievement of the nation's Founders, today virtually no aspect of life is free from government encroachment. A pervasive intolerance for individual rights is shown by government's arbitrary intrusions into private economic transactions and its disregard for civil liberties.

To counter that trend, the Cato Institute undertakes an extensive publications program that addresses the complete spectrum of policy issues. Books, monographs, and shorter studies are commissioned to examine the federal budget, Social Security, regulation, military spending, international trade, and myriad other issues. Major policy conferences are held throughout the year, from which papers are published thrice yearly in the *Cato Journal*. The Institute also publishes the quarterly magazine *Regulation*.

In order to maintain its independence, the Cato Institute accepts no government funding. Contributions are received from foundations, corporations, and individuals, and other revenue is generated from the sale of publications. The Institute is a nonprofit, tax-exempt, educational foundation under Section 501(c)3 of the Internal Revenue Code.

CATO INSTITUTE
1000 Massachusetts Ave., N.W.
Washington, D.C. 20001

2194